READING 1–2 PETER AND JUDE

Society of Biblical Literature

Resources for Biblical Study

Tom Thatcher, New Testament Editor

READING 1–2 PETER AND JUDE

A RESOURCE FOR STUDENTS

Edited by
Eric F. Mason and Troy W. Martin

Society of Biblical Literature
Atlanta

Copyright © 2014 by the Society of Biblical Literature

All rights reserved. No part of this work may be reproduced or transmitted in any form or by any means, electronic or mechanical, including photocopying and recording, or by means of any information storage or retrieval system, except as may be expressly permitted by the 1976 Copyright Act or in writing from the publisher. Requests for permission should be addressed in writing to the Rights and Permissions Office, Society of Biblical Literature, 825 Houston Mill Road, Atlanta, GA 30329 USA.

Library of Congress Cataloging-in-Publication Data

Reading 1–2 Peter and Jude / edited by Eric F. Mason and Troy W. Martin.
    p. cm. — (Society of Biblical Literature resources for Biblical study ; 77)
  Includes bibliographical references and index.
  ISBN 978-1-58983-737-9 (paper binding : alk. paper) — ISBN 978-1-58983-738-6 (electronic format) — ISBN 978-1-58983-940-3 (hardcover binding : alk. paper)
  1. Bible. Peter—Criticism, interpretation, etc. 2. Bible. Jude—Criticism, interpretation, etc. I. Mason, Eric Farrel. II. Martin, Troy W. III. Series: Resources for biblical study ; no. 77.
    BS2795.52.R43 2014
    227'.9206—dc23   2014002884

Printed on acid-free, recycled paper conforming to
ANSI/NISO Z39.48-1992 (R1997) and ISO 9706:1994
standards for paper permanence.

In memory of
Joseph W. Bennington and Samuel Adekanmi Oginni,
who contended for the faith (Jude 4)

Contents

Acknowledgments ix

Abbreviations xi

Introduction
    Eric F. Mason and Troy W. Martin 1

Gathering Apostolic Voices: Who Wrote 1 and 2 Peter and Jude?
    Lewis R. Donelson 11

The Literary Relationships among 1 Peter, 2 Peter, and Jude
    Jeremy F. Hultin 27

The Epistolary Rhetoric of 1 Peter, 2 Peter, and Jude
    Duane F. Watson 47

"Awaiting New Heavens and a New Earth": The Apocalyptic
Imagination of 1–2 Peter and Jude
    Kelley Coblentz Bautch 63

Reborn to a Living Hope: A Christology of 1 Peter
    Steven J. Kraftchick 83

Christians as Babies: Metaphorical Reality in 1 Peter
    Troy W. Martin 99

Be Holy, for I Am Holy: Paraenesis in 1 Peter
    Nancy Pardee 113

Ethnicity, Empire, and Early Christian Identity: Social-Scientific
   Perspectives on 1 Peter
   David G. Horrell 135

1 Peter and Postmodern Criticism
   Félix H. Cortez 151

1 Peter in Patristic Literature
   Andreas Merkt 167

Biblical and Nonbiblical Traditions in Jude and 2 Peter:
   Sources, Usage, and the Question of Canon
   Eric F. Mason 181

Are the Others Too Other? The Issue of "Others" in Jude and
   2 Peter
   Peter H. Davids 201

Searching for Evidence: The History of Reception of the Epistles
   of Jude and 2 Peter
   Wolfgang Grünstäudl and Tobias Nicklas 215

Bibliography 229

Contributors 257

Index of Ancient Sources 259

Index of Modern Authors 272

Acknowledgments

The editors wish to thank a number of people who have played vital roles in this project. Tom Thatcher, the New Testament editor for the Resources for Biblical Study series, was supportive of the volume from the outset and is an enviable model of energy, efficiency, and promptness for all of us in the discipline. Leigh Andersen, managing editor for the press, provided help and guidance as always at various stages in the process, as did Bob Buller, director of publications for SBL. Special thanks are due to Jeff Reimer for his excellent copyediting for this volume, and, of course, to the friends and colleagues who contributed their good work to this collection and made it possible.

In addition, we are grateful to Edmondo Lupieri, the John Cardinal Cody Chair of Theology at Loyola University Chicago, who hosted a seminar in conjunction with the early work on this project on March 28, 2012. The editors thank Loyola graduate students Jenny DeVivo, Jeremy Miselbrook, and Cambry Pardee for their insightful responses to initial drafts of the editors' papers and Jeffrey Tripp for his skillful organization of the seminar. Likewise, we appreciate the special assistance offered in the proofs stage by three Judson University undergraduate students, Jimmy Fowler, Timothy Kuhn, and Jonathan H. Sherwell. We would also like to thank Saint Xavier University for granting some release time to Troy for the completion of this project.

Finally, we are especially appreciative of our families for their support. We dedicate this volume to the memory of two men whose passings coincided with the early and late stages of our work on this book: Joseph Bennington, beloved adopted grandfather of the Martin family; and Sam Oginni, an inspiring friend and fellow church member of the Masons.

Abbreviations

Greek and Latin Sources

Adamantius
   Rect. fid.   *De recta in Deum fide* (*On the Correct Faith in God* or *Dialogues of Adamantius*)

Aristotle [and Pseudo-Aristotle]
   Gen. an.   *De generatione anamalium* (*Generation of Animals*)
   Poet.   *Poetica* (*Poetics*)
   Pol.   *Politica* (*Politics*)
   Rhet.   *Rhetorica* (*Rhetoric*)
   [*Virt. vit.*]   [*De virtutibus et vitiis* (*Virtues and Vices*)]

Augustine
   C. Jul.   *Contra Julianum* (*Against Julian*)
   Enarrat. Ps.   *Enarrationes in Psalmos* (*Enarrations on the Psalms*)
   Ep.   *Epistula* (*Letter*)
   Fid. op.   *De fide et operibus* (*Faith and Works*)
   Serm.   *Sermo* (*Sermon*)

Cicero
   Inv.   *De inventione rhetorica* (*On Invention*)
   De or.   *De oratore* (*On the Orator*)

Clement of Alexandria
   Hyp.   *Hypotyposeis* (*Outlines*)
   Strom.   *Stromata* (*Miscellanies*)

Dio Chrysostum
   Or.   *Oratio* (*Oration*)

Epictetus
   Diatr.   *Diatribai* (or *Dissertationes*; *Discourses*)

Eusebius
   Hist. eccl.   *Historia ecclesiastica* (*Ecclesiastical History*)

Galen
   UP   *De usu partium* (*On the Usefulness of the Parts of the Body*)
   Sem.   *De semine* (*On the Seed*)

Hesiod
   Theog.   *Theogonia* (*Theogony*)

Hippocrates
   Aphor.   *Aphorismata* (*Aphorisms*)
   Epid.   *Epidemiae* (*Epidemics*)

Irenaeus
   Haer.   *Adversus haereses* (*Against Heresies*)

Isocrates
   Demon.   *Ad Demonicum* (*To Demonicus*)

Jerome
   Epist.   *Epistula* (*Letter*)
   Vir. ill.   *De viris illustribus* (*On Illustrious Men*)
   Vit. Malch.   *Vita Malchi* (*Life of Malchus*)

Josephus
   Ag. Ap.   *Contra Apionem* (*Against Apion*)
   Ant.   *Antiquitates judaicae* (*Jewish Antiquities*)
   J.W.   *Bellum judaicum* (*Jewish War*)

Justin Martyr
   Dial.   *Dialogus cum Tryphone* (*Dialogue with Trypho*)

Leo the Great
   Serm.   *Sermo* (*Sermon*)

Origen (see also Rufinus)
   Cels.   *Contra Celsum* (*Against Celsus*)
   Comm. Jo.   *Commentarium in evangelium Joannis* (*Commentary on John*)
   Comm. Matt.   *Commentarium in evangelium Matthaei* (*Commentary on Matthew*)
   Hom. Jes. Nav.   *In Jesu Nave homiliae* (*Homilies on Joshua*)
   Princ.   *De principiis* (*First Principles*)

Philo
   Alleg. Interp.   *Legum allegoriae* (*Allegorical Interpretation*)
   Contempl. Life   *De vita contemplativa* (*On the Contemplative Life*)

Decalogue	*De decalogo* (*On the Decalogue*)
Embassy	*Legatio ad Gaium* (*Embassy to Gaius*)
Moses	*De vita Mosis* (*The Life of Moses*)
Posterity	*De posteritate Caini* (*On the Posterity of Cain*)
Rewards	*De praemiis et poenis* (*On Rewards and Punishments*)
Sacrifices	*De sacrificiis Abelis et Caini* (*On the Sacrifices of Cain and Abel*)
Spec. Laws	*De specialibus legibus* (*On the Special Laws*)

Pliny
   Ep.   *Epistula* (*Letter*)

Quintilian
   Inst.   *Institutio oratoria*

Rufinus

Orig. Comm. Rom.	*Origenis Commentarius in epistulan ad Romanos* (*Origen's Commentary on the Epistle to the Romans*)
Orig. Hom. Exod.	*Origenis in Exodum homiliae* (*Origen's Homilies on Exodus*)
Orig. Hom. Jos.	*Origenis Homiliae in librum Josua* (*Origen's Homilies on Joshua*)
Orig. Hom. Lev.	*Origenis Homiliae in Leviticum* (*Origen's Homilies on Leviticus*)
Orig. Hom. Num.	*Origenis in Numeros homiliae* (*Origen's Homilies on Numbers*)

Seneca
   Ep.   *Epistula* (*Letter*)

Soranus
   Gyn.   *Gynecology*

Tacitus
   Ann.   *Annales* (*Annals*)

Tertullian
   Nat.   *Ad nationes* (*To the Heathen*)

Xenophon
   Mem.   *Memorabilia*

Dead Sea Scrolls

CD	Cairo Genizah copy of the Damascus Document

1QS	*Rule of the Community*
1QH	*Hodayot (Thanksgiving Hymns)*
4QpIsaiah[b]	*Pesher Isaiah (4Q162)*

Pseudepigrapha

2 Bar.	*2 Baruch*
1 En.	*1 Enoch (Ethiopic Apocalypse)*
2 En.	*2 Enoch*
Jub.	*Jubilees*
Odes Sol.	*Odes of Solomon*
Pss. Sol.	*Psalms of Solomon*
Sib. Or.	*Sibylline Oracles*
T. 12 Patr.	*Testaments of the Twelve Patriarchs*
T. Levi	*Testament of Levi*
T. Mos.	*Testament of Moses*
T. Naph.	*Testament of Naphtali*

Apostolic Fathers

Barn.	*Barnabas*
Did.	*Didache*
Diogn.	*Diognetus*
Mand.	Shepherd of Hermas, *Mandates*
Mart. Pol.	*Martyrdom of Polycarp*
Pol. Phil.	Polycarp, *To the Philippians*

Other Early Christian Writings

Act. Scil.	*Acts of the Scillitan Martyrs*
Acts Thom.	*Acts of Thomas*
Apos. Con.	*Apostolic Constitutions and Canons*

Rabbinic Literature

Tg. Ps.-J.	*Targum Pseudo-Jonathan*
m. Sanh.	*Mishnah Sanhedrin*

Secondary Sources

AB	Anchor Bible
ACNT	Augsburg Commentaries on the New Testament
AnBib	Analecta biblica
ANF	*Ante-Nicene Fathers*. Edited by A. Roberts and J. Donaldson. 10 vols. Repr., Peabody, Mass.: Hendrickson, 1994. [orig. 1885–1887]
ANRW	*Aufstieg und Niedergang der römischen Welt: Geschichte und Kultur Roms im Spiegel der neueren Forschung*. Edited by H. Temporini and W. Haase. Berlin: de Gruyter, 1972–.
ANTC	Abingdon New Testament Commentaries
BBR	*Bulletin for Biblical Research*
BDAG	Bauer, W., F. W. Danker, W. F. Arndt, and F. W. Gingrich. *Greek-English Lexicon of the New Testament and Other Early Christian Literature*. 3rd ed. Chicago: University of Chicago Press, 1999.
BDF	Blass, F., A. Debrunner, and R. W. Funk. *A Greek Grammar of the New Testament and Other Early Christian Literature*. Chicago: University of Chicago Press, 1961.
BECNT	Baker Exegetical Commentary on the New Testament
BTB	*Biblical Theology Bulletin*
BETL	Bibliotheca ephemeridum theologicarum lovaniensium
Bib	*Biblica*
BNTC	Black's New Testament Commentaries
BZNW	Beihefte zur Zeitschrift für die neutestamentliche Wissenschaft
ca.	circa
CBET	Contributions to Biblical Exegesis and Theology
CBQ	*Catholic Biblical Quarterly*
CBQMS	Catholic Biblical Quarterly Monograph Series
CCSL	Corpus Christianorum Series Latina
ConBNT	Coniectanea biblica: New Testament Series
CSEL	Corpus Scriptorum Ecclesiasticorum Latinorum
CurTM	*Currents in Theology and Mission*
EvQ	*Evangelical Quarterly*
FC	Fathers of the Church
ForFasc	Forum Fascicles

FRLANT	Forschungen zur Religion und Literatur des Alten und Neuen Testaments
GBS	Guides to Biblical Scholarship
GRBS	*Greek, Roman, and Byzantine Studies*
HTB	Histoire du texte biblique
HTR	*Harvard Theological Review*
HUT	Hermeneutische Untersuchungen zur Theologie
IBC	Interpretation: A Bible Commentary for Teaching and Preaching
ICC	International Critical Commentary
JBL	*Journal of Biblical Literature*
JECS	*Journal of Early Christian Studies*
JETS	*Journal of the Evangelical Theological Society*
JNES	*Journal of Near Eastern Studies*
JTS	*Journal of Theological Studies*
JSNT	*Journal for the Study of the New Testament*
JSJSup	Journal for the Study of Judaism in the Persian, Hellenistic, and Roman Periods Supplement Series
JSPSup	Journal for the Study of the Pseudepigrapha Supplement Series
KJV	King James Version
LCL	Loeb Classical Library
LD	Lectio divina
LEC	Library of Early Christianity
LNTS	Library of New Testament Studies
LSJ	Liddell, H. G., R. Scott, and H. S. Jones. *A Greek-English Lexicon*. 9th ed. with revised supplement. Oxford: Clarendon, 1996.
LXX	Septuagint
MT	Masoretic Text
NAB	New American Bible
NASB	New American Standard Bible
NIBCNT	New International Biblical Commentary on the New Testament
NIDB	*The New Interpreter's Dictionary of the Bible*. Edited by K. Doob Sakenfeld. 5 vols. Nashville: Abingdon, 2006–2009.
NIV	New International Version
NovTSup	Supplements to Novum Testamentum

NPNF[1]	*The Nicene and Post-Nicene Fathers*, series 1. Edited by P. Schaff. 14 vols. Repr., Peabody, Mass.: Hendrickson, 1994. [orig. 1886–1889]
NPNF[2]	*The Nicene and Post-Nicene Fathers*, series 2. Edited by P. Schaff and H. Wace. 14 vols. Repr., Peabody, Mass.: Hendrickson, 1994. [orig. 1890]
NRSV	New Revised Standard Version
NTAbh	Neutestamentliche Abhandlungen
NTG	New Testament Guides
NTL	New Testament Library
NTTS	New Testament Tools and Studies
NTS	*New Testament Studies*
OTS	Old Testament Studies
PG	Patrologia graeca [= Patrologiae cursus completus: Series graeca]. Edited by J. P. Migne. 162 vols. Paris: Imprimerie Catholique, 1857–1886.
PTS	Patristische Texte und Studien
RB	*Revue biblique*
RSV	Revised Standard Version
SBLDS	Society of Biblical Literature Dissertation Series
SBLMS	Society of Biblical Literature Monograph Series
SBLRBS	Society of Biblical Literature Resources for Biblical Study
SBLSP	Society of Biblical Literature Seminar Papers
SBLSBS	Society of Biblical Literature Sources for Biblical Study
SBLSymS	Society of Biblical Literature Symposium Series
SBS	Stuttgarter Bibelstudien
SBT	Studies in Biblical Theology
SC	Sources Chrétiennes
SEAug	Studia ephemeridis Augustinianum
SemeiaSt	Semeia Studies
SecCent	*Second Century*
SJLA	Studies in Judaism in Late Antiquity
SNTSMS	Society for New Testament Studies Monograph Series
SP	Sacra pagina
s.v.	*sub verbo* ("under the word")
TDNT	*Theological Dictionary of the New Testament*. Edited by G. Kittel and G. Friedrich. Translated by G. W. Bromiley. 10 vols. Grand Rapids: Eerdmans, 1964–76.

TNTC	Tyndale New Testament Commentaries
TUGAL	Texte und Untersuchungen zur Geschichte der altchristlichen Literatur
TynBul	*Tyndale Bulletin*
VC	*Vigiliae Christianae*
WBC	Word Biblical Commentary
WUNT	Wissenschaftliche Untersuchungen zum Neuen Testament
ZNW	*Zeitschrift für die neutestamentliche Wissenschaft und die Kunde der älteren Kirche*
ZWT	*Zeitschrift für wissenschaftliche Theologie*

Introduction

Eric F. Mason and Troy W. Martin

The three New Testament epistles treated in this volume—1 Peter, 2 Peter, and Jude—have long been viewed as outliers in the New Testament canon by biblical scholars, even though the three books faced differing assessments in the early church. Second Peter, quite suspect throughout much of the patristic era, was further marginalized by some late nineteenth- to mid-twentieth-century scholars who claimed it exemplifies "early catholicism," a supposed calcification of the early church's vibrant faith into a cold, institutional, tradition-bound orthodoxy, and thus it is "perhaps the most dubious writing in the canon" (Käsemann 1964, 169).[1] Discussion of Jude and 1 Peter has normally been less caustic, but the modern perspective is captured well by the titles of two journal articles that appeared four decades ago. Douglas J. Rowston declared Jude to be "The Most Neglected Book in the New Testament" (1975), and just a year later John H. Elliott coined an oft-repeated moniker for 1 Peter when he wrote "The Rehabilitation of an Exegetical Step-Child: 1 Peter in Recent Research" (1976). Actually, Elliott went further and included "the remaining Catholic Epistles, Hebrews, and the Johannine Apocalypse" in his list of the "step-children of the NT canon" (1976, 243).

---

1. Typically three characteristics are cited for "early catholicism": fading hope for Christ's imminent return, increasing institutionalism with defined leadership offices, and the solidification of doctrine and tradition in order to preserve "the faith" against challenges like those posed by gnostics or Montanists. See Chester and Martin 1994, 148–51 and especially Bauckham 1983, 151–54 for rebuttals to Käsemann's characterization of 2 Peter (and Bauckham 1983, 8–11 for similar discussion in regard to Jude). Dunn (2006, 372–400) argues that numerous New Testament books (including Jude and 2 Peter, but also others like 1 Corinthians and Romans) have *certain* elements of early Catholicism.

In some ways things have changed significantly in the last few decades. Hebrews and Revelation have certainly garnered significant scholarly attention in recent years, and it is not coincidental that they were the first two texts addressed in the Resources for Biblical Study "Reading" volumes, which the present book now joins.[2] Elliott could offer a much more positive assessment of scholarly interest in 1 Peter by the time his Anchor Bible commentary on that epistle appeared a quarter century later (2000, 3–6). The bibliography of this present volume attests heartily to Elliott's personal contributions to that renaissance; the appearance of his commentary, combined with Paul J. Achtemeier's in the Hermeneia series (1996) just a few years earlier, represents a sea change of interest in this text.

As for 2 Peter and Jude, Richard J. Bauckham lamented in the preface to his important Word Biblical Commentary on those epistles that when writing he was "for the most part … unable to draw on the mass of recent research in articles and monographs which is available to commentators on most other NT books" (1983, xi). Although recent focus on 2 Peter and Jude has still not attained the levels now enjoyed by Hebrews, Revelation, and even 1 Peter, the situation has improved in subsequent decades (in part due to Bauckham's own contributions), and polemical charges of early Catholicism are much less common. Today one can affirm with Gene L. Green that "interest in these books is on the rise, and their study is experiencing a revival" (2008, xi).

Our goal is that this present volume will also contribute to greater interest in and appreciation for 1–2 Peter and Jude. Though readers have often considered these epistles confusing, mysterious, obscure, and even offensive, the chapters in this collection demonstrate that each of these three texts is a rich document with much to offer for scholarly investigation and contemporary reflection.[3]

The title of this book is *Reading 1–2 Peter and Jude: A Resource for Students*. Both phrases in this title are very important. The first part needs little explanation—this book is a scholarly investigation of key aspects of

---

2. See Barr 2003 on Revelation; Mason and McCruden 2011 on Hebrews. The third volume in the Resources for Biblical Study series concerns Romans (Sumney 2012), a text that has never lacked for interpreters' attention!

3. Perkins notes that the Catholic Epistles in general "should not be shoehorned into a story of early Christianity that has been established by the Pauline and deutero-Pauline letters and Acts" because they "instead … provide valuable evidence for the diversity of Christianity throughout the first century" (1999, 124).

these three epistles. Most of the contributors to the present volume are recognized specialists on the study of one of more of these epistles, as is evident in the bibliography at the end of the volume. Other contributors have not normally published on these particular texts but bring to the collection particular expertise from another field. All of our contributors engage current scholarship on these epistles and add to this discussion.

We assume that most readers of this book will study it alongside standard commentaries on one or more of the epistles. While this volume includes chapters on authorship and literary relationships among the three epistles, our focus has been to provide extended discussions of important issues that go beyond what is feasible in a typical commentary. We trust readers will find the chapters in this book informative, engaging, and enlightening.

This points to the significance of the second half of this book's title—"a resource for students." Our contributors have been charged not just to write chapters that engage the best of contemporary scholarship on these three epistles, but also to do so with the needs and concerns of student readers at the forefront. We have sought to write not only with an advanced undergraduate readership in mind but also in ways that will be beneficial for more advanced students in seminary or graduate school and indeed for any educated reader studying one of more of the epistles of Peter and Jude for the first time. This means we have been intentional about defining specialized terminology, providing relevant historical and cultural background information, and explaining tenets of the methodologies we utilize. While these epistles have been the subject of several very readable commentaries written by esteemed scholars (including some excellent volumes by contributors to this book), we are aware of no other student-oriented book on 1–2 Peter and Jude that addresses the breadth of issues with the range of perspectives that the present volume offers. We therefore trust that readers of various levels will find much of value in the chapters of this volume.

The chapters in this book fall into three sections: those addressing all three epistles, those addressing 1 Peter, and those addressing both Jude and 2 Peter. It has long been traditional to read these three epistles together in some manner, and this approach has certainly been fostered by factors such as the common attribution of authorship for 1 and 2 Peter and the significant overlap of content between Jude and 2 Peter. In recent decades, scholars have increasingly emphasized the importance of reading these books in light of their own distinctive contexts, yet it is still advantageous and even necessary to consider certain questions with all three epistles in view. As such, the first four chapters in this collection—on authorship and pseudonymity, literary relationships among the three books, epistolary rhetoric, and apocalyptic elements—consider important, foundational issues related to all three epistles. In many ways they lay the groundwork for the subsequent chapters.

Lewis R. Donelson addresses the tricky issues of authorship and pseudonymity in his opening chapter, titled "Gathering Apostolic Voices: Who Wrote 1 and 2 Peter and Jude?" Donelson briefly surveys the kinds of pseudonymous texts known in early Christianity and common scholarly explanations about how and why such texts circulated. He also notes the difficulty of substantiating assumptions about apostolic schools and even pseudonymous letters that were not written with the intent to deceive. Since "every general theory about the origin and motives of Christian pseudepigraphy has proven to be unsustainable," he deems it essential that each text be examined individually and that one also consider how to understand other features of these letters (such as identifications of the addressees and other personal references) if the ascribed author did not write the epistle. Ultimately, Donelson concludes that all three letters are pseudepigraphical but notes the plausibility of differing evaluations of the same data. Ultimately, "everyone reads these letters in much the same way regardless of the position taken on authorship," and their inclusion in the Christian canon authorizes them as "apostolic voices."

Next, Jeremy F. Hultin examines "The Literary Relationships among 1 Peter, 2 Peter, and Jude." He begins with the issue of common materials in Jude 4–18 and 2 Peter 2:1–3:3 by observing similarities of content, vocabulary, and sequence but not verbatim agreements. Hultin carefully evaluates proposals to explain these similarities, especially suggestions that Jude used 2 Peter, 2 Peter used Jude, or both used a common source. Hultin notes the strengths and weaknesses of each theory and concludes that 2 Peter's use of Jude is most likely, yet he also resists the idea that the problem is solved. "Theories serve best when they provoke ever more careful and creative engagement with the texts themselves," whereas consensus around one idea "may deaden interest in those pesky details that refuse to fit into any one model." Next, he considers the relationship between 1 and 2 Peter; he focuses not on authorship but instead on the reference to an earlier letter in 2 Pet 3:1–2 and thematic connections between the two books. Hultin concludes that 2 Peter knows 1 Peter and yet makes surprisingly little use of it.

At the end of the twentieth century, a sharp debate arose over the application of epistolary and rhetorical analyses to New Testament letters. Epistolary analysis views these letters as literary documents and compares them with other letters from the ancient world. In contrast, rhetorical analysis sees these letters as speeches in written form and compares them to ancient speeches and speech handbooks. In his chapter titled "The Epistolary Rhetoric of 1 Peter, 2 Peter, and Jude," Duane F. Watson takes the position in this debate that epistolary and rhetorical analyses are not mutually exclusive. He recognizes that these letters exhibit many of the conventions of ancient letters but that these conventions can serve rhetorical purposes. Thus the epistolary prescript and blessing-thanksgiving serve as the rhetorical *exordium* and *narratio* to build the relationship between the sender and the recipients as well as to introduce topics discussed in the body of the letter. The body of these letters functions as the rhetorical *probatio*, or argument for the authors' positions. The letter closing or postscript functions as the rhetorical *peroratio*, which builds goodwill and reiterates topics discussed in the letter. As such, Watson argues that these letters are essentially speeches in letter form.

In the final chapter of this first section, Kelley Coblentz Bautch brings her perspective as a specialist in Enochic and other Jewish apocalyptic literature to her chapter titled "'Awaiting New Heavens and a New Earth': The Apocalyptic Imagination of 1–2 Peter and Jude." Convinced that 1–2 Peter and Jude demonstrate "that end-time speculation and apocalyptic sensibilities … were important to early Christians and their communities," she offers a primer on key terms relevant for the discussion and surveys several prominent characteristics of apocalyptic. Then she considers how particular apocalyptic elements are present in each of our three epistles, including an interest in otherworldly beings and realms; the idea that the end times will resemble the primeval era; dualism; the Day of the Lord and judgment; and deliverance and the age to come. Coblentz Bautch is careful to demonstrate both the similar and differing uses of apocalyptic thought in our three epistles. She concludes that while each of the three epistles uses apocalyptic elements in distinct ways (and that these differences may reveal something about their specific audiences), overall "the apocalypticism of these three epistles fits well the apocalyptic tendencies of the entire New Testament."

The second section contains four chapters that focus exclusively on 1 Peter as well as two chapters that use this epistle to illustrate methodologies relevant to all three epistles. The first three chapters include discussions of the Christology, use of metaphor, and use of paraenetic materials in 1 Peter. The next two consider how social-scientific and postmodern approaches may be applied to that epistle.[4] A final chapter on 1 Peter addresses its reception in the patristic period.

Christology is an essential concern of Christianity, and Steven J. Kraftchick explores this aspect of 1 Peter. In his chapter "Reborn to a Living Hope: A Christology of 1 Peter," he declares 1 Peter to be "one of the most thoroughly christocentric writings in the New Testament" (quoting Achtemeier 1993, 176) but at the same time "thoroughly theocentric and ecclesiastically directed." The integration of ecclesiology, theology, and Christology moves 1 Peter away from systematic declarative affirmations and speculative statements to images that provide pastoral care for the letter's recipients who are suffering and need to understand their circumstances and identity. Kraftchick presents the epistle's Christology as functional, dynamic, and pastoral rather than abstract, formal, and logical. These christological images are "drawn from early Christian hymns, creeds, liturgical ceremonies, and interpretations of the Old Testament" and present Christ as the "agent of initiation" for the recipients' salvation and the "exemplar" of their faith. The goal of these images is "to have the readers interact *with* Jesus Christ rather than simply receive information *about*" him. The Christology of 1 Peter is thus participatory and invites the readers into the narrative world created by the text that will shape their own understanding of their circumstances and identity as Christians and offer them hope.

Metaphors are a prominent feature of 1 Peter and permeate the letter from its beginning to its end. Troy W. Martin thus explores 1 Peter's use of metaphor in his chapter "Christians as Babies: Metaphorical Reality in 1 Peter." He first surveys various definitions of metaphor that distinguish metaphor from other types of symbolic speech such as metonymy, allegory, parable, and simile. Metaphors are appropriately used in 1 Peter since they "give names to things that have none," and 1 Peter explains the new ontological reality of non-Jewish believers in Israel's God. Next, Martin describes some of the theories about metaphor that interpreters have applied to 1 Peter. The older notion of metaphor as a phenomenon of language is replaced by an understanding of metaphor as a phenomenon

---

4. For applications of these and other emerging methodologies to each of our three epistles, see especially Webb and Bauman-Martin 2007 (1 Peter); Watson and Webb 2010 (2 Peter); and Webb and Davids 2009 (Jude).

of thought, and interpreters seek to map the "salient and fitting characteristics" of source domains to target domains. Martin then investigates the specific metaphor of newborn babies to illustrate this new approach to the mapping of metaphors in 1 Peter. He points out that ancient physiology and in particular ancient conceptions of infant nutrition are necessary to map this metaphor. Martin concludes that the metaphors in 1 Peter describe the reality of its recipients' new status brought about by their becoming Christians. They have indeed been begotten by God in a very real sense, and the letter exhorts them to desire the very real blood of Christ in the Eucharist and to allow the word of God to shape them into the actual people of God's own making.

Another prominent feature of 1 Peter is its discussion of ethics. Nancy Pardee (who specializes in early Christian paraenetic literature outside the New Testament) investigates this aspect of the epistle in her chapter "Be Holy, for I Am Holy: Paraenesis in 1 Peter." She identifies encouragement as the primary goal of the letter and seeks to answer the question of how traditional moral exhortation functions in a text so focused on comfort and encouragement. She begins by explaining what paraenesis is and then distinguishes between Jewish and Greek elements in the letter's paraenesis. First Peter's moral expectations for its Gentile audience are based on Jewish concepts of holiness and sanctification. The letter integrates Greek ideas and terminology such as virtue/vice lists and household codes into these Jewish elements and so conflates Jewish and Greek moral traditions in its paraenesis. She concludes that the paraenesis in the letter is both traditional and adaptive. It draws from traditional Jewish and Greek paraenesis but adapts both the content and form to encourage the recipients of the letter in the context of suffering.

First Peter holds pride of place as one of the first New Testament documents to be interpreted as a whole according to a social-scientific approach, and in his chapter "Ethnicity, Empire, and Early Christian Identity: Social-Scientific Perspectives on 1 Peter," David G. Horrell describes some of the ways this approach helps illuminate the situation and strategy of this early Christian letter. Horrell first describes the pioneering social-scientific work of John H. Elliott, who argues that the recipients of the letter represented a conversionist sect distinct and separate from the world around it. The letter's strategy is to provide a home for these transient strangers or displaced persons. Horrell discusses the debate between Elliott and David Balch, who sees the letter as calling "for assimilation and greater conformity to the wider society" in contrast to the call for distinctiveness and resistance perceived by Elliott. Horrell views this debate as illustrative of the "great diversification of methods and perspectives within what may very broadly be seen as social-scientific criticism." Horrell then summarizes three brief case studies to show how social scientific resources help us "appreciate the significance of 1 Peter in the making of Christian identity." He explains the contributions of 1 Peter to the creation of Christian ethnicity, the postcolonial perspective of 1 Peter in conformity and resistance, and 1 Peter's redefining and reclaiming of the socially negative label "Christian."

The impact of postmodern biblical criticism should not be underestimated, and Félix H. Cortez helps us understand this interpretive movement and its influence on the analysis and interpretation of 1 Peter in his chapter "1 Peter and Postmodern Criticism." Cortez begins by describing this criticism not as "a method but rather a stance or a posture that uses different methods of analysis." It is essentially a resistance to modernism and is "antifoundational, antitotalizing, and demystifying." In biblical studies, postmodernism contests the historical-critical method, and Cortez surveys four postmodern studies of 1 Peter that address the postmodern concerns of "foundations, totalities, and objectivity." The first study exposes the constructed world of the assumed narrative in 1 Peter. Instead of providing a "real" foundation, the text projects a world and invites its readers into that world. The second study deconstructs the binary oppositions incoherently and inconsistently used by the text to construct a total system. The third study emphasizes that 1 Peter is shaped by political forces that serve the interests of one group or another. And the final study shows how 1 Peter and especially its household code have been used to further the interests of males to the disadvantage of females. Instead of focusing "on the historical meaning of the text and its genesis," Cortez concludes, postmodern approaches try "to pry open the political forces that have shaped interpretations of 1 Peter in order to focus attention on the current meaning of 1 Peter."

Bearing the authority of the apostle Peter, 1 Peter has been a significant document for the church, and Andreas Merkt traces the reception history of this letter in his chapter "1 Peter in Patristic Literature." In this literature, he notes, there was no doubt that the apostle authored this letter, and its canonicity was never in dispute. Initially it was placed first among the Catholic Epistles, but later it came to follow the Epistle of James (reflecting the order of Paul's list of "pillars" in Gal 2:9). Merkt surveys the reception of 1 Peter among the church fathers including Polycarp, who first quoted

1 Peter; Clement of Alexandria, who wrote the first brief commentary; and Didymus of Alexandria, who wrote the first comprehensive commentary on the letter. Read mostly in Easter liturgies and in the teaching of catechumens and neophytes, 1 Peter was understood to be "a letter about redemption, conversion, and its consequences," and Merkt illustrates this understanding by recounting the reception of "Christ's preaching to the spirits in prison in 3:19 and the term 'exemplum' applied to him in 2:21." Some fathers used the former to teach universal salvation, while others used it to limit salvation to the baptized only. The latter was central to the Pelagian controversy and exemplifies the patristic canonical approach to interpretation in which a verse is interpreted by links to other verses. Merkt thus sketches for us the importance of 1 Peter for the developing Christian tradition.

Finally, the third section of the book highlights issues of great significance for Jude and 2 Peter. Though both of these short epistles are treated in each chapter, the authors take care to highlight their distinctive characteristics, themes, and histories so as to avoid implications that the two letters are virtually indistinguishable or interchangeable. These chapters address the use in both books of biblical and nonbiblical sources and the questions this raises for understanding the idea of canon; the identity of the opponents in each of the two books; and the different reception histories of each epistle in the patristic period.

In his chapter "Biblical and Nonbiblical Traditions in Jude and 2 Peter: Sources, Usage, and the Question of Canon," Eric F. Mason notes that both epistles are steeped in references to biblical figures and events, yet the lone explicit textual quotation in either epistle is Jude's citation of Enoch. Also, the two epistles use and discuss traditional materials in differing ways. Jude ostensibly was written by a brother of Jesus but does not seek to exploit this status; prophecy is clearly authoritative, but the author does not explain why this is so. Second Peter, however, appeals to Peter's apostolic authority and testimony as well as the authority of Scripture; this author "is working with some consciousness of what is authoritative literature." Although 2 Peter does not retain the Enoch quotation from Jude, the author does not eschew nonbiblical texts (as is often claimed). Instead, "nothing in either Jude or 2 Peter allows one to distinguish between texts that later will be deemed biblical and nonbiblical," and this illustrates the difficulties of forcing later canonical sensitivities onto earlier writings.

Peter H. Davids highlights the importance of understanding the nature of the opponents in Jude and 2 Peter in his chapter titled "Are the Others

Too Other? The Issue of 'Others' in Jude and 2 Peter." Davids opens with a consideration of the diversity found in early churches (especially as seen in Paul's letters and Acts) when the movement grew to include peoples of differing cultural backgrounds. Naturally, varying practices and ideas appeared, even though our sources generally preserve only the perspectives of those whose preferences triumphed. "Some of these positions were inevitably viewed as acceptable differences within the movement, even if their proponents were viewed as wrong-headed, while others were viewed as serious enough to exclude their proponents from the movement." The communities of Jude and 2 Peter faced internal conflicts but of different sorts. The "Others" in Jude may be Hellenistic outsiders who reject the authority of the Torah that is valued by the "Beloved" in Jude's community, but their redemption is possible. In 2 Peter, however, the problem concerns community insiders who become "Others" because of their false teaching, and they have moved beyond the point of restoration.

Interest in Jude and 2 Peter paled in comparison to interest in the Gospels and Pauline Epistles in the early church, much as it still does today, yet the paths taken by these two books toward canonicity were very different. This is explained by Wolfgang Grünstäudl and Tobias Nicklas in the concluding chapter of this volume, titled "Searching for Evidence: The History of Reception of the Epistles of Jude and 2 Peter." Jude was accepted by many church authorities quite early but later survived significant opposition; the challenges arose in part due to its use of Enochic and other nonbiblical material. Second Peter was initially rejected due to its eschatology and differences from 1 Peter but was later embraced by orthodox leaders as a useful tool for affirming Paul's authority and countering millenarian interpretations of Revelation. Grünstäudl and Nicklas observe that "there is no clear evidence of the existence of 2 Peter in the time before Origen" (late second to mid-third century C.E.), and this lack of early attestation prompts their provocative thesis: 2 Peter might actually be *dependent* on—not a *source* for—two early second-century "postbiblical" texts, the *Dialogue* of Justin Martyr and the *Apocalypse of Peter*.

Gathering Apostolic Voices: Who Wrote 1 and 2 Peter and Jude?

Lewis R. Donelson

Almost all readings of texts include questions about the original author of the text. While readings of texts, especially biblical texts, have many purposes and methods, most readings at some point undertake an attempt to hear the voice and intentions of the original author. Part of what we want to do when we read is to understand the text as the author wanted it to be understood. Readers of biblical texts typically share this concern. We want to know who wrote 1 and 2 Peter and Jude and how they wanted their letters to be understood. It turns out that, for all three of these letters, these questions are not easy to answer.

At first glance, the authorship of these letters should not be a problem. First Peter names "Peter, apostle of Jesus Christ" as its author (1 Pet 1:1). Second Peter names "Simeon Peter, slave and apostle of Jesus Christ" (2 Pet 1:1). Jude names "Judas, slave of Jesus Christ, brother of Jacob" (Jude 1).[1] Many people think these named people are the historical authors.[2] However, there are reasons to hesitate in reaching this conclusion. Among early Christian documents, there are many that have the wrong name as author. These pseudepigraphical documents include numerous Gospels under false apostolic names (including a *Gospel of Peter*), various acts under apostolic names (including, again, an *Acts of Peter*), postresurrection dialogues with Jesus, various apocalypses (including an *Apocalypse of Peter*), and lots of pseudepigraphical letters (including a letter of Jesus to Abgar of Edessa). There is little or no debate about the pseudepigraphical status of most of these texts. However, the existence of these texts gives

---

1. See the discussion of the names Jude, Judas, James, and Jacob below.
2. See the discussions below on each letter.

space for the question of whether a text that claims to be written by Peter is, in fact, by Peter.

Even in the earliest centuries, Christians debated the authorship and authority of Christian texts. For instance, the early church historian Eusebius, who wrote his history of the church in about 325 C.E., divides early Christian documents into the undisputed, the disputed, and the spurious (*Hist. eccl.* 3.3.1–4; 3.25.3). For our purposes, it is interesting that Eusebius includes 2 Peter and Jude among the disputed (the so-called antilegomena).[3] Should any documents in the traditional canon be included among the many early Christian pseudepigrapha? In particular, did the apostle Peter really write 1 and 2 Peter? Likewise, did Jude the brother of James really write Jude?

The difficulty is that we do not know how to answer these questions with any confidence. Neither the early Christians nor readers since have agreed about how to determine when a text is pseudepigraphical. Part of the issue is that early Christian documents typically classified as pseudepigraphical are diverse in format and often have mysterious origins. For instance, some pseudepigrapha make no claim about authorship. The false names come from later attribution. Many later Christian Gospels are of this kind. Some texts make a false claim about their author not by making that claim explicitly but by including themselves, or being included, in authoritative collections. Second Isaiah and perhaps many of the psalms are of this kind. However, most pseudepigraphical texts make an explicit claim about authorship, and they make this claim for what seem to be all kinds of reasons. Thus it is not surprising that historians have produced no general explanation for why and how false names were used.

Pseudepigraphical letters are less diverse in how they claim authorship, typically naming an author explicitly.[4] They also typically name or address their recipients, even if the recipients are often addressed in such a way that they could be almost any ancient Christian. However, the origin and purpose of disputed letters has proven to be just as difficult to determine as for everything else (see Ehrman 2013, 69–148, for numerous examples). There are just too many possibilities, and the data are inconclusive.

Some scholars have proposed that most Christian pseudepigraphical letters emerged from groups of early Christians who were followers of

---

3. Among canonical texts, Eusebius also include James, 2 John, 3 John, and Revelation among the disputed texts.

4. The New Testament book of Hebrews is unusual in that it is anonymous.

Paul or Peter or other apostles (Soards 1988; Meade 1986, 9–11). These groups are typically portrayed as organized schools that were perhaps founded by historical friends or students of an apostle and studied the writings of their chosen apostle. It is further proposed that these followers wrote documents, including letters, in the names of these apostles as a way both to honor them and to continue their voice. Finally, it is usually assumed that these school letters were not written in the attempt to deceive other Christians.

It is suggested that both the authors and the original readers would have known that 2 Peter, for instance, was not by Peter. Rather, 2 Peter is an attempt by followers of Peter to imagine what Peter would say if he were still alive. These pseudepigraphical writers typically felt inspired by the Spirit to write in the spirit of the named apostle. Much of Jewish prophecy can be seen as instances of such inspiration, where oracles of diverse origin were published under the aegis, for instance, of Isaiah or Jeremiah. To give one's name as author would be to deny the power of the Spirit that funded these texts. It is more honest to place Peter's name on the text because Peter, by way of the Spirit, is the true author (See Aland 1961 for a fuller account of this proposal).

Of course, all of these proposals are contested. There is no direct evidence anywhere in early Christian texts of such apostolic schools. Their existence is extrapolated as a way to explain the existence of these pseudepigraphical texts. Thus, other scholars have suggested that there were no organized schools but only people in scattered locations who read and honored apostles and who chose for various reasons to speak in their names (See Soards 1988 and Elliott 2000, 124–34, for discussions of various options). Furthermore, there is no pseudepigraphical letter—in fact, no Christian pseudepigraphical document—that explicitly claims any self-understanding of the kind outlined above (Candlish 1391).

In fact, some scholars suggest that the usual motive for using pseudepigraphy in these apostolic letters was deception (See Ehrman 2013, esp. 149–54; Donelson 1986, 23–66). The original author wanted the original readers to think that 2 Peter, for instance, was really written by Peter. These scholars argue that, in the case of letters at least, this intention fits the ancient data. They point out that Christian documents written in the name of an apostle or Greek documents written in the name of an ancient philosopher lost their voice if they were suspected of being pseudepigraphical. Furthermore, they point out that early Christianity was devoted to apostolic authority. For any document to have authority, it had to be apostolic. The high status given to apostolic voices explains why there were so many pseudepigraphical documents in early Christianity.

In actual fact, these texts do not explain their motives for using pseudonymity. Thus, to detail such motives or to assume a theory of inspiration is simply to hazard a guess. It might be a good guess, but it is nonetheless a guess. There are many theories about the origin of these texts. Most of them are variations on the two options of inspiration and deception or, frequently, some combination of both. However, every general theory about the origin and motives of Christian pseudepigraphy has proven to be unsustainable. There is simply too much variety in these texts. Instead of proposing theories of inspiration or deception that might manage all these texts, we must look at each text individually, as each presents its own puzzle.

1 Peter

First Peter begins, as do 2 Peter and Jude, with a typical early Christian form of greeting. Ancient letters normally began with some form of "sender to recipient, greetings." Christian letters often expanded this greeting by adding attributions to both the sender and recipient and changing the Greek "greetings" to a theological invocation of, for instance, grace or peace. In 1 Peter, the sender is named simply "Peter, an apostle of Jesus Christ." This identification is a nice, clean, and classical naming, to which we shall return below. The greeting itself, "may grace and peace be multiplied for you," is also clean and traditional. It is the description of the recipients that receives the most elaboration and creates the initial puzzle for readers of 1 Peter.

The recipients are not really named. Instead of a name, we receive a theological description of a certain kind of people located over a large area of ancient Asia Minor. They are described initially as "exiles of the dispersion," and are, in 1:2, connected to a brief theological narrative that involves chosenness, sanctification, obedience, blood, and the Spirit. This open-ended theological address is given an extensive but not limitless geographical range. These exiles are those in "Pontus, Galatia, Cappadocia, Asia, and Bithynia," which are five contiguous Roman provinces in what is today western and northern Turkey.

It is not clear how these recipients should be understood. Such an open naming might be an effective way to compose a pseudepigraphical letter. The lack of specific names invites later readers to include themselves.

Anyone who thinks of oneself as an exile and as connected to this saving narrative can imagine oneself as a reader of the letter. The five Roman provinces are given because these are the areas where the letter was first published. Thus any Christian in those provinces would feel explicitly addressed by the letter. This scenario is certainly possible. However, there is nothing in the data itself that requires such a reading. As other people have pointed out, if the real Peter wrote a circular letter to Christians in these provinces, this description is precisely how he might have addressed them (Jobes 2005). The data can be configured several ways.

Peter's designation as "apostle of Jesus Christ" can be read two ways. On the one hand, this designation is the classic way the early church referred to Peter. Peter is an apostle. On the other hand, it is possible and even likely that Peter referred to himself in this way. We have no direct information on Peter's self-designation, unless 1 Peter is by Peter himself. Nevertheless, Paul's accounts of Peter (Gal 2:1-14; 1 Cor 9:5), whom he calls Cephas, make it likely that Peter would have thought of himself as an "apostle." Thus we learn nothing about authorship from this naming of Peter in the salutation.

Ancient letters often concluded with personal greetings and almost always with a final blessing of some kind. First Peter has both (1 Pet 5:12-14). The greeting begins by declaring that Peter "through Silvanus" has written "this short letter." This declaration is a standard way of noting the carrier of the letter, although some scholars have suggested (somewhat implausibly in my opinion) that the phrase "through Silvanus" means that Silvanus actually wrote the letter (see discussion in Elliott 2000, 123–24). In any case, Silvanus is named as the person who is delivering the letter to the communities scattered in these Roman provinces. The letter then conveys a greeting from literally "she who is co-elect in Babylon." "She" is usually and probably correctly understood as the church, and "Babylon" is probably Rome. The letter concludes with a brief greeting from Mark, a command to greet each other with the "kiss of love," and a final invocation of peace.

If the letter is written by Peter, all of these concluding elements are simple to understand. They read as a standard closing to an ancient letter. The comment about Silvanus would be a means of introducing or authenticating him as the deliverer of the letter. If the letter is pseudepigraphical, however, then it is less clear how to read this ending. Pseudepigraphical letters tend to have all the attributes of a normal letter, including personal greetings and biographical comments. Thus the presence of these greetings at the end of 1 Peter says nothing about whether the letter is pseudepigraphical.

Moreover, greetings in pseudepigraphical letters have many functions. Some letters use the details as theological or moral illustrations. Some letters seem to use such personal details for verisimilitude, as an attempt to make the letter seem real. Since Silvanus and Mark seem to have no other function in the letter, it is quite possible these references serve to make the letter appear real. However, there are other possibilities. For instance, many of the people who think 1 Peter was the product of a Petrine school in Rome suggest that Silvanus was still the actual carrier of the letter, even though it was not really Peter who wrote "through Silvanus" (see discussion in Senior and Harrington 2003, 152–53). There are in any case numerous plausible interpretations of the closing.

First Peter illustrates how difficult it is to use the personal references in disputed Christian letters to determine authorship. Consequently, decisions about authorship tend to be made by asking a rather broad question about historical probability. The guiding question is something like: Is 1 Peter a letter that we can imagine the historical Peter writing, or is it easier to imagine someone else writing it? A question like this can, of course, be answered in many ways and cannot, by its very nature, have a definitive answer. However, an appeal to historical probability is not a surrender to any and all opinions. The historical data must be addressed. Any account of authorship must have some sort of historical possibility. Nevertheless, the indeterminate nature of the data and the subjectivity of historical arguments in letters of this kind result in much debate and limited agreement.

There are good reasons for thinking that Simon Peter did not write 1 Peter. The portrait of Peter in both the Gospels and Paul portrays a Palestinian Jew whose native language is Aramaic, who was imbedded in the controversy about Jewish and Gentile Christians and the status of the law, who focused his ministry on Jews and Jewish Christians, and who, as one of the so-called Twelve, knew Jesus firsthand. The letter of 1 Peter, however, is written in a Greek style beyond what many scholars can imagine for Simon Peter. Furthermore, in 1 Peter, there is no reference to the historical life of Jesus; no interest in debates about the law; the audience seems to be former Gentiles, not Jews; the cosmic Christology of 1 Peter has little relation to that of the Gospels; and when the author refers to himself, he names himself surprisingly as "fellow elder" (1 Pet 5:1). Furthermore, the image of widespread persecution seems unlikely during the life of Peter.

The brief household codes are hard to imagine as coming from the Peter of the Gospels. All in all, the theology, the language, and the overall historical context of the letter fit awkwardly into the time and life of Simon Peter but easily into later Christian history. In fact, the letter fits more easily into the postapostolic world of the late first century. Thus, many historians conclude that the letter is more likely to be pseudepigraphical (for example, see list of such people in Elliott 2000, 125 n. 38).

However, many people still affirm authorship by the apostle Peter (Hillyer 1992; Jobes 2005; see list in Elliott 2000, 118 n. 35). A common response to the above argument is that it is simply not convincing. The letter can, to the contrary, be read quite easily as coming from Simon Peter. First Peter could have been written late in Peter's life, when he is living in Rome. His Greek has improved or, perhaps, people have helped him compose the Greek syntax of the letter. The issue of the law is fading. Peter is no longer bound by the imagery and theology of Palestine. He has participated in the growth and creativity of Christian theology. He has moved beyond his initial call to evangelize the Jews. Peter has taken on an unusual and perhaps unique position of authority in the church. He is using that authority to comfort and admonish Christians scattered throughout these Roman provinces. Furthermore, the early church seemed to have no real hesitation about Petrine authorship of 1 Peter, and they knew more about what is historically probable in the first century than any modern historian can ever know.

I think both sides have a good case. My opinion is that it is easier to read the letter as not having been written by Peter. Assuming an unknown author, who lived after the death of Peter and sometime around the end of the century and who used Peter's authority (and perhaps some Petrine traditions) to authorize and shape his letter, produces the most natural reading of the text. However, the plausibility of both of these readings (and others not detailed here) suggests a certain modesty about our conclusions of authorship.

It is often the case that knowing the identity of the author of a document assists and influences how the document is read. However, this is difficult to know in the case of 1 Peter. The imagery and theology of the stories of Peter in the Gospels and Acts do not overlap with the imagery and theology of 1 Peter (see Meade 1986, 172–77, for an argument in support of at least some overlap). Plus, the stories of Peter in the Gospels and Acts, which are framed within the theologies of the authors of those books, do not provide information about Peter's own theology that we might use to organize our readings of 1 Peter. Thus nearly all readers, no matter who they think the author was, read 1 Peter with minimal reference to the stories of Peter in the rest of the New Testament. The somewhat unexpected result is that people who think Peter wrote 1 Peter read the letter almost identically to people who think he did not.

It is not our portrait of the author that directs our reading of 1 Peter; rather, it is our reading of 1 Peter that directs our portrait of its author. Readers have long noted that when we read any text, we inevitably and necessarily create images of its author. This happens with 1 Peter. As we read it, we imagine a Christian living on the edges of the Roman and Christian world and composing this letter to encourage scattered and persecuted Christians. If Peter wrote the letter, then we learn something of what happened to him later in his life, long after his time with Jesus. This Peter is far from Palestine; he is embedded in the Roman world, not the Jewish, and he has changed and grown. If Peter did not write 1 Peter, then we have this same portrait, but it belongs to an unknown Christian who probably lived either in Rome or one of the named Roman provinces. In either case, all readers agree that 1 Peter creates a portrait of a fascinating and even brilliant author.

2 Peter

The debate about the authorship of 2 Peter is much less divided. Questions about the authorship of the letter began in the early church and persist to this day. Second Peter was rarely quoted and mostly ignored in the early church. When we do encounter it, it often comes with questions. As noted above, Eusebius lists 2 Peter among the "disputed" books. Writing at the beginning of the fifth century, Jerome (*Epist.* 120.11) noted the stylistic and theological differences between 1 Peter and 2 Peter and concluded that the two books could not have been written by the same person. Jerome's observation has proven to be largely persuasive.

Of all the books in the New Testament, 2 Peter is the book that is most often regarded as pseudepigraphical (e.g., Bauckham 1983; Kraftchick 2002; Senior and Harrington 2003; see Gilmour 2001 for a nice summary of the issues). This opinion is not, of course, unanimous. Some people point out, correctly I would add, that despite all the debate about 2 Peter, the book was accepted into the canon. It is doubtful that any letter that was generally considered pseudepigraphical would have been given this kind of status. The evidence suggests that the majority of early Christians considered Peter to be the author of 2 Peter, even if many of the academic elite had doubts (see the wonderfully nuanced analysis of Davids 2006, 121–58; see also M. B. Green 1987).

The letter opens by naming "Simeon Peter" as the author. The use of the Hebrew form "Simeon" (*Symeōn* in Greek) occurs only one other time in the New Testament (Acts 15:14). Peter's name usually has the Greek form, "Simon [*Simōn*] Peter." Some people have wondered if the presence of the Semitic form suggests the hand of Peter himself (see discussion in Davids 2006, 159–60). That could be true. Of course, many early Christians would have known the Hebrew form of Simon. Simeon Peter is then identified as "slave and apostle of Jesus Christ." While there is no evidence from Acts or the Gospels that Peter called himself "slave," the term "slave" (or "servant," as it is often translated) is a common self-designation in early Christianity.[5]

We noted above that one of the curiosities about 1 Peter is that it never mentions the Gospel stories of Peter and seems far removed from them. It is perhaps a bit ironic that 2 Peter, which is much less likely to have been written by Peter, actually includes a Gospel story. Second Peter 1:16–18 contains an abbreviated and curious version of the transfiguration story. In 2 Peter, there is no mention of Moses or Elijah. There is no cloud or command to listen. There is not even a hint of Peter's suggestion of tents. Second Peter focuses instead on the voice from heaven that is conveyed by "the majestic glory," which announces, "This is my beloved Son, in whom I am well pleased." The letter then moves into an examination of prophecy and inspiration.

There are many ways to think about this account. Most readers think the clipped nature of 2 Peter's story indicates that the author assumes the readers will be familiar with some version of the story (Bauckham 1983, 205–10). The author can evoke the whole story without explicitly repeating it. The absence of any mention of the peculiar role of Peter in the story suggests that 2 Peter is not trying to further the biography of Peter himself. Rather, 2 Peter uses Peter's presence at the transfiguration to make a claim about the nature of prophecy.

It is possible, of course, that if Peter is the author, he is herein laying claim to a unique authority that is based on his relationship to Jesus. However, this authority does not convey anything new about the person or

---

5. In Matt 10:24–25, for example, Jesus compares disciples to slaves, and Paul can call himself a slave (as in Rom 1:1 and Phil 1:1).

status of Jesus. Peter's familiarity with Jesus is not used to debate a theological point about the identity of Jesus. In fact, the authority given to Peter in 2 Peter does not come from Peter's relationship to Jesus. It comes from Peter's presence at the transfiguration. Peter is a witness, not to Jesus, but to an epiphany, to a heavenly voice. This gives him insight into how God conveys divine truth.

It is, of course, possible that Peter could be telling this story this way. However, this seems unlikely. Even though 2 Peter cites a Gospel story, the way the author structures the story seems contrary to the way the relationship between Jesus and Peter is narrated in the Gospels. The personal trust that Peter has in the person Jesus as the Messiah has become an account of worshiping the Lord in heaven. The Gospel citation seems contrary to the spirit of the Gospel story, and especially to Peter's role in the story. The use of this Gospel story actually *lessens* the possibility that Peter wrote this letter.

Second Peter has often been compared to a testament or to a farewell letter (Bauckham 1983, 131–35). The primary reason for this is 2 Pet 1:12-15, wherein Peter is described (or describes himself) as on the verge of death and as writing this letter as a reminder. "Peter" says that he knows that "the putting off of my tent is soon." He knows this because "Jesus Christ has disclosed [it] to me." Since he is about to die, he wants to remind his readers of "the truth" so that "even after my departure you are always able to remember these things." There are obvious parallels to both testaments and farewell letters, although in its overall form 2 Peter is different from both. The deathbed scene and family gathering at the heart of the testament genre is lacking here, as is the "farewell" of a farewell letter. However, 2 Peter is similar to testaments and farewell letters in that all of them imagine respected leaders on the point of death as they leave their final and thus essential teachings to their families or followers.

In this way, 2 Peter seems to be written as a way to preserve in letter form the reliable theology of the apostle Peter. Again, it is possible that Peter is writing this way himself, although what he chooses to inscribe to their memory is a bit contrary to genre. The teachings of the patriarchs in the *Testaments of the Twelve Patriarchs* are typically summaries of the moral life. In contrast, the content of 2 Peter is more particular than general. Second Peter does not seem like what Peter would have written if he were writing his testament.

Furthermore, if we can assume that 2 Peter is pseudepigraphical, it becomes a classic example of the Christian pseudepigraphical letter. Most

Christian pseudepigrapha (especially letters) are, at least in part, attempts to bring the voice and authority of departed apostles into the ongoing life of the Christian communities. Second Peter articulates the motivations perfectly: now that Peter is gone, we have access to his thought when we read this letter.

For all this, most people think Peter did not write 2 Peter because it does not seem like a letter Peter would have written. The Greek is probably the most complicated Greek in the New Testament. Furthermore, many of the arguments in 2 Peter show evidence of training in Greek rhetoric. It is hard to imagine that Peter, whose native language is Aramaic and who surely did not have a Greek education, wrote Greek this complex. Second Peter's probable dependence on Jude is a problem for authorship by Peter.[6] It is hard to picture Peter borrowing this kind of material in this way. Finally, the cosmic Christology, the lack of interest in the ministry of Jesus of Nazareth, the absence of debate about the law, and the aggressive attacks on other Christians in chapters 2 and 3 make it difficult to imagine how the Peter that we know from the Gospels could be the author of this letter. Furthermore, if we move the letter into the early second century and we envision the author as an unknown Greek-speaking Christian and not Simeon Peter, then the letter becomes easier to explain. Thus most modern readers of 2 Peter think the letter is pseudepigraphical.

Jude

Of the three letters considered here, Jude is certainly the most curious. Most of the letter consists of a rather vicious (and clever) attack on other Christians. It is not curious that Christians would attack each other this way; however, it is curious that such an attack found its way into the canon. In the early church, there clearly was some debate about Jude. Eusebius lists Jude among the "disputed" books. We know that Jerome and a few others had questions regarding its status. However, Jude, like 2 Peter, was eventually accepted as an authoritative text throughout early Christianity.

The letter is also curious because of the identity of Jude and how Jude is named. The letter opens with a typical naming of the author, "Jude, a servant of Jesus Christ and brother of James." The Greek actually names

---

6. See the chapter by Jeremy F. Hultin in this volume for discussion of the relationship between Jude and 2 Peter (and between 1 and 2 Peter).

the author as Judas (and James is actually Jacob in the Greek). English translations have traditionally rendered this "Judas" as Jude in order to distinguish this person from the other people in early Christianity named Judas.

We know of several early Christians named Judas. Luke 6:16 lists "Judas of James" as one of the Twelve.[7] The phrase "Judas of James" would normally be understood as "Judas son of James." The third bishop of Jerusalem is listed as "Judas of James" (*Apos. Con.* 7.46). We usually assume Luke and the *Apostolic Constitutions* refer to the same Judas. Furthermore, Eusebius says that the last Jewish bishop of Jerusalem was "Judas" (*Hist. eccl.* 4.5.3). In Acts, one of the people designated to convey the letter from the Jerusalem council to Antioch is Judas Barsabbas (15:22, 27, 32).

Other than Judas Iscariot, who is obviously not a candidate for the authorship of Jude, the best-known Judas in early Christianity was Judas Thomas. He is traditionally understood as "author" of the pseudepigraphical *Gospel of Thomas* and the *Acts of Thomas*. The most interesting thing about Judas Thomas is that the name Thomas in Aramaic means "twin." A tradition emerged in which this Judas was believed to be the twin of Jesus (as in, for example, *Acts Thom.* 31, 39). Finally, Mark 6:3 and Matt 13:55 list the brothers of Jesus as James, Joses (Joseph in the Matthew list), Judas, and Simon. Thus, one of the brothers of Jesus was named Judas, and thus this Judas would have a brother named James (Jacob).

Since the Judas of the Epistle of Jude is identified solely by his relationship to James, "Judas of James," who is included in Luke among the Twelve, and "Judas," who according to Matthew and Mark is brother of Jesus and James, are the most likely candidates for being the Jude of this letter. Given ancient care about paternity, it is unlikely that the author of Jude is confused about syntax. Thus Luke's "Judas of James" almost certainly means "Judas son of James." Thus, when the author of Jude identifies Jude as the "brother of James," he must mean the Judas listed in Mark and Matthew as the brother of Jesus and James. If this is the case, then Jude is connected to his brother in order to convey to this letter the unique status and authority that James, the brother of Jesus, had in the early church (on this James, see Chilton and Neusner 2001).

---

7. The authors of Matthew (10:2-4) and Mark (3:16-19a) do not include Judas of James in their lists of the Twelve.

While the preceding account seems plausible enough, it is curious that Jude is identified as brother of James and not brother of Jesus. Jesus, after all, has more status and authority than James. It is also curious and perhaps pertinent that in the letter of James, James is not identified as brother of Jesus or brother of the Lord, but as "a servant [or slave] of God and of the Lord Jesus Christ" (Jas 1:1).

Of the numerous explanations for not mentioning kinship with Jesus, two have received the most attention. First, in some early church traditions it is argued that Mary remained a virgin even after the birth of Jesus (see Bauckham 1990, 19–32, for a description of these traditions). In these accounts, the brothers and sisters of Jesus are, in fact, half brothers and sisters (or other relatives). Thus, it is surmised, Jude is not named the brother of Jesus because such an unexplained naming would misrepresent the relationship. Instead, Jude is connected to his famous brother James and thereby enjoys the credentials of James and the unstated implication of being in the family of Jesus.

Second, there may be theological modesty in this phrasing. To identify oneself or to identify someone else as a brother of Jesus is to undo the proper narratives of Christian faith. No one's relationship to Jesus is based on genealogy or membership in his nuclear family (see Matt 12:46-50; Mark 3:31-34; Luke 8:19-21). Jesus is, in the language of Jude (v. 25), not anyone's singular brother but the Lord of all of us, including Jude and James.

Assuming then that "Jude ... the brother of James" is referring to the brother of Jesus and James, the question remains whether the letter was actually written by him. I think it is unlikely that the letter of Jude would have gained its status unless most people in the early church thought it was written by Jude. The letter is, perhaps, a clever and creative attack on other Christians, but it does not have the theological weight or range to have gained authority on its own. Furthermore, its deep dependence on *1 Enoch* weighed against its acceptance.[8] While *1 Enoch* was influential in a wide range of Jewish and early Christian groups, eventually it was not included in the major canon collections in either the West or the East. The disputed status of *1 Enoch* raised questions about the status of Jude. Early Christians, such as Tertullian, Clement of Alexandria, Origen, Eusebius,

---

8. Jude 14b-15 quotes *1 En.* 1:9, and vv. 4, 6, 12-13, and 16 have clear allusions to *1 Enoch*.

and Jerome, were troubled by the fact that a canonical letter like Jude derives much of its theology from a noncanonical text (see Kelly 1969, 223–24, for citations). Thus it seems likely that Jude's eventual inclusion in the canon depended on the assumption in the early church that Jude the brother of James (and Jesus) really was the author.

All of this means that a decision about the authorship of Jude hinges on a judgment as to whether the Letter of Jude seems more likely to have come from the historical Jude, the brother of James, or from a later unknown author writing in his name. We know almost nothing firsthand about the historical Jude (although see Bauckham 1990). Given that he was a first-century Galilean Jew who became a follower of Jesus, we can guess certain things. But even if we should conclude that the historical Jude wrote the letter, this does not help us understand the content of the letter in any significant way. We really know nothing about what Jude might have thought. Thus, even more so than with 1 and 2 Peter, the character of the letter provides knowledge of the author, not vice versa.

Of the many issues about the identity of the author, two seem to have the most weight. Once again, we encounter Greek that is hard to imagine coming from the historical Jude. It is always possible that Jude somehow became quite learned in Greek and Greek rhetoric. Still, the letter is more likely to have come from a native speaker of Greek. Furthermore, Duane Watson has made a good case that the author of Jude uses classic Greek rhetoric to compose the letter (Watson 1988). All of this speaks against identifying Jude as the author (but see Davids 2006, 25–28). Second, the arguments of Jude are composed mostly by way of citations from or allusions to Jewish Scripture. Bauckham (and to some extent G. L. Green) has argued not only that the pattern in which Scripture is used is more typical of Jewish readings than Gentile, but also that Jude's midrashic style places it in the milieu of Palestinian Judaism (Bauckham 1990, 179–234; G. L. Green 2008, 9–16). This would, then, speak in favor of Jude's being the author. However, the usual concerns of Jewish Christianity, such as law and covenant, are lacking. Furthermore, many Gentile Christians became quite proficient in reading the LXX.

While G. L. Green, Davids, Bauckham, and others have made plausible arguments for Jude as the author, I think, in the end, it is difficult to make a case for the historical Jude as author (G. L. Green 2008; Davids 2006; Bauckham 1983). It is hard to conceive of all the curious sequences wherein a brother of Jesus managed to write a letter like this one—which then circulated on the edges of Christian literature with its authenticity being frequently doubted but which eventually made its way into the inner circle of Christian texts. However, it is easy to imagine an early second-century Christian, embroiled in deep and bitter divisions in his (!) church, who used the authority and credibility of a brother of Jesus to address these divisions. The author wants to give his voice apostolic authority. We do not know what happened in the short term, but ultimately the respect accorded to a brother of Jesus gave credence and voice to the letter. In this scenario, Jude becomes a typical early Christian pseudepigraphical letter.

Conclusion

In the discussion above I have probably underrepresented the energy of the debates about authorship, but I think this energy does not come from potential disagreements in how we understand the sentences and arguments (i.e., the actual content) in these three letters. As I claimed above, it is a bit curious that everyone reads these letters in much the same way regardless of the position taken on authorship. When there are debates about the meaning of these texts, disagreement about authorship is rarely the cause. Instead, I think we argue about authorship because we have serious disagreements about the nature of the canon, the history of early Christianity, and the proper force and structure of historical interpretations of texts. These issues are not idle questions. There is, in fact, much at stake. We cannot, of course, explore all of these questions here. However, a few comments by way of conclusion seem appropriate.

These letters say what they say no matter who wrote them. While we cannot reconstruct fully the debates in the early church about the authority of these texts (though see the two chapters in this volume that discuss the reception of these books in the early church), we do know the result. These texts are included in the standard Christian canons, and debates about authorship do not undermine their canonical status. Their status comes from the decision of early Christians to give these texts authority in the church. Furthermore, the presence of these texts in the canon, whether they are pseudepigraphical or not, witnesses to an ongoing need of Christian communities to have apostolic voices in their midst. Throughout history, Christian churches have looked for guidance and inspiration to the confessions and witness of the earliest Christian apostles, particularly of those who knew Jesus himself (e.g., Peter and Jude). Even if these letters are not from the hand of Peter and Jude, their presence in the canon represents the best attempt of the early church to identify apostolic voices among the many early Christian texts. These three letters, no matter who wrote them, should be read as belonging to those voices.

The Literary Relationships among 1 Peter, 2 Peter, and Jude

Jeremy F. Hultin

Someone encountering the New Testament for the first time would expect to find a greater affinity between 1 and 2 Peter than between 2 Peter and Jude. After all, both Petrine epistles say they are written by "Peter" (identified as an "apostle"), and 2 Peter even calls itself his "second letter" (2 Pet 3:1), suggesting an awareness of the first. Yet ever since antiquity, careful readers have been struck by how greatly 1 and 2 Peter differ in style and thought. Readers have also long noted that 2 Peter and Jude have a great deal in common. Indeed, the similarities between 2 Peter and Jude are so extensive that it appears one made use of the other or they both used a common source. The first part of this chapter will examine the relationship between Jude and 2 Peter; the second will consider the relationship of the two canonical epistles of Peter.

Jude and 2 Peter

The following table highlights most of the material shared by Jude and 2 Peter. I give a very literal translation so as to preserve resonances in the Greek that might be obscured in more polished English.

Jude	2 Peter
2: May mercy, <u>peace</u>, and love <u>be yours in abundance</u>	1:2: May grace and <u>peace be yours in abundance</u> in the knowledge of God and of Jesus our Lord.

3: Although I was making <u>every effort</u> to write to you of our common salvation, I find it necessary to write and appeal to you to contend for the faith <u>that was</u> … <u>passed on to</u> the <u>holy</u> ones.	1:5: For this very reason, give <u>every effort</u> to add to your faith virtue … 2:21: the <u>holy</u> commandment <u>that was passed on to</u> them.
4: Certain intruders <u>have snuck in among you,</u> who <u>deny</u> our only <u>Master</u> and Lord, Jesus Christ.	2:1: false teachers <u>among you,</u> who <u>will sneak in</u> destructive opinions … [and] will <u>deny</u> the <u>Master</u> who bought them
5: I desire <u>to remind you, though you are fully informed,</u>	1:12: I intend <u>to remind you</u> of these things, <u>though you know them already</u>
6: And the <u>angels</u> who did not keep their own position, but left their proper dwelling, he has <u>kept</u> in eternal <u>chains</u> [*desmois*] *in deepest darkness for the judgment* of the great day.	2:4: For if God did not spare the <u>angels</u> when they sinned, but cast them into Tartarus and committed them to <u>chains</u> [*serais*] of <u>deepest darkness</u> to be <u>kept</u> for the <u>judgment</u>.
7: <u>Sodom and Gomorrah</u> and the surrounding <u>cities,</u> … serve as an <u>example</u> [*deigma*] by undergoing a punishment of eternal fire	2:6: Turning the <u>cities</u> of <u>Sodom and Gomorrah</u> to ashes, he condemned them to extinction and made them an <u>example</u> [*hypodeigma*] of what is coming to the ungodly
8: Yet in the same way these dreamers also <u>defile</u> the <u>flesh,</u> reject <u>lordship</u> [*kyriotēta*], and <u>slander glories.</u>	2:10: those go after the <u>flesh</u> in <u>defil</u>ed lust, and who despise <u>lordship</u> [*kyriotētos*]. DARing and willful, they are not afraid to <u>slander glories.</u>

9: But when the arch<u>angel</u> Michael contended with the devil and disputed about the body of Moses, he did <u>not DARE</u> <u>to bring against</u> him <u>a judgment of slander</u>, but said, "The Lord rebuke you!"	2:11: whereas <u>angels</u>, though greater in might and power, do <u>not bring against</u> them <u>a slanderous judgment</u> from the Lord.
10: <u>But these people slander whatever they do not understand</u>; and what they know by <u>instinct</u>, <u>like irrational animals</u>, by these things <u>they are destroyed</u>.	2:12: <u>But these people</u> are <u>like irrational animals</u>, mere creatures of <u>instinct</u>, born for capture and destruction. They <u>slander what they do not understand</u>, and in their corruption, <u>they</u> also <u>will be destroyed</u>.
11: Woe to them! For they have gone in the <u>way</u> of Cain, and abandoned themselves to <u>Balaam's error</u> for <u>wages</u>, and perished in Korah's rebellion.	2:15–16: They have left the straight road and have <u>erred</u>, following the <u>way</u> of <u>Balaam</u> son of Bosor, who loved the <u>wages</u> of doing wrong
12: These are rocks [*spilades*] in your love-feasts [*agapais*], <u>while they feast with you</u> without fear, feeding themselves.	2:13: They are blots [*spiloi*] and blemishes, reveling in their dissipation [*apatais*] <u>while they feast with you</u>
12–13: [<u>These are</u>] <u>waterless</u> clouds carried along by the winds; autumn trees without fruit, twice dead, uprooted; wild waves of the sea, casting up the foam of their own shame; wandering stars, <u>for whom the deepest darkness has been reserved</u> forever.	2:17: <u>These are waterless</u> springs and mists driven by a storm; <u>for whom the deepest darkness has been reserved</u>
16: These are grumblers and malcontents; they indulge their own <u>lusts</u>; they speak <u>bombastic</u>	2:18: For they utter <u>bombastic</u> nonsense, and with licentious <u>lusts</u> of the flesh they entice

things, showing partiality for advantage.	people who have just escaped from those who live in error.
17–18: <u>beloved</u>, <u>remember the words spoken beforehand by the apostles of</u> our <u>Lord</u> Jesus Christ, for they said to you,	3:1–3: <u>beloved</u>, … <u>remember the words spoken beforehand by the</u> holy prophets, and the commandment of your <u>apostles</u> of the <u>Lord</u> and Savior. First of all you must understand this, that
"<u>In the last time there will be scoffers, indulging their own</u> ungodly <u>lusts</u>."	<u>in the last days scoffers will come</u> in scoffing and <u>indulging their own lusts</u>

Two initial observations about the pattern of these parallels will help make sense of the major ways of explaining the relationship between Jude and 2 Peter that I consider below. First, the similar material is not evenly distributed throughout the two epistles. Almost everything they share in common occurs in Jude 4–18 and 2 Pet 2:1–3:3. The beginning and ending of Jude (vv. 1–3, 19–25) exhibit only a few similarities with 2 Peter. In the case of 2 Peter, even larger portions—the entire first chapter and most of the third chapter—show little relationship to Jude. Whether one of these authors depended on the other or they used a common source, clearly the dependence was limited to a circumscribed portion of their compositions.

Second, it is important to note that there are similarities in the *content* (e.g., the reference to the fall of the angels [Jude 6//2 Pet 2:4]); the *vocabulary* (slandering "glories" [Jude 8//2 Pet 2:10]; rejecting "lordship" [*kyriotēs*] [Jude 8//2 Pet 2:10]); and the *sequence* of related phrases (Jude 11//2 Pet 2:15–16 is the one real exception). Yet there is no extensive *verbatim* agreement between Jude and 2 Peter, such as is found among the Synoptic Gospels or between Ephesians and Colossians.[1]

Instead of word-for-word agreement, Jude and 2 Peter often describe the same details with different words (e.g., Jude 6//2 Pet 2:4 both mention the detail that the angels were shackled, but they use different words for the chains). Such minor stylistic variations are not at all surprising. What *is* surprising is that these two texts sometimes express *different* ideas with

---

1. Callan 2004 offers interesting statistical analysis of the common vocabulary.

very *similar* words. For instance, in the descriptions of the intruders at Christian meals (Jude 12//2 Pet 2:13), Jude labels them *spilades*, a word that in other Greek literature means "rocks" or "squalls."[2] The author of 2 Peter calls them *spiloi*, a straightforward word for "blemishes" or "stains." Obviously the words look and sound a great deal alike, but they do not have the same meaning. In the same verse, Jude says that the intruders "feast with you at your *agapai*," using the plural of the Greek word for "love" (*agapē*) as the name of the meal (literally "at your loves," hence the common translation "love feasts"). The author of 2 Peter says that the intruders "feast with you in their *apatai*," that is, "in their *deceptions*" or "their *pleasures*"—again expressing an entirely different thought with a word that looks and sounds similar.

Major Hypotheses for Understanding the Relationship between Jude and 2 Peter

Several hypotheses have been proposed to account for these remarkable and puzzling parallels. I discuss the three major approaches below, but two others deserve brief mention here. A few scholars (most famously Robinson 1976, 192–95) have claimed that the *same author* wrote both letters, but the differences in Greek style tell strongly against this position. Some others (including Bartlet 1899, 518–21) have argued that the passages in 2 Peter that are similar to Jude were actually added to 2 Peter after its composition (i.e., the Jude-like material is an interpolation). However, it is clear that all of 2 Peter is a literary unity, which would not be the case had material been added to 2 Peter. There is, furthermore, no manuscript evidence to support interpolation theories. Most scholars have rejected both of these proposals and instead have argued for some kind of literary dependency: Jude used 2 Peter, 2 Peter used Jude, or both used a common source.

Jude Used 2 Peter

Prior to the nineteenth century, it was generally believed that Jude used 2 Peter.[3] By the end of the nineteenth century, rigorous examination of

---

2. LSJ, s.v. σπιλάς (A) and (C), respectively. Most translations of Jude render *spilades* "blemishes," but they do so primarily because of the parallel with 2 Pet 2:13 (cf. LSJ, s.v. σπιλάς [B]).

3. The earliest surviving comment on their relationship is found in the commen-

the question of dependence began to turn the tide toward the view that Jude was the earlier document. In response, several scholars who sought to uphold the traditional belief in the priority of 2 Peter were forced to muster evidence for their view, since it could no longer be taken for granted. Although the priority of 2 Peter is now a minority view, there are some impressive arguments that point in this direction.[4]

First, Jude often reads like an improvement of 2 Peter.[5] Virtually all scholars agree that the Greek style of Jude is far clearer than that of 2 Peter.[6] To give but one example, Jude 10 is concise, balanced, and clear, but the corresponding passage in 2 Pet 2:12 is not only ungainly but actually unclear. (The ambiguities of the Greek are not conveyed in English versions because translators are forced to choose one of the possible meanings.) It is easier to imagine that Jude simplified and improved awkward expressions from 2 Peter than to imagine 2 Peter muddled phrase after phrase. Furthermore, examples of Jude's "improving" 2 Peter are not limited to matters of style. For instance, it is easy to imagine that Jude 11 would have changed "Balaam of Bosor" (2 Pet 2:15) to "Balaam" (Jude 11), since Balaam's father (or nationality?) is nowhere else called "Bosor."

Second, certain passages in Jude make a great deal of sense if one imagines that they were written when both the author of Jude and his readers had 2 Peter in mind. For instance, 2 Peter *predicts* (using the future tense) that heretics and "scoffers" will arise and infiltrate the church and then describes the "judgment against them" (2 Pet 2:1-3; 3:3). Thus when Jude states that heretics who were "written down for this judgment" *had arrived* (Jude 4), and Jude reminds his readers that the apostles warned that "scoffers" would come (Jude 17-18), this statement and reminder appear to fit hand in glove with 2 Peter.

---

tary of Pseudo-Oecumenius (PG 119:708, 712, 720), dated sometime between the eighth and the tenth centuries. The priority of Peter is assumed.

4. The most thorough defense of Petrine priority in English is still that of Bigg 1902, 217-25.

5. Gerdmar (2001, 116-23) demonstrates how Jude can be read as a stylistic improvement on 2 Peter. In the end, Gerdmar concludes that mere literary dependence is inadequate to explain the similarities between the two letters; rather, he thinks that they must have originated in a similar milieu (Gerdmar 2001, 331, 338).

6. It is hard to overstate the disdain many scholars have expressed for 2 Peter's Greek. Even those who have sought to defend 2 Peter usually acknowledge that its Greek is often "laboured, turgid, involved, and obscure" (Bigg 1902, 225).

Third, there are a few subtler—and in the end not as compelling—arguments for the priority of 2 Peter. For instance, Jude has some specifically Pauline vocabulary. Perhaps it is easier to imagine that Jude unconsciously introduced such terminology than that 2 Peter carefully sifted out each Pauline expression. Similarly, Jude's letter opening could be interpreted as a combination of Petrine and Pauline elements (Bigg 1902, 217–18).

Why have these arguments not persuaded more people that Jude depended on 2 Peter? It is hard to explain why Jude would have drawn only from the middle section of 2 Peter. Why would he have passed over all of the theologically rich material in 2 Peter 1 and 3? Why quote Peter's prediction that "scoffers" would come (Jude 17–18//2 Pet 3:3) without ever stating what they were scoffing about (see 2 Pet 3:4–13)?[7] Also, if 2 Peter were written first, why would early Christians have bothered to preserve Jude? Almost everything Jude says would already have been contained in the lengthier letter by a more illustrious figure! More reasons to doubt the priority of 2 Peter will be seen below when considering the arguments for the priority of Jude.

If Jude did use 2 Peter, what are the implications, and what can be discerned in the ways he adapted his source? For one thing, it would appear that Jude took a particularly harsh stance against his opponents. In the midst of 2 Peter's list of previously punished sinners, there are also examples of God's readiness to "rescue the godly," such as Noah and Lot (2 Pet 2:5, 7–9; cf. 3:8–9). Jude would have skipped these, and retained only the record of God's acts of judgment.

Conversely, although Jude would have entirely passed over 2 Peter's engagement with the scoffers' teachings, Jude would have *added* references to the intruders' "dreaming" (Jude 8) and to their lack of the Spirit (Jude 19). Would these additions suggest that Jude was countering opponents who claimed Spirit-inspired dreams and visions?

Finally, one must ponder whether there was any theological (as opposed to stylistic) reason that Jude would have added the examples of Cain and Korah (Jude 11), expanded 2 Peter's metaphor of waterless

---

7. One response to this criticism is to claim that Jude wanted only one specific thing from 2 Peter, namely, to show that the *apostles* had already warned that *heretics* would one day infiltrate the church. Hence, Jude confined himself to using this warning, and omitted the description of what the scoffers were scoffing about. If what Jude needed was the authority that only an apostolic testimony could offer, however, why did he not *name* Peter as his source?

springs (Jude 12-13), or introduced a sizeable quotation from *1 En.* 1:9 (Jude 15–16).

2 Peter Used Jude

For nearly one hundred years, the overwhelming consensus of critical scholars has been that 2 Peter used Jude.[8] Proponents of this position typically include the following arguments.

First, 2 Peter was probably written later than Jude. Many scholars believe that this can be shown on grounds independent of the question of priority. If true, then Jude obviously could not have used 2 Peter. However, use of a common source would still be possible.

Second, since Jude is so brief and has so little content apart from what is found in 2 Peter, it is hard to imagine why Christians would have preserved it unless it was already known prior to being used by 2 Peter.

Third, it is generally easier to imagine the rationale for 2 Peter's substantive changes to Jude than the other way around. This applies especially in the case of their most obvious difference, namely, the larger scope of 2 Peter. It is easier to imagine the author of 2 Peter borrowing from Jude's artful polemic (Jude 4–18) for a *single* portion of his letter than to imagine that Jude omitted so much material from 2 Peter. As a rule, the same principle applies in smaller units of discourse.[9] Although such arguments are always subjective, it is hard to deny the cumulative force of observations like the following:

a. 2 Peter, unlike Jude, presents the record of God's judgments in their biblical sequence, and it seems unlikely that an author would disturb this if it were present in a source.

Jude	2 Peter
Israel in Wilderness (Jude 5)	—
Fallen Angels (Jude 6)	Fallen Angels (2 Pet 2:4)
—	Flood (Noah saved) (2 Pet 2:5)

---

8. Thurén 2004 summarizes just how dominant this position has come to be.
9. Watson 1988 provides a passage-by-passage analysis. Although he admits that there are sections in which it is hard to determine the likelihood of priority, it is easier to imagine in most cases that 2 Peter has changed Jude.

Cities of Plain (no mention of Lot) (Jude 7)	Cities of Plain (Lot saved) (2 Pet 2:6-8)
Cain (Jude 11)	—
Balaam (Jude 11)	Balaam (2 Pet 2:15-17)
Korah (Jude 11)	—

It is not only the order that suggests Petrine redaction. The mention of the flood in 2 Pet 2:5 prepares the way for him to cite the flood again in 2 Pet 3:5–7, where it is adduced as evidence of God's ability to undo creation. Furthermore, mentioning the salvation of Noah and Lot (2 Pet 2:5–9) prepares for the claim in 2 Pet 3:9 that God longs for the salvation of all. Thus both 2 Peter's conformity to the biblical order and the connections to themes he develops later in his letter would suggest that 2 Peter has modified the examples he found in Jude.

b. Second Peter does not contain Jude's citation of *1 En.* 1:9 (Jude 14–15) or its allusion to an episode from the *Assumption* (or *Testament*) *of Moses* (Jude 9). Some early Christians were definitely troubled by Jude's citation of texts that ultimately came to be considered noncanonical.[10] Might 2 Peter have avoided Jude's references for the same reason? Since 2 Peter dwells on the inspiration of the prophetic word (1:19–21) and compares Paul's letters to "other scriptures" (3:15–16), some scholars argue that 2 Peter was concerned with the boundaries of what counted as biblical and thus deliberately avoided Jude's references (but see the discussion of this issue in Eric F. Mason's chapter in this volume). Whatever the motivation, it is generally easier to imagine that these references were eliminated by 2 Peter than that they were added by Jude.

c. Some have perceived in Jude an incredibly intricate structure, including an ingenious series of subtle allusions to other ancient texts. Such a structure would be virtually impossible to achieve if Jude were starting with a block of material from 2 Peter that lacked these intertextual allusions. Bauckham (1990, 179–234) offers the most developed form of this argument, but the complexity he perceives in Jude is not always persuasive.

---

10. See discussion in Hultin 2010.

d. Although Jude is generally clearer than 2 Peter, there are some cases where 2 Peter looks like it is simplifying Jude. To take an example mentioned above, Jude's use of *spilades* ("rocks" or "squalls") might naturally be changed to 2 Peter's *spiloi* ("blemishes"), but it is very hard to imagine Jude would replace 2 Peter's familiar word and straightforward image with something so perplexing as "rocks at your meals." Other examples could be added.

e. Even a few of 2 Peter's awkward expressions look like they resulted from trying to combine an expression from Jude with his own themes. For instance, Jude 17 has the straightforward phrase "remember the words spoken beforehand by the apostles of our Lord" (Jude 17). Second Peter 3:2 seems to have added to Jude's verse references to the prophets (cf. 2 Pet 1:19–21) and to "the commandment" of the Lord (cf. 2 Pet 2:21): "Remember the words spoken beforehand by *the holy prophets and the commandment* of the Lord and Savior through your apostles."

f. The author of 2 Peter shifts between future-tense predictions that heretics would one day come (2:1–3; 3:3, 17) and present-tense descriptions of what they were already saying and doing (2:10–22; 3:5, 9, 16). Some think this inconsistency shows that 2 Peter has tried to pass itself off as the apostolic warning mentioned in Jude 17–18 (so Jülicher 1904, 237–38; Dibelius 1936, 208–9).

It is important to consider the implications of this position. If 2 Peter used Jude, the former author added a great deal to his source, above all to engage more fully with the content taught by his opponents. However, the fact that 2 Peter says so much more raises some questions about the parts of Jude's polemic that it omits. To take just one example, why would 2 Peter skip Jude's reference to Cain (Jude 11)? In some ancient Jewish traditions, Cain was portrayed as a skeptic who doubted that God judged the world justly or would offer reward and punishment in the world to come.[11] Many scholars argue that 2 Peter was written to combat this type of theological skepticism.[12] If so, however, why would the author pass over this example from Jude?

---

11. Such skeptical opinions are attributed to Cain in several of the Aramaic translations (called "targumim") of Gen 4:8. The date of the traditions in these targumim is difficult to determine, but several scholars have argued that they are as old as the first century c.e. For details, see Vermes 1975, 96–99.

12. For such a profile of the opponents in 2 Peter, see especially Neyrey 1980.

Another question often lurking in the background of discussions about the relationship between Jude and 2 Peter is that of authorship. The view that 2 Peter used Jude has definitely contributed to the belief that 2 Peter is pseudepigraphical.[13] Some defenders of Petrine authorship, however, see nothing inherently problematic with the idea that the real Peter admired what he read in Jude and therefore made use of it.[14]

Jude and 2 Peter used a Common Source

The similarities between Jude and 2 Peter could also be explained as the result of both using a common source. Many scholars mention this possibility only to dismiss it as superfluous.[15] Why invent a hypothetical source—of which no other trace survives—when there is a simpler explanation at hand?[16] What could the genre of such a source be, since it would consist of little more than an assortment of vitriolic invective and illustrations of God's wrath? Finally, the source would appear to be almost coextensive with Jude, which raises the question of why Jude would have used a source to which he added nothing besides an epistolary framework (vv. 1–3, 24–25) and a brief exhortation (vv. 20–23)?[17]

Since at least the eighteenth century, a slender minority of scholars have nevertheless pointed out that a common source might resolve problems the other explanations cannot.[18] It would indeed be superfluous to propose a source if the differences between Jude and 2 Peter clearly resulted from one's editing of the other. As has been seen, however, there are some passages that suggest 2 Peter redacted Jude, and others that suggest Jude redacted 2 Peter. This ambiguity is exactly what we would expect if they both made their own independent use of a common source.

Neyrey regards the targumim of Gen 4:8 as evidence for traditions going back to the first century C.E. (1980, 412–13, 422).

13. See the opinions of several scholars cited by Gloag 1887, 254.
14. So Gloag 1887, 220–21; Carson, Moo, and Morris 1992, 436.
15. Not atypical is the verdict of Chase 1902a, 2:802: "The hypothesis that both writers borrowed from a third document, though it has found stray advocates, may be put aside at once."
16. So, for instance, Kraftchick 2002, 79–80.
17. An objection noted by Thurén 2004, 452; and Davids 2006, 142.
18. E.g., Sherlock 1725, 203–30; Robson 1915; Reicke 1964, 148, 189–90; Spicq 1966, 197 n. 1, 228; M. B. Green 1987, 58–64.

There are other aspects of Jude and 2 Peter that would result from their use of a common source. For instance, both books contain some "Semitisms," words or phrases that are awkward in Greek because they represent the vocabulary or syntax of Hebrew or Aramaic.[19] As a rule, competent writers of Greek tended to reword Semitisms into idiomatic Greek. Both Jude and 2 Peter write Greek that is generally free of Semitisms, and yet they each have Semitic expressions in places where they would not have derived them from the other.

For example, the following Semitisms in 2 Peter could not have come from Jude.

> 2 Pet 2:1: "heresies of destruction" = "destructive heresies"[20]
> 2 Pet 2:10: "lust of defilement" = "defiled lust"
> 2 Pet 2:14: "children of curse" = "accursed children/people"
> 2 Pet 2:18: "enormities of vanity" = "vain enormities" or "bombastic nonsense"
> 2 Pet 3:3: "scoffers will come in scoffing."[21]

Jude also has Semitisms he could not have derived from 2 Peter.

> Jude 9: "judgment of slander" = "a vituperative verdict"
> Jude 16: "marveling at appearances" = "showing partiality"
> Jude 18: "living by their own desires of ungodlinesses" = "ungodly desires."

Most of the Semitisms listed here do not occur in the Bible, so they cannot be explained as imitations of the LXX or as direct translations from biblical Hebrew or Aramaic. Hence, Semitisms are clearly a problem for both of the theories of direct dependence. Defenders of such positions must claim that when 2 Peter or Jude borrowed directly from the other epistle,

---

19. For a clear and concise discussion of Semitisms, see Moule 1959, 171–72.

20. In several of these examples, a noun in the genitive case (e.g., "of defilement") functions as an adjective ("defiled"). This is quite common in Hebrew (and in Greek translated from Hebrew). Although such a construction is possible in Classical and Koine Greek (a so-called genitive of quality), it is rare; hence, grammarians identify it as a Semitism. See BDF §165; Moule 1959, 174–75; and Turner 1963, 212–14.

21. On the Hebrew background of this particular construction, see Moule 1959, 177–78.

they carefully eliminated many of the awkward Semitisms they found—only to introduce new ones of their own devising! However, if Jude and 2 Peter used one common source that was dense with Semitisms and they both modified its language independently, this would account for why they both exhibit *different* Semitic expressions in *different* places.

Numerous smaller details also support the theory of a common source. For instance, both 2 Peter and Jude make ample use of the words derived from *asebēs* ("ungodly"). If the author of 2 Peter used Jude, why would he have occasionally *omitted* this word where it appeared in his source (e.g., Jude 18//2 Pet 3:3), and then *added* it where Jude lacked it (2 Pet 2:6; cf. 2:5, 3:7)? The exact same problem must be faced if Jude used 2 Peter.[22] However, a common source that was strewn with the vocabulary of "ungodliness" would explain why such terminology appears in *different* places in Jude and 2 Peter.

As for the genre of this putative source, it might resemble some of the Dead Sea Scrolls that gather together biblical quotations and apply them to contemporary opponents.[23] It is generally agreed that Christians used similar collections of prophetic "proof texts."[24] Alternatively, some have argued that rather than positing a written source, we should think of oral tradition, perhaps in the form of catechesis, or of a sermon denouncing heretics (M. B. Green 1987, 62; Reicke 1964, 148, 189–90).

There is one final point in favor of the view that Jude and 2 Peter made independent use of a common source. Namely, a common source best explains why neither of them mentions the other.[25] Neither of the other theories of literary dependence can account for why one finds such exten-

---

22. Someone might argue that Jude 7 passed over *asebēs* from 2 Pet 2:6 because Jude wanted to avoid overuse of the term. A glance at Jude 15—"the ungodly deeds done in an ungodly way ... by ungodly sinners"—suggests Jude was not troubled by frequent use of the word.

23. So Spicq 1966, 197 n. 1, 228, who drew attention in particular to the pesher of Habakkuk (1QpHab). Other relevant texts from Qumran include 4QFlorilegium (= 4Q174) and 4QTestimonia (= 4Q175). Both 1QpHab and 4QFlorilegium give biblical quotations and then apply them to contemporary circumstances with the expressions "this is ..." or "these are...." Cf. Jude 10//2 Pet 2:12. For detailed analysis of this method of interpretation, see Bauckham 1990, 179–221.

24. See the surveys of Hodgson 1979; Albl 1999; and Lincicum 2008.

25. The fact that 2 Peter does not mention Jude has more often been cited as evidence of Petrine priority; but, as Mayor (1907, xxiii) notes, the fact that Jude does not mention Peter could point in the opposite direction.

sive borrowing without some attribution of the source in order to establish authority. Even when we acknowledge that ancient authors had somewhat different norms regarding intellectual property than are common today, the silence is still puzzling. If Jude used 2 Peter because he sought the authority of an apostolic witness (Jude 17), he ought to have *named* Peter for greater effect (note how robustly Jude introduces his quotation of Enoch). Similarly, 2 Peter speaks warmly of the letters of "our beloved brother Paul" even though Paul is never quoted. Why borrow so much from Jude and fail to mention him in like manner? If both writers were employing an anonymous tract or sermon, the lack of any "citation" ceases to be problematic.

The theory of a common source is more compelling than is usually acknowledged, but it certainly has its own problems. One of the most serious obstacles is offering a more specific account of its genre, for when one looks closely at the details of the material Jude and 2 Peter share, it becomes harder to imagine *what kind of text* the source could have been. For instance, the source would have had to include direct address to readers or an audience (Jude 5//2 Pet 1:12), something that would hardly fit a collection of *testimonia*.

Conclusion

The view that Jude was written first and 2 Peter made use of it has won widespread scholarly support. One of the positive results of this consensus is that it has encouraged redactional analysis of 2 Peter, or careful research into how and why 2 Peter made the changes he did. In evaluating the different hypotheses, however, it is important to remember that each theory has its strengths and weaknesses. Theories serve best when they provoke ever more careful and creative engagement with the texts themselves. When repeated often enough, a theory that was first put forth tentatively can become an "assured result of scholarship," at which point it may deaden interest in those pesky details that refuse to fit into any one model.

1 Peter and 2 Peter

The relationship between 1 Peter and 2 Peter has often been approached with the question of authorship in mind. The two letters exhibit considerable differences in vocabulary, style, and content. According to Jerome (*Vir. ill.* 1), already in antiquity this "dissonance" led many to doubt that

Peter could have written them both.[26] Yet, as Jerome noted (*Epist.* 120.11), differences in vocabulary and style might simply indicate that Peter relied on different interpreters (*diversis interpretibus*) when composing the two letters.[27] In addition, differences in subject matter are not surprising in letters written for different occasions. Paul's letters vary enormously in the topics they cover, and the major themes of some letters go virtually unmentioned in others.

What makes the relationship between the Petrine epistles truly puzzling is not that there are differences, but rather that despite all their differences, 2 Peter appears to refer to 1 Peter and to claim that both letters were written to the same readers and with the same purpose (2 Pet 3:1–2). By taking this passage as a starting point, we can consider the letters' relationship without being preoccupied solely with the question of authorship.[28] Regardless of who wrote either letter, 2 Peter appears to offer a glimpse of how someone—Peter or an author writing in his name—understood and appropriated 1 Peter (see Boobyer 1959).

The critical passage in 2 Pet 3:1–2 reads as follows: "This is now, beloved, the second letter I am writing to you; in them I am trying to arouse your sincere intention by reminding you that you should remember the words spoken in the past by the holy prophets, and the commandment of the Lord and Savior spoken through your apostles" (NRSV).

The author proceeds to cite the prediction that scoffers would come deriding the return of Christ (2 Pet 3:3–4), and this prediction appears to be part of the prophetic and apostolic message readers are to remember. Thus, the author of 2 Peter claims that both 2 Peter itself and a "first" letter are chiefly reminders of the words of the prophets and the command of Christ delivered through the apostles, with special attention to predictions of heretics.[29]

---

26. Interestingly, Origen and Eusebius, who expressed doubts about the authenticity of 2 Peter, did *not* mention its style as a problem (noted by Bigg 1902, 229).

27. Indeed the phrase "writing *through* Silvanus" (1 Pet 5:12) has sometimes been taken to mean that Silvanus was Peter's secretary, although it probably means he was the letter's *carrier* (see the discussion in Achtemeier 1996, 349–52).

28. This lack of preoccupation is not to deny that their literary relationship has *implications* for the question of authorship, some of which will be noted here. The question of the authorship is treated directly by Lewis R. Donelson in his chapter in this volume.

29. Some translations place a break between 2 Pet 3:1 and 3:2 and treat them as distinct thoughts. So the NIV: "[3:1] Dear friends, this is now my second letter to you.

On the face of it, this simply does not sound like a description of 1 Peter, which is not a letter of reminder; it neither mentions heretics nor cites a "command" of Christ. Such observations have led some to conclude that 2 Pet 3:1 cannot have 1 Peter in mind and must instead allude to a letter that did not survive (so recently M. B. Green 1987, 134–35). This option is certainly possible. Paul refers to letters that have not survived (1 Cor 5:9), and there are patristic references to lost writings of Peter. (See discussion of the latter in the chapters on reception of 1 and 2 Peter in this volume.)

Thematic Connections between 1 Peter and 2 Peter

Despite the issues just noted, most scholars continue to affirm that 2 Peter refers to 1 Peter. If so, in what sense did 2 Peter find in 1 Peter a treatment of "the words of the prophets," "the commandment of the Lord," or the reality of Christ's return?

Words of the Prophets

Interest in the phenomenon of prophecy is actually one of the most impressive similarities between both epistles. Both 1 Pet 1:10–12 and 2 Pet 1:19–21 emphasize that prophets were merely the vehicle for the Spirit of God, who spoke through them. This correspondence is not likely to be an accident, for the nature of prophetic inspiration is not a topic discussed elsewhere in the New Testament, and in fact 2 Peter speaks of the Holy Spirit only in this context.

Although both letters share an interest in the dynamics of prophetic inspiration, nevertheless their appropriation of prophetic texts—and of the Old Testament in general—is one of their most striking differences. Second Peter, on the one hand, has at most five biblical allusions, only one of which is introduced as a citation (2:22).[30] First Peter, on the other hand,

---

I have written both of them as reminders to stimulate you to wholesome thinking. [3:2] I want you to recall the words spoken in the past...." This break has the effect of limiting what is claimed for the joint purpose of the two epistles to one thing only, namely, "stirring up your pure mind," which might more obviously be said of 1 Peter.

30. Even here, it is not clear if 2 Peter is trying to cite a *biblical* proverb or just a well-known saying. The first half of 2 Pet 2:22 resembles Prov 26:11, but the second half is a common adage.

is saturated in Scripture: there are more than thirty allusions, as well as lengthy citations (1:24–25; 2:6; 3:10–12; 5:5) and formal citation formulas (1:16; 2:6).

The Commandment of the Lord

The context in 2 Peter suggests that "the commandment of the Lord and Savior" (2 Pet 3:2) is a summary of Christ's demand for a godly life. In the author's view, the opponents used "freedom" as a pretext for "licentious desires of the flesh" (2 Pet 2:18–19). They thereby abandoned "the way of righteousness" and "the holy *commandment*"—both shorthand expressions for the morally upright Christian life. Indeed, a theme of 2 Peter is the responsibility of Christians to respond to God's call by growing in virtue (2 Pet 1:5–11).

Although 1 Peter does not use the vocabulary of "commandment," it constantly exhorts believers to lead holy lives. Furthermore, both letters are concerned that Christian conduct should not damage the church's reputation. This concern is especially prominent in 1 Peter, but compare also 2 Pet 2:2; both letters even show a predilection for the same word when discussing good or bad "conduct" (*anastrophē*).

Thus one can see how 2 Peter could find in 1 Peter a reminder of Christ's command, but it should also be noted that much of the language and imagery the two epistles use for this theme is different. Most notably, 1 Peter speaks often of *imitating* Christ, especially in the model Christ gave by his honorable endurance of suffering (1 Pet 1:6–7; 2:11–25; 3:9–17; 4:12–19; 5:10). The absence of any such imagery in 2 Peter has often struck scholars as odd.

Certainty of Christ's Return

Second Peter responds to doubts about Christ's second coming by noting that the apparent delay was the result of God's distinct sense of time (2 Pet 3:8) and merciful *patience* (2 Pet 3:9, 15). Since the end would eventually come when least expected (2 Pet 3:10; cf. 2:2, "*sudden destruction*"), Christians should occupy themselves by striving to be holy (2 Pet 3:14).

First Peter also speaks of eschatology and cites divine judgment as motivation for good behavior (1 Pet 4:18–19). Yet, what 2 Peter refers to as the *parousia* ("arrival"), 1 Peter describes as Christ's "revelation" (1 Pet 1:5, 7; 5:1). The differences go deeper than terminology. The discussion in

2 Peter is a more philosophical attempt to make a difficult Christian teaching intellectually palatable. In contrast, eschatology is a matter of existential urgency for the suffering addressees of 1 Peter (1 Pet 1:6-7). Whereas 2 Peter tries to make sense of the *slowness* of the consummation, 1 Peter declares without hesitation that "the end of all things is near" (1 Pet 4:7).

The present discussion suffices to show that, despite the two letters' profound differences in style and even content, it is not impossible to see how 2 Peter could claim that 1 Peter also had the function of recalling the words of the prophets, of emphasizing Christ's commandment for holy life, and of addressing the coming revelation of Christ.

Other Significant Similarities between 1 Peter and 2 Peter

Two other noteworthy points of contact deserve mention.[31] In citing Noah as an example, both letters share certain words or details. The author of 1 Peter says that Christ *preached* (*ekēryxen*) to spirits who disobeyed in the days of *Noah*, and the letter notes that *eight* people were *saved* in the ark, when God showed *patience* (*makrothymia*; 1 Pet 3:19-20). The author of 2 Peter says that *Noah* was a *preacher* (*kēryx*) of righteousness and was saved "as the *eighth*" (2 Pet 2:5), and later the author mentions God's *patient waiting* (*makrothymei*) for the *salvation* of all (2 Pet 3:9).[32]

The other interesting parallel occurs in the letters' opening salutations, which use an identical—and not very common—greeting.

> 1 Pet 1:2: "*May grace and peace be yours in abundance.*"
> 2 Pet 1:2: "*May grace and peace be yours in abundance* in the knowledge of God and of Jesus our Lord."[33]

---

31. Mayor (1907, lxviiii–cv) gives an exhaustive list of the possible points of contact. In most cases, the words shared by both epistles are too common to demonstrate a relationship, and some of the rare words used by both epistles are actually used in different ways. Thus, after thirty-seven pages of minute analysis, Mayor concludes that although 1 and 2 Peter are not as dissimilar as they are sometimes made out to be, it is still clear that "at all events the Greek of the one is not by the same hand as the Greek of the other" (1907, lxxiv). For a different assessment of the parallels, see Bigg 1902, 224–36.

32. Bauckham (1983, 146) sees 1 Pet 3:20 and 2 Pet 2:5; 3:9 as the *only* real point of contact between 2 Peter and 1 Peter.

33. Although the salutations are similar, one should note that 2 Peter has a unique form of Peter's name, *Symeōn* Peter, in 2 Pet 1:1. Many scholars point to such diver-

Conclusion

In the end, we can only speculate as to why, if the author of 2 Peter knew and referred to 1 Peter, he did not reproduce more of its language or themes. In fact, 2 Peter's relationship to 1 Peter is not unlike its relationship to Paul. The author of 2 Peter knows Paul's letters and holds them in the highest esteem (2 Pet 3:15–16), but the former shows hardly a trace of distinctively Pauline phraseology or thought. Thus it appears that the author of 2 Peter made only a limited use of the authorities explicitly named—the inspired prophets, 1 Peter, and Paul—and yet, according to the regnant paradigm, drew quite extensively from Jude, who is never mentioned at all.

Concluding Thoughts on the Relationships between 1 Peter, 2 Peter, and Jude

The links between these three letters have been recognized for a long time. Indeed, even in the earliest known manuscript of these texts, they survive *together*.[34] In the case of 1 Peter and 2 Peter, the question has always been why the vocabulary and themes of 2 Peter are so different from 1 Peter. I have tried to show that the two epistles share a few of the same concerns and details, while acknowledging that even in their commonalities there are surprising differences.

In the case of Jude and 2 Peter, the question is how two letters that never mention each other could have so much material in common. We have seen that there are several good arguments in support of the majority view that 2 Peter is directly dependent on Jude. But we have also noted that not all the details point in this direction, and we should be reluctant to say that the puzzle has been "solved."

---

gences of style as evidence for the authenticity of 2 Peter, on the grounds that a "forger" would have stuck closer to the wording of a well-known letter of Peter in hopes of passing off his own composition as genuine (so Guthrie 1990, 820).

34. All three writings are found in P[72], part of the Bodmer Miscellaneous Codex. It should be noted that the three letters do not occur sequentially in this codex; 1 and 2 Peter occur together, as the final two writings in the codex, and Jude occurs several books earlier. For details, see Horrell 2009a; Wasserman 2005.

The Epistolary Rhetoric of 1 Peter, 2 Peter, and Jude

Duane F. Watson

There are many types of Greek and Roman letters contemporary with the New Testament that developed in different contexts for different purposes. The relationships of friendship, family, and client-patron form some of the contexts that generated these letters. Ancient epistolary handbooks classify letters into their many types, including friendship, family, praise and blame, and exhortation and advice. These classifications and others are ideal types that can be amplified and mixed to better serve their purposes within different contexts (Stowers 1986; Malherbe 1988; Klauck 2006).

These Greek and Roman letters were influenced by rhetorical conventions. They can also be classified according to the three species of rhetoric: judicial (accusation and defense), deliberative (persuasion and dissuasion from a given course of action), and epideictic (praise and blame; Watson 2010b, 25–47). For example, accusing and apologetic letters are judicial, letters of advice and exhortation are deliberative, and letters of recommendation and praise are epideictic.

Early in the twentieth century, Adolf Deissmann made the questionable, yet persistent, distinction between nonliterary or documentary letters and literary letters. The former were situational and private, while the latter were written for posterity, and with rhetorical sophistication for public use. He classified the letters of the New Testament as nonliterary (Deissmann 1901, 3–59; 1927, 146–251).

However, rhetorical analysis of these letters has demonstrated that they fall between his rigid categories, as they are situational yet also public and written with rhetorical finesse. The more the letters of the New Testament are compared with literary letters, the more their rhetorical sophistication becomes apparent. Many facets of rhetorical argumentation, arrangement, and style found in literary letters are also found in the letters of the New Testament, although not necessarily in the same degree or kind as in a speech (Anderson 1999; Lampe 2010; Martin 2007; 2010a; Watson 2010a). Early Christian letters generally are a mix of the ideal types of letters and species of rhetoric, and usually they are not adequately classified by using only one letter type or rhetorical species. Since letters were influenced by rhetorical conventions, determination of a letter's type and rhetorical species are interdependent, as will become clear below in the analysis of 1 and 2 Peter and Jude (Aune 1987, 183–225; Watson 1997, 650).

The Epistolary Form of Early Christian Letters

Greek letter writing was heavily guided by long-standing conventions (White 1972; 1984; 1986; 1988; Aune 1987, 158–82). Christian letters are constructed according to the conventions of Greek letters, but with adaptations suited to the Christian experience (Doty 1973; Berger 1974; Schnider and Stenger 1987; Watson 1997, 650–51). These letters commence with the letter opening or prescript composed of the formulaic salutation: sender (*superscriptio*) to recipient (*adscriptio*), greetings (*salutatio*). Often Christian letters amplify the salutation by describing the sender and recipient in relation to God (e.g., "apostle," "chosen by God"). The opening of a Greek letter employs a verb of greeting (*chairō*) in the *salutatio* and a wish for the recipients' health (*hygianō*), but in Christian letters "grace" (*charis*) and "peace" (*eirēnē*) replace them, often in the form of a benediction ("may grace and peace be yours"; S. A. Adams 2010, 33–55; Tite 2010).

As just mentioned, the salutation in the Greek letter is usually followed in the letter opening by the sender's wish for the recipients' health (*hygianō*), but it also often includes an expression of joy at the receipt of the letter from the recipients (also *chairō*); a thanksgiving for the recipients' good health and deliverance from disaster using a verb to rejoice (*eucharisteō*); and a report of the sender's prayer for the recipients (*proskynēma*) and/or a mention that the sender remembers the recipients (*mneia*). In Christian letters these conventions are often subsumed into a thanksgiving that also introduces the key topics of the letter (Arzt-Grabner 2010; R. Collins 2010).

The body of Greek letters comprises three main parts: the body-opening, body-middle, and body-closing (White 1972, 1; for discussion and assessment, see Martin 1992, 69–75; 2010b, 191–94). The body-opening reaffirms and elaborates the common ground between the sender and recipients by alluding to shared information or by disclosure of new information. The body-opening discloses the main occasion or purpose of the letter and introduces some of the main points that the letter will develop. The letter's purpose can be expressed in at least one of three ways: (1) a full disclosure formula that gives the sender's wish or command that the recipients know something ("I want you to know that") and that consists of a verb of disclosure such as "wish" or "want" (*thelō, boulomai*) and a verb of knowing (*ginōskō*); (2) a motivation for writing that uses the verb for writing (*graphō*); or (3) a petition that the audience take some course of action, composed of a verb of petition (*parakaleō, erōtaō*) and a reason for the petition.

The body-middle both develops the topic(s) introduced in the body-opening as well as new topics. Like the body-opening, it often begins with a disclosure formula that conveys that the sender desires or commands the recipients to know something. The body-closing reiterates the main motivation for writing and opens channels to future communication. It often starts with the imperative form of the disclosure formula using the verb for knowing (*ginōskō*) followed by responsibility statements urging the recipients to be attentive to the content of the letter and respond as requested. It may also notify the recipients of the sender's intention to visit, a visit motivated by a desire to talk face-to-face rather than using pen and ink. It may also contain a recommendation of a third party who will deliver the letter.

The letter closing or postscript maintains contact between sender and recipients and enhances their mutual friendship. This relational maintenance is accomplished using greetings (*aspazomai*), a health wish, and/or words of farewell. In Christian letters, a reference to a holy kiss, a wish for peace, a doxology, or benediction can replace the latter two components (Weima 2010).

The Rhetorical Form of Early Christian Letters

Early Christian letters were substitutes for giving an oral address in person. They were designed to be read to the recipients and were in many ways speeches in letter form. Greco-Roman rhetorical conventions had influenced letters by the first century and are found in abundance in ancient letters, especially of a more literary nature. No less is true of early Christian letters. These conventions are preserved in rhetorical handbooks, most notably those of Aristotle (*Rhetorica*), Cicero (*De inventione, De oratore*), and Quintilian (*Institutio oratoria*). These conventions were discussed under the broad categories of invention, arrangement, style, memory, and delivery. The first three of these categories are useful for analyzing early Christian letters (Kennedy 1984, 12–30; Watson 1988, 13–28; 2010a, 119–39; Martin 2010a).

Invention concerns the stasis, or basis of the main issue at hand (Martin 2010a, 78–92), as well as the types or species of rhetoric appropriate to address the stasis: judicial, deliberative, or epideictic (Watson 2010b). These types or species are the rhetoric appropriate to the courtroom, political arena, or public ceremony respectively. Judicial rhetoric is used to accuse and defend in regard to past actions. Deliberative rhetoric is used to persuade and dissuade an audience regarding a course of action to take in the future. Epideictic rhetoric applies praise and blame based on communal values to individuals and actions to affirm or challenge them.

Invention is primarily the creation of proofs in argumentation. These proofs may be inartificial or artificial, that is, not created or created by the rhetor. Inartificial proofs include previous judgments of the court; in the New Testament inartificial proofs include eyewitness testimony and quotations of the Old Testament. Artificial proofs include ethos (the moral character of the speaker), pathos (emotional appeal), and logos (propositions and supporting arguments).[1] Proof from logos can be from induction or deduction, or example and argument respectively. Examples used in proof in the New Testament letters are typically derived from the Old Testament, Jewish tradition, and nature. Arguments in the New Testament letters are often enthymemes, which, in simple terms, are propositions with one supporting premise stated and one left unstated (Martin 2010a, 95–102).

Arrangement concerns the best way to structure an oral presentation, typically as *exordium* (introduction touching on main topics to be discussed), *narratio* (facts of the issue at hand), *partitio* (list of propositions to be developed), *probatio* (argumentation about the issue at hand and development of topics), *refutatio* (refutation of the argumentation of any opposition), and *peroratio* (recapitulation of the argumentation and appeal to emotion; Martin 2010a, 50–78). Style is the use of language to support the argumentation, and includes figures of speech and thought among other

---

1. For detailed discussion of artificial proofs, see Martin 2010a, 94–113 and various essays in Olbricht and Eriksson 2005; Olbricht and Sumney 2001; and Eriksson, Olbricht, and Übelacker 2002.

things (Watson 2010a). Important figures of style in the New Testament letters include antithesis, metaphor, and irony.

The Epistolary Rhetoric of 1 Peter, 2 Peter, and Jude

First and Second Peter and Jude conform to the conventions of the Greek letter tradition and its adaptation by early Christian letter writers. These works also exhibit a variety of rhetorical conventions from the Greek and Roman rhetorical traditions. However, the degree of their conformity to either letter or rhetorical traditions varies by the type of these letters, their incorporation of elements of other literary genres, and their use of rhetoric to best address the needs of their recipients. Modifications, substitutions, deletions, and additions to letter and rhetorical conventions are common, especially because these letters, like all those in the New Testament, were more elaborate and, as noted above, much more akin to a speech than the typical Greek letter.

1 Peter

The recipients of 1 Peter are suffering persecution (1:6–7; 2:19–23; 3:13–17; 4:19; 5:9–10) because their conversion has so changed their lives that their neighbors are offended by their withdrawal from drunken parties and idolatrous practices (4:4). The persecution is mainly verbal (2:12, 15; 3:16; 4:4, 14, 16), but physical abuse is also indicated (1:6; 2:23; 3:9, 13–17; 4:12). The letter stresses that good conduct is the best approach to persecution because it renders any accusation groundless (3:13–17) and may lead to the conversion of the persecutors (2:12–17). Besides, such conduct is an outworking of the recipients' new nature as obedient children of God (1:14–16). The letter also stresses that persecution is a part of the Christian life, a testing from God (4:12, 19) and an opportunity for imitation of Christ (2:21–23; 3:18).

Of the many types of letters in the Greco-Roman world, 1 Peter is a paraenetic or hortatory letter intended to teach the recipients and persuade them to follow a prescribed course of action (Stowers 1986, 96–97; Martin 1992, 81–134; Sandnes 2005). It is also a circular letter sent to recipients in several churches. It has been described more specifically as a Diaspora letter, a designation for letters sent from the Jews in Jerusalem to those in exile (see 1:1) in Babylon (Jer 29:1–23), Assyria (*2 Bar.* 78–87), Egypt (2 Macc 1:1–10a; 1:10b–2:18), and elsewhere (see also the discussion of the address of this letter in Martin 1992, 144–61). While the Diaspora letter is not a specific genre in the larger Greco-Roman world, the circular letter that early Christians sent to other congregations is analogous. Other examples besides 1 Peter include the Letter of James, which was possibly sent from Jerusalem to neighboring churches (Jas 1:1), and the letter of the Jerusalem Council sent from Jerusalem to the church at Antioch (Acts 15:23–29).

First Peter exhibits many, but not all, of the conventions of the ancient letter (Thurén 1990, 79–88; Martin 1992, 41–79; Watson and Callan 2012, 10–12). The letter opening (1:1–12) begins with a salutation referring to the sender (Peter) and the recipients (exiles of the Dispersion) with theological descriptors (1:1–2a), a greeting in the guise of a benediction (1:2b), and a blessing taking the place of a thanksgiving (1:3–12). The body of this letter comprises 1:13–5:11. The body-opening of 1:13–2:10 begins with "therefore" (*dio*). The body-middle of 2:11–4:11 begins with a vocative and a petition, "beloved, I urge you" (*agapētoi parakalō*), although a petition is more common to the body-opening. The body-closing of 4:12–5:11 commences in 4:12 with the vocative "beloved" (*agapētoi*) and another petition (*parakalō*) in 5:1 that introduces a series of exhortations functioning as responsibility statements (5:1–11). The letter closing of 5:12–14 is indicated by the commendation of the messenger and the message (5:12a), the motivation for writing (5:12b), greetings from a third party and the sender (*aspazomai*, 5:13–14a), a reference to a kiss (15:14a), and a wish for peace (5:14b).

First Peter does not closely follow the conventions of Greco-Roman rhetoric in its invention and arrangement, but many of those conventions are present. Formal and highly structured arrangement and argumentation are replaced by the development of topics alone and in various combinations, and by exhortation appropriate to the topics that are developed. Primarily the status of the audience before God is developed in a series of metaphors (e.g., exiles and resident aliens in the Diaspora, the household of God, and spiritual temple and holy priesthood to God), and then exhortation to behave in a way appropriate to that status is given, particularly with Jesus Christ and others offered as exemplars of such behavior (Martin 2007, 67–71; Watson and Callan 2012, 10–12).

Parts of the letter do function like parts of the ancient speech, but not all (Thurén 1990; Campbell 1998). The letter prescript (1:1–2) and blessing-thanksgiving (1:3–12) function as the *exordium* and *narratio* of the letter. Like an *exordium*, they work to build the relationship of the sender and recipients, here through elaborating the blessings that they share in

Christ. Like a *narratio* they elaborate topics to be discussed in more detail in the body of the letter, particularly God's gifts in salvation.

The body of the letter (1:13–5:11) functions as the *probatio*. It is divided into three main parts by the vocative "beloved" in 2:11 and 4:11. The first part, the body-opening, comprises 1:13–2:10 and develops topics related to God's provision of salvation and Christians' status before God. It contains a call to be holy as God is holy (1:13–16) and a motivation to respond to this call—the living hope based on the death, resurrection, and exaltation of Christ (1:17–21). The next section of 1:22–25 loosely argues from the premise that the recipients have purified their souls by obedience to the truth, to the conclusion that they should exhibit mutual love. That is, as those having been born again as children of God, they need to love the rest of their new family (1:3, 14, 17).

The following section of 2:1–3 begins with "therefore" (*oun*), which introduces imperatives based on what has already been said (as in 4:1, 7; 5:1, 6). Having purified their souls and been born again (1:22–25), the recipients are exhorted to grow into salvation. The final section is 2:4–10, which compares the fate of those who come to Christ, the living stone, with those who reject him; this further establishes the new Christian identity as God's people and as a priesthood to God.

Verse 4 introduces the topic of the living stone, which is subsequently developed in 2:4–8 using quotations from the LXX that contain the word "stone" (Isa 28:16; Ps 117 [LXX 118]:2; Isa 8:14). Verse 5 introduces the topic of the people of God that is subsequently developed in 2:9–10 with a mix of texts from the LXX that refer to God's mercy and the people of God (Exod 19:5–6; Isa 43:20–21; Hos 1:6–7, 9; 2:1[LXX 1:10]; 2:25 [LXX 2:23]).

The second part of 1 Peter, the body-middle, comprises 2:11–4:11 and concerns how to live among the Gentiles. It begins with an appeal in 2:11–12 to live honorably among the Gentiles so that their accusations against the recipients will be groundless and the Gentile accusers will come to glorify God. This appeal is followed in 2:13–3:7 by a household code that describes the behavior appropriate for members of a household toward one another and toward the authorities. The household code was a common feature of Greco-Roman moral instruction. Here it is presented to help Christians live in ways that will decrease hostility with Gentile neighbors, silence their neighbors' criticism, and hopefully lead to their neighbors' conversion.

The first relationship discussed is Christians to civil authorities (2:13–17). Christians should do good because the emperor has authority from God to maintain order. The second relationship is that of masters and slaves (2:18–25). Slaves are exhorted to be subject to their masters regardless of how they are treated, with the motivation that if they suffer for doing the will of God, they will be rewarded by God (2:18–19). This exhortation is followed by the example of Christ, who suffered unjustly so that Christians may live for righteousness (2:21–25). The third relationship is that of husband and wife, specifically a Christian wife and a non-Christian husband (3:1–7). The wife's conversion to Christianity is a blow to the honor of her husband since a wife was expected to follow his religion. Here she is encouraged to behave in a way that does not give her non-Christian husband any further reason to suspect that she is disloyal—like dressing in a way that indicates she is looking for another man. Christian husbands are then addressed to honor their wives so that their prayers will be heard by God. The household code is followed in 3:8–12 by an exhortation to practice mutual love and peace with all. The exhortation is an extensive quotation of Ps 33:13–17a LXX (MT 34:12–16a), which amplifies the need for good behavior, both within the community and with those outside.

The next section of 3:13–22 exhorts the recipients to do good rather than evil in the midst of suffering (3:13–17) by following Christ's example, which makes all such suffering victorious (3:18–22). This section is loosely ordered like 2:18–25, with a premise (2:18; 3:13), exhortation about appropriate Christian behavior while suffering (2:19; 3:14–16), affirmation that doing good is the correct moral choice (2:20; 3:17), and presentation of Christ as the example of one who suffered for doing good and was victorious (2:21–25; 3:18–22; Achtemeier 1996, 228–29). This section is followed by 4:1–6, which repeats the focus on suffering for doing good at the hands of the unredeemed (3:13–17; 4:1–4) and the vindication of this suffering as exemplified and made possible by Christ (3:18–22; 4:5–6). It compares the former sinful life of the recipients with that of their sinful persecutors, a life they left behind because in Christ they have finished with sin (3:18, 21; 4:1–3).

This second part of 1 Peter ends in 4:7–11, with an exhortation on the need for mutual responsibility in light of the coming consummation (4:7–10) and a doxology (4:11). It forms an inclusio with the opening of this second part of 1 Peter by repeating the topic of the end (2:12; 4:7) and by giving God glory (2:12; 4:11). This part of the letter has focused on how Christians are to relate to those outside their faith and, in this final section, now turns to how Christians should relate to one another as motivated by the coming consummation. The topic of the consummation will become prominent in the third and final part of 1 Peter.

This third part of 1 Peter, the body-closing of the letter, comprises 4:12–5:14. It reiterates topics developed so far, often expanding them and interconnecting them in new ways. The first section of 4:12–19 further develops the topic of suffering (1:6–7; 2:18–25; 3:9–18; 4:1–4) with the additional points that suffering is integral to being a Christian and that its presence in the life of the Christian community is a sign that the consummation is near. The next section of 5:1–11 consists of concluding exhortations that define the responsibilities of the recipients as first outlined in 4:7–11, responsibilities that are especially needed in light of the coming judgment just described in 4:12–19.

The letter closing or postscript is 1 Pet 5:12–14, which functions as a *peroratio* of the letter by working to build goodwill with the audience and by reiterating topics. Here there has been great effort to create an inclusio with the beginning of the letter by repeating the topics of Christ (1:1; 5:14), chose/chosen together (1:1–2; 5:13), resident foreigners and Diaspora (1:1) or Babylon (5:13), grace (1:2; 5:12), and peace (1:2; 5:14).

2 Peter

Second Peter is a testament to the skill of its author in the art of Greco-Roman rhetoric (Watson 1988, 81–146). The letter is written to address a crisis of eschatology caused by the delay of Christ's return and the appearance of false teachers among the recipients (2:1). In light of the delay, these false teachers reject the apostolic preaching of the Parousia (1:16–21; 3:1–4, 8–13) and the judgment that was expected to accompany it (2:3b–10; 3:1–7). This denial results in immoral behavior (2:10b–22). The author relies on all three species of rhetoric in his argumentation. He employs deliberative rhetoric to persuade the recipients to cling to the promises of Christ and the apostolic tradition and to dissuade them from exchanging the truth for the teaching and behavior of the false teachers; judicial rhetoric to refute the propositions of the false teachers and support the apostolic tradition of the Parousia and its judgment (1:16–2:10a; 3:1–13); and epideictic rhetoric to dishonor the false teachers and destroy their ethos (2:10b–22).

Second Peter is a farewell speech or testament (Bauckham 1988, 131–35). In Jewish and Christian testaments, a leader announces his impending death and instructs those over whom he has charge to remain faithful after his death to the traditions they share as a community, often by referring to the future appearance of false teachers who will try to change those traditions. Second Peter is a testament in an epistolary form, which is not a common mix. This combination allows the author writing long after Peter's death to portray Peter as communicating over time to the recipients of the letter that the author wants to instruct.

The letter opening of 2 Peter begins with the salutation referring to sender and recipients and a blessing (1:1–2), followed by elements borrowed from the testament genre. The first element is the rehearsal of shared traditions as a miniature homily (1:3–11), which replaces the standard thanksgiving of a letter. The second element is the announcement of the impending death of "Peter" (1:12–15), which functions as the body-opening of the letter (1:12–15), for reminding the recipients of tradition functions like a full-disclosure formula ("I wish you to know that") and a motivation for writing. The body-middle of the letter (1:16–3:13) develops the testamentary commonplace of the coming of false teachers and refutes their unwanted modification of tradition. The body-closing (3:14–18a) is indicated by the vocative "beloved" and a responsibility statement (3:14), while a doxology serves as the postscript (3:18b).

Within this epistolary framework, the sender works with Greco-Roman rhetoric to persuade the recipients with what is essentially a speech in letter form. The letter opening (1:1–2), which is common to the letter genre, and the rehearsal of shared traditions (1:3–11) and announcement of impending death (1:12–15), which are common to the testament genre, constitute the *exordium* of the speech. In the *exordium*, the rhetor tries to make the audience attentive, receptive, and well-disposed, and he introduces important topics to be developed in the main body of the speech. Here in the letter opening, the sender defines his own authority and the positive spiritual status of the recipients (1:1), and he gives a blessing (1:2)—all of which promote the functions of the *exordium*.

The rehearsal of shared traditions as a miniature homily (1:3–11) and the announcement of impending death (1:12–15) introduce topics central to the rhetoric. Like an ancient homily, it contains a historical and theological portion, rehearsing God's acts in salvation history (1:3–4), exhortations based on this salvation history (1:5–10), and a concluding promise of salvation or threat of judgment (1:11). Topics introduced include godliness/ungodliness (*eusebeia/asebēs* and related words, 1:3, 6–7; 2:5–6, 9; 3:11; cf. 2:13; 3:14), promise (*epangelma*, 1:4; 3:4, 9, 13), escaping corruption (1:4; 2:12, 20–22), knowledge of God and Jesus (*gnōsis* and *epignōsis*,

1:2–3, 5–6, 8, 20; 2:20–21; 3:8, 18), and being established/unestablished (*stēriktos/astēriktos*, 1:12; 2:14; 3:16–17).

Next comes the body-middle (1:16–3:13), which functions like the *probatio* of a speech in which the rhetor seeks to persuade the audience of the truth of his case through a presentation of propositions and accompanying proofs and refutations, many of which were introduced in short form in the *exordium*. Here in 2 Peter, the sender uses judicial and deliberative rhetoric to refute the false teachers' rejection of the apostolic preaching of Christ's Parousia and judgment and to dissuade the recipients from accepting the doctrine and practice of the false teachers (1:16–2:10a; 3:3–13). He also uses epideictic rhetoric to destroy the ethos of the false teachers (2:10b–22).

The sender launches into a series of accusations of the false teachers and his own refutations of those accusations.

> First Accusation and Refutation (1:16–19)
>> Accusation of the False Teachers: The apostolic proclamation of the Parousia is a cleverly devised myth (1:16a).
>> Refutation of the Sender (1:16b–19)
>>> Proof of eyewitness testimony: Peter and other apostles saw Jesus' transfiguration, which was a proleptic vision of God's installation of Jesus as his eschatological vice-regent. Jesus will exercise this authority at the Parousia (1:16b–18).
>>> Proof from a document: Apostolic testimony of the Parousia is reliable because it depends on Old Testament prophecy (1:19).
>
> Second Accusation and Refutation (1:20–21)
>> Accusation of the False Teachers: The Old Testament prophecy that underlies the apostolic proclamation of the Parousia is unreliable because such prophecy is dependent on the prophet's own interpretation, not inspiration (1:20–21).
>> Refutation of the Sender: Proof from an enthymeme. The Old Testament prophecy that underlies the apostolic proclamation of the Parousia has to be reliable because all such prophecy is inspired (1:20–21).
>
> Counteraccusation of the Sender (2:1–3a)
>> The false teachers are accused of standing in the tradition of false prophets, not that of the apostles, and they will be

judged by God for it. As a prophecy within a testament, this counteraccusation functions like a proof from example, and more specifically a judgment based on a supernatural oracle. "Peter" is portrayed as long ago prophetically condemning the very false teachers that have appeared in the church, and this prophecy is now a judgment within the sender's rhetorical scheme.

Third Accusation and Refutation (2:3b–10a)
Accusation of the False Teachers: Divine judgment is idle, and divine destruction is asleep (2:3b).
Refutation of the Sender: Proof from example and comparison of examples that divine judgment has been active in the world. These traditional examples include the casting of the Watchers into Tartarus, the judgment by flood of the wicked generation spawned by the Watchers, and the destruction of Sodom and Gomorrah (2:4–10a).

Digression of the Sender (2:10b–22)
Having given three accusations of the false teachers and refuted them, the sender digresses to amplify their evil nature in order to undermine more completely their ethos and the authority of their arguments. He associates them with all kinds of evil characters in the Old Testament and Jewish tradition and links them as well to a variety of sins and visual images of sins.

Transition of the Sender (3:1–2)
This passage is a transition from the digression back to the *probatio* proper and reminds the recipients of the tradition from the Old Testament prophets and the apostles concerning the Parousia and its accompanying judgment—the main topic prior to the digression (especially 1:16–21).

Fourth Accusation and Refutation (3:3–13)
Accusation of the False Teachers: The accusation is presented as a prophecy of "Peter" within a testament, a proof from example of the type of supernatural oracle. The false teachers are presented as arguing that there has never been a judgment

of God since creation, so the promise of Christ's coming in
judgment is mute (3:3–4).
Refutation of the Sender (3:5-10)
    Proof from enthymeme (3:5–7)
        Premise: God stored water for judgment at the flood
        (3:5–6).
        Premise: Likewise, God has fire stored for judgment
        (3:7).
        Unexpressed conclusion: God has and will intervene
        in history with judgment.
    Proof from a document (Ps 90:4 (LXX 89:4]). There is no
    delay in the Parousia from God's perspective (3:8).
    Proof from an enthymeme (3:9)
        Premise: God delays the Parousia because he does not
        want anyone to perish (3:9b).
        Conclusion: God is not slow about his promise (3:9a).
    Proof from the ethos of "Peter" in the form of an affirma-
    tion of the Parousia (3:10)
Ethical exhortation based on the reality of the coming Parousia and judgment (3:11–13)

Finally, 3:14–18 forms the body closing of this letter and acts like the rhetorical *peroratio* in recapitulating the main points of the argumentation in the *probatio* and seeking to elicit the emotion of the recipients so that they will respond as desired by the sender.

JUDE

The situation is the appearance of teachers within the church with a theology and ethics that diverge from apostolic tradition; they have gathered a following (vv. 4, 19, 22–23), primarily for financial gain (vv. 11–13). Possibly based on their claim to prophetic revelation (v. 8; cf. v. 19), they deny the authority of the law of Moses (vv. 8–10) and Christ himself (vv. 4, 8), and as a consequence they are immoral, especially sexually immoral (vv. 6–8, 10, 16). The sender believes that this situation is acute because the appearance of this group was prophesied by Enoch and Christ as a precursor of the eschaton (vv. 14–15, 18); the eschaton is thus near (vv. 14–16, 17–19, 21, 23), and those who follow these teachers will be destroyed (vv. 14–15, 23). The sender has to prove to the recipients of the letter that the opponents they face are ungodly—the very ungodly about which prophecy had forewarned—and that following them puts the recipients in jeopardy at the coming judgment.

This letter is designed to meet this challenge with a sophisticated mix of epistolary and rhetorical conventions (Watson 1988, 29–79; Charles 1993, 20–64). Jude begins with a letter opening describing the sender and recipients and a benediction (vv. 1–2). It is followed by the letter body (vv. 3–23) divided into the body-opening (vv. 3–4), body-middle (vv. 5–16), and body-closing (vv. 17–23), with all three sections beginning with the transitional vocative "beloved" (*agapēte*). The body-opening (vv. 3–4) provides the occasion for the letter, here as a petition (*parakaleō*, v. 3) and the reason for the petition (v. 4). The body-middle (vv. 5–16) provides further background for the petition and begins with a full-disclosure formula that employs the idea of wishing (*boulomai*) that the recipients know (*oida*) something. The body-closing (vv. 17–23) begins with the imperative form of the disclosure formula "remember" (*mnēsthēte*) and contains many responsibility statements in the form of exhortations. The letter ends with a letter closing in the form of a doxology (vv. 24–25).

While this book has been described as a homily or a midrash, it is better to understand Jude as a rhetorically sophisticated letter (Bauckham 1983, 3–6). Within the epistolary framework, the sender uses deliberative rhetoric to advise and dissuade an audience with reference to a particular action, here to "contend for the faith" (v. 3), with support from epideictic rhetoric that appeals to emotion. The false teachers are portrayed negatively as a way to discredit them and make contending for the faith more advisable.

The letter opening describes the sender and the recipients according to their relationship with God (v. 1) and provides a benediction (v. 2). The letter opening functions like an *exordium* by seeking to increase the ethos of Jude, who is described as a "servant of Jesus Christ and brother of James," and to increase the goodwill of the recipients, who are designated as "beloved in God the Father and kept safe for Jesus Christ." This designation also points to the subject of the letter by stating up front that God in God's love will keep Christians safe for Jesus Christ in the midst of this diversion from the truth posed by the false teachers (vv. 21, 24).

By providing the occasion for the letter as a petition (v. 3) and the reason for the petition (v. 4), the body-opening (vv. 3–4) functions as the *exordium* and the *narratio* of this letter. The petition of verse 3 is the *exordium* and refers to "the salvation we share," a reference that supplies the common ground between the sender and the recipients and the basis for the petition to "contend for the faith that was once for all entrusted to the saints." The background to the petition in verse 4 is the *narratio*, which supplies the background of the case: the teachers in the church who deny Christ's authority are ungodly, and they are the ungodly of prophecy.

By providing further background for the petition, the body-middle (vv. 5–16) functions as the *probatio* of the letter by using three proofs from example to prove that the teachers are ungodly and the ungodly of prophecy. The first proof from example (vv. 5–10) begins in verses 5–7 with mention of three ungodly groups that were linked together in Jewish and Christian argumentation to prove that that sin incurs judgment: the unfaithful of Israel in the wilderness who died there, the Watchers of Gen 6:1–4 who fathered the wicked generation of Noah and are imprisoned in deepest darkness, and the cities of Sodom and Gomorrah that were punished by fire. Then in verses 8–10 the behavior of the false teachers is compared with that of these ungodly groups who were punished: they defile the flesh like the Watchers and inhabitants of Sodom and Gomorrah, they reject authority like all three groups, and they revile angels like the Sodomites. The comparison then emphasizes the caliber of the false teachers' disregard for divine authority, for while they curse angels associated with giving the Mosaic law, even the archangel Michael would only act within his God-given authority when dealing with the devil himself over possession of the body of Moses (*Testament of Moses*).

The second proof (vv. 11–13) is one from prophecy or supernatural oracle, a subgroup of the proof from example. First, a prophecy (woe oracle) of the judgment of the ungodly is given (v. 11), and then it is applied to the false teachers (vv. 12–13). The prophecy incorporates three ungodly people from the Old Testament who, according to Jewish tradition, enticed others to sin: Cain taught others to sin (Josephus, *Ant.* 1.52–66; Philo, *Posterity* 38–39), Balaam persuaded Balak to lure Israel into sexual sin and idolatry (Philo, *Moses* 1.295–300; Josephus, *Ant.* 4.126–130; *L.A.B.* 18.13; *Tg. Ps.-J.* Num 24:14, 25), and Korah led a rebellion against the authority of Moses (Num 16:1–35; 26:9–10). The application of the prophecy to the false teachers amplifies their sinful nature, destructive leadership and teaching, and the judgment that will come upon them.

The third proof (vv. 14–16) is one from prophecy, that is, from example. First, a prophecy of *1 En.* 1:9 is quoted (vv. 14–15), and then it is applied to the opponents (v. 16). The prophecy of Enoch proclaims that the Lord will come to exercise judgment on the ungodly, especially those who have spoken against him. This prophecy is then said to be fulfilled with the appearance of the false teachers in the church and their coming judgment at the Parousia. This application, with the designation "grumblers and malcontents," associates the false teachers once more with the Israelites in the wilderness and with Korah's rebellion.

With its opening disclosure formula "remember" (*mnēsthēte*) and many responsibility statements in the form of exhortations, the body-closing (vv. 17–23) functions as the *peroratio* of the letter by serving to reiterate the main points of the *probatio* and to elicit the emotion of the audience. The reiteration primarily comes in verses 17–19 and the emotional appeal primarily in verses 20–23. The reiteration is a proof from example, with a summary of the predictions of Christ and the apostles that those rejecting authority and indulging their own lusts could appear in the last days (vv. 17–18) and with an application to the false teachers (v. 19). The emotional appeal amplifies the need for the faithful to be strong and to rescue those following the false teachers in light of the imminent judgment. The letter closing in the form of a doxology concludes the letter; it reiterates the topic that God can keep the Christian from falling and reaffirms that the power and authority denied God by the false teachers does in fact reside with God (vv. 24–25). It therefore functions like the *peroratio*.

Conclusion

The letters of 1 and 2 Peter and Jude illustrate the complex interaction of epistolary and rhetorical features as these features are mustered by the authors to address the needs of their respective audiences. Type of letter chosen, adaption of the letter form for oral presentation, and types of arrangement and argumentation incorporated show these letters to be far more literary than Deissmann proposed. The interplay between the status of the Christian and exhortation to good works in 1 Peter, the more conventional Greco-Roman rhetorical invention and arrangement in 2 Peter, and the heavy reliance on images and examples in Jude demonstrate the creativity of their authors as they strove to address their diverse audiences. It is this creativity that reminds us as interpreters to guard against simplistic analyses of these letters and expect a greater degree of sophistication than our predecessors.

"Awaiting New Heavens and a New Earth": The Apocalyptic Imagination of 1–2 Peter and Jude

Kelley Coblentz Bautch

Near the end of 2 Peter, the author makes an intriguing statement that should catch the attention of any modern reader: "In accordance with his promise, we wait for new heavens and a new earth, where righteousness is at home" (2 Pet 3:13 NRSV). Indeed, this is not the only language in the book that likely seems foreign to modern audiences. The Day of the Lord? Revelation of the deeds of humankind, both good and bad, and portending judgment? Obliteration of the heavens and earth that we know? Some readers of Scripture may find such claims extravagant, eccentric, or marginal to contemporary sensibilities.[1] In light of the Hebrew Bible and New Testament, however, such sentiments were not so out of the ordinary, as they recall the writings of the Hebrew prophets (e.g., Isa 13:6–16; 65:16b–17) and of other early Christians (Mark 4; 13; 1 Thess 5:1–11; Rev 21:1). In the ancient context, the views expressed in 2 Peter would have found support from many Jews and Christians who also expected that the world as we know it will be changed and that this transformation will be related to divine intervention and judgment of humankind.

Their expectation is not to suggest, however, that there was a full consensus about such topics in antiquity; the diminutive missive 2 Peter is especially concerned to vigorously challenge those who do *not* share the same expectations (2 Pet 3:1–5). Yet 1 Peter and Jude also feature with 2 Peter an apocalyptic outlook. E. G. Selwyn notes how important endtime views are to 1 Peter's message: "There is no book in the New Testament where the eschatology is more closely integrated with the teaching of

---

1. See DiTommaso (2011, 223–41) for a recent critique of apocalyptic dualism and Freyne (2011, 259–60) for a counterview.

the document as a whole" (1954, 394). With regard to Jude, Duane Watson sees this epistle's imminent eschatology conveyed through its view of false teachers (scoffers) as a sign of the last time (Jude 14–15, 18), and he also calls attention to strong intertextual connections with apocalyptic texts and other Jewish writings that provide "examples, emotive images and warrants for its proof" (2002, 188). We can discern from 2 Peter's concerns and also from 1 Peter and Jude that end-time speculation and apocalyptic sensibilities (defined further below) were important to early Christians and their communities.

Students of the New Testament are well served by considering how these three Catholic Epistles express various end-time perspectives and expectations that some scholars maintain are inseparable from early Christian theology. Indeed, Ernst Käsemann famously remarked that apocalyptic "was the mother of all Christian theology" (1969, 102). From an ideological perspective, the numerous manifestations of apocalyptic motifs and language locate these books among other early Jewish and Christian works (Bauckham 1983). In that respect, 1–2 Peter and Jude are not at all marginal writings. We will briefly explore the nature of apocalyptic language and perspectives and then examine how these motifs occur in our three texts.

The "Apocalyptic Imagination": Key Terms Related to End-Time Traditions

It is important to begin with an orientation to several terms related to end-time traditions that are commonly used in studies such as ours. These terms include *revelation* (and its related term *apocalypse*), *eschaton*, *eschatology*, *eschatological*, *apocalypticism*, and *apocalyptic*.[2] Many scholars finely parse these terms and use them in specialized ways.

Our contemporary word *apocalypse* comes from the Greek *apokalypsis* ("revelation"). A "revelation" is conventionally understood as a disclosure of some sort whereby information that would otherwise be inaccessible is made known. A number of texts in early Judaism and Christianity present a heavenly mediator with special knowledge who reveals such

---

2. Excellent resources that can assist students in navigating these terms and apocalyptic literature in general include J. J. Collins 1998 (whose title is reflected in the subheading above) and also Lewis 2004; S. L. Cook 2003; and Murphy 2012. See also Webb 1990, who assesses the various attempts to define these terms.

information to select individuals (see especially Rowland 1982). Hence, the term *apocalypse* is applied to texts of this genre to underscore the importance of revelation in these literary works.

The classic example of the apocalypse genre is the Revelation of John, which designates itself as the *apokalypsis* (Rev 1:1). Other examples of the apocalypse genre may be found outside the Hebrew Bible or New Testament, and some probably predate John's Apocalypse by at least 250 years. One early example is the Book of the Watchers, which is classified by many scholars as an apocalypse because angels provide a pious forefather (the patriarch Enoch; see Gen 5:21–24) with information about extraordinary realms and future judgment.[3] An apocalypse, then, typically provides information to readers that they would not otherwise have the means of knowing (e.g., what will happen after death). Angels, messengers from the divine, are sanctioned to disclose data to those who are elect, which would by extension include the text's audience.

Because apocalypses often look to the future for resolution and concern judgment and the afterlife, another important term for this study is the Greek word *eschaton*, which means "last" (as related to time) and "at the extremities or edge"; the term could refer to the last days (of the current age) or being at the edge of a time of transition to a new age. Many texts in Jewish and Christian literature follow certain prophetic presentations of divine visitation and judgment. These traditions often anticipate a time in which God will intervene to change the nature of the present mode of existence by ushering in a period of divine rule. Often the scenarios sketched in biblical texts present a world that is out of order but then returns to the state of the world before its corruption.

The German scholar Hermann Gunkel (1895) observed that many nonbiblical ancient Near Eastern texts also associate the latter days with the primeval period. In addition, Gunkel observed a tendency in both

---

3. The definition of apocalypse that has become widely used among scholars is that of J. J. Collins (1979, 9): "'Apocalypse' is a genre of revelatory literature with a narrative framework, in which a revelation is mediated by an otherworldly being to a human recipient, disclosing a transcendent reality which is both temporal, insofar as it envisages eschatological salvation, and spatial insofar as it involves another, supernatural world." This definition was later supplemented with reference to how the author of an apocalypse interprets earthly circumstances in light of the otherworld and future, and how such literature is intended to influence its audience on the grounds of its authority (A. Y. Collins 1986, 7).

biblical and Babylonian texts to envisage cosmic combat between forces representing order and chaos.[4] He famously stated that "in der Endzeit wird sich wiederholen, was in der Urzeit gewesen ist" ("the occurrences of the primordial age will recur in the end time"; 1895, 370). Thus, many early Jewish and Christian writings that concern the return of the divine to set the world in order (expressed often in prophetic literature as "the Day of the Lord") present a new age that recalls the pristine quality of early times, comparable to life in Eden, the verdant garden of God (see Gen 2–3).

The term *eschatology*, which is related to the word *eschaton*, refers to the study of or teachings about the last (or final) things. When a text addresses the final epoch of the world as we know it, or even what happens to individuals upon death (i.e., the "end" with respect to individuals), we may speak of the eschatology of the work (see Arnold 2010, 24–29). Literature that concerns death and the afterlife, the last days, or a time of judgment may be described as "eschatological."[5]

The term *apocalypticism* is often used to refer to a social ideology or movement (J. J. Collins 1998, 2), but the adjective *apocalyptic* appears in many guises. Typically it describes traits of literature with eschatological concerns, but the term can convey even more about a text's religious perspective and what it communicates to its audience.[6] An apocalyptic worldview tends to reflect the following. First, apocalyptic literature concerns a reality that is unseen (a transcendent reality) but not static. Rather, the otherworld, like our world, is moved by events, and the otherworld has the means of affecting our world. Apocalyptic literature is universal and cosmic in scope. Second, the literature often communicates through use of symbols. Protagonists are directed by means of visions, dreams, and revelations from the divine, especially about the end of a distinctive time or phase in history or the end (the *eschaton*) of the world as we know it.

---

4. Gunkel found this tendency in both cosmogonies and apocalyptic texts. Cosmogonies are texts that discuss the nature and structure or contents of a world, whether terrestrial or heavenly. See also the definition of *apocalyptic*.

5. Wright (for example, 1992, 320–38) has argued that language evoking cosmic disaster in the New Testament refers to sociopolitical and historical changes rather than to the obliteration of the world. E. Adams (2007, 5–16) challenges this view and argues that apocalyptic writings indeed speak to the passing away of heaven and earth and posit destruction and re-creation on a macro scale.

6. J. J. Collins (1998, 2, 11) clarifies the adjective *apocalyptic* by speaking of "apocalyptic eschatology" that seeks "retribution beyond the bounds of history."

Third, the literature conveys a dualistic view of the world. Entities of our world and the otherworld are aligned with either good or evil, which stand in sharp opposition. Fourth, the present time has been corrupted in some manner, and the world—seemingly controlled by evil forces—is in need of repair. In contrast, a future time, the age to come, will be controlled by the divine. The assurance of divine intervention speaks also to the idea that contrary to appearance, events do not occur haphazardly; instead they are determined in advance by God. Fifth, the divine will intervene to destroy forces of evil and will prevail over evil. Judgment against the forces of evil, especially an otherworldly antagonist (variously called Satan, the devil, or Belial), is assured. A new order is established—one marked by restoration or deliverance and related to the rule of God—with a reversal of the former state of affairs. Judgment extends to humankind, both the living and the dead.[7]

Overall, such a list of apocalyptic features or motifs is meant to provide a heuristic way to approach a number of ancient texts with shared traits. Numerous scholars have attempted to define apocalyptic discourse, and readers should consider this enumeration of qualities as "a flexible set of resources that early Jews and Christians could employ for a variety of persuasive tasks" (Carey 1999, 10). Many ancient writings include apocalyptic traits or suggest an apocalyptic worldview, even if they do not fit the formal genre classification of apocalypse. For example, Mark 13 is not formally designated an apocalypse, but it utilizes apocalyptic language.

Similar to texts of the genre of apocalypse, apocalyptic literature also conveys information that would not otherwise be known by humankind, especially about the course of time and the *eschaton*. In that light, both the genre of apocalypse and apocalyptic literature can reveal information about the otherworld and its inhabitants who serve as intermediaries in bringing revelations.

Readers of apocalyptic literature (and for the purposes of this collection, of 1–2 Peter and Jude) may observe overlaps with other writings from antiquity, including other genres of literature in Scripture. Indeed, apocalyptic perspectives resemble aspects of prophecy in the Hebrew Bible in that both mediate assurance of God's control over the present and the promise of divine intervention to right wrongs and overturn a contem-

---

7. Recent helpful articulations of apocalyptic traits include those of Murphy 2012 and Carey 1999, 4–5.

porary social evil.[8] Likewise, other characteristics of apocalyptic literature recall aspects of the wisdom literature of ancient Israel. These characteristics include speculations on the otherworld and transcendent realities, and information communicated through revelation and other extraordinary means (such as the ability to "read the signs of the time").[9] References to mantic wisdom, to otherworldly beings (e.g., angels, either virtuous or malevolent), and to dualism have encouraged exploration of the roots of apocalyptic in traditions outside of ancient Israel as well.[10]

Scholars also examine the relationship between apocalyptic literature and social context and consider how the authors or initial audiences may have perceived themselves in situations of crisis but found some comfort and instruction through an apocalyptic worldview (see, e.g., Webb 1990, 124–25). In such a scenario, the community members identify with the righteous protagonist or the elect in a given apocalyptic work; they understand their own present difficulties as part of a larger cosmic drama in which they are guaranteed a favorable resolution.

While apocalyptic literature has been examined through each of these lenses (as related to prophetic or wisdom literature, as rooted in either Israelite or foreign traditions, or as emerging from contexts of crisis), shrewd interpreters also understand that apocalyptic literature derives from a complex matrix of varied literary, cultural, and social influences. This observation is certainly relevant for the Epistles of 1–2 Peter and Jude as well.

The student of the New Testament has access to excellent resources to assist her or him when exploring the apocalyptic perspectives of 1–2 Peter and Jude. From analysis of apocalyptic rhetoric in these Catholic Epistles to study of how these texts mediate earlier apocalyptic motifs, there are many points of entry for this topic (see especially Webb 2007, 72–110; Callan 2010, 59–90; Watson 2002; and Dubis 2002, 37–45).

---

8. For scholarship that explores and roots apocalyptic literature within prophetic traditions of the Hebrew Bible, see, for example, Hanson 1975.

9. Von Rad (1993, 263–86) was an early proponent of the view that apocalyptic literature shares a deterministic view of history with wisdom literature.

10. While it is common to find speculation about Persian influence (or the influence of Zoroastrianism) on apocalypticism, an extensive body of scholarship has demonstrated overlap or shared features of the latter with Near Eastern traditions that are Babylonian, Akkadian, and Sumerian in origin. See, for example, VanderKam 1984, esp. 1–75; Clifford 1998, 1–38; and Kvanvig 2011.

Comprehensive commentaries on the letters also make clear the unique way apocalyptic features are employed in each of these writings.[11] While this chapter examines key features of apocalyptic literature in 1–2 Peter and Jude, students are encouraged to study each epistle on its own terms in order to discern how particular authors engage and tailor apocalyptic features.[12]

Apocalyptic Features in 1–2 Peter and Jude

The Unseen World: Otherworldly Beings and Otherworldly Realms

Like other apocalyptic writings, 1–2 Peter and Jude speak of otherworldly beings and otherworlds. The authors take for granted that their audiences share this belief in unseen worlds and unseen beings. Moreover, the literature is concerned not with a limited geographical perspective but with the cosmos, the created universe (Dennis 2008, 158). The angelology in 1 Peter might not surprise the modern reader, but it reminds one that the author's belief in otherworldly beings and their role in the world at hand are related to his apocalyptic worldview.

First, the epistle makes reference to Jesus, who sits at the right hand of God with angels, authorities, and powers subject to him (3:22). This articulation of different kinds of celestial beings recalls the elaborate angelology of other apocalyptic texts and of other early Christians.[13] Second,

---

11. On 1 Peter, see, for example, Davids 1990, 17; Michaels 1998, xlvi–xlix (though he views the apocalyptic nature of 1 Peter as distinctive from other Second Temple apocalypses); and Achtemeier 1996, 107.

12. Webb (2007) provides a very extensive list of apocalyptic features and how they appear in 1 Peter.

13. Michaels (1998, 220) notes that 1 Peter already hints at Christ's elevation above the angels in 1:12. Numerous terms are used to name otherworldly beings in Second Temple and late antique Judaism and Christianity. Designations reminiscent of 1 Pet 3:22's "angels," "authorities," and "powers" appear in a number of contemporaneous texts, many with apocalyptic perspectives. For example, *1 En.* 61:10 (from the Book of Parables, *1 En.* 37–71) makes reference to "angels of the power" and "angels of the principalities." Along with the thrones and angels of the presence of the Lord, *T. Levi* 3:1–8 names the powers of the hosts, authorities, and angels. Moreover, we find the same classifications for heavenly beings among the letters of Paul. See, for example, 1 Cor 15:24 and Rom 8:38. See also Michaels 1998, 220. Donelson, in con-

with regard to the good news preached through the Holy Spirit sent from heaven, 1 Peter describes the mysteries of salvation as a matter into which the angels, like the prophets of old, wished to look (1:12). Third, the epistle warns its audience to resist the devil, who is presented as the opponent of the community (5:8) and who prowls like a lion searching for someone to devour.[14]

Jude, followed by 2 Peter, refers to angels ("messengers") and glorious beings ("glories") and also indicates familiarity with more extensive accounts involving angels. In fact, the very topic of angels provoked some sort of controversy for the communities behind these epistles.[15] Jude 8 seems concerned, for example, about people ("dreamers") who blaspheme glorious beings (likely angels of the heavenly court who are given the title "glorious" because of their proximity to God's glory; cf. Heb 9:5). These people also defile the flesh and scorn authority.[16] Though Jude does not elaborate on the charge of the slander of glorious beings, the misdeed likely relates to insulting or defaming speech.[17] Second Peter

---

trast, suggests that 1 Pet 3:22 intends to denote simply cosmic powers that Christ overcomes. Rather than naming distinctive categories, the terms denote comprehensive evil cosmic powers that oppose God (Donelson 2010, 114–15; so also Elliott 2000, 686–88). I disagree here with the approach of Donelson and Elliott because various types of heavenly beings and hierarchies with whom a visionary or mystic was thought to interact appear in Second Temple and late antique texts (see, e.g., figures in the Parables of *1 Enoch* and *2 Enoch*).

14. On the figure of the devil (*diabolos*) here and the conflict sketched in the letter between the devil and the people of God, see Michaels 1998, 298–99; and Elliott 2000, 854–59.

15. While the Greek expressions *angeloi* and *doxai* could be used as well to indicate respectively human "messengers" and exalted figures ("glorious ones") in the community, the context here would seem to suggest that the authors of Jude and also of 2 Peter have in mind otherworldly beings. See, for example, Bauckham 1983, 57; Donelson 2010, 183; and Neyrey 1993, 69.

16. In discussing Jude 8, Bauckham (1983, 57) and Neyrey (1993, 69) rightly call attention to examples of angels given the title or designation "glorious ones" in early Jewish literature (see 1QH 10:8; *2 En.* 22:7, 10; Philo, *Spec. Laws* 1.45). These examples also provide reminders that certain Second Temple and late antique communities actively reflected on angels, their role in the heavenly court and heavenly liturgy, and their different classifications. Such a focus (construed perhaps as "worship" of angels; see Rev 19:10; 22:8) did not sit well with all early Jewish and Christian communities (see Col 2:18; 1 Tim 1:4), however, and this focus provides a plausible context for the controversy indicated in Jude 8. See also Frey 2009.

17. See Neyrey 1993, 69. Neyrey also considers the idea that the opponents may

2:10b reiterates the charge that some slander "glorious ones" even though they do not understand them (2 Pet 2:12). In contrast to these malefactors, angels (who are greater in might and power than humans) do not bring slanderous judgment against the slanderers (2 Pet 2:11).[18]

This last sentiment is underscored by Jude 9, which recounts an episode from the *Testament of Moses*, or *Assumption of Moses* (on this account, see Bauckham 1983, 65–76; and Donelson 2010, 184–85). Michael contends with the devil over the body of Moses in this tradition (Jude 9), yet even the archangel did not dare "slander" (or reprimand directly) the devil. Michael instead asks the Lord to rebuke the devil; he does so by means of an allusion to the language of Zech 3:2 (where an angel and the accusing angel, or adversary, contend over the case of Joshua, here a representative also for the people of Israel). In this manner, the archangel manifests humility before God (see also Neyrey 1993, 66).

There are other references to angels in 1–2 Peter and Jude that indicate awareness of Second Temple–period literature, especially writings associated with Enoch, a patriarch of the primeval era.[19] Jude and 2 Peter mention

---

be promoting "an overly realized eschatology" that denies not only a future judgment but also a role in that judgment for the angels who accompany Christ at the Parousia, the second coming of the Son of Man (e.g., Matt 24:3). This denial could constitute for Jude an insult against the heavenly beings (Neyrey 1993, 31–32). Bauckham (1983, 58–59) and Donelson (2010, 183–84) contemplate two other plausible explanations for charge of slander: Christians, asserting superiority over angels (see 1 Cor 6:3 and Heb 2:7), could be placing themselves above angels in the cosmic order, or Christians could be denying the role of angels in giving the law and instead be adopting certain antinomian positions that offend Jude (see also Reicke 1964, 201–2). Of these possible explanations, the most plausible to my mind are that the opponents are challenging what they perceive to be excessive speculation involving angels (cf. Col 2:18) or that the opponents are imagining themselves to have a higher status than angels.

18. These verses are exceedingly difficult to parse, due in part to unclear syntax in the biblical text. Commentators offer various possible readings (see, e.g., Donelson 2010, 250–51). Bauckham suggests that 2 Peter offers a new reading of Jude so that here the opponents are false teachers who are not adequately fearful of malicious angels who could tempt or lead them astray in matters of morality (1983, 260–64). For a comparison of passages in Jude and 2 Peter and how the latter uses the former, see Bauckham 1983, 259–60.

19. There are many different writings attributed to Enoch, a patriarch who is described in Gen 5:21–24 and who becomes a figure of much speculation in Second Temple period texts. Many of these writings, produced between the third (or perhaps fourth) century B.C.E. and the first centuries B.C.E./C.E., are to be found now in the

angels who are imprisoned for wrongdoing, and their lack of elaboration implies that they assume their respective audiences know the tradition. In Jude 6, the author describes angels who deserted their proper dwelling and are now kept in chains until judgment; and in 2 Pet 2:4, the author describes angels who have sinned and subsequently are confined by means of chains to darkness until judgment. Traditions about angels (sometimes called "watchers" in the ancient literature) who left their heavenly home to cavort with mortal women were well known in the Second Temple period and appear in apocalyptic texts such as the Book of the Watchers and the Animal Apocalypse (from the Enochic Book of Dreams). Both of these Enochic texts predate the New Testament epistles by a couple of centuries.[20]

In terms of exploration of otherworlds, the letters assume the existence of unseen realms that are within the control of the divine and that nonetheless concern the inhabitants of this world (Dennis 2008). While the epistles do not treat these realms as the objects of contemplation (in contrast to, for example, chapters 17–36 of the Book of the Watchers or the later apocalypses that describe tours of heaven and hell), they are most interested in discussing the netherworld or places of punishment for hortatory purposes to get the attention of their audiences.[21] For example, 2 Pet 2:4 describes the angels who sinned as cast into darkness, an expression that was synonymous with the "realm of the dead" (see also 2 Pet 2:17), and into Tartarus, a place where only the most wicked would go for punishment in the afterlife according to Greco-Roman traditions (Bauckham 1983, 53, 248–49; Neyrey 1993, 198).

The account of angels subject to punishment in a type of liminal place appears also in 1 Pet 3:19, in a brief reference to Jesus' preaching to imprisoned spirits. While exegetes have considered a wide range of interpretative

---

anthology of *1 Enoch*, a much later collection of these texts in Ge'ez (a language of ancient Ethiopia). Students interested in this literature and its history should consult VanderKam 1995.

20. See the chapter in this volume by Eric F. Mason for a helpful study of the ways Jude and 2 Peter draw on and use traditions associated with the angels who descend to earth. See also Nickelsburg 2001, 86, 123–24. On the numerous traditions associated with the fallen watchers, see various chapters in Harkins, Coblentz Bautch, and Endres 2014, especially Mason 2014.

21. See Bauckham (1998, 49–96) on traditions of the netherworld in Jewish and Christian literature. Dennis (2008, 157) makes the case that cosmology serves the theology of these letters and especially discussion of God's salvific work by means of Christ.

possibilities for this enigmatic Petrine text, the consensus today is that the passage also refers to the tradition of angels imprisoned in a liminal space, a tradition that underscores justice and divine judgment (see, e.g., Mason 2014, 71–79 ; also Dalton 1989; Michaels 1998, 205–10; Achtemeier 1996, 255–62; Elliott 2000, 655–61; Dennis 2008, 163).

Endzeit wird Urzeit: How the End Times Resemble the Primeval Era

Discussion of the angels who are punished in some manner relates as well to the tendency in apocalyptic writings to explore the end times in light of earlier events, especially those occurring in the primeval era. The fallen angels in these traditions are otherworldly beings thought to have descended to earth during the primeval era; in fact, the tradition of these celestial beings shares a connection of some sort with the "sons of God" in Gen 6:1–4 who mate with the "daughters of men," just prior to the great flood.[22] In the literature of the Second Temple period, these angels are typically presented in a way that suggests that they have rebelled against God and are subject to judgment. Jude 6–7 links the angels who illicitly abandoned their heavenly home with the people of Sodom and Gomorrah, associating the sexual impropriety of one with the other. The author also connects the rejection of divinely ordained order by both with that of the false teachers. That is, the angels, the people of Sodom and Gomorrah, and the opponents of Jude are out of place (see, e.g., Perkins 1995, 150).[23]

In linking events of the primeval era with end-time warnings, the authors of Jude and 2 Peter draw on a traditional schema of divine judgment on sinners, and the examples derived from the Pentateuch are meant to discourage the audience against such behavior (see, e.g., Watson 2002, 188; Bauckham 1983, 46–47; Neyrey 1993, 59).[24] For Jude, the infamous exemplars consist of the wilderness generation, the disobedient angels, and Sodom and Gomorrah (vv. 5–7). The author of 2 Pet 2:4–8 also

---

22. See Seeman (2014, 25–38) on the relationship between early Enoch literature, traditions of the angels' descent, and Gen 6:1–4.

23. Reicke (1964, 199) reminds that fornication regularly signals idolatry or polytheism and reflects the apostasy of the opponents. See also Neyrey 1993, 60–61.

24. The pattern may be observed in Sir 16:7–10; CD 2:17–3:12; *3 Macc.* 2:4–7; *T. Naph.* 3:4–5; and *m. Sanh.* 10:3.

treats three instances of judgment but employs in this traditional schema the fallen angels, the "ungodly" overcome by the flood, and Sodom and Gomorrah.[25] Jude 13 makes reference to other actors associated with the primeval period and judgment by mentioning the so-called wandering stars. While there are no obvious scriptural antecedents for these wandering stars, the Book of the Watchers describes in detail the place where deviant stars are imprisoned as well as their punishment.[26] The purpose in sharing these examples is to call attention to how God punishes sin so that these may serve as a warning to contemporary audiences (see 2 Pet 2:6; Watson 2002, 189).

The classic articulation of the primeval era/end-times typology suggests that the chaos and strife accompanying theogony (stories of the beginnings of deities) are revisited in the eschaton. To the extent that the New Testament letters call attention to particular end-time scenarios, one can see hints of the *Urzeit* drama as well. For example, in 2 Pet 3:10–12 the dissolution of the world as we know it through commotion and fire calls to mind Hellenistic and Roman ideas about primal forces or elements that interact with the result of world creation.[27] Likewise, the explicit reference to the re-creation or imparting of new heavens and a new earth in 2 Pet 3:13 recalls the creation account in Genesis and the renewal after the flood.[28]

The author of 1 Peter also expresses an interest in protology by calling the audience's attention to events that occurred at the very beginning of time. References to the "foreordination of Christ's suffering from before the foundation of the world" (1:20), "the election of believers" (1:1–2), and "the predestination of unbelievers" (2:8) remind readers that the apocalyptic drama connects the end of time with the beginning (Dubis 2002,

---

25. Donelson (2010, 241) distinguishes these exemplars in Jude and 2 Peter. He notes that the focus in Jude is on sin and disobedience leading to the certainty of God's punishment; in 2 Peter the emphasis is on God's unique ability both to save and to punish.

26. See Bauckham 1983, 89–91. See Coblentz Bautch 2003, 47–48, 147–49, on the precedents upon which Jude draws.

27. Perkins (1995, 190–92) notes how the themes of the elements dissolving would resemble the Stoic teaching of elements dissolved in fire. For different readings of this text, see Bauckham 1983, 303.

28. Bauckham (1983, 326) describes the cosmic dissolution as a renewal of creation: a "return to the primeval chaos, as in the Flood (3:6), so that a new creation may emerge."

40; see also Elliott 2000, 376). Just as the other epistles draw on primordial events as paradigms for judgment, 1 Peter calls attention to the theme of judgment through reference to the punishment of the rebellious angels, the flood, and the deliverance of the righteous as signified by the example of Noah and his family (1 Pet 3:19–20; Dubis 2002, 40).

Dualism

Like other texts associated with apocalypticism, 1–2 Peter and Jude present a view of the world that is colored by dualism, one that typically contrasts this world and its limitations with the realm of the divine. Moreover, these texts present distinctive communities—those on the side of the divine and those opposed—with clear demarcations or boundaries between them.

First Peter offers many striking distinctions between the world at hand and a true home (or inheritance safeguarded by the divine; 1 Pet 1:4; 2:11) and between darkness and light (1 Pet 2:9; Elliott 2000, 440–41). Further, 1 Pet 1:4 calls its audience to an inheritance that awaits them that is imperishable, undefiled, and permanent.[29] The people addressed are to be born anew of imperishable seed, in contrast to that which is perishable (1 Pet 1:23). Similarly, the crucifixion of Jesus is presented as a "death in the flesh," whereas Jesus is made alive in the spirit (1 Pet 3:18), though commentators typically resist assigning to this verse any sort of anthropological dualism.[30] Overall, the audience of 1 Peter is estranged from the world at hand, and as "aliens" and "exiles" they are to remember their true home (see 1 Pet 1:1, 17; and 2:11 on desires and transitory existence that wage war against the soul).[31]

---

29. See Elliott 2000, 336–37, on the development of the idea of a transcendent inheritance.

30. Dalton (1989, 135–42, esp. 138) takes up the matter of a "flesh/spirit" dichotomy in the New Testament, which he concedes appears often. He concludes that the contrast is not between body and soul (incorporeality and corporeality) but rather between two orders of being: human nature (represented by flesh) and the influence of the divine and the spirit of God. With Dalton, a number of scholars do not discern in 1 Peter (and other instances of the flesh-and-spirit pairing in New Testament writings) a Platonic view of the world that would distinguish between the material and immaterial or between reason and passions; instead the *Weltanschauung* taken for granted is that presented in the Hebrew Bible. On the view of the body and soul from the perspective of the Hebrew Bible and early Judaism, see J. B. Green 2006, 1:283–85.

31. Elliott (2000, 463–65) suggests that the author is intending to distinguish

In condensed manner, Jude presents two groups that are sharply distinguished: those beloved of the author and the apostates.[32] Members of the latter abandon themselves to error (v. 11), are rebellious (v. 11), complain (v. 16), scoff (v. 16), and cause divisions (v. 19). Jude also differentiates the world of the apostates from the world of the beloved. Apostates live on the natural plane (*psychikoi*) and are devoid of spirit (v. 19).[33] Moreover, Jude thinks about the body as an outer garment, one that can be stained by the flesh (v. 23). Neyrey (1993, 87–92) emphasizes that instead of separating the physical (or material) and spiritual worlds, the author of Jude contrasts pollution (through vices and passions) with holiness.

The author of 2 Peter shares a similar view of the world. The world is a realm of corruption and lust that is opposed to the divine nature; with this

---

between the audience's former way of life (as Gentiles; see 1 Pet 1:18; 4:3–4) and their new context. References to "resident aliens" and "sojourning" complicate our understanding of the work, its audience, and the challenges of the audience. For example, recent scholars discuss how to read 1 Peter within the genre of Diaspora letters, much like 2 Macc 1:1–10a; 1:10b–2:18; *2 Bar.* 78–87; cf. Jas 1:1 (Michaels 1998, xlvi–xlvii; Martin 1992, 144–61). Elliott (1981, 41–49) in particular has challenged a spiritualizing reading of the theme of sojourning in 1 Peter and thinks instead that the references to aliens refer to the social status of the audience. Not all are convinced by Elliott's claim that the epistle does not also refer to the journeys or travails of the people of God in a metaphorical sense (Martin 1992, 142–43). See Donelson 2010, 10–11, and Achtemeier 1996, 56, for excellent summations of positions regarding the language of resident aliens; Achtemeier also notes the ambiguities in the letter that thwart identification of the audience (1996, 50). Michaels (1998, 8) observes that early Christian literature regularly describes churches as "sojourning" at a particular place (see, for example, the prologue of *1 Clement*) to the extent that the expression is almost a technical term. Even though 1 Peter is at the threshold of these developments, Michaels notes, the use of the language of sojourning and living as aliens reveals something about the church "as a certain kind of community: a people not quite at home in the places where they live." Moreover, Michaels (1998, 62) reads 1 Pet 1:1 in light of temporal situations of Christians, sojourning in this present life and anticipating an inheritance kept in heaven. See also Martin 1992, 150–58.

32. Jude's comparison (*synkrisis*) of positive behavior with disapprobation is understood also as a common rhetorical device. See Forbes 1986, 2–8. Neyrey (1993, 27), following Watson (1988, 40–77), sees the author as arguing a case by means of forensic rhetoric that contrasts "virtue with vice, praise with blame, honor with shame." See also Neyrey, 1993, 37–38, 85; and Webb 1996, 151.

33. Frey (2009, 323, 329) understands expressions like *psychikoi* to derive from Hellenistic Judaism, and he proposes that their use in Jude reflects a larger conversation about rival claims related to pneumatic orientation.

example, 2 Peter provides a contrast between vice and wholeness, impurity and holiness (2 Pet 1:4; Neyrey 1993, 153–54). Using language familiar from writings emerging in a Hellenistic setting (see *Diogn.* 6:8 or 2 Cor 5:1–4), the body is presented as a temporary dwelling, as "a tent" (2 Pet 1:13–14; cf. Isa 38:12; Wis 9:15) to be put aside. More strongly, 2 Pet 2:10 suggests that those who follow the flesh with its depraved desire (sexual immorality) show contempt for divine authority. The ultimate desire is to seek entry into the eternal kingdom of Jesus Christ (as opposed to the world; 2 Pet 1:11), which is incorruptible and holy (Neyrey 1993, 157–58), and to decline the defilement of the world (2:20) in favor of the ways of righteousness (2:21). Still, the dualism expressed in 2 Peter is not one contrasting a defiled materiality with a heavenly existence. Edward Adams (2007, 255) reiterates that like the Hebrew Scriptures, 2 Peter and other apocalyptic writings assume a positive valuation of creation and the created world.

The dualism of apocalypticism (which contrasts two parties or two ways) works well with the generic nature of 2 Peter, which is apologetic and polemical (Watson 1988, 81–146). The concern of the letter/testament is to challenge opponents the author regards as false teachers who introduce destructive heresies (2 Pet 2:1–22). Whereas the author and the author's allies have eyewitness accounts and a reliable prophetic message (2 Pet 1:18–19), the opponents portrayed by the letter have only devised myths (2 Pet 1:16). In contrast to the letter's way of truth (2 Pet 2:2), the opponents offer fabrications (2 Pet 2:3). These false teachers are called slaves of corruption; they once had escaped the defilements of the world through the knowledge of the Lord, but subsequently they have become entangled (2 Pet 2:1, 20).

The Day of the Lord and Judgment

Apocalyptic literature is best known for conveying views about the eschaton and judgment. The authors of 1–2 Peter and Jude work in different ways to express convictions about divine intervention and hope for a new age that is at hand. In fact, in 2 Peter the author's apocalyptic orientation (3:7–13) and the opponents' denial of a final judgment (2:9; 3:4) seem to prompt the apology that makes up the core of the letter. While engaging both the Hellenistic milieu and vocabulary (see, e.g., Neyrey 1993, 202, 241; Bauckham 1983, 154; E. Adams 2007), these Catholic Epistles are also indebted to the worldview of Jewish apocalypticism, especially on the matters of judgment and renewal.

Jude expresses the expectation for God's intervention by drawing on traditional language that describes the coming of the Lord as a divine warrior accompanied by celestial hosts. While the image is familiar from the Hebrew Bible (see, e.g., Isa 26:21), here Jude cites *1 En.* 1:9, an outstanding example of early Jewish apocalyptic literature.[34] In terms of the theme of judgment, Jude juxtaposes divine decrees against infamous evildoers from the Hebrew Bible with warnings about the fate of the contemporaneous opponents. Webb argues that the references to past judgment are in fact intended to move Jude's audience to proclaim "the intruders" as guilty (1996, 144, 149–50). Looking back, Jude gives the example of the angels who abandoned their proper abode, and he notes their current imprisonment and also their future condemnation (v. 6). Moving to the author's own context, Jude remarks that many of the "intruders" who perturb the community were long ago designated for judgment. This statement also recalls the theme of a predetermined plan of the divine within apocalyptic literature and the temporal axis of an apocalyptic worldview (v. 4; Neyrey 1993, 55; but compare Bauckham [1983, 35–36], who associates the claim of a judgment given beforehand with earlier [pre-Christian] prophecy).

Second Peter likewise presents the latter days as a time of judgment and recompense. Comparable to Jude, 2 Peter underscores that the impious opponents of God are detained until the day of judgment, when a final punishment is meted out (2 Pet 2:9). An example provided by 2 Peter to epitomize this claim is that of the angels who had sinned. Reflecting but also adapting Jude 6, this epistle notes that the sinful angels are kept in the chains of Tartarus until judgment. Similarly, the punishment of Sodom and Gomorrah anticipates the sort of judgment that awaits the "ungodly" (2 Pet 2:6). For 2 Peter, the eschaton is ushered in by the coming of Christ. Thus those who deny the Parousia, the triumphal appearance of Jesus, or the visitation of God are troubling for the author of the epistle (2 Pet 3:1–13; Davids 2006, 264). The scoffers ask about the promise of the coming of the Lord, and they suggest that there is no precedent for the end of one age, the beginning of a new distinctive age, and all the changes that would accompany this transition (2 Pet 3:4).[35] The author of 2 Peter looks to the

---

34. See Mason's chapter in this volume for discussion of the use of biblical and nonbiblical traditions in Jude and 2 Peter.

35. Watson (2002, 212) argues that the author of 2 Peter is borrowing materials from other sources in order to support the Parousia and is less immersed in a context of apocalyptic fervor than Jude.

account of the flood (see Gen 6–9) as an earlier instance of judgment and punishment on a worldwide scale (2 Pet 3:5–7).

Second Peter provides a description of the eschaton as a time when heaven and earth will be destroyed by fire (2 Pet 3:12). The heavens, set ablaze, will pass away with a loud noise; elements and earthly entities will be dissolved with fire (2 Pet 3:10–11; E. Adams 2007, 200–234). From the vantage of 2 Peter, traditions about the eschaton and examples of divine punishment serve a hortatory function by encouraging people to think about leading holy and godly lives (2 Pet 3:11; see also 2 Pet 2:6; Davids 2006, 287–88). At the same time, the author of 2 Peter is able to draw on Stoic traditions about world cycles and conflagration that coincide with eschatological expressions familiar from Jewish traditions (see, e.g., Isa 34:4; Mal 4:1; 1QH 3:29–35; cf. Matt 3:10; Perkins 1995, 164–65; Neyrey 1993, 240–41; E. Adams 2007, 216–18).

The epistles further communicate a view of an eschaton that is imminent or has begun. One way proximity is charted is through the community's experience of different challenges or trials that presage the end of an era. These "birth pangs" are often presented as necessary suffering prior to divine intervention or advent (cf. Dan 12:1–2; *T. Mos.* 8; 10; Matt 24:7). First Peter articulates these trials—in fact, persecutions—in different ways (see especially Webb 2007, 88–95; Dubis 2002, 63–95, 172–85; Watson and Callan 2012, 8–9). Significantly, the epistle notes that its audience suffers various trials that will only last a little time before the revelation of Jesus (1 Pet 1:6–7).[36] In this regard, the eschaton is heralded by Jesus made manifest (1 Pet 1:20; Michaels 1988, 67–68).

For Jude, the scoffers indulge "their own ungodly lusts," cause divisions, and are devoid of the Spirit. Their presence in the community's midst is proof that the era of the last times (or the eschaton) has commenced (v. 18; Davids 2006, 87–88).[37] Following Jude, 2 Peter also affirms that the presence of those who scoff at the Parousia is a prerequisite of the last days (2 Pet 3:3), with the implication that the eschaton is at hand. Still, however, 2 Peter takes a cautious approach toward putting the eschaton on

---

36. First Peter uses the language of "revelation" in a distinctive manner. Here, an "apocalypse" is not a disclosure of information to recipients but a revealing of Jesus at the Parousia. See also 1 Pet 1:13 and Michaels 1987, 272–73.

37. The term "scoffers" appears as an epithet for opponents in Isa 28:14 as well as in texts from the apocalyptic-minded community behind the Dead Sea Scrolls; see, for example, CD 1:14 and 4QpIsaiah^b 2:6–10.

a time line. The epistle prompts the audience to adopt a more expansive view of time by imagining how God envisages the length of day (2 Pet 3:8; cf. Ps 90:4). Recalling a refrain familiar from other New Testament writings ("the day of the Lord will come like a thief"; see Matt 24:43; 1 Thess 5:2; Rev 3:3), the author keeps the audience poised to expect the return at any time (2 Pet 3:10). The author anticipates questions as to why the Parousia and eschaton have not yet occurred; there has been a delay to provide more time for people to repent (2 Pet 3:9). This theme of a merciful delay is also present in other Jewish apocalyptic traditions (Bauckham 1980, 19–28).

Deliverance and the Age to Come

Apocalyptic literature provides a strong rationale for encouraging the right response to the divine, but it also gives comfort to communities in peril or facing perceived crises. Deliverance and restoration are anticipated for the communities of 1–2 Peter and Jude.

In 1 Peter, soteriology is presented as a living hope and as a goal of one's faith (1 Pet 1:3, 9; Michaels 1988, 16). Salvation is an inheritance that is imperishable, kept in heaven, and safeguarded for the community (1 Pet 1:4; on the transcendent nature of this reality, see Elliott 2000, 336). This inheritance consists of being in the presence of the eternal glory of God (1 Pet 5:10).[38] Moreover, salvation includes deliverance at the time of final judgment (1 Pet 1:9) of the living and the dead (1 Pet 4:6; Achtemeier 1996, 67; Elliott 2000, 337–38). This salvation, by means of the Parousia, is revealed in a future, final time (1 Pet 1:5–7; Michaels 1988, 23) and brings blessings with the return of Jesus (Achtemeier 1996, 95, 107).

Jude speaks of the "salvation we share" or "our common salvation" (v. 3; Bauckham 1983, 31). Within the epistle, salvation suggests freedom from slavery (v. 5) and corruption (v. 25; Neyrey 1993, 54). Perkins (1995, 147–48) associates this salvation with the "renewed moral life, the gift of the Spirit and participation in communal fellowship." She also observes that the word "salvation" had a certain cachet in secular Greek culture of the time, such that it could refer to the welfare or security of the community (1995, 147–48). Salvation also concerns the Parousia that brings

---

38. See Feldmeier (2009, 203–13) for more in-depth discussion of the salvation of the soul. He understands soteriology with regard to the soul in 1 Peter to be consistent with Hellenistic anthropology.

about the mercy of the Lord and leads to eternal life (v. 21; Webb 1996, 140–41).

Second Peter gives more elaborate pictures of this salvation. Ancient exemplars recall how God intervenes to deliver the devout from trials (2 Pet 2:9; Watson and Callan 2012, 180–81). God preserved the righteous Noah and his family (2 Pet 2:5) and the righteous Lot (2:7–8), thus God can deliver the righteous in 2 Peter's audience from challenges and trials as well (Perkins 1995, 183; Bauckham 1983, 256–57).

Deliverance also concerns a better world for the communities behind these letters (E. Adams 2007, 259). The end of the old heavens and earth presage for the author of 2 Peter the arrival of a new heavens and new earth where righteousness is at home (2 Pet 3:13; cf. Isa 65:17; 66:22; *1 En.* 72:1; 91:16; *Jub.* 1:29; 4:26; Rev 21:1). This inheritance is not perishable (Perkins 1995, 165). Salvation in 2 Peter offers the righteous the means to participate in God's glory (Perkins 1995, 165; Davids 2006, 291–93).

Conclusion

When examining the apocalypticism of 1–2 Peter and Jude, we are struck by the following. Both Jude and 2 Peter have a special interest in angels and a concern with those who disparage these otherworldly beings (Jude 10; 2 Pet 2:10–11). The author of 1 Peter may be asserting Jesus' preeminence over angelic beings by contrasting him with fallen angels (1 Pet 3:19; Donelson 2010, 115) and by placing him beyond the angels of the heavenly realms (1 Pet 3:22; cf. Watson and Callan 2012, 15). In fact, even the recipients of 1 Peter are superior to the angels (1 Pet 1:12; Watson and Callan 2012, 29, 93). This last view may reflect Pauline tendencies (see 1 Cor 6:3; Frey 2009, 314–15, 328). Jude's apocalyptic is not self-conscious but rather part of the world he and his audience take for granted (Bauckham 1983, 11). The audience of 2 Peter, however, may not be as steeped in an apocalyptic worldview. For example, the author responds to opponents who challenge eschatology (2 Pet 3:3–7), and he also uses Greek *topoi* when describing the otherworld (e.g., Tartarus in 2 Pet 2:4).

The apocalypticism of these three epistles fits well the apocalyptic tendencies of the entire New Testament. This is not the place to discuss the broader question of the New Testament and apocalypticism, but such tendencies include references to the reign of God, the coming Son of Man, eschatological woes that precede deliverance, the wrath of God's judgment, the imminence of the Parousia, the dualism of two ages, and resurrection from the dead. These features of apocalypticism are present in 1–2 Peter and Jude to varying degrees.

This brief study suggests the many ways the epistles of 1–2 Peter and Jude are apocalyptic in orientation. From acceptance of the role of the otherworld and otherworldly beings in our sphere of being, to views of time in which the eschaton resembles creation, to a dualistic perspective toward the world and distinctive communities, these epistles communicate a worldview shared by many other Jews and Christians in antiquity. Especially striking are the ways the letters speak to divine intervention, judgment, and deliverance, all of which are essential aspects of the apocalyptic imagination. Whether expressed in the language of the last days, Parousia, or a new heavens and a new earth, apocalyptic perspectives were significant to these epistles and their theologies.

Reborn to a Living Hope: A Christology of 1 Peter

Steven J. Kraftchick

Schubert Ogden begins his book *The Point of Christology* by observing, "Without a doubt the question christology answers *is* the question 'Who is Jesus?' But what certainly is wrong in this understanding is what it in effect denies in assuming that this is the *only* question that christology answers." Ogden states this to ensure that Christology will attend to the question of who Jesus is (or was), but *also* to the difference that answers to that question have for understanding God and ourselves. This statement requires that in constructing a Christology one must always ask, directly or indirectly, two other questions: "the question 'Who is God?' understood as asking about the ultimate reality upon which we are dependent for our own being and meaning as human persons … [and] the question 'Who are we?' or better, 'Who am I?' which we are each led to ask more or less explicitly insofar as we are concerned not to miss but to attain our own authentic existence as human beings" (Ogden 1982, 27–28).

First Peter reflects a similar understanding of Christology, and this letter connects the purposes of God with the actions of Jesus in order to define the identity of the church and the individual. The letter's portraits of Jesus as the Christ reveal God and the church, and in a reciprocal manner, the convictions about God and the church influence its author's presentation of Jesus Christ. Thus 1 Peter is "one of the most thoroughly christocentric writings in the New Testament," with a "highly developed Christology" (Achtemeier 1993, 176). The letter is also thoroughly theocentric and ecclesiastically directed.

As a consequence, the letter's Christology is dependent on the author's understanding of God and God's actions in the world, and it is shaped by the author's perspective on the circumstances facing his audience as they live their faith commitments in private and public social settings. This intricate relationship of ecclesiology, theology, and Christology means that a Christology of 1 Peter will not be a set of declarative systematic sentences, but a combination of images. The letter's christological "affirmations are not speculative statements about Jesus, but illuminate and provide the basis for the readers' own Christian existence" (Boring 1999, 97). The Christology of 1 Peter is, therefore, functional and dynamic rather than abstract and formal. Each of its images and conceptions of Christ is influenced by the pastoral desire to help the church understand its identity. They are presented as invitations for reflection, not as linear, logical proofs intended to produce tightly woven formal arguments.

Readers of 1 Peter experience a wealth of images of Jesus Christ that are drawn from early Christian hymns, creeds, liturgical ceremonies, and interpretations of the Old Testament. The cumulative effect is almost overwhelming in its diversity and reach. Just in the first twelve verses, Jesus is portrayed as: the one the churches obey because they have been sprinkled with his blood (1:2; cf. 1:18–19); the Son of God, raised from the dead, and the basis for the church's living hope (1:3; cf. 1:13, 21; 3:15); the one unseen, but soon to be revealed in glory and honor (1:7–9; cf. 1:13; 4:13); and the one sought by the prophets, urged on by the "Spirit of Christ" within them (1:10–11; cf. 3:18–19).

This cascade of imagery is not restricted to the letter's opening, but continues throughout the epistle. Some recur, especially the images depicting the future revelation of Jesus in glory (1:7, 13; 4:13) and those recalling Christ's endurance of trials and suffering (2:21–23; 3:18; 4:1, 16; 5:1). Just as many, however, appear only to give way to other evocative images such as Christ the "living stone" (2:4) and "chief shepherd" (5:4).

This cascade creates a constellation of images and ideas that appear more like an architect's watercolor conceptual sketch than the precise lines of a building blueprint. Lewis Donelson expresses the effect of the letter's rhetoric when he notes that

> the gathering of diverse theological and ethical figures, and even the shift from specific to general audience—all this is frequent in the letter. This mixed rhetoric means that the letter lacks extended, sequential theological argument. Instead, the letter's theology is built more by gathering than by sustained argument. It takes the readers to complete the argument, since the readers must decide, for instance, how Jesus' footsteps might be followed in their own lives. (Donelson 2010, 86)

The author's goal was to have the readers interact *with* Jesus Christ rather than simply receive information *about* Jesus Christ. The letter does not develop a christological argument or provide unique ideas about Jesus so much as provide a "narrative world" in which readers

> are met not only with statements, commands, and promises, but by an understanding of reality, a world that has a particular narrative shape, that may be different from their own and that challenges it. The narrative world is itself a continuing call to decide which is the real world that determines the life of the reader: the everyday world assumed by the culture and common sense, or the world projected by the text. (Boring 2007, 24)

The narrative world reconfigures the "lived world" of the letter's readers and enables them to comprehend and respond to the challenges they were experiencing because of their new faith. The Christology 1 Peter presents is not a neutral account about Jesus but a proclamation of Jesus as the Christ influenced by, and directed to, the needs of its initial addressees. It is intended to present the *meaning* of Christ, not to prove that Jesus is the Christ or to explicate theories of Christ's atoning sacrifice.

Because of the letter's interrelated depictions of Christ, God, and the church as well as its pastoral goals, we must first sketch the contours of the social situation and the author's strategy for addressing it to discern its Christology. Two dominant features of the Christology illustrate the letter's understanding of Christ's foundational work for God's purposes (1:17–21) as well as the pattern Christ creates for those who trust in him (2:21–24).

The Occasion of the Letter

Questions concerning the authorship of 1 Peter, as well as its date and provenance, put any fine-grained portrait of its audience beyond our reach.[1] However, the author's use of newborn and infant imagery (1:3, 14, 23; 2:2) suggests that the recipients were recent converts who had left devotions to pagan deities and sworn allegiance to Christ (1:18; 2:12; 4:3). Based on the opening and closing verses of the letter, we can also suppose they were formed into small congregations spread throughout Asia Minor (1:1) and were struggling to maintain their existence as social and spiritual communities (5:6–10, 12).

---

1. For detailed discussions of the issues, see commentaries such as Achtemeier 1996; Elliott 1990; 2000; Kelly 1969; Michaels 1988; and Selwyn 1947.

The change in their religious orientation, as well as the changes in their social behavior this caused, likely alienated non-Christian friends, associates, and in some cases family (4:1–6). As a result, they were experiencing resistance in the form of social distancing, charges of following an illegitimate religion, and perhaps accusations of crimes against the state (Horrell 2007a, 376). These broken relationships are referenced repeatedly when the recipients are described as "suffering various trials" (1:7), "being maligned as evil doers" (2:11), "suffering unjustly" (2:19), "suffering for doing what is right" (3:13, 17), facing a "fiery ordeal" (4:12), "suffering as a Christian" (4:16), and surprisingly, "suffering in accordance with God's will" (4:19). The repeated descriptions of these broken relationships demonstrate how critical the situation had become.

The Author's Strategy

Our author's purpose was to provide a narrative by which the readers could understand, endure, and respond to the social ostracism they were experiencing. This purpose required an explanation of the nature and ends of their social suffering, and the author provides four interconnected approaches to the audience's experiences of social difficulties, each having a distinctive emphasis.

First, suffering that results from misbehavior or sin is distinguished from unmerited suffering (2:19–21; 3:17; 4:15–16). Second, different ends are assigned to suffering: (1) a sign that God's people are obedient to the will of God (2:15; 3:17; 4:1, 19); (2) a natural result of changing allegiance from the "futile ways of the ancestors" to the "will of God" (1:6; 2:11, 19, 20; 3:14, 17; 4:4, 16); (3) an opportunity to express the ethical truth of their faith (3:15–16); and (4) preparation for and enhancement of trust in God, who redeems and vindicates the people of God (4:12–14, 19). Third, the author explains that although current suffering feels like an overwhelming experience, it is in fact only a temporary affliction (1:6; 4:7, 12, 17; 5:10), especially compared to the glory that is to come (1:7; 3:16; 4:13–14; 5:1, 10). By juxtaposing the finite experience of suffering with the "imperishable, undefiled, and unfading" (1:4) inheritance at the end of time (1:6; 5:10), the author is able to reframe their experience in terms of God's plan and will.

Fourth and most importantly, the author identifies suffering as an essential part of Christian existence and defines it as "following the footsteps of Jesus Christ" (2:21). Because Christ has suffered in the flesh

(4:1) at the hands of those who did not understand him, Christians are to accept that this result could be their fate (3:18). Indeed, they share in Christ's sufferings (*pathēmata*, 4:13; cf. 1:11, 5:1, 9) as they attempt to follow Christ's example. Not only do Christians share in Christ's suffering, but they can also respond to it as Christ did (2:21). Indeed, this response is the essence of "doing good" (*agathopoieō*, 2:15, 20; 3:6, 17), both as part of one's religious commitments and as a witness to God's judgments (cf. Zerbe 1993, 270–90; Van Unnik 1980, 83–105). In this regard, suffering properly understood and responded to is faithful existence *in* and faithful proclamation *of* God's good news (2:12, 15, 18–25; 3:3, 9, 13–18; 4:1–6, 14, 16, 19).

The last of these approaches distinguishes 1 Peter's thought from other ancient Hellenistic and Jewish responses to suffering. Our author is not interested in valorizing suffering, nor is he insisting that it be sought as a mark of discipleship. Rather, his focus is on the responses to unmerited suffering and their efficacy. It is at this juncture that the Christology of 1 Peter is most evident, for Christ is the model and foundation for those responses. As Eugene Boring recognizes:

> Unjust suffering is not just a strategy in 1 Peter. It is inherently right, as revealed in Christ. The nature of God and the universe embraces unjust suffering. This is the polar opposite of saying that Christians may cause, contribute to, or excuse unjust suffering. But when they are called upon to endure it, they can do so as a grace of God, as was the cross itself (2:19–10; 5:12). (Boring 1999, 120)

The author of 1 Peter argues that the manner in which Christ responded to social rejection and suffering defines the life of the disciple. The Christ model allows the audience to understand its own experiences of suffering (2:21–25; 3:13–18; 4:1, 12–16). The author consistently returns to this aspect of Jesus Christ's nature and makes it "the theological center and fulcrum of the letter" (Boring 1999, 120).

Theological Presuppositions

The beginning and ending point for 1 Peter's theology is the "holiness of God" (1:15–16). God is both merciful Father (1:3; 2:10) and impartial judge (1:17; 4:17–18). Invoking God as Father requires acknowledging both elements, which the author implies when he asserts that God's people should live in "reverent fear" (*phobos*, 1:17) and be "aware of God" (2:19), which means adhering to God's will (1:17; 2:17; 3:2, 14), proclaiming God's glory (4:1–2, 11), and "doing good" especially in response to evil. This response is the divine nature revealed in Christ (2:15, 20; 3:6, 17–18; 4:19).

There are thirty-nine instances of the term "God" in this relatively short epistle (105 verses), and numerous other "divine passive" verbs are used to indicate God as the active force behind occurrences in history. As with the christological claims, a strategy of portrayal rather than argument is used to present a multifaceted picture. It is through God's initiative that the communities of believers came into existence (2:10; cf. 1:3, 23; 2:2), are sustained and protected (1:5; 4:14; 5:10), and will be vindicated (1:9; 2:12; 4:17; 5:6). God foreknew and predestined the redemptive activity of Christ including Christ's death and subsequent glorification (1:20a). It is God who raised Christ from the dead (1: 13; 3:18), "the quintessential demonstration of God's animating and saving power and the basis for hope and trust in God despite adversity" (Elliott 2000, 334).

God initiates, empowers, and wills the redemption of human beings through the agency of Christ. Christ enacts, through his death and resurrection, the divine character of the merciful judge who establishes right relationship between humans and God. Christ's death initiates this relationship, and by trusting in Christ, Christians are sustained until their hope becomes realized at Christ's return (1:3, 18, 21; 2:21, 24; 3:21; 4:16). All of these benefits are catalyzed by the appearance of Christ in human history (Richard 1986, 131–32), but 1 Peter has focused attention on the two aspects of Christ's reality that make them possible: Christ's suffering and death, and Christ's revelation in future glory. These aspects locate the experience of ostracism in a larger context and encourage the church's mission of lived witness.

Christological Contours

As we have noted, there are many features of Christ's being and actions that the author does not emphasize because they were not pertinent to his audience. Three features of the letter underscore this lack of emphasis: the images 1 Peter emphasizes compared to those he mutes, the foundational role of Christ, and Christ as exemplar.

Many christological images that are frequently found in other New Testament documents do not appear in 1 Peter. For example, 1 Peter never refers to the "son of God," although this title is implied when God is called Jesus' Father (1:3). He does not use the title "Savior" even though he refers to the salvation of believers (1:5, 9–10; 2:2). In 1 Peter, the term "Lord" only occurs eight times, and only twice is the term used as a title for Jesus (1:3; 3:15). Undoubtedly, Christ was Lord for the author of 1 Peter, but the author's tendency is to "blur the distinction between Christ and God" (Boring 1990, 90). In the same manner, while there are no direct references to the preaching of Jesus or quotations from his teaching, there are references to the "word" of God. However, "instead of citing a saying of Jesus, as one might anticipate from an eyewitness disciple, the Petrine point is made by citing Scripture (e.g., 3.14, 4.8, 14). In the narrative world of 1 Peter, Scripture and its prophetic authors speak, but the earthly Jesus does not" (Boring 2007, 29).

More important than what 1 Peter omits is what the letter emphasizes. The author uses early Christian motifs portraying the death of Christ but customizes them to meet the needs of his audience. In particular, the author prefers to speak of the "suffering of Christ" rather than "Christ's death," because it is the unmerited suffering and Jesus' response to it that provide the addressees with actions and speech they can emulate if not reduplicate.

This concern produces two christological motifs that dominate the letter: Christ as initiating catalyst for the relationship believers enjoy with God (1:21, 23; 2:5; 3:21) and the suffering Christ as an exemplar (1:10–11; 2:19–23; 3:14–18; 4:1–2, 14–16; 5:10). These images of Christ form the core of 1 Peter's thought and provide the lenses through which his other christological images can be viewed. "Christ as agent of initiation" depicts the actions of God in or through Jesus Christ that inaugurate the relationship between believers and God. "Christ as exemplar" centers not only on the suffering that Jesus endured in his trial and crucifixion but also on the rejection of Christ that continues in history. These two images, the agent of initiation and exemplar, are fundamental for understanding 1 Peter's christological motifs.

Christ as Agent of Initiation

We noted above the fundamental and foundational character of God for this letter's ethics and Christology, and that Jesus Christ is the central figure in the world that God has created and will redeem. Christ as agent of initiation brings these two tenets into one focus. Preordained by God, his death and resurrection are the events through which the new existence of "trust in God" has been initiated, and it will be with his future revelation that Christians will attain its culmination of glory.

An important facet of the image of Christ as initiator is that the Christ event divides chronological time and existence. First Peter emphasizes this division of time with his contrasts between "then" (*pote*, 2:10; 3:5, 20) and "now" (*nyn*, 1:12; 2:10, 25; 3:21).[2] The Christ is pivotal, dividing human history and separating those who are known by God from those who refuse to acknowledge God's sovereignty. The event is not limited to Jesus' time on earth; it is located beyond time, "destined before the foundation of the world" (1:20), revealed as the turning point of the ages (1:20), and enduring beyond time (4:11; Feldmeier 2008, 119). As Boring observes, "The central event of Jesus Christ who was crucified and raised at a particular time in history modulates into other events in such a way that it cannot simply be located at one point on the chronological line" (Boring 2007, 24).

The focus on the historical yet transtemporal reality of Christ centers human chronology in cosmic reality and distinguishes present existence from eternal existence. The Christ event inaugurates the possibility of the Christian life, communal and individual, and is a pledge toward full existence with God, which is itself inaugurated by the revelation of Jesus at the end of time (1:5, 7; 4:13–14; 5:1, 4). Christ functions as catalyst both in the sense of inaugurating the new age by his death and resurrection (1:21; 2:9–10, 22–25; 3:18) and by bringing it to culmination with his revelation in his glory (1:7, 11, 13; 4:13; 5:1, 4, 10).

The integration of the resurrection of Jesus and the final coming of Christ is underscored by three stylistic techniques. First, the verbs used for resurrection and the future revelation of Christ are typically in the passive voice, implying that Jesus is the means by which God enacts a new moment in human existence. Second, the actions are understood as God's established plan for the cosmos and not a revision of God's initial purpose. Third, Christ's actions are usually viewed in light of the past and the future; that is, the author looks back to what Christ has done and forward to what Christ will do. At this moment, between the time of their becoming "a new people" and when they will be fully redeemed at the eschaton, the primary role of Christ is as example and model.

Christ as Exemplar

Christ as exemplar focuses on the critical moment of Jesus' final suffering and death. The author does not refer to the ministry or deeds of the

---

2. On this important motif, see Achtemeier 1988, 232–33.

earthly Jesus but to the suffering and death of Jesus, especially the manner in which he responded to those who effected these offenses. There are at least fifteen explicit references to this constellation of events in the letter: three report the suffering and death without comment (3:18; 4:1, 13), but the others provide redemptive interpretations of Jesus' death. Our author refers to the death of Jesus as: suffering "for you" (2:21); a ransom enacted (*lytroō*) through the sprinkling of blood (1:2, 18–19); the bearing of human sins that enables believers to live righteously (2:24; 3:18); and the stone that serves as the foundation for God's spiritual people and as the stumbling block for God's opponents (2:4–7). However, the main focus of the author's references is to Christ as the one who endured suffering for others in order to be the example to others.

Christ as exemplar pertains not only to the suffering Christ endured but also to the nonretaliatory response to this abasement and to the vindication by God. Christians who endure unjust suffering by following Christ's pattern will also be vindicated at the consummation of the age (1:4–7, 21; 2:21–24; 3:9, 16; 4:13–15, 19; 5:6, 10).

Implications of Christ as Initiator and Exemplar

Focusing on the past and future in order to comprehend the present is typical of 1 Peter and informs the readers that their existence is not confined to or defined by their present circumstances. By extending the horizon of their vision and encouraging them to look behind and beyond the present, the author defines their place in God's plan of salvation. Quite literally, theirs is a "living hope" maintained by what God has done in Christ and expressed in their imitation of Jesus, because the power of God that raised Jesus from the dead protects them and ensures their future salvation. Although they do not experience it in complete form, they are now in effect sharing in a new life inaugurated by the resurrection of Jesus from the dead and concluding in the "salvation of their souls" (1:9) when Christ reappears to initiate the final judgment.

The letter addresses the readers as "exiles of the Dispersion" (1:1; 2:11) and refers to them as "legal aliens" in a hostile environment (2:11).[3] However, the author urges his audience to expand their horizon beyond their

---

3. Whether these metaphors of alienation were intended to help the early Christian communities adapt to or else resist the pressures of the Roman social system is a matter of some debate. These two options are well defined by the written exchanges

geographic and temporal locales by reminding them that they are not alone in their distress (5:9). More importantly, he asserts that the temporal and spatial limits of physical location are not the limits of their true existence in God. They are a "spiritual dwelling" (2:4) with an "imperishable inheritance kept in heaven" (1:4). They are reminded that present circumstances are fleeting and that their true identity is based in the "word of the Lord," which endures forever (1:25). The realities of their existence may be hidden, but they still trust the one who remains invisible at this time (1:8) without fear of shame (2:6) because he is sovereign over both the seen and unseen inhabitances. As the raised and vindicated one, Christ proclaims God's victory over all opposition (3:19), stands as the judge of the living and the dead (4:5), and now "is at the right hand of God, with angels, authorities, and powers made subject to him" (3:22). These metaphors ground the communities in "hope" (1:3, 13, 21; 3:15), even, or especially, in the midst of resistance and suffering, for Christ has overcome these forces and rules over them.

Two passages are especially illustrative of these christological ideas and expressions: (1) 1:17–21, where God's ransoming act through Christ is depicted as a transformation of Christian believers from the futility of their heritage into a people who revere God; and (2) 2:21–25, where Christ is presented as a model or pattern to be followed as the church endures persecutions and suffering and as the means by which reverent life in God is attained. While these are not the only passages with christological importance, they are central to the author's concepts and concerns and present the letter's christological dynamic.

1 Peter 1:17–21

Verses 17–21 form one sentence in Greek that highlights the commitments of "being holy" (1:17) as well as providing the christological warrant for those commitments (1:18–21). The readers "already know" these convictions, but they are recast to remind them that God has acted through the Christ event "for your sake" (1:20) and will continue to act so that "your faith and hope are set on God" (1:21). The "passage embodies the fundamental theological argument that underlies and undergirds all

---

between Elliott (1986; 1990) and Balch (1986). A mediating path between the two polar positions is offered by Horrell (2007a).

that follows in this letter, whether hortatory or theological" (Achtemeier 1996, 123).

The letter's opening highlighted the regeneration of believers, calling it a "living hope." The next section of the letter (1:13–21) expands on that theme by repeating the word "hope" (*elpis*, 1:13, 21) and the terms for "conduct" (*anastrophē* and *anastrephō*, 1:15, 17, and 18; cf. 3:1, 16).[4] The author links convictions to actions by arguing that the eschatological hope of salvation, ensured through Christ's death and resurrection, is the reason for a new form of life, one that displays appreciation and awe for the power of God (1:17–18). The author calls this "living in reverent fear" (*en phobō ... anastraphēte*, 1:17) and contrasts it to living in "conformity to former ignorance" (1:14) and "the futile ways inherited from your ancestors" (1:18).

The pattern of God's working through Christ is exhibited in 1:18–21. Christians are ransomed by God through the "blood of Jesus," a metonym for "Jesus' life" (cf. Gen 9:4; Lev 17:11). The verb *lytroō*, which refers to the monies paid to manumit slaves or redeem property, is rare in the New Testament and occurs only here, at Luke 24:21, and at Titus 2:14, although the idea of Christ's redemptive death is far more prevalent (see Mark 10:45; Rom 3:24–25; Heb 9:12).[5] The notion of ransom is funded by the tradition of Israel's redemption from bondage in Egypt and the Babylonian exile (see Exod 6:6; Isa 51:11) and especially by Isa 52:3–4, where Israel is referred to as God's people who were "residing as aliens" in Egypt (*paroikēsai*; cf. 1 Pet 2:11, *paroikous*). The release from Egypt was celebrated at Passover, and this tradition may be in the background of the references to Christ as "a lamb without defect and blemish." Nevertheless, the reference to redemption by blood and not by money in 1:18 appears to be an echo of Isa 52:3, which, along with the clear influence of Isaiah's Suffering Servant motif on 2:21–25, suggests that the lamb image may be a reflection of Isa 53:7, "the lamb led to slaughter," even though no mention is made of its perfection in that text (see Elliott 2000, 374–75; and Achtemeier 1996, 128–29, for more detailed discussion). In any event, the dominant idea stems from Jesus' death itself and the early Christian interpretations of that death as redemptive (e.g., Acts 20:28; Rom 3:24–25).

---

4. The verb *anastrephō* is used here to indicate a manner of life conducted according to particular principles (BDAG 72–73).

5. The verb *lytroō* is an aorist passive indicating God's definitive action on behalf of humanity.

In this instance, Christians have been released from the futility of the ways of their ancestors (1:18) to live according to the will of God (cf. 1:14–15; 2:11–12; 4:1–4). Three elements of the ransom are underscored, each relating a christological conviction: it is costly and unique (1:18–19); it is perfect, without defect (1:20); and it has been central to God's design and being since before creation (1:20). The contrast of "former" and "present" life is mirrored in the contrast between a ransom paid with the world's most valuable commodities and one procured through the "precious" blood of Jesus. The point stresses the difference between the effects of human commerce and traditions and God's power through the distinct action in Christ.

Verses 20–21 supply further details concerning God's initiation of the Christ event. This initiation is signaled by the passive participles "destined" (*proegnōsmenon*) and "revealed" (*phanerōthentos*) used to modify the noun *Christou*, which ends verse 19 in the Greek text. The author asserts that Christ's sacrificial ransom was not an afterthought or an ad hoc solution to the human plight but instead a fundamental part of God's eternal purposes. The role of the entire Christ event (and by implication Christ's being) existed before the "foundation of the world" and is revealed at "the end of the ages." The language allows the author to express the cosmic scope of the event and so remind the readers of the profundity of God's actions on their behalf—actions that were in place before their own existence (cf. 1:2, where "destined" is also used). The term "revealed" (*apokalyptō*) here refers to Jesus' death, while in 5:4 it refers to Christ's appearance at the end of history. Christ plays both roles, and the author's use of "revealed" links Christ's roles as Judge and Shepherd to his sacrificial death for others (see 1:5, 7; 4:13; 5:1, where *apokalyptō*, "to reveal," and *apokalypsis*, "revelation," are used to make this connection). These verses focus on the fundamental role of Christ's death, hidden since before the creation but now revealed. Its significance and ultimate status are signified by Christ's resurrection from the dead to live in glory (1:21). It is this pattern of suffering followed by vindication that serves as a pattern of exhortation to the "communities in exile" (4:13–16; 5:1).

1 Peter 2:21–25

The interconnectedness of Christ and the church is a fundamental motif in 1 Peter, as 2:4–10 illustrates. Like Christ, the church is a "living stone" (2:4), "rejected by mortals" (2:4, 7). As the foundation stone of the believers' "spiritual building," Christ's sacrificial pattern establishes the community's identity. The author "is not thinking only of the Jewish leadership's rejection of the historical Jesus ... , but of the continuing rejection of Jesus by human society" (Boring 1999, 97). The audience experiences this same form of rejection from their neighbors and associates. Yet like Jesus, they are "chosen" by God (1:1; 2:4, 6, 9) and "precious in God's sight" (2:4, 7), and like him they will be vindicated if they respond to their present suffering in the manner he did.

The pattern of the suffering and rejected Christ as the foundation for the church is best represented in 2:21–25, where Christ's suffering and response are once more interpreted. The interpretation is not a theological apology for the suffering, but an exhortation that focuses on Christ's response to suffering. Donelson has suggested that 1 Peter's "portrait of Jesus is traditional and credible, and what is at stake is whether and how Christians are to suffer" (Donelson 2010, 78). This passage is part of the author's exhortations to household slaves (*oiketai*), but it functions as a general exhortation to the entire community of believers, as similar advice recurs in 3:16–18 (see Achtemeier 1996, 194; Boring 1999, 117). "The point is that just as a slave in that society could hardly avoid suffering, even unjust suffering, so the Christian in that society could expect a similar fate" (Achtemeier 1988, 229–30). Consequently, this pericope "takes the reader to the heart of 1 Peter's theology: it asserts not only that unjust suffering is an inevitable aspect of the Christian life, but also that such suffering constitutes the essential character of the Christian life" (Donelson 2010, 83). Here, as in 3:16–18, the christological claims are the basis for the exhortation to endure unrighteous suffering through a consciousness of the nature of God (2:18–19).

Verses 21–25 are drawn from an early Christian reinterpretation of the Suffering Servant tradition found in Isaiah 53.[6] They present the Christ as one who suffered unjustly but who relied on God for vindication, and it is to this same form of trust that Christians have been called (2:21). The call is to discipleship, not imitation, for as we have noted above, following Christ is not a matter of reduplication but of accepting the path of resistance that faithfulness to God may entail. As Christ suffered for them, they

---

6. The parallels are: 2:22 (Isa 53:9); 2:24 (Isa 53:4–5, 11–12); 2:25 (Isa 55:6, 10). While there is no verbal parallel, the thought of Isa 53:7 could have informed the use of *anteloidorei* ("he did not return abuse") in 2:23. The influence of the motif on 1 Peter has been explored fully in Achtemeier 1993, 176–88.

will be called to suffer for "doing good" in their devotion to him. Donelson rightly notes that according to 1 Peter, "The suffering of Christ does not end Christian suffering; the suffering of Christ calls for more suffering" (Donelson 2010, 83).

Beside the comparison to the Suffering Servant motif and the depiction of Christ as redeemer and guardian, there is another aspect of this passage that merits our attention: Christ as "exemplar," whose actions and response Christians should follow (2:21). To appreciate it, we need to consider these two terms and then delineate the elements of suffering that Christians are to exhibit. The term "exemplar" (*hypogrammon*) appears only here in the New Testament and refers to tracing a pattern to teach children to write (BDAG 1036). Here the idea is not to follow the exact details of Christ's trials, but to follow Christ's direction of innocent suffering, nonretaliation, and reliance on God for vindication (Kelly 1969, 120). The second phrase, "to follow in Christ's footsteps" (*epakolouthēsēte tois ichnesin*), also unique to 1 Peter, is used epexegetically to further define Christ's "pattern." Christians do not mimic Jesus mechanically, but as disciples they make their "own creative adaptation of the pattern" (Boring 1999, 121).

We can draw three conclusions about these verses. First, even though the Christians may suffer with Christ, this suffering is not a matter of reduplication but discipleship. Christ's suffering is unique, the sole redemptive moment in human history (1:2, 18–19; 2:21, 24; and especially 3:18). One follows the path of Christ, but the suffering that one will endure will not be identical to that of Christ.

Second, it is not simply Christ's suffering that is the pattern, but that he suffered for doing good (and therefore unjustly) and that in this suffering he did not respond in kind, but with more benevolence (2:23). Unmerited suffering does not call for a reprisal or quietude, but further acts of good, trusting the one who judges all to mete out justice. This same pattern marks the Christian's response, which is to suffer for doing good and in so doing present an example to those who inflicted the suffering (2:15; 3:15–18; cf. 3:1). This response to suffering shares in the suffering of Christ (4:13) and is a form of preaching Christ to the world (2:11, 15).

Third, unmerited suffering is intrinsic to discipleship (cf. 3:17; 4:14–17), not simply because of social friction but because it is an element of Christ's own existence. The Christ was "destined" for suffering (1:11, 20), and so he determines the ethos of the people called "Christ followers" (*Christianoi*, 4:16; cf. Lohse 1986). Christ is not a moral epitome, but the exemplar of the very nature of God's will for humanity: to express acts of love through mutual sacrifice. As Boring aptly suggests, "'Jesus suffered as an example' and 'Jesus suffered for others' are two sides of the same *christological* coin" (1999, 122).

Conclusion

Our chapter began with Ogden's important reminder that a Christology must speak not only of Christ but also of "who we are." Thus, having pointed to the dominant role that 1 Peter gives to the experience of suffering and the response that faithfulness to Christ requires, it is important for us to consider the role of 1 Peter in a contemporary setting. First Peter's portraits can be important moments of encouragement, and they should embolden modern Christians to persist in their faithful witness in the face of social pressure. At the same time, in many areas of the world the Christian church is not a minority group or perceived as a threat to society's security. Neither is identification as a Christian perceived as an oddity; indeed, often it is taken as a given. Rather than being perceived as an opponent to the cultural, ethical, and social norms, being a Christian is almost essential to being received as a legitimate public spokesperson about moral and ethical matters. Thus, to appropriate 1 Peter's Christology requires adapting it to contemporary settings. The call to "do good" is still a present and essential need, but the manner in which this call is carried out will certainly be different.

To "do good" or "follow the pattern of Christ" must entail critical reflection on the surrounding society's values and practices as well as those of the church, for as 1 Peter reminds its readers, "the judgment of God begins with the household of God" (4:17), and this judgment requires a self-directed scrutiny of the church's values and internal behaviors.

First Peter also refreshes the church's memory of its true status as "aliens in this world," and its Christology calls for a greater identification between the church and other members of society who are ostracized for resisting the "given" structures of our commonwealths. To recapture the response of Christ as a model for proper discipleship will require the church to take stances on social issues and behaviors that will not always cohere with the majority norm. There will be resistance to these stances, and at these moments 1 Peter's christological image of Christ as witness must loom large in the church's conscience.

Finally, it cannot be emphasized enough that while it focuses on the suffering Christ followers' experience, 1 Peter is not a call to suffer for suffering's sake. It is an exhortation to respond to unmerited suffering with an embodied witness to God's mercy (3:8–17). The suffering to which the church is called is a result of persistent and quiet resistance to societal behaviors and norms that betray wholesome community life and demean individual worth. Such a call is not easily answered, and this is why 1 Peter's concluding remarks remain pertinent for today's church: "Resist [your adversary the devil] in your faith, for you know that your brothers and sisters in all the world are undergoing the same kinds of suffering. And after you have suffered a little while, the God of all grace, who has called you to his eternal glory in Christ, will himself restore, support, strengthen, and establish you" (5:9–10, my translation).

Christians as Babies:
Metaphorical Reality in 1 Peter

Troy W. Martin

Metaphors permeate 1 Peter from the very beginning, where the Christian recipients are described as "elect sojourners of the Diaspora," to the end, where the sender and his community are identified as the "co-elect [Diaspora] of Babylon."[1] The author of 1 Peter is quite fond of metaphor, and an informed interpreter of this document as well as of the New Testament as a whole needs some understanding of metaphors and how they function in thought and communication. R. Melvin McMillen notes, "Petrine scholars are well-advised to think deeply and read widely in the field of metaphor, not only because of its importance, but also because of its often unnoticed complexities" (2011, 3).

Aristotle, in explaining the nature of metaphor, also provides an explanation for the abundance of metaphors in 1 Peter. He states, "Metaphors must not be far-fetched, but we must give names to things that have none by deriving the metaphor from what is akin and of the same kind, so that as soon as it is uttered, it is clearly seen to be akin" (*Rhet.* 3.2.12 [1405a], LCL). First Peter addresses those "who formerly were *no people* but now are the people of God" (1 Pet 2:10). These recipients are non-Jews who have left their former life and now believe in the Jewish God (2:9).[2]

---

1. All translations of ancient texts are mine unless otherwise noted. The term "diaspora" is lacking from 1 Pet 5:13 but should probably be supplied because of the connection between "elect" in 1:1 and "co-elect" in 5:13. The term "brotherhood" may also be supplied from 5:9. See Martin 1992, 145–46.

2. Scholars still debate whether the recipients are Jews, non-Jews, or a mixture of both. Dunn (2009, 1158–60) most recently makes the case for Jewish recipients. Several passages (such as 1 Pet 1:14, 18; 2:10; and 4:3–4), however, persuade the majority of interpreters that the letter is addressed to non-Jews.

They are neither Greek nor Jew but a new race of humans as specifically mentioned in *Diogn.* 1. Consistent with Aristotle's explanation, metaphors are therefore necessary to "give names" to these recipients and to describe their new unique status. Indeed, one metaphor, "Christian" (4:16), which this text uses perhaps for the very first time, will become the common designation not only for these recipients but also for all who belong to this new human race (Horrell 2007b, 361–81).

Considering the importance of metaphors in 1 Peter, this essay will first survey various definitions of metaphor. Next, it will describe some of the recent theories about metaphor that interpreters have applied to 1 Peter. It will then investigate the specific metaphor of newborn babies to illustrate the metaphorical reality of the recipients' new life in Christ.

Defining Metaphor

All speech is symbolic, but not all speech is metaphorical, and distinguishing metaphor from other symbolic speech requires definition. Metonymies are often confused with metaphor but can be distinguished because they only name a constituent part in reference to the whole. Numerous metonymies occur in 1 Peter and include "house" for the household (4:17) and "tongue" and "lips" for speech (3:10; Howe 2008, 368–69). Allegories and parables do not play a significant role in 1 Peter, but they are nonetheless figurative speech and are sometimes understood as extended metaphors. A simile is an expression that uses "like" or "as" to make a comparison, and simile is often contrasted with metaphor that uses copulative verbs to join the two comparative entities. However, Aristotle states, "The simile also is a metaphor; for there is very little difference. … Similes must be used like metaphors, which only differ in the manner stated" (Aristotle, *Rhet.* 3.3.4 [1406b], LCL). The close connection of simile and metaphor is illustrated in 1 Peter, which uses both a metaphor ("exiles," 1:1) and a simile ("as exiles," 2:11) to compare its recipients to exiles. It is thus customary in Petrine studies to include similes such as the recipients as children (1:14) and newborn babies (2:2) when discussing the epistle's use of metaphors. These and other types of symbolic speech necessitate defining metaphor.

The Greek word *metaphora* means "transference," and transference is essential to the definition of metaphor. Aristotle writes, "A metaphor is the application of a word that belongs to another thing: either from genus to species, species to genus, species to species, or by analogy" (*Poet.* 21.7, LCL; cf. *Rhet.* 3.10.7). Until recently, his definition determined the definition of "metaphor as 'the transfer of a name,' with emphasis on metaphor as an isolable word or phrase" (Aune 2003, 301). Modern theorists, however, deem Aristotle's definition of metaphor and indeed the entire previous approach to metaphor as inadequate and operating on the faulty assumption that metaphor is primarily a phenomenon of language.

Instead of defining metaphor as the transfer of a word, modern theorists define metaphor as a phenomenon of thought. George Lakoff explains that "the word 'metaphor' has come to mean a cross-domain mapping in the conceptual system" (1993, 203; quoted in Howe 2008, 68). This shift in understanding leads to this working definition: "The essence of metaphor is understanding and experiencing one kind of thing in terms of another" (Lakoff and Johnson 1980, 5; quoted in Howe 2008, 60). Michael Kimmel gives a more detailed and functional definition: "Metaphor is a mapping of certain salient and fitting characteristics of one domain to another domain, so as to give rise to a set of systematic correspondences. In order to characterize the directional nature of this mapping, we speak of a topical Target domain and a Source domain from which new structures are adduced" (2002, 26; quoted in McMillen 2011, 32). The notions of source and target domains as well as mapping have become essential to the modern treatment and definition of metaphor.

Current definitions of metaphor are numerous, and no single one has gained consensus. McMillen notes, "The difficulty of defining metaphor is complicated by the fact that not all metaphors have identical features: some, for example, are based on shared attributes, while others depend on common relationships" (2011, 32). These diverse definitions and understandings of metaphor give rise to numerous modern theories about metaphor, but some notion of transference remains a common aspect of all of them.

Theories of Metaphor

The complexity of metaphor is demonstrated by the explosion of studies and investigations since 1970 (Hoffman 1985; Noppen and Hols 1990; both cited in McMillen 2011, 2 n. 4). The myriad of studies reveals that no single approach to metaphor has gained consensus and makes it difficult to integrate the diverse and competing theories. Nevertheless, some general observations can be made, and evaluation of the strengths and weaknesses of specific theories used in the study of 1 Peter is possible.

When I began to work on 1 Peter for my dissertation in the 1980s, modern theories about metaphor were only in their infancy. I relied on the theory of Harald Weinrich (1976, 276–341), who distinguished between an image-contributor and an image-receptor (Martin 1992, 147). The recent studies of 1 Peter by Bonnie Howe (2008) and R. Melvin McMillen (2011) intentionally apply modern metaphorical theory to 1 Peter and adopt the language of source domain and target domain instead of the terms I took from Weinrich.[3] These studies criticize my dissertation for relying on an older conception of metaphor and for not giving more attention to the theory of metaphor (Howe 2008, 271–72 nn. 10–11; McMillen 2011, 7–8). In the 1980s, however, the metaphor theory applied by each of these scholars to 1 Peter was not fully available to me, and both of these scholars have made important theoretical advances to the study of metaphors in 1 Peter.

The thesis of Howe's work "is that conceptual metaphor, grounded in basic embodied human experience, makes possible a shared moral language and discourse between the New Testament writers and readers of the New Testament today" (Howe 2008, 5). Her goal is to minimize the old hermeneutical gap between what 1 Peter meant then and what it means now so that the epistle can function as an exemplar and speak more directly to modern readers (Howe 2008, 2). She adopts conceptual or cognitive metaphor theory (CMT) and attempts to map the source domains to the target domains of the metaphors in 1 Peter. She describes the source domain as the "sensorimotor domain" and the target domain as the "non-sensori-motor" domain. Thus metaphor is experientially based in "basic bodily experience" and social interaction (Howe 2008, 81). Since human bodies do not differ much from ancient to modern times and several social interactions are similar, she thinks that the distance between the metaphors in 1 Peter and today is not as great as the traditional hermeneutical gap has supposed (Howe 2008, 349, 352–53). Obviously, Howe is correct that human bodies have not changed much. However, the perception and understanding of the human body has changed a great deal from when 1 Peter was written to now, and Howe's study needs to be more sensitive to this change.

Howe's method is far too complex to summarize completely here, but it can be illustrated by her treatment of the newborn baby metaphor in 1 Pet 2:1–3, where the recipients are exhorted to desire the "logical, undiluted milk" as newborn babies so that they can grow into salvation.

---

3. Other terms for the image-receptor or target domain are "target," "topic," "tenor," "subject," and "focus." The image-contributor or source domain is variously called "base," "source," "vehicle," and "frame." See McMillen 2011, 17.

She describes this metaphor as blended from two source domain frames. Howe defines "frames" as "structured understandings of the way aspects of the world function" (2008, 64). The two frames on which this metaphor relies are the household frame and the body frame (Howe 2008, 280–86, 294–304).

Regarding the household frame, she comments, "When Christian believers as a group constitute the target domain, they are fitted into selected slots in the Household Frame." She states that Christians "are fitted into the Child slot: they are 'little children, infants' whose desire to grow 'into salvation' is expressed as a 'longing for the pure, spiritual milk.'" She then concludes, "Infantile longing for milk is mapped onto adult desire to 'grow' into salvation" (2008, 286). Regarding the body frame, she explains that an infant's longing for milk is a clear example of good desire, for "we know what it is for newborns to want milk … not only for growth, but for life itself" (2008, 303). Thus Howe's conceptual metaphor theory allows her to map the source and target domains of the metaphor of newborn babies in 1 Pet 2:1–3 and to observe some salient features of this metaphor.

Her attempt to minimize the hermeneutical gap in her analysis, however, limits her treatment of this metaphor. She assumes that modern understandings of how infants are produced in a household and how they long for milk are the same as ancient understandings. Perhaps some aspects are the same, but some may be different. Ideas about how babies are conceived and how they grow in the womb have certainly changed in the past two thousand years. Notions of nutrition are most definitely different today than they were at the time of the writing of 1 Peter.

Mapping metaphors requires an accurate understanding of not only the source domain but also the target domain. Howe's treatment of the metaphors in 1 Peter is frequently lacking in such an understanding, as John H. Elliott observes,

> The method of cognitive metaphor analysis as presented by Howe holds much promise, I believe, for ethicians and exegetes and deserves our immediate attention. It is regrettable that the method so lucidly exposed in the first half of the book is not coupled with a vigorous exegesis of 1 Peter and sound hermeneutical reflection in the study's second half.

He concludes, "The combination of cognitive metaphor analysis with exegesis and ethics remains a promising idea in search of an adequate method" (2007b, n.p.).

McMillen agrees with Howe that conceptual metaphor theory makes a significant contribution to the analysis of metaphors in 1 Peter, but he thinks her method needs supplementing with structure mapping theory (SMT; McMillen 2011, 11).[4] SMT is a type of comparative metaphor theory that "directly links Source and Target concepts" (McMillen 2011, 81). Its primary objective is to identify "the system of *relations* in the Source that correspond to a system of relations in the Target" (McMillen 2011, 66). He quotes Dedre Gentner (1989, 201): "The central idea in structure-mapping is that an analogy [or metaphor] is a mapping of knowledge from one domain (the base) into another (the target) which conveys that a system of relations which holds among the base objects also holds among the target objects" (quoted in McMillen 2011, 66). McMillen prefers SMT theory because it "encourages interpreters to study all forms of similarity within a document, rather than artificially abstracting specific ones from its overall conceptual and textual context" (2011, 81).

McMillen (2011, 83–105) adapts SMT as well as other theories into his own major metaphor model. His method is even more complicated than Howe's and cannot be summarized completely here, but, like Howe's, it can be illustrated by his treatment of the newborn baby metaphor in 1 Pet 2:1–3. Consistent with his method, McMillen describes as many structural similarities as he can between the source and target domains of this metaphor.

First, he links 2:1–3 with the Father-God metaphor of 1:13–17 and sees a Father-God structure in the newborn baby metaphor in 2:1–3 (2011, 174–76). He identifies the "milk" as the Father-God's mercy and grace offered to his children who must desire it with humility. McMillen sees humility "implied in the Source of craving milk in terms of both its content and the desperate need" (2011, 175). This humility is "essential in relationship to Father-God and his family" (2011, 175). Second, McMillen observes a mental structure in the imperative "long for" (*epipothēsate*) in 2:2, and he proposes that the "logical milk" must include "God's Word, to the exclusion of all other objects of desire, leaving little doubt that filling the mind with its truth is enjoined" (2011, 176–77). Third, he sees a spatial structure in the "putting off" of sinful attitudes (2:1) as external clothing in contrast to the spiritual nourishment that God's children ingest. McMillen

---

4. McMillen relies on the numerous works of Dedre Gentner. See a list of her publications in McMillen 2011, 291–92.

now understands the "logical milk" as spiritual nourishment (2011, 178). Finally, he perceives a conflict structure in this metaphor by hypothesizing "a Petrine view of God's Word as a weapon in cosmic spiritual battle" (2011, 179). By earnestly desiring the "logical milk" of God's Word, the recipients of the letter nourish "hope and trust in their father" and "grow towards the salvation that is its content" (2011, 180).

As his treatment of the newborn baby metaphor in 1 Pet 2:1–3 demonstrates, McMillen's method is far more productive of meaning than Howe's. As with Howe, however, McMillen's method assumes modern understandings of objects in the source domain of this metaphor. He does not investigate whether the ancients had a different understanding of "instinctual cravings" than moderns have (2011, 176). Furthermore, his shifting referent for "logical milk" from "God's grace and mercy" to "God's Word" and then to "spiritual nourishment" opens the question of whether the source domain could convey these meanings to ancient readers. In the end, McMillen admits, "No claim is made that this is the final, perfect template applicable even to First Peter's metaphors, either in terms of content or structure" (2011, 83).

The studies of Howe and McMillen raise important issues in the application of modern metaphor theories to 1 Peter. First and most obvious is the determination of which theory of metaphor to apply. Howe's cognitive metaphor theory and McMillen's structure mapping theory yield very different exegetical results. Selection of any one of the dozens of possibilities thus has important exegetical consequences.[5] Second, their studies warn us to avoid obscuring the text of 1 Peter behind a plethora of analytical terms and concepts. The heuristic test of a method or theory is the clarity it provides. Modern metaphor theory is useful to the degree that it clarifies the text of 1 Peter. To the degree that it does not, it is not helpful. When the method becomes an obstacle to understanding a text, it loses its functionality. Third, their methodologically focused studies demonstrate that no method is a substitute for a thorough understanding of the ancient source domains of the metaphors in 1 Peter, which is absolutely necessary for an

---

5. McMillen notes, "The development of theories of metaphor continues with no signs of exhaustion" (2011, 25). Elsewhere he admits, "On the one hand, the content and structure of First Peter invites a comprehensive metaphorical analysis; on the other hand, the burgeoning field of metaphor studies today has not yet reached any clearly defensible consensus on many of the key issues critical to its application to a text such as First Peter" (2011, 16).

adequate mapping of these metaphors. Finally, their studies also confirm that mapping metaphors is of crucial importance and that many of the disagreements among Petrine scholars arise from differences in mapping the individual metaphors.

Mapping the Newborn Baby Metaphor

Discussing all the specific metaphors in 1 Peter would far exceed the limitations of the present article, and so I shall limit the remaining investigation to a single illustrative metaphor, namely Christians as babies (2:1–3). This expression is technically a simile, but the literature on 1 Peter both treats it as and calls it a metaphor (Howe 2008, 286, 303). This metaphor illustrates the importance of thoroughly understanding the ancient source domain for mapping the analogous characteristics 1 Peter transfers to its recipients. The metaphors in 1 Peter describe the ontological reality of these non-Jewish believers in Israel's God, and mapping each metaphor including the newborn baby metaphor is necessary for an informed understanding of 1 Peter's description of its recipients.

This metaphor of desiring the "logical, undiluted milk" as newborn babies in 1 Pet 2:1–3 occurs with other metaphors related to the elect household of God (1:14–2:10; Martin 1992, 161–88). The themes of divine election and its corollary, the elect people of God, are prevalent in the Jewish Diaspora (Martin 1992, 163 n. 91). The Jews of the Diaspora considered themselves to be the elect people of God. First Peter takes this prevalent Diaspora theme and applies this designation to its recipients. In their Diaspora sojourn, they are none other than the elect people of God. This metaphor of newborn babies' desiring the "logical, undiluted milk" thus fits in and contributes to the overarching and controlling metaphor of the Diaspora.[6]

---

6. When I began writing my doctoral dissertation in the 1980s and investigating metaphors in 1 Peter, previous scholarship largely studied each metaphor in the letter individually, with few attempts to understand how the metaphors related to each other or worked together to communicate the message of 1 Peter. As I tried to "map" the conceptual field of these metaphors, some emerged as overarching metaphors that provided a conceptual framework for the others. I labeled these overarching metaphors "metaphor clusters" and identified them as "the elect household of God" (1 Pet 1:14–2:10), "aliens in this world" (2:11–3:12), and "sufferers of the Dispersion" (3:13–5:11; Martin 1992). I then identified the Diaspora as the controlling metaphor that provides coherence for these metaphor clusters and indeed for all the metaphors

In 2:2–3, the letter instructs its recipients to yearn for "the logical, undiluted milk" (*to logikon adolon gala*) as newborn babies (*hōs artigennēta brephē*) yearn for the logical, undiluted milk in order that by this milk they might grow into salvation if they have tasted that the Lord is wholesome (*chrēstos*).[7] Mapping this metaphor has proven difficult (Achtemeier 1996, 145 n. 33). Some map the *newness* of newborn babies and conclude that the recipients are new converts (Kelly 1969, 84) or recently baptized (Boismard 1956, 196). Others struggle over how to understand the adjective "logical" when applied to milk. Achtemeier comments, "The proper understanding in this context of the adjective λογικός ... is difficult to determine" (1996, 146–47). Still others wonder what the milk and in particular the undiluted (*adolon*) milk signifies and reflect on what the recipients are instructed to desire. Are they to desire the word of God or the eucharistic food (Achtemeier 1996, 147–48)? Recent metaphor theory and an understanding of ancient physiology help to resolve some of these problems encountered by the interpreters of this metaphor.[8]

The source domain of this metaphor is not simply newborn babies but a blend of newborn babies and nutrition. The metaphor assumes that the recipients are familiar with infant nutrition and can transfer the appropriate analogy to their own conduct. To make the appropriate transfer to

---

in 1 Peter. In particular, my identification of the Diaspora as the controlling metaphor generated a lively debate among scholars that continues to the present. A few deny altogether a controlling metaphor for 1 Peter (Michaels 1993, 359; J. B. Green 2007, 218 n. 60; Howe 2008, 268 n. 4, 309), while the majority agrees there is one but thinks it other than the Diaspora (see the list in McMillen 2011, 8–17). Still others agree with my identification of the Diaspora as the controlling metaphor (Tite 1997, 32, 43 n. 27).

7. Not all milk was useful or wholesome for the nutrition of the baby. Aristotle (*Gen. an.* 4.8 [766a]) states that a mother's milk only becomes useful (*chrēsimon*) after the seventh month of gestation when the mother's blood nutrition is adequately shifted from her uterus to her breasts. Hippocrates (*Epid.* 2.3.17) says that this shift occurs in the eighth month. Soranus (*Gyn.* 2.11–15) discusses several types of unwholesome milk. Translating *chrēstos* as "wholesome" thus fits the milk metaphor better than other possible translations.

8. Tite (2009, 371–400) has recently investigated this metaphor from the source domain of ancient breast-feeding and infant moral development. Tite is a former student of mine, and I have for years been suggesting to my students an investigation of this metaphor from the ancient physiological source domain. Tite has investigated the source domains of breast-feeding and moral development, but I would like to focus more specifically on the physiological source domain of this metaphor.

the behavior of the recipients of 1 Peter, an informed interpreter of this metaphor thus needs an understanding of the conception and nutrition of a child in the womb and immediately after birth.

Ancient explanations of conception and birth began with the reproductive fluid of mother and father (Martin 2011, 179–80). The mother's blood collects in her body and is discharged monthly until the introduction of the father's semen, which concocts, congeals, or sets the blood of the mother in the womb. Aristotle likens the process to the curdling of cheese by the introduction of rennet. He explains:

> The action of the semen of the male in "setting" the female's secretion in the uterus is similar to that of rennet upon milk. Rennet is milk which contains vital heat, as semen does, and this integrates the homogeneous substance and makes it "set." As the nature of milk and the menstrual fluid is one and the same, the action of the semen upon the substance of the menstrual fluid is the same as that of rennet upon milk. (*Gen. an.* 2.4 [739b], LCL)

Aristotle's analogy is appropriate because ancients thought that male semen was blood that is frothed or concocted more perfectly than the female's blood in the uterus (Aristotle, *Gen. an.* 1.19 [727a]; 1.20 [728a]; Galen, *UP* 14.10–11; *Sem.* 1.12). The added heat of male semen thus enables it to be the agent that "sets" or congeals the more watery blood of the female and causes a pregnancy to occur. Aristotle states, "The female always provides the material, the male provides that which fashions the material into shape" (*Gen. an.* 2.4 [738b], LCL). In Aristotle's terms, therefore, the blood semen of the male provides the formal, efficient, and final causes, while the female blood serves as the material cause.

As long as the child remains in the womb, the mother does not discharge blood each month.[9] Instead, this blood goes to her womb and nourishes the child as it hardens, congeals, and forms the child's body according to the power of the male blood semen (Aristotle, *Gen. an.* 4.8 [776a–b]; Galen, *UP* 14.10–11). Galen notes that the uteri and breasts are connected by vessels, and then he comments:

> Now when a woman is at the prime of life, in the time before conception Nature each month evacuates through the vessels extending to the uteri

---

9. If she does menstruate during pregnancy, Hippocrates (*Aphor.* 5.60) says that the embryo must be unhealthy.

whatever surplus accumulates, but when she is pregnant, it is through these vessels that the embryo attracts nutriment. Since this surplus accumulates in these common vessels during the whole of pregnancy as if in reservoirs of nutriment, enlarging and distending them to the limit and, as it were flooding them, it seeks some place to go. But there is no place other than the breasts, into which the distended, burdened veins conduct it. (*UP* 14.8; May 1968, 638–39)

Hippocrates (*Aphor.* 5.52) states that copious flows of milk from the breasts of a pregnant woman are a sign that the baby in the womb is weak. Galen (*UP* 14.8) explains that it is weak because it is undernourished. The blood that should be going to it is being diverted to the breasts and frothed into milk.

After the child is born, the mother still does not menstruate or only has light flows because her blood is now directed to her breasts, which froth her blood into milk. Soranus comments, "The uterus itself brings the seed to perfection, whereas the breasts prepare milk as food for the coming child; and menses occurring, the milk stops, whereas lactation occurring, menstruation appears no more" (*Gyn.* 1.15; Temkin 1956, 14).[10] Aristotle writes, "It is clear that milk is possessed of the same nature [substance] as the secretion out of which each animal is formed. ... And this material ... is the bloodlike liquid, since milk is concocted ... blood" (*Gen. an.* 4.8 [777a], LCL). Likewise, Galen writes, "No newborn animal could at that time digest solid food, and so for this reason Nature has prepared for it nutriment drawn from the mother, just as she did when it was still a fetus" (*UP* 2.292; May 1968, 625). Thus the child in the womb is nourished with the blood of its mother, and this child upon birth continues to be nourished with its mother's blood, frothed or concocted, as milk. A newborn baby's desire for its mother's milk is therefore logical, and the author of 1 Peter refers to this milk as "logical, undiluted milk" (*to logikon adolon gala*, 2:2).

The addition of the adjective "undiluted" (*adolon*) probably distinguishes this milk from the colostrum, a watery, milky substance that the breast emits a few days before and after birth, and other types of "corrupted" milk that are not fit for infant nutrition. Aristotle says that the

---

10. See also Hippocrates (*Aphor.* 5.39), who connects lactation with suppressed menses and recommends (*Aphor.* 5.50) applying a cupping-glass to the breasts and suctioning out the milk to suppress menstruation.

former and later milk is unfit for use (*achrēston de to prōton kai hysteron*, *Hist. an.* 3.20 [522a]). Any milk produced before the seventh month of gestation is not useful according to Aristotle (*Gen. an.* 4.8 [776b]). Soranus (*Gyn.* 2.11–15) discusses numerous reasons milk might not be useful or wholesome for the baby including its being too watery, too thick, or mixed with various juices from the foodstuffs ingested by the mother or wet nurse. The milk that a newborn desires is the pure, undiluted, uncorrupted, wholesome milk that "comes in fully" a few days after the baby is born when the mother's blood fully shifts from her uterus to her breast. This blood, or "logical, undiluted milk" from its mother's blood, nourishes the baby and enables it to grow just as the mother's blood did in her uterus.

The ancient physiology of infant nutrition as the source domain of this metaphor in 1 Pet 2:1–3 indicates some connection between the conception and begetting of these recipients and the "logical, undiluted milk" that they as newborn babies are supposed to desire. This connection is provided in 1 Pet 1:23–25. The recipients were begotten not from perishable seed but imperishable seed (*ouk ek sporas phthartēs alla aphthartou*, 1:23). Since seed or reproductive fluid was frothed blood according to ancient physiology, ancient readers were more likely than modern readers to understand blood as the material source of the new begetting of these recipients. Indeed, the blood of Christ is not included among the perishable things (*ou phthartois*, 1:18–19) but is imperishable, and this imperishable blood was sprinkled on the recipients (*rhantismon haimatos Iēsou Christou*, 1:2) as a result of their election and inclusion as the people of God (1:1).

Furthermore, ancient readers would likely have understood the word of God as the (male) active principle that shapes the recipients begotten from this blood into the new people that God intends. God is certainly the agent or father who begot these recipients anew (*anagennēsas*, 1:3), but the intermediate agency of their begetting is the living and remaining word of God (*dia logou zōntos theou kai menontos*, 1:23).[11] The blood of Christ is thus the material source of the new begetting of these recipients, and the word of God is the active power or principle that shapes this blood into the new life created by this begetting. Reinhard Feldmeier comments, "This as

---

11. Achtemeier (1996, 139) sees no significance in the shift of the preposition *ek sporas* to *dia logou* in 1:23. The interpretation offered here, however, follows LaVerdiere (1974, 92), who takes *ek* as indicating origin or source and *dia* as expressing extrinsic principle or agent.

well is again a relatively daring image: The divine word is described in its action in analogy to human sperm. Just as this makes possible biological life, so the word—which itself is 'living and remaining'—communicates its livingness and imperishability so that those newly born by it are removed from the general transience" (2008, 123–24).

Given their understanding of ancient physiology and especially infant conception and nutrition, the ancient recipients could understand the source domain of this metaphor more immediately than modern readers can. The metaphor is productive for them in communicating the mutual effectiveness of both word and sacrament. The blood of Christ received in the sacrament provides the substance for the new life, while the word of God shapes that life into a childlike form. The imperative for the recipients to desire the "logical, undiluted milk" (2:2) is thus conditioned by the circumstantial participle (*apothemenoi*, 2:1). This participle indicates that desire for this milk is conditioned by putting away all badness, guile, hypocrises, envyings, and evil-speaking (2:1a). Since all of these vices are prohibited by the word of God and lacking in newborn babies, the recipients must put them away so as to realize a childlike desire for the "logical, undiluted milk" (Martin 1992, 174–75).

This imperative is contextualized by the expression, "if you have tasted that the Lord is wholesome" (*ei egeusasthe hoti chrēstos ho kyrios*, 2:3), connecting intertextually with Ps 33:9 LXX, "Taste and see that the Lord is wholesome" (*geusasthe kai idete hoti chrēstos ho kyrios*). Early Christians sang this psalm or recited parts of it in the eucharistic liturgy (*Apos. Con.* 8.13; Cyril of Jerusalem, *Catechetical Lecture* 23.20 [= *Mystagogic Catechesis* 3.20]; Jerome, *Letters* 71.6). The change in 1 Pet 2:3 from the LXX imperative *geusasthe*, which gives a command, to the indicative *egeusasthe*, which makes a statement, as well as the omission of the LXX words "and see," indicates that 1 Peter uses this psalm eucharistically, perhaps for the first time in Christian literature (Kelly 1969, 87).

Psalm 33 is important to the message of 1 Peter, which will quote or allude to it again in 2:4 (Ps 33:6) and in 3:10–12 (Ps 33:13–17). This psalm is a testimony of God's rescue from all of the psalmist's sojournings (*ek pasōn tōn paroikiōn mou*, Ps 33:5 LXX). The psalm therefore probably resonated with the recipients of 1 Peter, which describes them as sojourners and exiles (*paroikous kai parepidēmous*, 1 Pet 2:11) who are in need of rescue (1:5, 10–12) from their own Diaspora sojourn (1:1).

Understanding modern metaphor theory and the ancient physiological source domain of this metaphor therefore helps resolve the sharp debate among modern commentators about mapping the "logical, undiluted milk" to the word of God or to eucharistic food. The metaphor blends both ideas with the milk that images the eucharistic food and is then shaped and formed by the word of God in the lives of the recipients.[12] Since the recipients were begotten from the blood of Christ, it is "logical" for them to desire this blood in the Eucharist as a means of continued nutrition so that they may grow into the salvation provided by Christ.

Conclusion: Metaphorical Reality

Metaphor is sometimes understood as figurative in contrast to literal or real language. Modern theories about metaphor, however, emphasize that metaphor is a way of thinking about and expressing reality. The metaphors in 1 Peter describe the reality of its recipients' new status brought about by their becoming Christians. They have indeed been begotten by God in a very real sense. The letter exhorts them to desire the real blood of Christ in the Eucharist and to allow the word of God to shape them into a real people of God's own making (*laos eis peripoiēsin*, 2:9). Achtemeier notes a "dynamic element in the author's understanding" in that "the Christian community is under way toward being God's peculiar people" (1996, 166). The metaphors and similes in 1 Peter express this real ontological status of its recipients (Martin 1992, 143–44). On the basis of who these recipients really are, the letter exhorts them to act accordingly and to live as the people of God. Using various metaphors to describe their new status, 1 Peter creates new language to express the ontological reality of its recipients' new life in Christ (Feldmeier 2008, 128–29). In many ways, this language and these metaphors are still with us today as are the religious realities they name and express.

---

12. The negative connotations of milk in 1 Cor 3:1–3; Heb 5:12; and 6:2 and the mapping of milk to elementary instruction or catechesis are lacking in the context of 1 Pet 2:2.

BE HOLY, FOR I AM HOLY: PARAENESIS IN 1 PETER

Nancy Pardee

Amid the struggles of daily life and the pain of life's tragedies, people often look for comfort and strength. This search, perhaps above all else, is at the heart of 1 Peter. The letter presupposes ongoing conflict between the recipient communities and the surrounding pagan society; thus encouragement was an important, if not the primary, goal of the letter.[1] The precise nature of the attacks is not specified, but references to slander (*katalaleō*, 2:12), insult (*loidoria*, 3:9), defamation (*blasphēmeō*, 4:4), and reproach (*oneidizō*, 4:14) point to an oppressive social environment rather than to any government-sponsored prosecution.[2] Yet the stress experienced by the converts was enough to raise concern that their commitment to the gospel might be jeopardized (Martin 1992, 156–58). Indeed, the sense that the situation is critical pervades the letter (see especially 1 Pet 3:13–17; 4:1–5, 12–19; 5:9–10).

Given this context of suffering, it may seem odd to modern readers that so much of the epistle is concerned with paraenesis, that is, moral exhortation.[3] The recipients are told to "discipline yourselves" (1:13), "live

---

1. Among recent supporters of this view, Elliott sees this encouragement in the author's attempt to strengthen the communities' sense of their unique, Christian identity and lifestyle so as to enable their continued resistance to outside pressures (2000, 104–5; 2007a, 40–42). Alternatively, Dryden, though acknowledging the theme of suffering, thinks the letter's primary purpose was to promote the growth of Christian moral character among the Gentile converts (2006, 39–41).

2. For a discussion of persecution against Christians and its relevance for 1 Peter, see especially Achtemeier 1996, 23–36; and Holloway 2009, 40–73. Elliott (2000, 90) envisions the communities as rural and thus even more susceptible to *local* suspicions "with Rome playing no role at all."

3. Elliott (2000, 67) lists the features that create the "predominantly hortatory tone of the letter." Among these is the use of participles with an imperatival sense,

in reverent fear" (1:17), and "conduct yourselves honorably" (2:12).[4] They are advised to maintain the traditional societal subordination of slave to master (2:18), wife to husband (3:1), and youth to elders (5:5). The communities are warned against "licentiousness, passions, drunkenness, revels, carousing, and lawless idolatry" (4:3). Was the situation really so dissolute in these communities? The overall positive tone of the letter does not lead to this conclusion. Will good behavior, then, serve to alleviate their suffering? Though this claim sometimes appears (2:12, 15; 3:13, 16), the author of 1 Peter does not really believe that it will (2:19–21; 3:14–18; 4:12–19; 5:9–10). What, then, is the function of traditional moral exhortation in a text so focused on comfort and encouragement?

While the intended *audience* of 1 Peter is (at least predominantly) Gentile, the pervasive Jewish imagery, the thorough familiarity with Jewish Scriptures and Jewish beliefs and practices, and the consistent application of Jewish concepts in the epistle show that the church of *origin* for this letter is Jewish-Christian.[5] Yet the letter exhibits a level of Greek language and rhetorical composition that could only be generated from someone with a formal Hellenistic-style education. Thus a historical understanding of 1 Peter and its emphasis on paraenesis must be sought in the context of Hellenistic Jewish-Christianity and its mission to Gentiles.

What Is Paraenesis?

The Greek abstract noun *parainesis* is derived from the verb *paraineō*, "exhort, recommend, advise" (LSJ 1310). Although scholars still debate the precise definition, the following description by David Aune is generally representative of paraenesis in the Greco-Roman world.[6] *Paraenesis*

---

for which he provides the relevant literature. Martin (1992, 90–92) and Achtemeier (1996, 117) urge caution in translating participles in this way. For a discussion of the paraenetic features of 1 Peter, see Martin 1992, 85–103.

4. Biblical quotations are from the NRSV unless otherwise noted.

5. For identification of the audience as largely (if not entirely) Gentile, see 1 Pet 1:14, 18; 2:10; 4:3–4, and discussions in Achtemeier 1996, 50–51; Elliott 2000, 95–97; and J. B. Green 2007, 5. For the argument that the readers are primarily Hellenistic Jewish-Christians, see Witherington 2007, 23–37; and Dunn 2009, 1158–60.

6. Current discussions can be found, for example, in Starr and Engberg-Pedersen 2005, especially the proposed definitions on 3–4 and the essay by Engberg-Pedersen, 47–72. The phenomenon of "paraenesis" can also be used more broadly to include a wide range of texts from the ancient Near East. The 1990 publication *Paraenesis: Act*

refers to moral exhortation that (1) "is traditional, reflecting conventional wisdom generally approved by society"; (2) "is applicable to many situations"; (3) "is so familiar that it is often represented as a 'reminder'";[7] (4) "can be exemplified in exceptional people who are models of virtue";[8] (5) "is usually transmitted by people who are regarded as socially and morally superior to those they address" (Aune 2003, 334).[9]

Ancient Greco-Roman paraenesis is found in epistolary and other texts that represent personal communication, whether real or fictive.[10] It is distinct from the moral instruction of legal and didactic works and sayings collections in that the primary function of paraenesis is not the communication of *new* information but rather the iteration and application of *traditional* values by a mentor to a protégé who, in reality, already knows and accepts those principles. In addition, the more *general* character of paraenesis is to be differentiated from advice given for *specific* circumstances, a distinction illustrated, for example, by comparing Paul's "fruit of the Spirit" in Gal 5:22–23 with his instruction on marriage in 1 Corinthians 7.

The modern study of paraenesis in biblical texts begins with Martin Dibelius and his work on the Epistle of James. Dibelius questioned the classification of James as an epistle because the text itself provided no specific

---

and Form (*Semeia* 50), for example, included in its purview texts from "the ancient Near Eastern world of Egypt, Sumeria and Babylonia to the Mediterranean world of the Roman Empire" (Gammie 1990, 41–42).

7. As an example, Malherbe notes the recurring phrase "as you know" (1986, 125).

8. Family members, in particular the father, are often used as examples (Malherbe 1986, 125).

9. See also Malherbe 1986, 124–25. Popkes adds a situational aspect to this definition: "The present time is a time of decision which implies an element of transition," and includes under this Christian conversion and baptism (2005, 17–18).

10. According to Malherbe, paraenesis is transmitted especially via "speeches, letters … and tractates which may assume some epistolary features" (1986, 124). Today many scholars characterize *paraenesis* more broadly as a "style" (Fiore 2009, 4:382; Aune 2003, 334) rather than a specific genre (but see Gammie 1990, esp. 47). The fact that the use of letters as vehicles for paraenesis became widespread in the ancient world, however, leads Aune (2003, 334) to suggest that a distinction be made between "epistolary paraenesis, which is found in defined concluding sections of some Christian letters" (e.g., Rom 12:1–15:3; Col 3:1–4:6), and "paraenetic styles, which permeate letters" (e.g., 1 Thessalonians, Galatians, and Colossians). Indeed, today some scholars identify 1 Peter specifically as a paraenetic letter (Stowers 1986, 96–97; Martin 1992, 85–134, 270; Elliott 2000, 11; Sandnes 2005; Dryden 2006).

occasion for writing, exhibited no epistolary characteristics subsequent to its opening, and lacked a train of thought (Dibelius 1976, 2). It is, however, replete with moral exhortation, a phenomenon Dibelius observed also in parts of the Pauline Epistles, in Hebrews 13, in the speeches of Jesus, in the *Mandates* of the Shepherd of Hermas, and in the Two Ways instruction found in the *Didache, Barnabas,* and the *Doctrina apostolorum*—all texts with a Jewish background. He suggested that Jewish paraenesis of the Hellenistic period, as heir to Israel's wisdom tradition but also very influenced by Greek thought, provided early Christianity with the moral instruction needed to secure the continuation and growth of the new communities. Indeed, he found paraenesis elsewhere in works such as Tobit and the *Testaments of the Twelve Patriarchs* (a text he considered to have a Jewish *Vorlage*) as well as Pseudo-Phocylides and possibly Pseudo-Menander. (Dibelius considered the two latter texts "openly Hellenistic in language and terminology" [1976, 3–4].) Thus Dibelius turned to the Greeks to find a better understanding of the moral instruction of James.

Dibelius cited as the earliest examples of paraenesis in Greek texts the *Ad Nicoclem* and *Nicocles* of Isocrates (436–338 B.C.E.) and the contemporary *Ad Demonicum* of Pseudo-Isocrates, and scholars today still begin their study of paraenesis with these texts.[11] Indeed, *Ad Demonicum* is the first text to identify itself as a paraenesis (*Demon.* 5). The author distinguishes his work, which he describes as promoting virtue (*aretē, Demon.* 7, 45–46, 48), from ones that simply teach rhetorical skills; he variously labels the latter *logos protreptikos* (*Demon.* 3) and *paraklēsis* (*Demon.* 5). *Ad Demonicum* is personal in nature—the author characterizes it as a "gift" (*dōron*) bestowed out of friendship with the recipient's father (*Demon.* 2). Its tone is one of advice rather than command, and its counsel is based on traditional Greek values: virtue and its components, modesty (*aischynē*), justice (*dikaiosynē*), and temperance (*sōphrosynē*; *Demon.* 15). To bolster his instructions, Pseudo-Isocrates includes examples for Demonicus to emulate, heroes such as Hercules and Theseus (*Demon.* 8) as well as Demonicus's own father (*Demon.* 9–12). Further support comes through the quotation of (sometimes still identifiable) precepts and maxims.

From this beginning, the use of paraenesis and eventually the paraenetic letter increased in the ancient world and found its way into Jewish

---

11. All three texts are conveniently found in *Isocrates* 1928–45, vol. 1.

literature as well.[12] A clear example can be found in Tobit's deathbed "testament" to his son Tobiah (Tob 4:5–19), where just as in Greek paraenesis, the instruction comes from a mentor to a protégé, appropriates traditional and widely applicable instruction (reverence to the Lord and upright behavior), and presents models to be emulated (Noah and the patriarchs), all in a very eclectic and asyndetic arrangement (see also Tob 12:6–10). The content here is Jewish, but the paraenetic style is very much Greek.

Jewish and Greek Elements in the Paraenesis of 1 Peter

The Jewish Context of 1 Peter

This synthesis of Jewish and Greek traditions in Hellenistic-Jewish paraenesis is found also in 1 Peter. On the one hand, the Jewish character of 1 Peter is so prominent that Achtemeier sees the author's identification of the church with Israel as the "controlling metaphor" of the work (Achtemeier 1996, 69; compare Martin 1992, 139–61). Indeed, the salutation of the letter (1:1–2) describes the Gentile readers with language traditionally applied to Israel. They are *parepidēmoi* ("sojourners, resident aliens, visitors"), an identification repeated in 2:11, where it is coupled (as in both its occurrences in the LXX) with the nearly synonymous and more common word *paroikoi* ("sojourners, aliens"), a cognate of which is also found in 1:17 (*paroikia*, "residing in a foreign land"). Elliott takes these terms literally and envisions the communities of 1 Peter as including resident aliens subject to the typical harassment experienced by such peoples at the hands of native populations (Elliott 2000, 94, 312–13, 476–83). Most scholars, however, see these terms as symbolic of the new spiritual identity of the Gentile converts.[13] In the LXX *paroikos* and cognates often designate the status of Israelites and Jews as resident aliens in a foreign place—for example, Abraham and other patriarchs, the Israelites in Egypt, and the exiles in Babylon.[14] This literal sense can still be found in

---

12. The development of the paraenetic letter is shown in the fact that, while the earliest extant handbook on epistolography, *Epistolary Types* (first century B.C.E.), does not include paraenetic letters among its 21 categories, the author of the later *Epistolary Styles* (fourth to sixth centuries C.E.) lists the paraenetic letter *first* among 41 types.

13. For example, see the discussion in Martin 1992, 188–92.

14. That *paroikos* is a particularly Jewish term is seen not only in the number of times it is found in Jewish literature but also in the additional fact that two synony-

the New Testament, when *paroikeō* and *parepidēmeō* are used in parallel to describe the patriarchs (Heb 11:9, 13). Over time, however, these terms also took on metaphorical meanings, including that of mortal life on earth apart from God (K. L. Schmidt and M. A. Schmidt 1967, 5:844, 847–50). This metaphorical usage is perhaps the meaning in 1 Pet 1:1, 17; and 2:11, which characterize the Gentile audience as "sojourning" while awaiting salvation (cf. 1:4–9; Martin 1992, 152–56).

In the salutation, 1 Peter also identifies its Gentile readers as living in the Diaspora, a term rare in secular Greek but used technically in the LXX and other Jewish literature to refer to the many communities of Jews existing outside of Palestine.[15] Moreover, the recipients are *eklektoi* ("chosen"; see 1 Pet 5:13). First Peter transfers to the church the theological concept of Israel as the chosen people of God, an image found beginning in Deuteronomy (Debrunner et al. 1967, 4:159). Their "election," moreover, is "in accordance with the foreknowledge of God" (*kata prognōsin theou*) and has been accomplished "by the sanctification [*hagiasmos*] of the Spirit" (1:2; author's translation). The term *hagiasmos* and its cognates appear almost exclusively in biblical and related literature and occur in the New Testament primarily in connection with Gentile Christians (Procksch and Kuhn 1964, 1:113) for whom faith in Christ has resulted or should result in their sanctification and subsequent holy living.[16]

Indeed, the readers of 1 Peter have been sanctified "for the purpose of obedience" (*eis hypakoēn*) and "for the sprinkling [*rantismon*] of the blood of Jesus Christ" (author's translation). *Rantismos* is rare outside of Judeo-Christian literature and alludes either to Jewish rites of purification/ consecration or to the ratification of the covenant of Moses in Exod 24. In 1 Pet 1:2 the phrase *rantismon haimatos* refers to the ultimate purification of the Christian Gentiles as indicated by its position at the end of a series

---

mous and related nouns, *paroikia* and *paroikesia*, are found virtually only in Jewish (and Christian) texts.

15. In secular Greek the noun occurs several times only in Plutarch (46–ca. 122 c.e.). See Schmidt 1964, 2:98–99. Elliott again takes the term literally in 1 Peter to refer to the geographical location of the communities (2000, 314).

16. On the attestation of *hagiasmos* and cognates, see Procksch and Kuhn 1964, 1:111–13; BDAG 9–10; and the *Thesaurus linguae graecae*. See Rom 6:19, 22; 1 Cor 1:30; and 1 Thess 4:3–4, 7, for its use by Paul in the context of Gentile Christians. See also 1 Tim 2:15; Heb 12:14; and 2 Thess 2:13 (the latter with *en hagiasmō pneumatos* as in 1 Pet 1:2).

on the stages of salvation (divine foreknowledge, election, sanctification of the Spirit, and obedience).[17]

The identification of the readers with Israel continues in the blessings section (1:3–12), where it takes on a sense of comfort. They have received an "inheritance" (*klēronomia*), a term used often in the Hebrew Bible to designate the land of Canaan as Israel's promised possession but later used with eschatological notions such as the possession of the entire earth (e.g., *Jub.* 32:19) or of life beyond this earth (*Pss. Sol.* 14:10; *1 En.* 40:9; *4 Ezra* 7:9, 17; see Foerster and Herrmann 1965, 3:779–81 for further examples). This latter notion is also found in 1 Pet 1:4, where the inheritance is "preserved" or "guarded" (*tetērēmenēn*) in heaven. Indeed, 1 Peter tells its converts to rejoice in their suffering, for it is only a "test" and will ultimately result in reward from God (1:6–9). One final reassurance comes from the assertion that their salvation has been predicted by the prophets of old (1:10–12).

Beginning in 1:13, however, the author follows up his words of comfort with a lengthy paraenetic section that, broadly speaking, lasts until the conclusion of the epistle. In the author's view, the Gentile readers should act properly *because* of their identification as Israel. They are to "gird up the loins of their minds," that is, to be prepared, a thoroughly Jewish use of Exodus imagery (Achtemeier 1996, 118).[18] They are to live holy, obedient lives in accordance with the fundamental premise "you shall be holy for I am holy" (1 Pet 1:16; cf. Lev 11:44–45; 19:2; 20:7, 26). They are to "live in reverent fear," a usage of *phobos* that is rare in Greek literature but common in Judaism. Such obedience brings sanctification (*hagnizō*, 1:22), a term related to *hagios* and thus to the holiness of 1:15–16 (Achtemeier 1996, 136, cf. 138). This characterization is further heightened in the author's descriptions of them as "a holy priesthood" (2:5); "a chosen race, a royal priesthood, a holy nation, a people of his own" (2:9); and, quoting Hosea, "God's people" (2:10).

Thus the opening passages of the epistle and the self-identification of the author as Peter make it highly likely that the community of origin for 1 Peter is Jewish-Christian and that its moral expectations for its Gentile audience are based on Jewish concepts of holiness and sanctification (1:2,

---

17. See a similar series of the stages of salvation in Rom 8:30. Apart from 1 Peter, *rantismos* and cognates occur only in Hebrews in the New Testament, and there only once in reference to Christians. According to Hunzinger, the references in Hebrews and 1 Peter are to baptism (1968, 6:983–84).

18. This metaphor is found also in Luke 12:35 and in a negative form in *Did.* 16:2.

15–16; 2:5, 9; 3:5, 15), purity/purification (1:2, 22), and obedience to God (1:2, 14, 22; cf. 3:6). These moral expectations are supported especially by the promise of eschatological reward (1:3–9, 13, 21, 23; 2:2; 3:9; 4:13; 5:4, 6, 10) and of finding approval with God (2:19–20; 3:4, 12; 4:14; 5:5).

THE GREEK CHARACTER OF 1 PETER

The Virtuous Life

Within the Jewish context of 1 Peter one also finds Greek paraenesis, both in content and form. The readers are addressed by an authority figure and urged to lead a holy (i.e., virtuous) life, the specifics of which they already know but need to be reminded of because of the present troubling circumstances.[19] The teaching is general; scriptural "precepts" are cited, and role models (particularly Christ) are presented. Moreover, 1 Peter exhibits what Malherbe calls the "complex" stand of Christian authors regarding the surrounding pagan society. While at certain points Gentile converts were told to shun their former life, elsewhere the text "presupposed an *agreement* with the standards of their society" (1986, 14, emphasis mine) and encouraged them to imitate the best of pagan morality.

An example of this conflation of Jewish and Greek moral tradition is found in 1 Pet 1:13–16. The Jewish metaphor "girding up the loins" is juxtaposed with the Greek verb *nēphō*, literally "to be sober; drink no wine," but here, as elsewhere in Greek literature, it is best understood in the metaphorical sense: "be self-controlled; be sober and wary" (LSJ 1175). The audience is warned to refrain from the "desires" (*epithymiais*) of their preconversion lives, an example of the increasingly negative connotation that the term *epithymia* gained beginning with the Stoic philosophers. Clearly Greek ideas and terminology are a natural part of the thought world of our author.

Greek Paraenetic Forms

Beyond the rather general instruction of 1 Peter (1:13–22; 2:11–12; 4:1–2; 5:8–9, 12), the influence of Greco-Roman moral exhortation is seen even

---

19. Contra Witherington, who, referring to 1 Pet 2:11–3:12, sees the author as "calling for a change in behavior to some extent" (2007, 128, cf. 126–32, 142), and emphasizes the freedom of the readers to make a choice for or against the advice of the author.

more readily in the "stereotyped pararenetic forms" (Aune 1987, 194) in which it is expressed, namely, lists of vices and/or virtues and codes of proper relationships within the household (*Haustafeln*), both of which have their source in Greco-Roman tradition.[20]

Catalogs of Virtues and Vices

Lists ("catalogs") of virtues or vices are more common than *Haustafeln* and are attested in a wider range of New Testament texts. Rare in the Old Testament, they became common in Greek literature beginning about the fifth century B.C.E. (Aune 2008, 3:671) and are found in a variety of texts, including within paraenetic works (Malherbe 1986, 133–39). One example is seen in Pseudo-Aristotle's *Virtues and Vices* 1.3–4, a work contemporary with the New Testament.

> If in accordance with Plato the spirit is taken as having three parts, wisdom is goodness of the rational part, gentleness and courage of the passionate, of the appetitive sobriety of mind and self-control, and of the spirit as a whole righteousness, liberality and, great-spiritedness; while badness of the rational part is folly, of the passionate ill-temper and cowardice, of the appetitive profligacy and uncontrol, and of the spirit as a whole unrighteousness, meanness and smallmindedness. (*Virt. Vit.* 1.3–4, LCL)

Such lists are common in the writings of Greco-Roman moral philosophers (see, e.g., Dio Chrysostom, *Or*. 2.75–76).

The adoption of this catalog form by Hellenistic Jewish authors is seen, for example, in Philo, *Alleg. Interp*. 1.63, where the four rivers of Gen 2:10–14 are interpreted in terms of the four cardinal virtues (wisdom/prudence, justice, courage, and temperance). These cardinal virtues originate with Socrates/Plato and are a central tenet of the "Koine ethic." However, Philo also knows vices, and in *Sacrifices* 32 he provides what is perhaps the longest vice list in the ancient world, with 147 items (Aune 2003, 90). Interestingly, scholars point out that in Judaism (and Christianity) vice lists often reflect the overall impression held by Jews that Gentiles were

---

20. Aune (1987, 194–97) also lists as a third form, the "two-ways tradition," but this is better classified more broadly as a motif.

immoral (and idolatrous; cf. passages like Wis 14:25–27 [ca. 100 B.C.E.] with Paul's argument in Rom 1:28–31).

Aune observes that this preoccupation with Gentile immorality is also seen in the fact that vice lists are more common and generally longer than virtue lists in the New Testament (2003, 90), and he suggests that where the two occur together ("double catalogs") in Jewish and Christian works, an initiatory context perhaps lies in the background (1987, 195). Indeed, support for this suggestion is seen in some "Two Ways" texts, that is, works that present lists of virtues and vices and use the image of a choice between two paths as a metaphor for deciding for a life of good or evil. Although the Two Ways figure is seen in earlier biblical texts (e.g., Deut 30:15–20; Jer 21:8), its increased and more developed appearance in Jewish texts of the Greco-Roman period is generally attributed to the influence of Iranian and Greek "Two Ways" materials (McKenna 1981, 357–59, 386–87). A Jewish Two Ways text, possibly used in the context of initiation, is found among the Dead Sea Scrolls in the *Rule of the Community* (1QS IV 2–11), while in Christianity a Two Ways text is attested in several renditions: *Barn.* 18–21, the Latin *Doctrina apostolorum*, and the *Did.* 1–6. The latter text is explicitly part of a prebaptismal instruction for Gentiles.

Given that 1 Peter is primarily directed toward Gentiles and keeping in mind Aune's observation cited above, there are, not surprisingly, three vice lists in the letter (2:1; 4:3, 15) while only one is devoted to virtues (3:8). The first vice list, in 2:1, follows upon the call in 1:22 for *philadelphia*, "love of the brothers," a notion much valued in the Greco-Roman world. It instructs the readers to "rid yourselves" (*apothēmenoi*) of "all malice, and all guile, insincerit[ies], env[ies], and all slander." While *apotithēmi* had been used in reference to vices since Demosthenes (BDAG 124), Achtemeier notes that it also appears widely in early Christian moral texts due to the connection of its literal meaning ("to remove clothing") with the baptismal catechism and ritual.[21] The pattern here of a recurring adjective "all" (*pas*) plus a mixture of singular and plural nouns is also common within Christian moral texts, as are the individual vices themselves. Lewis Donelson points out that there is nothing explicitly Christian about any of them (2010, 56).[22] Yet Aune notes that while Greco-Roman paraenesis

---

21. Achtemeier denies a direct relationship (1996, 144); Donelson advises caution (2010, 56). Elliott sees the term as likely to be connected at least with the baptismal catechism but perhaps only later with an actual ritual (2000, 395–96).

22. On the traditional character of these vices, Achtemeier makes the interesting

tended to emphasize *personal* vices, Christian lists focused on *social* vices (1987, 195) as in 1 Pet 2:1, where such behaviors would certainly inhibit the community love advised in 1:22.[23]

A short list of virtues appears in 1 Pet 3:8: "unity of spirit [*homophrōn*], sympathy [*sympathēs*], love for one another [*philadelphos*], a tender heart [*eusplanchnos*], a humble mind [*tapeinophrōn*]." Just as with the vices of 2:1, this list is intended for the entire community and comes at the conclusion of more individualized instruction on household relationships in 2:18–3:7 (see below). This list extends the emphasis on subordination in those relationships into a sense of mutuality within the community at large (Achtemeier 1996, 223).[24] While the sentiments here are Christian (Achtemeier 1996, 222) and perhaps even reflect a common tradition shared by Rom 12 (Elliott 2000, 601–2), four of the five adjectives of 1 Pet 3:8 are unique forms in the New Testament and the other one is rare (Achtemeier 1996, 222; Elliott 2000, 600). These unique and rare terms are surely a sign of the author's own hand.

Noteworthy is the fact that some of the "virtues" vary from what would have been considered proper in Greco-Roman society. *Eusplanchnos* was certainly a quality more valued in Judaism than in Greek culture. While it is found one other time in the New Testament (Eph 4:32) and more often in Hellenistic-Jewish and extrabiblical Christian texts, it occurs only rarely in pagan literature. Further, *tapeinophrōn*, a trait much prized in the Jewish and Christian tradition, was generally viewed negatively in Hellenistic culture (Achtemeier 1996, 223 n. 42). Elliott states that "in the highly competitive and stratified world of Greco-Roman antiquity, only those of degraded social status were 'humble,' and humility was regarded as a sign of weakness and shame, an inability to defend one's honor" (2000, 605). Thus once more in 1 Peter, one finds that paraenesis is a combination of traditional Greek and Jewish terminology, concepts, and forms that are adapted to fit Christian needs.

---

observation that most of those found in 1 Pet 2:1 are also included in the more extensive list of *Did.* 5:1 (1996, 144 n. 20).

23. Achtemeier 1996, 144–45; Elliott 2000, 394–98. Elliott sees these vices as particularly relevant to the communities of 1 Peter that, in his view, are socially and ethnically mixed (2000, 398).

24. Elliott (2000, 601, 617), however, denies that subordination is the overall theme of 2:13–3:12.

Of the remaining two vice lists in 1 Peter, that of 4:3 provides specific examples of human "desires" (*epithymiais*) that conflict with the will of God (4:2): licentiousness, passions (*epithymiais*), drunkenness, revels, carousing, and idolatry. Again, these are vices stereotypically applied to Gentiles from a Jewish or Christian point of view (Elliott 2000, 721, 725). The list of alcohol-related vices (drunkenness, revels, carousing) culminating in idolatry is thought by many to refer to Gentile social gatherings, either explicitly religious or as part of the practices of pagan guilds and associations. Sins of a sexual nature may be implied by "licentiousness" (Donelson 2010, 119) and "passions" (Achtemeier 1996, 282–83). In some cases, such practices were portrayed in a negative light by secular moralists as well (Achtemeier 1996, 281–82; Elliott 2000, 722). Achtemeier voices the suspicion that the recipients' question as to whether some limited activity in pagan worship was allowable is lurking behind the author's statement in 1 Pet 4:3 that the converts have spent *enough* (*arketos*) time in their earlier behaviors (1996, 281), an idea perhaps supported by the fact that the author puts *arketos* as the first word in this sentence for emphasis. The answer given by the author clearly excludes any such compromise.

Finally, a brief list of "offenders" is found in 1 Pet 4:15: "Let none of you suffer as a murderer, thief, criminal [*kakopoios*], and mischief-maker [*allotriepiskopos*]." The sense of the first two words is clear; both are considered by Jews, Christians, and Gentiles alike to be illegal. The more general *kakopoios*, however, does not necessarily denote *illegal* activity and could simply denote "evildoer" (Achtemeier 1996, 310; Donelson 2010, 136) or "wrongdoer" (Elliott 2000, 784–85).[25] Moreover, the term *allotriepiskopos* is found only here in the Greek literature of our period. Elliott derives the translation "a meddler in the affairs of others" from the word's components (2000, 785–88), though, alternatively, some suggest a reference to financial misconduct (BDAG 47; Achtemeier 1996, 310–13). Whatever the precise definition of *kakopoios* and *allotriepiskopos*, all four terms from 4:15 certainly denote activities universally deemed immoral—there is no disparity here between Judaism, Christianity, and Greco-Roman society. As many Hellenized Jews had been eager to point out, Judaism shared important virtues with Greco-Roman moral philosophy and, as shown here, one of

---

25. The verb form *kakopoieō* also occurs three times in 1 Peter (2:12, 14; 3:17) and can be contrasted with the use of *agathopoieō* in the epistle (see below p. 128).

the goals of 1 Peter was to encourage Christians to demonstrate the type of behavior universally seen as honorable.

Household Codes

The other paraenetic topos taken over by Jews and Christians from secular society was the household code (German *Haustafel*), instruction specifying proper behavior among members of the ancient household (Greek *oikonomia*, "to manage [*nomō*] a household [*oikia*]"). According to Aune, "the household was widely thought to constitute the basic unit of society, and a well-ordered household was the necessary prerequisite for a well-ordered state" (2003, 221–22). Similarly, Elliott notes that maintaining order in society was the "replication of an ordered universe" (2000, 486). Thus New Testament scholars locate the origin for such codes in Greek philosophy; previously they thought it originated in Stoicism, but now (following especially the work of David L. Balch) they trace such instruction to Aristotle (see Balch 1988). One finds in *Pol.* 1.3, for example,

> Seeing then that the state is made up of households, before speaking of the state, we must speak of the management of the household. The parts of household management correspond to the persons who compose the household, and a complete household consists of slaves and freemen. Now we should begin by examining everything in its fewest elements; and the first and fewest possible parts of a family are master and slave, husband and wife, father and children. (Aristotle 1885)[26]

Among writings contemporary with the New Testament this topos can be found in works of the Stoic philosopher Epictetus (e.g., *Diatr.* 3.2) and the Roman Stoic Seneca, the latter even assuming that the study of philosophy would include advice on "how a husband should conduct himself towards his wife, or how a father should bring up his children, or how a master should rule his slaves" (*Ep.* 94.1; translation Malherbe 1986, 127). Since such an organization of authority in Hellenistic society coincided with Roman sensibilities, the model became the general expectation for

---

26. Scholars note that the emphasis on conduct within society (Aune 1987, 196) and on mutuality (Achtemeier 1996, 52) found in works such as the *Politics* is more comparable to Christian *Haustafeln* than Stoic works whose emphasis was always on the individual. A convenient review of research on the precedents of the Christian *Haustafeln* can be found in Balch 1988.

good citizenry in the Roman world and any deviation from this structure "would ultimately be seen as a challenge to the Roman political order" (Achtemeier 1996, 52).

That such ideas found their way also into Judaism can be seen from the writings of Philo.

> In the fifth commandment on honouring parents we have a suggestion of many necessary laws drawn up to deal with the relations of old to young, rulers to subjects, benefactors to benefited, slaves to masters. For parents belong to the superior class of the above-mentioned pairs, that which comprises seniors, rulers, benefactors and masters, while children occupy the lower position with juniors, subjects, receivers of benefits and slaves. (*Decalogue* 31.165–166 LCL)[27]

The oldest New Testament household code, Col 3:18–4:1, with its threefold advice for wife/husband, child/father, and slave/master, was used directly by the author of Ephesians (5:21–6:9) and is also foundational for later Christian codes (Aune 2003, 221, citing Crouch 1972, 36). As compared with earlier codes, the precise form of the Christian *Haustafel* in Colossians is distinctive (Boring 2007, 905), in particular in its address to entire classes (rather than the "individual"), in its *direct* address to slaves and women (rather than as a part of the instruction given to masters/husbands; Elliott 2000, 552), and in its address first to the subordinate partner of each pair (Balch 1988, 46–47; Achtemeier 1996, 190).[28]

In some New Testament examples, the purview has been extended beyond the household to the social structure of the Christian community itself (*Gemeindetafeln*), as in 1 Pet 5:1–5, where advice on leadership is given to presbyters coupled with a reciprocal directive to younger members to heed their authority (cf., e.g., 1 Tim 2:11–14; 5:1–2). Other examples, including 1 Pet 2:13–17, bring into Christianity the secular notion of subordination to governmental authority. According to 1 Peter, Christians should "accept the authority of every human institution" (2:13) and "honor

---

27. See Elliot (2000, 506) for additional examples of household codes in Jewish literature.

28. On the reversal of the traditional Hellenistic order within the pairs, the emphasis on the subordination of the social inferior rather than on the authority of the social superior in 1 Peter and elsewhere in early Christian literature, and the sense of mutuality implied by both phenomena, see Elliott 2000, 507–9.

everyone; love the family of believers; fear God; honor the emperor" (2:17; cf. 1 Tim 2:1–2; Rom 13:1–7).[29]

Scholars often note the contrast between "fearing" God and merely "honoring" the emperor. Achtemeier sees 1 Pet 2:13–17 as reflecting the growth of the imperial cult in Asia Minor and the desire to provide a basis for Christians to show civic respect without participating in the associated religious rites (1996, 180–83). An interesting suggestion by J. Ramsey Michaels (1988, 122–23; followed by Witherington 2007, 130–31) is that such a preface to the *Haustafel* in 1 Peter, in contrast to those of Colossians and Ephesians, immediately creates a context that extends beyond the Christian community, a world of believers as well as nonbelievers that should also be understood for the household instructions that follow (1988, 122).

Within the household code proper (2:18–3:7), the author of 1 Peter assumes a schema reminiscent of (though clearly independent from) Colossians and Ephesians. It uniquely begins not with wives, as in the other two, but with slaves. As appropriate to their subordinate legal status, slaves are to be submissive to their masters "in all fear," even when treated unjustly. Though grammatically ambiguous, many scholars see this "fear" as directed toward God rather than the masters. They cite in particular its earlier occurrence in 1:17 and its position here between the command to "fear" God in 2:17 and the "mindfulness of God" recommended in 2:19 (see Achtemeier 1996, 194–95; Elliott 2000, 516–17; Donelson 2010, 81).

Going even further on the basis of this interpretation, Achtemeier suggests the intent that slaves be obedient to their masters *only* when there is no conflict with Christian values. In a society where slaves would be expected to participate in the religion of their owners (Balch 1981, 68 [citing Bömer 1958–63, 4:247–48]; Elliott 2000, 516), this expectation would be problematic for Christian slaves serving pagan masters. Finally, in the midst of unjust treatment, slaves are to look to Christ in his suffering as a role model, advice that is supported in 1 Pet 2:22–24 by references to Isa 53.

Without any word to masters, the author of 1 Peter proceeds to address wives. Like slaves, Christian wives are to submit to their husband's authority as per traditional societal expectations. They are reminded of what con-

---

29. Elliott sees this passage as directed literally to legally "free persons" as a group (2000, 496).

stitutes proper, modest decorum in appearance and conduct (cf. 1 Tim 2:9-10). Modesty was a trait highly valued in women in Greco-Roman society as well as in Judaism and Christianity.[30] Though such instruction is surely intended for all wives, the hope that proper behavior will win husbands to the faith in 3:1-2 shows that at least a portion of the audience is composed of Christian women married to nonbelievers. This situation was particularly difficult since women in general were already so vulnerable to divorce and were not even considered part of the husband's family until they bore a son (Elliott 2000, 577, 579). Moreover, the fact that a Christian wife would ignore the social obligation to follow her husband's religion not only resulted in a stressful situation for the individual woman but also opened up the entire church to criticism from outside.[31]

As with slaves, wives too are encouraged to follow a model, in this case the matriarch Sarah (3:5-6). They are her "children" if they "do right" (*agathopoiousai*) and are not afraid. The verb *agathopoieō* (and its cognates), prominent in 1 Peter, is often understood here and elsewhere in the epistle as synonymous with doing God's will (Achtemeier 1996, 184-85, and n. 62; Elliott 2000, 491, 494-95; more recently Sandnes 2005, 373-403). As with his view on the submission of Christian slaves, so too Achtemeier interprets 3:6 as specifically instructing wives to act in accordance with their Christian beliefs, even when this conduct brings intimidation from a nonbelieving spouse (2000, 216-17).

The household code concludes in 1 Pet 3:7 with brief instructions to Christian husbands on the treatment of their wives: men are to act "with consideration" (*kata gnōsin*) and honor (*timēn*) toward their wives as "weaker vessels" (*asthenesterō skeuei*).[32] Elliott notes that the author does

---

30. For references illustrating the value of modesty in the Greco-Roman world see Achtemeier 1996, 211-12; and Elliott 2000, 561-62. Considering the widespread acceptance of this view, Donelson suggests that its use in 1 Peter "may be an appeal to a value already shared by the women in his audience" (2010, 91).

31. See references in Balch 1981, 99; Achtemeier 1996, 211; Elliott 2000, 557-58. Balch even envisions the pagan husbands here as instigators of such criticism (1981, 99, 102).

32. The general meaning of *gynaikes* is simply "women"; thus Achtemeier maintains that the instruction extends to *all* the women in the household (2000, 217 and n. 162). Elliott acknowledges this as grammatically possible but argues that the context warrants the limitation to wives alone (2000, 575). Donelson seems to leave the matter open, though he makes the interesting statement, "Women are obligated and subject to men other than their husbands" (2010, 88).

not refer to "control" of wives, as was conventional in Greco-Roman and Jewish culture (2000, 574–75). Though the wife is physically weaker, the overall sense of 3:1–7 shows that the author does not consider women morally or intellectually inferior, as was widely believed in Greco-Roman society (Achtemeier 1996, 217; Elliott 2000, 576–78).[33]

Indeed, Achtemeier sees in the reference to the sharing of eternal life by both spouses the presence of gender equality within the Christian community and views the remark about ineffectual prayer in 3:7 as a warning that such equality must be taken seriously. Because he thinks the point of the household code in 1 Peter is primarily to lift up slaves and wives as representational for the suffering of the community as a whole (1996, 218–19), Achtemeier sees the inclusion of the instruction to husbands as solely for the purpose of reminding men of the equality of the sexes within the church (1996, 218–19). In contrast, Elliott denies that there was complete gender equality within the early Christian communities and prefers terms such as "equity" and "commonality" to describe the relationship (2000, 580–81). In his view, "the behavior of wives as well as the harmony of Christian households serves as a model for the conduct and cohesion of the entire household of God" (2000, 583).

As with the preface to the household code (2:11–17), the author concludes with an address to the entire community and emphasizes the importance of mutuality as a way of life among the members of the Christian "family" (3:8–9). Such conduct pleases God and will result in divine blessing, a notion supported by reference to Ps 34:13–17 (3:9–12).

The *Haustafel* of 1 Peter is clearly traditional in form and content, yet it exhibits differences from other such codes. Are there clues here for a historical reconstruction of the communities of 1 Peter? Does the absence of instruction for parents and children, for example, mean that the letter represents an early period in the church in which the communities did not yet constitute entire families?[34] Does the lack of instruction for masters show that there were only slaves in the communities, that there were no Christian masters (Michaels 1988, 122; Elliott 2000, 516), and that the converts of 1 Peter were generally of a low socioeconomic status? Does the more extensive and detailed instruction directed to wives than that to

---

33. As with the ambiguous *en phobō* in 2:18, Achtemeier sees *kata gnōsin* in 3:7 as referring to divine requirements (1996, 218).

34. Elliott suggests, however, that this category is represented by 1 Pet 5:1–5 (2000, 507).

husbands—a stark contrast to the even-handedness of Col 3:18–19 and to the greater instruction given to husbands in Eph 5:22–33—indicate that women made up the majority of community members; that most of the female converts were married to nonbelievers; that Christian women were a particular source of criticism from outsiders; that liberated Christian wives needed reining in; and/or that a (reversion to a) repressive environment for women was beginning in the churches?[35]

Scholars are often dubious that much can be determined about the historical situation reflected in a household code. The prominence of slaves and wives in the household code of 1 Peter is, in Balch's view, simply a reflection of the particular vulnerability of these groups to suspicion from those outside and should not be taken as an indicator of the social makeup of the communities (1981, 96–97). He maintains that the household code in 1 Peter represents an attempt to alleviate Roman suspicion that Christianity, like other foreign religions, caused social disorder. Balch cites contemporary texts from writers like Josephus and Dionysius of Halicarnassus who employ such material in an apologetic manner and compares this with the advice in 1 Pet 3:15 that one should be prepared to make a defense of Christianity to any challengers. He concludes that the household code in 1 Peter is likewise apologetic and encourages a "selective acculturation" on the part of Christians with respect to Greco-Roman culture (Balch 1981, 73–76, 81–116; 1988, 29, 33).

Achtemeier also cautions against drawing the conclusion from the focus on slaves and wives that they formed the greater part of the congregations. Instead, he maintains that the primary purpose of the household code in 1 Peter was to present *models* of oppressed individuals as examples of appropriate behavior for *all* community members as people suffering from a sometimes cruel society (1996, 54–55, 192, 209).[36] Elliott as well sees slaves and wives as paradigmatic for the community. Observing that 1 Peter is the only place among all of the New Testament *Haustafeln* where slaves are addressed first, he notes that "their uprootedness from home,

---

35. On the last three ideas, see the summary and critique of Balch (1981, 65–116) and Schüssler Fiorenza (1983, 260–66) in Elliott 2000, 584.

36. See also Lohse 1986, 44; Balch 1981, 96. Similarly, Elliott sees the household slaves as "paradigmatic of the entire oikos of God" (most recently 2000, 542, with other references). Achtemeier supports this view and cites the reference to the community as "slaves of God" in 1 Pet 2:16. One should note, however, that the term *doulos* used there differs from the term *oiketēs* in 2:18.

lack of kin-group support, and exposure to the whims and abuse of their superiors, together with their suffering even when doing what is right typified the entire community's vulnerability in a hostile society" (2000, 540). Contra Balch, both Elliott and Achtemeier deny that the household code, or 1 Peter in general, advises "accommodation" to societal norms (Achtemeier 1996, 53; Elliott 2000, 509–10).

Still, Achtemeier does draw some historical information from the code in 1 Peter. He cites the use of the term *oiketai* for slaves rather than *douloi* (as in the comparable passages in Colossians and Ephesians) as an indication that the addressees were household slaves of a higher social level (1996, 55, though he seems to reverse this conclusion on 194; see also Elliott 2000, 513, 542). In addition, he reads the instructions regarding female attire to imply the presence of relatively wealthy women within the community (1996, 55, 212; contra Elliott 2000, 564). Thus the extent to which the household code reflects the social makeup of the Christian communities addressed by 1 Peter remains an open question.

As with the virtue and vice catalogs, the *Haustafel* of 1 Peter exhibits the characteristics of paraenesis in several ways. The instruction is largely traditional and, as Donelson notes, remarkably general (2010, 78). The tone is one of advice and encouragement rather than command. Scriptural "precepts" are cited to support the instruction given. Finally, well-known or well-respected persons are presented as role models.

Conclusion

The content and form of the paraenesis in 1 Peter is both traditional and adaptive—the author has utilized paraenetic forms and material already available, both Greco-Roman and Jewish, but in the selection and formulation has made the tradition applicable to Christians and to a particular audience. As to the purpose of this paraenesis, especially in the context of suffering, scholars differ. While 1 Peter is at times optimistic that right conduct may serve the practical purposes of staving off persecution (2:12, 15; 3:13, 16) or of persuading nonbelievers to convert (3:1–2), one can see that the author does not really believe such arguments (2:19–21; 3:14–18; 4:12–19; 5:9–10). Instead, he moves the basis for encouragement elsewhere—to the promise of eschatological reward (1:3–9, 13, 21, 23; 2:2; 3:9; 4:13; 5:4, 6, 10) and of approval with God (2:19–20; 3:4, 12; 4:14; 5:5); to the argument that it is better to suffer for doing right (3:17), noting that others are suffering (5:9) and that Christ suffered the ultimate injustice to bring salvation (2:21–23; 3:18; 4:1, 13); and to the consolation that, in the end, their persecutors would be judged by God (4:5, 17).

Scholars of 1 Peter have at times suggested that the paraenesis was part of an actual baptismal homily or liturgy or that it was taken from an underlying early Christian (baptismal) catechism, but today many find the arguments for these theories unconvincing.[37] As mentioned above, Balch, dealing strictly with the household code, suggests an apologetic function that encourages the communities to conform with Greco-Roman expectations (1981, 87–88), but neither the code itself nor the paraenesis in the rest of the epistle really supports this hypothesis.

J. de Waal Dryden sees the paraenesis of 1 Peter as intended, first and foremost, to foster character development among neophytes, a function he suggests was typical of Greco-Roman philosophical paraenesis (2006, 43–47, 193–94). Yet while paraenesis does assume that the author occupies a superior social position, 1 Pet 5:1–4 shows that not all of the readers are new converts, and Dryden must qualify his position by saying that "the ideal audience category of 'young converts' is how the author has chosen to envision the status of his audience" (Dryden 2006, 45 n. 25).

Charles Talbert suggests that the paraenesis of 1 Peter "is what is deemed necessary for them to survive (a) as a group (b) in a hostile environment" (Talbert 1986, 146). In his view, paraenesis was directed both internally, to promote group cohesion, and externally, to provide the adaptation necessary to exist in the larger society. Achtemeier, essentially agreeing with Talbert, maintains that there would have been only two possible responses to pressure from outside—isolation or accommodation; it is the latter that is attested by 1 Peter. Still, this accommodation is qualified, and, as noted above, both Elliott (2000, 510) and Achtemeier (1996, 53) defend the author as someone who, while seeking to emphasize the values shared by the church with the society at large, is still ultimately unwilling to compromise Christian values.

Amid all these theories, perhaps something more underlies the paraenesis of 1 Peter. Malherbe notes that "*consolation* was regarded by rhetoricians

---

37. For the rejection of 1 Peter as a baptismal sermon or liturgy on form-critical grounds, see Martin 1992, 81–83. Further, Achtemeier states, "That baptism is a major theme of the letter is not borne out by the evidence" (2000, 60). Even the idea of an underlying catechism in 1 Peter could not be sustained when comparisons with other, similar texts showed too great a disparity among all of them. For an overview of these theories, see Balch 1981, 10–13.

and practiced by moralists as belonging to paraenesis" (1986, 82, emphasis mine), and this raises the question as to whether the function of the paraenesis in 1 Peter was one of comfort. As demonstrated by *Ad Demonicum* above, ancient moral exhortation could be classified as *paraklēsis*, *paraenesis*, and *protreptic* (Fiore 2009, 4:382). The term *paraenesis* never actually occurs in 1 Peter; rather, the author characterizes his communication using the verb *parakaleō* at key points (2:11; 5:1; and, in a summary statement, 5:12). It is often noted that Philo uses *paraklēsis* and *paraenesis* synonymously (*Contempl. Life* 12), and Fiore adds that "Paul uses the term *paraklesis* [*sic*], even when he engages in parenesis" (2009, 4:382; see also Engberg-Pedersen 2005, 62–70).

The range of meaning for the verb *parakaleō* (and cognate noun *paraklēsis*) in the literature of our period includes "call for, summon," "beseech," "exhort," "encourage," and, interestingly, "comfort" (LSJ 1311, 1313; BDAG 764–66; Schmitz and Stählin 1967, 5:773–99). According to Schmitz and Stählin, this last meaning originated in the fact that consolation in antiquity often consisted of advice to "be tough" and thereby created a fine line between exhortation, encouragement, and consolation (1967, 5:776, 779–80, 782–83, 796–97). While the surface meaning "comfort" is rare in Greek overall, Stählin suggests that "the imperative element in *parakaleō* ('to admonish') is always more or less plainly accompanied by the indicative 'to console' and *vice versa*" (Schmitz and Stählin 1967, 5:779).[38]

Moreover, in the LXX texts, there appears to be a clear dichotomy. Schmitz observes that when *parakaleō* and *paraklēsis* appear in texts that have been *translated* into Greek from the Hebrew, the meaning is *primarily* "comfort." In contrast, when *parakaleō* and *paraklēsis* occur in works written *originally* in Greek, they exhibit the wider spectrum of meaning found in ordinary Greek usage but virtually *never* have the sense of divine or human consolation. Outside of the LXX, Philo and Josephus generally reflect the secular Greek usage, while texts such as the *Testament of the Twelve Patriarchs* and *4 Ezra* also exhibit the meaning "comfort," likely influenced by the LXX (Schmitz and Stählin 1967, 5:776–79, with one exception in Josephus, *J.W.* 1.667). All of the meanings can be found in

---

38. Schmitz notes, "In the *rare* instances in which the verb and noun mean 'to comfort' or 'comfort' respectively in *ordinary* Greek usage, the consolation is mostly at the level of exhortation or encouragement to those who sorrow." He calls this phenomenon "philosophical consolation" (Schmitz and Stählin 1967, 5:776, emphasis added).

the New Testament (Schmitz and Stählin 1967, 5:793), including instances where those experiencing hardship, especially those suffering for the gospel, are "encouraged" and "comforted" via "exhortation" to right conduct.[39]

In times of disorder, one is comforted by images of order. In the Greco-Roman era, the behavior of the individual and of the community were thought to be intimately tied to the orderly working of the world. In this context, perhaps the paraenesis of 1 Peter was a very natural and much-needed reminder of Christian *order* that, in conjunction with other authorial strategies, served to bring comfort and reassurance to weary communities.

---

39. See also Heb 12:5; Rom 15:4; 2 Thess 2:16–17 (Schmitz and Stählin 1967, 5:797).

Ethnicity, Empire, and Early Christian Identity: Social-Scientific Perspectives on 1 Peter

David G. Horrell

New Testament studies has become a highly diverse discipline with a wide range of methods and approaches. Among the many contemporary approaches, what has come to be known as social-scientific criticism has an important place, even if, as I shall suggest below, it is now too diverse and too integrated into the discipline as a whole to be easily identified as one specific and particular method.

The immediate origins of social-scientific criticism lie in the early 1970s, although there are earlier precursors, including an interest in social history (see further Horrell 2002). Two important landmarks may be identified. One is the series of essays on both the Jesus movement and the Pauline communities published in the 1970s by Gerd Theissen (see Theissen 1979, with English translations in Theissen 1982 and 1992). The second is the formation in 1973 of a Society of Biblical Literature group devoted to the study of the social world of early Christianity. Notable publications to emerge from this early phase in the United States include those by Wayne Meeks (1972), Robin Scroggs (1975), and John Gager (1975).

Interest in this area continued to grow in the early 1980s, and something of a division developed. Some followed a more model-based approach rooted especially in cultural anthropology, for which Bruce Malina's *The New Testament World* (2001; first edition in 1981) provided a fundamental stimulus. Others saw themselves more as social historians drawing on social-scientific theories as and where they were helpful (notably Meeks 1983). Since that time, this distinction has to some extent continued, though it is questionable whether it is helpful or cogent. The "social-scientific" approach associated with Malina and the Context Group concentrates on using models to understand the New Testament within the social and cultural world of traditional Mediterranean society. In contrast, the so-called social historians favor a more eclectic and interpretative use of social-science approaches, though in my view the latter approach is equally "social-scientific" in character (see Horrell 2009b).

What has certainly also occurred is a great diversification of methods and perspectives within what may very broadly be seen as social-scientific criticism—whether or not the practitioners of such approaches would use that label of their work. For example, some draw on social-identity theory from the field of social psychology (Esler 1998; 2003), while others focus on economic models and socioeconomic stratification (Friesen 2004; Longenecker 2009; 2010). Some use political science and postcolonial theory to probe the political dimensions of the early Christians' engagement with the Roman Empire (Horsley 1997; 2000; 2004a; 2004b), while others draw on anthropology and comparative ethnography to illuminate the cultural values and practices evident in New Testament texts (Lawrence 2005).

More generally, the pioneers of social-scientific criticism have broadly achieved their aim—to reconnect "body and soul," that is, to root the study of the New Testament texts more firmly in their social world. A few decades ago, it was novel to explore the Gospel of John as reflecting a sectarian outlook or to consider the extent to which honor and shame were important cultural values in the New Testament world. Now such perspectives are commonly part of any mainstream discussion of such texts and their social contexts. Consequently, what might be identified as social-scientific perspectives have found their way into much of the broadly historical investigation of the New Testament texts.

In relation to 1 Peter, the most important pioneering study using a social-scientific approach is John H. Elliott's monograph *A Home for the Homeless* (1981). Although social-scientific studies had been gaining momentum since the early 1970s, Elliott's study was among the first to develop a social-scientific approach to a specific New Testament document as a whole. Subsequent early examples include Petersen (1985) and Esler (1987). Such an approach, Elliott proposes, entails an attempt to understand both the situation and the strategy of the document in question.

The starting point for Elliott's investigation is a study of the terms *paroikos* ("stranger") and *parepidēmos* ("alien"); the precise translation and nuance of the words is open to considerable discussion. They are used in 1 Peter to denote the identity of the recipients (1:1; 2:11; cf. 1:17). Contrary to a long history of interpretation that took these terms to refer to a metaphorical or spiritual identity as strangers or pilgrims on the earth,

Elliott argues that they refer instead to "the actual social and political condition of the addressees"; both before and after their conversion they were "resident aliens [*paroikoi*] and transient strangers [*parepidēmoi*]," literally "displaced persons" (Elliott 1981, 35–37, 48). This thesis provides the basis for a study of the "social profile" of the addressees and suggests that they were predominantly based in rural locations, a mixture of both Jews and Gentiles (with the latter probably in the majority), and generally in a vulnerable socioeconomic position (Elliott 1981, 59–73).

Elliott then draws on studies of contemporary religious sects, particularly by the sociologist Bryan Wilson, to depict the situation of the communities addressed by 1 Peter. They were in conflict with the wider world, as is typical of a conversionist sect with its membership based on individual conversion and with its stance of exclusivity (Elliott 1981, 73–84). The conflict evident in the letter, Elliott argues, was not due to any official Roman policy or criminalization of Christianity but to "the sectarian exclusiveness of Christianity itself" (Elliott 1981, 80, see also 74, 78).

In exploring the letter's strategy, related to the perceived situation of the addressees, Elliott considers 1 Peter as "a response to those problems with which conversionist sects in general must struggle" (Elliott 1981, 102). Thus the letter constitutes an attempt to sustain and promote the solidarity of the community, to maintain its distinctiveness and separation from the world (Elliott 1981, 106–48). In particular, the letter accomplishes its aim through its positive focus on the image of the household (*oikos*). Indeed, Elliott's key claim is that there is a crucial correlation to be drawn between the terms *paroikos*, which denotes the readers' displaced status in society, and *oikos* (*tou theou*), which denotes the new "home" in which they have found a place of belonging and identity (Elliott 1981, 200–233). The title of his book (*A Home for the Homeless*) thus captures concisely his central thesis about the strategy of 1 Peter (see Elliott 1981, 288). Finally, Elliott explores this strategy as an expression of the ideology and self-interests of the letter's producers, a Petrine circle based in Rome (Elliott 1981, 267–88).

Elliott's pioneering work has undoubtedly exerted considerable influence in shifting perceptions of 1 Peter. It helped to generate a focus on the concrete social conditions that the letter addresses and on its strategic attempt to sustain the vulnerable Christian groups in the face of hostility from the world.

Needless to say, not all of Elliott's arguments have been found fully persuasive. The majority of scholars, for example, are not convinced that the terms *paroikos* and *parepidēmos* refer to a sociopolitical identity held both before and after conversion (see, e.g., Feldmeier 1992, 203–10; Bechtler 1998, 64–83; Achtemeier 1996, 174–75). Some also question whether the *oikos* is as central to the letter's strategy as Elliott claimed. Troy Martin proposes "diaspora" as the letter's "controlling metaphor" (Martin 1992, 144–61), while Paul Achtemeier sees "Israel" as the central motif (Achtemeier 1996, 69–72), and Andrew Mbuvi claims that "temple imagery undergirds the entire letter" (Mbuvi 2007, 71). Some other issues of debate are mentioned below, but the importance of the shift in perspective achieved by Elliott's work remains, despite such disagreements on the substantive arguments.

The change in subtitle from the first (1981) to the second edition (1990) of *A Home for the Homeless* is significant. "Sociological exegesis" in the first edition becomes "social-scientific criticism" in the second. This change reflects both the developing sense of this subdiscipline's identity and also Elliott's involvement in the Context Group and its focus on Mediterranean cultural values (see also Elliott 1993), a focus evident in some of Elliott's later publications on 1 Peter.

In an essay from 1995, for example, Elliott explores the ways in which the letter is infused with the language of honor and shame, which are cultural values held to be central to the ancient Mediterranean (Elliott 1995; 2007a, 51–86). He argues that the letter, addressed to those who were abused and shamed by those around them, affirms their honorable status as God's elect people and turns their apparent shame into glory and honor. Elliott's work on 1 Peter is most comprehensively presented in his magnum opus in the Anchor Bible commentary series (Elliott 2000), a work in which his social-scientific perspectives decisively shape the interpretation of the letter and illustrate the way in which these perspectives have shaped the mainstream output of contemporary New Testament studies.

Since the first publication of *A Home for the Homeless*, scholars have drawn on an increasingly wide range of social-scientific perspectives to shed light on various New Testament texts, such that today there is no one approach that constitutes *the* "social-scientific" reading of 1 Peter. In the following sections, I shall offer three brief case studies that illustrate just some of the ways in which social-scientific resources can help us to appreciate the significance of 1 Peter in the making of Christian identity. Identity has become a prominent focus in recent New Testament study, and this focus mirrors a similar emphasis on identity in various areas of the social sciences and humanities. It is important to stress, however, that these are examples from among a wide range of possibilities, and different priorities or different theoretical resources could lead to very different engagements with the letter.

Ethnicity and Identity: 1 Peter 2:9

Identities rooted in a sense of race or ethnicity loom large in some of the most intractable conflicts in the modern world. Studies in "ethnopolitics" attempt to grapple with the complex historical and contemporary dimensions of these tensions. Religion plays a prominent role in many of these conflicts, albeit in varied ways, and is often deeply connected, at least in the minds of those whose identities are at stake, with historical claims about the rootedness of this identity in the past, near or distant. Indeed, a wide variety of factors, including religion, may play a role in constituting a sense of racial or ethnic identity. Which of these factors is salient in any given context is highly variable.

Recent social-scientific discussions have stressed that ethnic and racial identities are inevitably social constructions, matters of belief rather than anything objective or real. Max Weber's classic definition of ethnic groups illustrates this well: "human groups (other than kinship groups) which cherish a belief in their common origins of such a kind that it provides a basis for the creation of a community" (cited in Stone 2003, 32). What makes such identities so important and powerful is precisely the profound extent to which they are *believed* to be real. Kevin Avruch comments,

> For scholars of the postmodernist persuasion the great insight into ethnicity—ethnic identity, nationalism, culture, history, or most anything else that is social, for that matter—is that ethnicity is socially constructed: It is not a given but rather a thing which is made and thus potentially unstable, inconstant, and negotiable. ... But what makes this insight worth pursuing (and it is, at least in the long run, essentially correct), is that it so sharply flies in the face of what most ethnic "actors," the players themselves, believe. (Avruch 2003, 73)

Contemporary scholars disagree about the extent to which race remains a useful category for analysis and whether it is to be distinguished from ethnicity. Modern use of the term *ethnicity* has been traced to the United States in 1941–42, when, as Werner Sollors comments, "the term [ethnicity] ... was intended to substitute for 'race' at a time that the older word had become deeply compromised by 'racism,' a word coined, perhaps, by

Magnus Hirschfeld in 1938" (Sollors 1996, xxix). This substitution suggests that both race and ethnicity denote essentially the same thing. Contrary to any view of race in particular as biologically or geographically determined, both are therefore equally socially constructed and discursively maintained facets of human social identity.

What does all this have to do with 1 Peter? One verse is particularly notable. In 2:9, at the culmination of an important passage rich in scriptural phrases (2:4–10), the author describes the identity of the addressees as follows:

> But you are a chosen race [*genos eklekton*], a royal priesthood, a holy nation [*ethnos hagion*], a people [*laos*] for his own possession, that you may proclaim the excellencies of him who called you out of darkness into his marvelous light. (ESV)

It is striking that we find here three words—*genos*, *ethnos*, *laos*—that are commonly used to denote what we would call ethnic groups (see further Horrell 2012; 2013, 133–63). This is most clearly the case with the word *genos*, in which the idea of descent is often present.

All three words are used to describe the people of Israel in the LXX and in Jewish literature of the Roman period. The term *laos* is particularly common in the LXX (e.g., Exod 5:23; Lev 26:12; Deut 7:6), while *ethnos* (often in the plural form) is most frequently used of other nations (e.g., Exod 34:24; Lev 18:24; Deut 7:6–7). The word *genos* emerges as a prominent designation of the people of Israel in later texts (e.g., Judith, 2–3 Maccabees) as well as in Josephus (e.g., *Ag. Ap.* 1.1–2, 59, 106) and Philo (e.g., *Embassy* 3–4, 201). Indeed, it is clear that the author of 1 Peter is taking fundamental identity-designations of the Jewish people—chosen race, holy nation, God's own people—and applying them to the Christian communities addressed in the letter (cf. Deut 7:6–7; Exod 19:5–6; Isa 43:20). This appropriation of course raises challenging questions about the extent to which early Christianity implicitly or explicitly regards itself as replacing the Jews as the people of God (see further Horrell 2008, 102–5; Bauman-Martin 2007).

The importance of this move for the making of early Christian identity may be seen when we set 1 Peter in the context of the New Testament and other early Christian writings. First Peter 2:9 is the only place in the New Testament where the significant term *genos* is applied to the Christians, and it is the only place where *genos*, *ethnos*, and *laos* occur together. This verse and Matt 21:43 (rather less direct) are the only two places in the New Testament that describe followers of Jesus Christ as members of an *ethnos*. Equally significant is the observation that talk of Christians as a *genos* became established in the second century, sometimes in the context of a threefold distinction of Greeks, Jews, and Christians (*Diogn.* 1; Clement of Alexandria, *Strom.* 5.14.98.4; see further Buell 2001; 2002; 2005; Lieu 2002, 49–68; 2004, 239–68). Also emerging during this period is the notion that Christians explicitly constitute a "third race" (*triton genos*; Latin *tertium genus*). This expression is used both positively by Christians (possibly in the *Kerygma Petrou* [in Clement of Alexandria, *Strom.* 6.5.41.6–7]; also Pseudo-Cyprian, *De Pascha computus* 17) and critically by their opponents (Tertullian, *Nat.* 7–8; see Harnack 1904, 300–352).

First Peter therefore stands at the beginning of an influential discourse in which early Christian identity is described in explicitly ethnic or racial terms. This raises some questions about a long-established tendency to depict Christianity as a nonethnic and universal religion that transcends the ethnic particularism of Judaism (see Johnson Hodge 2007, 3–7). Yet the modern social-scientific emphasis on the constructed nature of ethnic and racial identities also raises questions about the tendency in scholarship to depict Christian ethnic terminology as fictive, spiritual, or metaphorical as opposed to "real." If all forms of racial and ethnic identity are constructed through discourse and social practices, such that they are "believed" rather than objectively real, then the distinction between "real" and "fictive" breaks down.

Instead, we see early Christian writers, including the author of 1 Peter, using what Denise Kimber Buell calls "ethnic reasoning" to construct what is in some ways an ethnic identity, even if this does not necessarily mean that previous ethnic identities are erased (see further Buell 2005; Johnson Hodge 2007; Sechrest 2009; Horrell 2012). Naturally this raises a series of complex questions about what constitutes a specifically ethnic identity and how such identities can be construed in both restrictive and open or universal terms.

What seems clear nonetheless is that concepts of ethnic or racial identity formed an important part of the discourse by which early Christian identity was articulated. Buell comments that "early Christians perceived ethnicity/race as concepts flexible enough to encompass both the radical transformation of identity attributed to the conversion process and the stability of identity hoped for in its wake" (Buell 2002, 436). The use of *genos*, *ethnos*, and *laos* in 1 Peter to denote Christians draws on Jewish

Scriptures and identity markers and represents a move that was of considerable significance in the development of Christian identity.

Estranged in the Empire: a Postcolonial Perspective

One of the most prominent debates in the history of 1 Peter scholarship took place in the 1980s following the publication of two monographs that took very different views of the letter, and in particular of its stance toward the wider world. We have already discussed the arguments of the first of these monographs, John Elliott's *A Home for the Homeless* (1981), which draws on a sectarian typology to position the communities addressed by 1 Peter as representative of a conversionist sect that is clearly distinct from the world. The author's strategy, Elliott insists, is "to reinforce a sense of distinctive Christian identity and solidarity" (1981, 106).

The second monograph, also published in 1981 (though based on a 1974 doctoral dissertation), is David Balch's *Let Wives Be Submissive*, a study of the domestic (or "household") code in 1 Pet 2:11–3:12. Balch sees the function of the domestic code in terms of an apologetic attempt to lessen criticism and hostility directed toward members of the Christian movement (especially women and slaves) by instructing them to conform more closely to the social norms of the time, namely, submitting to masters and husbands.

In two papers presented at the SBL Annual Meeting in 1982 (and subsequently published in 1986), Balch and Elliott debated their different approaches to 1 Peter. Balch (1986) drew on social-scientific studies of the ways in which minority or immigrant groups adapt to a dominant culture through assimilation and acculturation. Elliott, by contrast, rejected this reading of the letter and reiterated his own view.

> Nothing in 1 Peter, including its discussion of household duties, indicates an interest in promoting social assimilation. It was precisely a temptation to assimilate so as to avoid further suffering that the letter intended to counteract. … The letter affirms the distinctive communal identity and seeks to strengthen the solidarity of the Christian brotherhood so that it might resist external pressure urging cultural conformity and thereby make effective witness to the distinctive features of its communal life, its allegiance and its hope of salvation. (Elliott 1986, 72–73, 78)

These two important studies clearly offer contrasting perspectives on 1 Peter's social strategy. Where Balch sees a call for assimilation and greater conformity to the wider society, Elliott sees distinctiveness and resistance to external pressures. Yet despite their significant disagreements, both authors acknowledge that there is some material in 1 Peter that points in each direction. This suggests both a concern for distinctive identity and some degree of accommodation to the world. The question is how best to grasp the dynamic of the author's perspective.

In an earlier essay (Horrell 2007a; see also 2013, 211–38), I have argued that we might fruitfully look to theoretical resources that could help us appreciate the particular dynamics of the sociopolitical context in which 1 Peter was written, namely, the context of the Roman Empire. I suggest that postcolonial studies may be particularly helpful (see also Bauman-Martin 2007). Postcolonialism does not constitute one particular or defined theory, nor is it a field only associated with the social sciences. Indeed, its main proponents have often come from the field of literary studies (for introductions see Ashcroft et al. 2000; 2002; Gandhi 1998). While postcolonial studies focus primarily on European colonialism from the sixteenth century onward, their main concern—to analyze the impact of colonialism and imperialism on societies and cultures—can appropriately be applied to the effects of the Roman imperial project (see Webster and Cooper 1996).

One of the key points to emerge from this area of studies is that the relations between colonizer and colonized are complex and ambivalent, with resistance and complicity often inextricably intertwined. The "space" of interaction creates a place for new, hybrid identities in which both colonizer and colonized become something other than they were before (Bhabha 1994, 36–39, 110–15). Also, the disturbance of colonization can dislocate people, both physically and/or culturally, such that the language of diaspora and exile finds a prominent place in postcolonial reflection (see, e.g., Ashcroft et al. 2006, 425–59). "Postcolonialism thus invites us to read 1 Peter as a literary product of a colonial/imperial context, with our ears attuned to the ways in which this letter constructs the identity of the people to whom it is addressed and offers one particular way of negotiating existence in the empire, between conformity and resistance" (Horrell 2007a, 123).

One aspect of the way in which the letter constructs its readers' identity is evident in the opening and closing of the letter. The addressees are identified as elect strangers in the Diaspora (1:1), by an author who sends greetings from "Babylon," most likely a cryptic reference to Rome (5:13; see Hunzinger 1965). In these few words that significantly frame the letter, the readers are dislocated or alienated from the world, labeled as those who do not "belong" as citizens in the empire. The empire itself is cast into the role of Babylon, a designation that may be taken to evoke "the very epitome and type of an ungodly and domineering city" (Kuhn 1964, 1:515). Even though the author of 1 Peter has a different stance from that of the writer of Revelation, he says enough, I would argue, to show that he shares certain aspects of a critical perspective on the empire and on Christian existence within it. His stance is more conformist and polite than is implicit in the hostile apocalyptic imagery of Revelation, but it is nonetheless a stance of resistance.

Corresponding to the critical dislocation of the readers from a sense of being "at home" within the empire is the articulation of their positive and honorable new identity as the elect people of God, something that reaches a literary climax in 2:4–10, as we have already seen. Without there being any explicitly anti-imperial or anti-Roman polemic, the author's words are sufficient to indicate that the basis for positive identity and future hope lies not in belonging as citizens of the empire but elsewhere. Elliott's stress on the author's attempt to reinforce a positive and distinctive identity for the readers in this sense seems correct (see Elliott 1981, 106–7, 148, 225–26, 270).

When it comes to practical instructions on how to live, the author both reiterates the sense of distinction from the world (2:11–12) and, as Balch suggests, urges conduct that would conform to established social values concerning what counts as "good" (2:12–3:17). The author's optimistic hope is that "good" conduct on the part of Christians will ultimately convince their opponents and persecutors to revise their negative judgment (2:12–15; 3:1–2, 13–17). Yet he does not entirely recommend behavior in conformity to societal (and specifically imperial) expectations.

In 2:17, the author makes a significant distinction between "worshiping God" (*ton theon phobeisthe*) and "honoring the emperor" (*ton basilea timate*; see Horrell forthcoming). Although scholars commonly see here only the absence of any critical stance toward Rome (e.g., Michaels 1988, lxiii; Elliott 2000, 502; Bechtler 1998, 50), the specific terminology is crucial. As a number of somewhat later sources show, the Christians' refusal to offer the kind of cultic obeisance demanded of them (despite their willingness to honor the emperor) was regarded as a form of resistance sufficient to warrant execution. When testing accused persons to ascertain whether they were Christians (ca. 111–12 C.E.), Pliny, governor of

Pontus-Bithynia, required them to reverence the gods and the emperor by offering wine and incense to the emperor's image. Pliny knew that no true Christian would do this (*Ep.* 10.96.5–6). Whether Pliny's letter, and the later Christian sources mentioned below, reflect a similar situation to that presumed in 1 Peter is certainly open to debate. But in my view, the distinction drawn in 1 Peter between "worshiping" (only) God and "honoring" the emperor most likely reflects a context similar to the one Pliny refers to, and similar to those reflected in some later Christian texts, namely, those where hostility against Christians led to their accusation and appearance in court (see further Horrell 2007b; 2013; Williams 2012a). This context explains why the author formulates this carefully and concisely worded instruction.

Somewhat later, for example, Polycarp, bishop of Smyrna, draws a comparable distinction, explaining to the proconsul that "we [Christians] are taught to render all due honor [*timē*] to rulers and authorities appointed by God." However, Polycarp refuses to "swear by the Fortune of Caesar [*tēn kaisaros tychēn*]," and he is consequently martyred (*Mart. Pol.* 10.1–2).

Even later, the Scillitan martyrs (180 C.E.) draw precisely the same verbal distinction found in 1 Peter between "honor" for Caesar and "worship" for God alone (*Act. Scil.* 8–9). Other martyr accounts and apologies also reflect the influence of 1 Peter, in recording a willingness to "honor" the emperor, but equally a refusal to "worship" him (e.g., *Martyrdom of Apollonius* 3, 6, 37; Theophilus, *Ad Autolycum* 1.11). The verbal similarities do not of course prove that the situations are the same, and we should be cautious about retrojecting a later context into the time of 1 Peter. But a persuasive case can be made, I believe, that there is an essential continuity in terms of the legal status of Christians, from the time of Nero to that of Decius (third century; see Horrell 2013, 183–97; Williams 2012a, esp. 180–226). Like these later martyrs, the author of 1 Peter was willing to urge a degree of compliance with Rome's demands, and to promote conduct that would be recognized as honorable and "good," but he was not willing to "go all the way" (*pace* Carter 2004) in acquiescing to imperial domination by worshiping the emperor or the gods of Rome. Adopting a postcolonial perspective does not by any means require that we come to this conclusion, which is based primarily on assessment of the relevant historical evidence (contrast the perspective of Bird 2011). What it does offer is a way to appreciate and understand the dynamics of interaction between colonizer and colonized, and specifically the complex negotiations by the colonized of a stance that lies between conformity and resistance.

A Strategy of Social Creativity:
Claiming the Label "Christian" (1 Peter 4:16)

The label "Christian" has, needless to say, become the definitive label for members of the movement that began around Jesus of Nazareth, even though it is scarcely evident in the New Testament (occurring just three times: Acts 11:26; 26:28; 1 Pet 4:16). It becomes prominent only from the second century onward. The Greek word *Christianos* is a Latinism; that is to say, its formation (with the ending *-ianos*) indicates an origin in, or under the influence of, the Latin language. Indeed, as most scholars agree, the name most likely originated with outsiders (quite possibly Roman officials) rather than with the Christians themselves (see Elliott 2000, 790–91, with n. 609). From a postcolonial perspective, these initial observations should already spark our interest. In a sense, "Christian" identity is a kind of hybrid identity, one constructed in the space of the (often hostile) encounter between the imperial power (and its language) and the colonized.

The context in which the term appears in 1 Peter is also significant. In the section that begins at 4:12, the readers' suffering, which is a theme throughout the letter (1:6; 2:19–20; 3:14–17; 4:1, 12–19; 5:9–10), is most vividly and fully described. Specifically, it seems that the kind of insults and hostility they endure "for the name of Christ" (4:14) include their being labeled as "Christian," an accusation comparable to other terms used to label wrongdoers such as murderer, thief, evildoer, or busybody (4:15–16). The setting, in other words, is one of hostility and suffering, where members of the Christian communities are ridiculed and slandered because of their allegiance to Christ. The appearance of the specific name *Christianos* in this context is not accidental, since it represents an outsiders' label that is used in a negative way to denote members of this deviant superstition, as external sources referring to the "Christians" confirm (Pliny, *Ep.* 10.96; Tacitus, *Ann.* 15.44; Suetonius, *Nero* 16.2).

In the history of scholarship on 1 Peter, there have been different views as to whether these contexts of suffering should be seen as the result of "official" Roman persecution or "unofficial" public hostility. Contemporary scholarship on 1 Peter has largely come to a consensus that "the persecution of 1 Peter is local, sporadic and unofficial, stemming from the antagonism and discrimination of the general populace" (Dubis 2006, 203; see also Webb 2004, 383). In some recent work, however, a number of scholars, including myself, have argued that the sufferings to which the readers were subject may well have included judicial trials and possible execution as well as informal slander and hostility (e.g., Horrell 2007b, 370–76; 2013; Holloway 2009, 4–5, 40–66; J. G. Cook 2010, 240–46; Williams 2012a; for an overview see Williams 2012b). Indeed, to pose "official" and "unofficial" sources of suffering as alternatives is to misconstrue the legal situation that pertained throughout this period. As Pliny's famous letter makes clear, Christians came to the attention of magistrates due to accusations brought by members of the public (i.e., there was no official or inquisitorial policy to seek out Christians). Yet, if a governor were so minded, the charge of being Christian, if upheld, was sufficient in itself to warrant the death penalty. Indeed, in such contexts the name "Christian" acquires particular significance: "I am a Christian" (*Christianos eimi*) is the crucial and fatal confession (see *Mart. Pol.* 10.1; 12.1; Pliny, *Ep.* 10.96.3; Eusebius, *Hist. eccl.* 5.1.20; further Lieu 2002, 211–31).

Whatever the kind of suffering that is in view, the author of 1 Peter clearly attempts to revalue the label "Christian." Instead of this label being a source of shame (*mē aischynesthō*), the name should gladly be borne as a means to glorify God (*doxazetō de ton theon en tō onomati toutō*, 4:16). The significance and dynamics of this literary intervention can be illuminated through the use of social-identity theory (see Horrell 2007b, 376–80; 2013, 197–209).

This theoretical perspective, developed in the field of social psychology particularly by Henri Tajfel and his collaborators and successors, has been fruitfully applied by a number of scholars to various New Testament texts (e.g., Esler 1998; 2003; Marohl 2008). The key focus for such theorists is the various facets of *social* identity—that is, those aspects of an individual's self-identity that derive from group membership. In particular, social-identity theorists have attempted to understand how and why groups form, why certain features of identity become salient in certain contexts, and how groups fulfill the psychological need to provide their members with a positive sense of their group identity, something regarded as crucial to the ongoing existence of social groups (see Tajfel and Turner 2001, 101).

Henri Tajfel and John Turner discuss what they see as the possibilities for those facing negative social identity because of their group membership and allegiances. Depending on the operative social assumptions in any particular context, these possibilities fall broadly under two categories: "social mobility" and "social creativity" (Tajfel and Turner 2001, 95–96). In situations where it is deemed possible, the former entails leaving the group, something that was clearly a pressure (or a temptation) for early Christians faced with negative social pressure and various forms of hostility. Hence there are warnings against apostasy, such as Heb 6:4–8, and the efforts of the author of 1 Peter to offer hope and consolation and to urge people to "stand firm" (5:12).

The latter strategy, "social creativity," is defined by Tajfel and Turner as one in which group members "seek positive distinctiveness for the in-group by redefining or altering the elements of the comparative situation" (Tajfel and Turner 2001, 104). As a "classic example" they note the slogan "Black is beautiful" (Tajfel and Turner 2001, 104). In other words, some quality or name that is seen by outsiders (and perhaps felt by insiders too) as negative, a form of stigma, is redefined and reclaimed so as to give it positive value in engendering a sense of the worth of group membership.

Something similar can be seen to be operative in 1 Peter, where the author attempts to claim the label "Christian" as a name to be gladly and honorably owned, a source of glory rather than shame. As such, 1 Peter makes a rather crucial contribution to the process by which the label "Christian" came to be accepted and used by insiders as a positive and identity-defining name.

Conclusion

These three case studies have illustrated some of the ways in which a range of resources drawn broadly from the social sciences can illuminate and inform our understanding of some of the dynamics of 1 Peter, particularly in terms of the letter's contribution to the construction of early Christian identity. It is important to stress once again that these studies are but examples from a potentially enormous range of possibilities and that the conclusions drawn are open to disagreement and debate. The letter draws on Jewish Scriptures, traditions, and identity markers in its declarations about the esteemed and honorable status God has bestowed upon its readers. It also reflects some of the pressures of negotiating existence and maintaining positive social identity in the face of a hostile empire and an often critical wider public.

In particular, the author of 1 Peter makes a number of moves that turn out to be crucial for the formation of early Christian identity. He is the first to describe his addressees as a *genos*, a move that laid the path for later discussion of Christians as a new "race," a *tertium genus*. He sets out a stance toward the empire that steers a course between conformity and resistance, one that would be broadly followed by later martyrs and apologists. Finally, he makes the first move to claim the outsiders' label "Christian" as one that insiders can positively own as a badge of membership that brings glory to God.

In these and other respects, the ongoing legacy of 1 Peter is ambivalent. The letter raises critical questions to consider about its positioning of the church as Israel. For example, does this appropriation imply replacement of the Jews as the people of God? Also, have the letter's appeals for submission—even in suffering—legitimated imperial domination and the abuse of women and slaves? Yet whatever our assessment of 1 Peter's theological and moral impact, its historical contribution to the emergence of what came to be known as Christianity is very considerable. This relatively short letter is pivotal to the making of Christian identity, and therefore it deserves more attention than it has traditionally received. Social-scientific perspectives cannot determine the correct answers to historical and exegetical questions about 1 Peter, but they can help us understand better the contributions of this important early Christian letter.

1 Peter and Postmodern Criticism

Félix H. Cortez

An array of diverse methods loosely characterized as postmodern has emerged in the area of biblical studies in the last thirty years. The purpose of this chapter is to introduce the reader to the basic tenets of postmodern criticism and its related methods and to survey briefly its impact on the analysis and interpretation of 1 Peter.

What Is Postmodern Biblical Criticism?

We should begin by saying that postmodern biblical criticism is not a method but rather a stance or a posture that uses different methods of analysis, and some of these methods at times may even be contradictory (Adam 1995, vii; Bible and Culture Collective 1995, 8–9). Thus not everyone agrees on which kind of interpretations should count as postmodern and which should not. In fact, postmoderns are not interested in defining who or what should determine an interpretation as postmodern. (That determination would be of interest to moderns, not postmoderns.)

Postmodern biblical criticism is mostly a movement of resistance (Adam 1995, 1). Its name suggests that it is a resistance against modernism. So, in order to understand what postmodernism is, we first need to understand modernism.

The symbolic moment that marked the transition from ancient to modern hermeneutics was probably the winter semester of 1513–14 at the University of Wittenberg.[1] Martin Luther was preparing his first lectures

---

1. Luther's text of the Psalms is more a symbol of the birth of a new age than the moment of its conception. It is, in fact, difficult to date modernity. Most scholars identify modernity with the Enlightenment of the eighteenth century. The impulses of modernism are noticed, however, much earlier. It is probably better to date the

as professor of theology. The topic was the book of Psalms, and Luther wanted to ensure that each one of his students had a copy of the biblical text to read. The Bible that was normally studied in those times was a commented text—the *Glossa Ordinaria*—in which notes and commentaries from the church fathers surrounded every verse or section of Scripture. In a literal sense, Scriptures were immersed in the traditions of the church, and it was expected that students would read the biblical text through that filter. Luther, however, instructed Johann Grunenberg, the university printer, to produce an edition of the Psalms with broad margins and plenty of space between the lines of the text. This blank space would be for students to write Luther's interpretative comments and reflections as well as their own.

This decision by Luther heralded an important shift in the way Scriptures were understood and read. The Reformation led to a crisis of authority. How should the correctness or legitimacy of an interpretation be determined? Before the modern era, one could resolve an argument by appealing to the testimony of ancient authorities. Moderns argued, however, that it was not agreement with the ancient authorities that legitimated a conclusion but the method in which the inquiry was done. The conclusions were true if the study proceeded rationally—that is, in a scientific, scholarly, or properly reasoned way. So, more than two centuries later, during the Enlightenment, the academic discipline of biblical studies arose in Germany out of this crisis, and its dominant approach was the historical-critical method. The study of the Bible became, then, a science—a *Wissenschaft* (see Kugel 2007, 1–46; Legaspi 2010, 3–26). Thus modernity embodies confidence in reason and science as guides to truth; it questions the authority of ancient interpreters and assumes that historical criticism provides the only legitimate criteria for judgment (Adam 2006, 20; see also Lyotard 1984, xxiii).

Modernism was optimistic about human destiny. Led by reason, the scientific revolution of the sixteenth and seventeenth centuries was expected to liberate humanity from the darkness of superstition and to lay the foundation for progress. Technology would make it possible to control and harness nature for the benefit of human beings, producing wealth and raising our standard of living. Market economies would spur economic

---

beginning of modernism to the era that goes from 1470 (the beginning of the Italian Renaissance) to the start of the Enlightenment in the 1700s. See Legaspi 2010, 3–26.

growth, supply social and material needs, and make possible a truly free and genuinely happy life. Similarly, a rational method for the study of the Bible would make it possible to go behind the traditions accumulated over centuries in order to discover the original historical situations in which biblical documents were written, that is, to find out "what had really happened." A scientific study of the Bible would make it possible to arrive at objective truth and to know what the authors originally meant (Barton 1998, 9–18). Charles Augustus Briggs, the famed coeditor of *The Brown-Driver-Briggs Hebrew and English Lexicon*, clearly shared this enthusiasm at the start of the twentieth century. He wrote:

> Holy Scripture, as given by divine inspiration to holy prophets, lies buried beneath the rubbish of centuries. It is covered over with the débris of the traditional interpretations of the multitudinous schools and sects. … Historical criticism is digging through this mass of rubbish. Historical criticism is searching for the rock-bed of the Divine word, *in order to recover the real Bible*. (quoted in Kugel 2007, 664)

The goals of modernism, however, did not materialize as expected. Science did provide great benefits to humanity, but it also gave birth to weapons of mass destruction, which led to staggering losses in human life in the First and Second World Wars. Technology raised the standard of living but also made possible the horrors of the Holocaust. Market economies spurred economic growth but also the Great Depression of the 1930s.

The failure of reason and science to prevent the great social, political, and economic tragedies of the first half of the twentieth century created a backlash against modernism. Postmodernism arose as a movement of resistance galvanized by deep distrust of the claims of modernism. Its main objective was to point out that the modern worldview's claims to truth were in fact not legitimate (Adam 1995, 5).

Cornel West identifies three important characteristics of postmodernism: it is antifoundational, antitotalizing, and demystifying. Thus, against the claims of modernism, postmodern thinkers point out that (1) there is not, and there cannot be, an unassailable starting point to establish truth; (2) any theory that claims to account for everything is suppressing examples or applying warped criteria; and, finally, (3) any claim based on assumptions that are "natural" or "objective" conceals ideological agendas (Adam 1995, 5). Let us look at each of these three characteristics of postmodernism more closely.

Postmodernism Is Antifoundational

Philosophical tradition has claimed that one needs to have some undoubtable, unshakeable truth with which to support one's arguments. Postmoderns do not doubt the existence of starting points or foundations, but they will point out that foundations are always problematic. In fact, some postmoderns assert that undoubtable, unshakable foundations do not exist at all. The problem is that philosophical foundations are human constructions, and this problem implies two troublesome things. First, foundations are built on the basis of human perception, and human perception is fallible. For example, human perception is vulnerable to optical illusions and false memories. Second, philosophical foundations are communicated through words and symbols, but words and symbols are ambiguous. Therefore, since philosophical foundations depend on imperfect perception and are communicated through ambiguous means, they remain always problematic and open to critique. Postmodern biblical criticism, then, will often question the philosophical foundations that buttress the claims to truth of modern approaches to biblical studies (e.g., historical-critical approaches).

Postmodernism Is Antitotalizing

A claim to truth is also an assertion about a totality. Such an assertion may be about the universe, a set of things, or even an individual. It is often argued that these entities are "naturally" or "logically" formed, and so claims to truth about them are "natural" or "logical." The problem with totalities is that they differentiate between members and nonmembers. Who decides, however, what should be included in that totality and what should not? When a person makes an assertion about patriotic people, for example, who gets to say who is patriotic and who is not? Would any assertion about human beings really include all human beings or just those whom interest groups want to legitimate? How does one define a person? Is a person with multiple personalities really one person? Is a person whose personality changed because of a stroke the same person he or she was, or is this now a different person? Postmodern biblical criticism, then, will often point out that the totalities about which some truths are claimed are in fact artificial. Therefore, they cannot serve as self-authenticating warrants for the truths they assert.

Postmodernism Is Demystifying

Finally, postmodern biblical criticism points out that any assertion of inclusion or exclusion from a totality, any assertion of truth, or any intellectual discourse is, in the final analysis, not disinterested or pure. Wittingly or unwittingly, things like group interests, political agendas, other motives, or simply honest beliefs and preconceptions color the way we see things. Our perception is never raw but instead is always filtered. Therefore, postmodern biblical criticism will often question the objectivity of modern approaches to biblical studies by prying into the motives behind their discourse, and it will argue that in the final analysis every interpretation—including its own—amounts to a power play (Bible and Culture Collective 1995, 3–5). Thus postmodern biblical critics constantly raise the question of who benefits from a particular interpretation (whether that be an individual or a group).

Cornel West's analysis of postmodernism is certainly helpful, but it is not the only one or the most influential. Other descriptions of postmodernism, however, mostly correlate with his analysis. Probably the most influential of these is Jean-François Lyotard's statement that postmodernism is "incredulity toward metanarratives" (Lyotard 1984, xxiv). A metanarrative is a story we tell about the nature and destiny of humanity (e.g., that we are evolving to universal recognition of human rights and political democracy; Adam 1995, 16). So metanarratives justify—or legitimize—the actions performed toward the fulfillment of those same metanarratives (e.g., actions that are exerted so that other nations become democratic) and help define and enforce totalities (e.g., assertions that those who support democracy are "reasonable" while those who do not are "unreasonable"). Metanarratives, however, may help conceal the cracks in the legitimation of those actions (e.g., that actions to further democracy in other nations may in fact serve interests other than the pure promotion of democracy). So, the postmodern attitude is that of suspicion toward grand arguments that legitimate actions.[2]

---

2. Lyotard argues that postmodernism can be identified in three trajectories. The first is aesthetic, emphasizing the constructed nature of a work of art. The second is epistemological, questioning the legitimacy of the modern discourse. The third is political, exploring the social, political, and ecological consequences of modern discourse. See Bible and Culture Collective 1995, 9–10.

Postmodernism versus Historical Criticism

Postmodern criticism, then, approaches the claims of historical criticism with suspicion.[3] The historical-critical method is concerned with the "plain sense" or "natural sense" of the text (Barton 1998, 17). Its aim is to conduct a disinterested analysis of the text so as to arrive at objective truth. It focuses on the original meaning of the text—what it meant to its first readers—and therefore asks genetic questions about biblical texts: when and by whom the biblical books were written, who the original readers were, and what the stages by which they came into being were (Aichele, Miscall, and Walsh 2009, 395). Postmodern criticism, however, is concerned with debunking the absolute or totalistic claims to the meaning of the text made by historical criticism. Its aim is to pry open the political forces that shape the interpretations of a text. It focuses on the current meaning of texts and therefore emphasizes the concerns of readers today, the forces that shape their readings, and the political impact of such readings. Postmodernism limits itself by showing that human reason is fallible and that this fallibility is inherent to the human condition. Postmodernism, however, does not suggest new philosophical foundations or new methods for theoretical discourse. In fact, it builds its critique with the same assumptions of modernism. Thus Zygmunt Bauman is right when he says,

> Postmodernity is no more (but no less either) than the modern mind taking a long attentive and sober look at itself, at its conditions and its past works, not fully liking what it sees and sensing the urge to change. Postmodernity is modernity coming of age: modernity looking at itself at a distance rather than from inside, making a full inventory of its gains and losses, psychoanalyzing itself, discovering the intentions it never before spelled out, finding them mutually cancelling and incongruous. Postmodernity is modernity coming to terms with its own impossibility; a self-monitoring modernity, one that consciously discards what it was once unconsciously doing. (Z. Bauman 1991, 272; quoted in Bible and Culture Collective 1995, 3; cf. Carroll 1998, 57)

This is why Lyotard argues that postmodernity is, in fact, part of modernity. "A work [e.g., of art] can become modern only if it is first postmodern. Thus understood, postmodernism is not modernism at its end, but in

---

3. See Barton (1998, 9–20) for a brief defense of the historical-critical method in the face of postmodern challenges.

a nascent state, and this state is recurrent" (Lyotard 1993, 12–13). Others write similarly:

> Postmodernism is not something "other" than modernism, as though they were two distinct historical eras or philosophical movements. Postmodernism cannot exist apart from modernism. Nevertheless, postmodernism does not uncritically accept the modern myth or its inclusions and exclusions. As noted previously, the basic mode of postmodernism is that of suspicion, and this includes, indeed it foregrounds, critical self-suspicion. It resists the desire for mythic metanarratives and prefers instead a multiplicity of partial, little narratives. (Aichele, Miscall, and Walsh 2009, 397–98)

Thus the same kind of suspicion that gave birth to modernity also drives the agenda of postmodernity.

Postmodernism in Biblical Studies

Postmodernism was still an "infant" in biblical studies at the beginning of the twenty-first century (Carroll 1998, 57). In several papers he presented at Society of Biblical Literature meetings in the mid-1980s, Gary Phillips first called attention to this emerging trend in literature and how it should help Bible critics rethink their work (S. D. Moore 2010, 9).[4] Stephen D. Moore began to write on literary criticism and poststructuralism around this time, and he became an important figure in the field.[5] In the 1990s, new seminars at professional meetings, journals, and monograph series were developed to explore innovative ways of reading the Bible. The journals *Semeia: An Experimental Journal for Biblical Criticism* (1972–2002) and *Biblical Interpretation: A Journal of Contemporary Approaches* (1993–),

---

4. One of the most important of these presentations was titled "The Authority of Exegesis and the Responsibility of the Critic: The Ethics and Ethos of Criticism" (Phillips 1989).

5. In 2010, the Society of Biblical Literature Resources for Biblical Study series published a collection of Moore's essays under the title *The Bible in Theory: Critical and Postcritical Essays*. Here he not only describes different approaches and discusses them but also shows how they work. Other important works are *Literary Criticism and the Gospels: The Theoretical Challenge* (1989); *Mark and Luke in Poststructuralist Perspectives: Jesus Begins to Write* (1992); and *Poststructuralism and the New Testament: Derrida and Foucault at the Foot of the Cross* (1994).

along with their respective monograph series, became the most prominent forums for the dissemination of postmodern approaches. Another important moment in the development of postmodern biblical criticism was the publication in 1995 of *The Postmodern Bible*. This volume was written by a group of writers who called themselves the Bible and Culture Collective. They introduced, illustrated, and critiqued seven prominent approaches to biblical criticism normally associated with postmodernism.

Probably the best place for a student to get a quick taste of how postmodern approaches actually influence the interpretation of the biblical text is through David J. A. Clines's fascinating article "Psalm 23 and Method: Reading a David Psalm" (2010). In this brief and highly interesting piece, Clines reads Psalm 23 from six different approaches, succinctly explains their methodologies, and illustrates how they influence the meaning of the text. Another good resource for sampling postmodern approaches is A. K. M. Adam's book *Postmodern Interpretations of the Bible: A Reader* (2001).

Postmodern Criticism and 1 Peter

John H. Elliot famously complained in 1976 that 1 Peter suffered "second-class status in the estimation of modern New Testament exegetes" (Elliott 1976, 243). He suggested that 1 Peter (together with other Catholic Epistles, Hebrews, and the Apocalypse of John) was benignly neglected as a "stepchild" of the New Testament canon. Nevertheless, a little more than two decades later he celebrated the "sizable body of research on 1 Peter" as he introduced his commentary on that epistle (Elliott 2000, 4).

This new interest in the letter has both increased the number of studies on its different aspects and incorporated new approaches to its study. Among the latter, probably the most important contribution has been the volume edited by Robert L. Webb and Betsy Bauman-Martin titled *Reading First Peter with New Eyes: Methodological Reassessments of the Letter of First Peter* (2007). From the point of view of methodology, this collection includes essays that fall naturally into three main groups: narrative criticism, rhetorical and socio-rhetorical criticism, and postcolonial criticism. The third group is normally considered a postmodern approach, and sometimes the first as well (Bible and Culture Collective 1995, 70–118). Beyond this volume, other scholars using postmodern approaches to 1 Peter have written from the perspective of feminist criticism.

In the following discussion I survey four postmodern methodologies and emphasize the way in which each methodology addresses the main concerns of postmodern criticism (foundations, totalities, and objectivity). I briefly describe the methodological approach, give an example of an essay that uses it, and consider the impact each approach has on the reading of 1 Peter.

Narratology: 1 Peter and the Impact of Its Narrative World on Contemporary Readers

Narratology is a method of analysis normally applied to narratives. It differentiates between (1) the events themselves (called *story*); (2) the narratives that have been told about those events (called *discourse*); and (3) the act of narrating those stories (referred to as *narrating*; Bible and Culture Collective 1995, 8). Narratology, then, is different from historical criticism in several ways. Historical critics are concerned with answering the question of what really happened. Thus they want to know the "real" or the "historical facts" behind any narrative. Historical critics want to approach as much as possible the "real event," the "objective fact." Narratology, however, is concerned with answering the question of what was said and how. Thus narratology is not concerned with the "real event" but with "the event as it was perceived." Its goal is not bringing into light the "objective fact" but putting "the perceived fact" under the microscope so as to analyze its plot, characterization, point of view, focalizers and defocalizers, and so on.[6]

Postmodern critics often assert that we do not have access to "real" or "objective" facts but only to "perceived" facts. Narratology highlights the difference between "real events" and "perceived events" by bringing into focus the difference between story, narrative, and narrating and the possible relationships among them (see Bible and Culture Collective 1995, 95–110). In fact, narratologists argue that "real events," those that happen outside the narrative, are either "irrelevant, unknowable, or methodologically off-limits" (Boring 2007, 22). Narratology is, then, amenable to the interests of postmodernity, which focuses more on the effects of texts, the political forces that shaped them, and the power interests they serve rather than on finding the "objective facts" behind those texts. Thus the tools

---

6. Focalizers and defocalizers are aspects of a narrative (or discourse) that we analyze to understand how the author wanted the events themselves to be perceived by the reader/audience.

of analysis that narratology provides are especially helpful to the goals of postmodernity.

M. Eugene Boring approaches 1 Peter from a narratological point of view in his article "Narrative Dynamics in First Peter: The Function of Narrative World" (2007). This is an interesting move because 1 Peter is not a narrative. He argues, however, that "1 Peter projects a narrative world composed of all the events it assumes to be real" and takes care to explain the methodology so as to identify that narrative world in the text (Boring 2007, 8).[7] He suggests that the narrative world of 1 Peter is a simple diachronic structure that "stretches from creation to consummation, with world history bifurcated into 'BC' and 'AD' by the revelation of Jesus Christ as the definitive denouement" (Boring 2007, 24). First Peter designates the first age as "once, previously" (*pote*, 2:10; 3:5, 20) and the second as "now" (*nyn*, 1:12; 2:10, 25; 3:21). He suggests that this narrative world compels "serious readers/hearers to examine their own understanding of reality" and invites them indirectly "to live their lives in the world projected by the letter" (Boring 2007, 8).

Boring identifies several benefits that this methodology provides to the study of 1 Peter. One is that narratology helps the interpreter better discern the author's strategy of communication. In other words, narratology provides an additional basis for rhetorical analysis. Another is that it helps us understand how 1 Peter fits in the canon of the New Testament. He argues that despite the variety of genres it contains, the Bible is held together by narrative, a single story line that includes numerous mini-narratives and subplots (Boring 2007, 35). So, even though 1 Peter is not a narrative, it projects a narrative world that is coherent with the grand narrative the Bible projects. Finally, another benefit that the narratological approach provides is that it gives new life to material that historical-critical methods had relegated to the category of "paraenesis"—advice or exhortation no longer relevant for modern readers. Bonnie Howe notes, "Boring's narratological approach helps explain the currency, the liveliness, and the challenge of 1 Peter for contemporary readers" (Howe 2009).

---

7. Boring had first outlined the narrative world of 1 Peter in appendix 1 (183–201) of his commentary on 1 Peter in the Abingdon New Testament Commentary series (1999).

Deconstruction: 1 Peter and Totalities

The goal of deconstruction is not to arrive at some sort of valid interpretation of the text. Instead, deconstruction's goal is to show us that "any interpretation, any sort of communication or even thinking entails serious risks, which we customarily avoid recognizing" (Adam 1995, 27). Deconstruction argues that any meaning, system, communication, or interpretation is not "natural" or "logical" but has, in fact, been created or constructed. Meanings or systems are built on the basis of binary oppositions, which make possible a process of construction through selection and exclusion (Bible and Culture Collective 1995, 120). The problem is that these oppositions are not natural, logical, or real but are determined on political or other grounds. Thus deconstruction searches for those points within a system that expose the non-natural, nonlogical, nonreal foundations of the system.

Deconstruction, then, does not have as its objective the creation of meaning but the deconstruction of meaning. Its purpose is to unmask incoherencies in the meanings suggested in a given reading, and in fact that meaning is not inherent in the text. "Meaning is what we make of texts, not an ingredient of texts" (Adam 1995, 27). This observation implies, then, that nobody holds "exclusive rights to legitimacy" in the interpretation of a text, that all of our interpretations are, in the final analysis, partial or biased. Yet deconstruction does not provide a better way to arrive at the unbiased meaning of something. Anything suggested could be in turn deconstructed. What deconstructionists want to promote is humility—awareness of the limitations of our own readings (see Bible and Culture Collective 1995, 129–31).

Betsy Bauman-Martin's article "Speaking Jewish: Postcolonial Aliens and Strangers in First Peter" (2007) provides a postcolonial reading of 1 Peter. Her article, however, is deconstructive before being postcolonial, and I will introduce it here as an example of a deconstructive reading of 1 Peter.

First Peter was written to believers who experienced imperialism (an ideology that legitimizes the economic and political control of one group by another) and colonialism (the settlement of the dominant group in the space or country of the dominated group, mostly with purposes of control). Bauman-Martin suggests that "the author of 1 Peter uses his letter primarily to define his readers as 'chosen' in order to strengthen their identity and enhance group cohesion in the face of local social harassment" (Bauman-Martin 2007, 160). This strategy is important, and the author uses it to help his readers resist the imperialistic power strategies of the Roman Empire in which they live as "exiles of the Dispersion" (1 Pet 1:1). Thus the creation of the binary oppositions "empire-subjugated" and "colonizer-colonized" is basic to the purpose of promoting resistance in 1 Peter.

Empires typically subjugate people, deprive them of freedom, inculcate the values of the empire, and seize the cultural heritage and property of the subjugated. The "empire/colonizer" normally has its own myth and an imperial ideology that validates its right to dominate and dispossess others. The irony, however, is that 1 Peter adapts the "chosen" language and other identity markers from Judaism as a strategy to resist the imperialist ideology of Rome. The letter itself, then, becomes an imperialistic, colonizing power toward Judaism. In this way, the author of 1 Peter "critiques and subverts the effects of imperialism that causes his readers to suffer, yet participates in the (colonizer-like) plundering of the cultural resources of another subaltern group [the Jews] solely for the purpose of the creation and maintenance of a superior identity" (Bauman-Martin 2007, 147). Thus Bauman-Martin claims that "1 Peter is a supersessionist text, and that supersessionism itself might be better understood from a postcolonial viewpoint as a strategy that posits an 'other' to better delineate one's own group, plunders the resources of a marginalized group to delineate the self in relation to the colonial power and leaves that other group in a position of no value or status" (Bauman-Martin 2007, 149–50).

First Peter appropriates several important identity markers of Judaism. Believers are the Jewish "Diaspora" (1 Pet 1:1). The Septuagint uses the term *paroikos* to refer to Israel as resident aliens in Egypt and to describe Abraham's life in Mesopotamia. The author of 1 Peter appropriates this term, however, to describe Christian believers (2:11). Believers are also the "household of God," a group that replaces the temple (4:17). Believers are now God's elect (1:1; 2:4–10; 5:13) and have been "sprinkled with his [Jesus'] blood," a reinterpretation of Jesus' death as the inauguration of the new covenant promised to Israel (1:2). Believers are the "royal priesthood" (2:5) and the Suffering Servant (2:21–25). The most aggressive example of this reappropriation is that 1 Peter uses the term "Gentile" to refer to anyone who does not believe Jesus is the Messiah.

Bauman-Martin has shown that the system built in 1 Peter on the binary opposition empire/subjugated or colonizer/colonized is in fact incoherent and inconsistent. The reading that promotes resistance and portrays Rome as a colonizing power in order to stimulate resistance actually masks, in fact, the colonizing actions of the subjugated. This is what deconstruction does. It brings into the open the cracks in the edifices of meaning we build.

Postcolonial Readings: 1 Peter and Political Legitimation

Postcolonial criticism engages the textual, historical, and cultural productions of societies that have been disturbed by the reality of a colonial power (Horrell 2007a, 119). Postcolonial criticism does not offer a "unified theoretical package" or model that can be unhesitatingly applied to texts. It is more properly an orientation, or a set of conceptual tools that help us understand the imperial/colonial situation and the relationships it produces. In biblical studies, it can take any of three directions. It may study the historical setting of the texts of early Judaism and Christianity in their imperial or colonial contexts, the history of biblical interpretation in the context of European colonial expansion, or the tendencies of contemporary readers in the context of centers of power. Some texts (or their interpretations) promote ideologies that legitimate imperial or colonial forces. Other texts (or their interpretations) foster ideologies that help victims resist imperialistic or colonizing powers. In short, postcolonial criticism analyzes how centers of power shape texts or their readings in one way or another. This approach is responsive to postmodern criticism, which claims that any text or any reading of a text has been shaped by political forces that often are hidden from immediate perception. Wittingly or unwittingly, every discourse promotes certain ideologies that benefit the interests of a class or a group.

David Horrell's article "Between Conformity and Resistance: Beyond the Balch-Elliott Debate Towards a Postcolonial Reading of First Peter" (2007a) suggests that a postcolonial approach could help one understand better the message of 1 Peter. During the 1980s, David L. Balch and John H. Elliott used social-scientific approaches to study the position of 1 Peter toward the Roman Empire, but they arrived at contrasting conclusions. Balch, on the one hand, suggested that 1 Peter used the domestic code (2:13–3:9) to urge Christians to conform as closely as possible to Hellenistic social forms without compromising their commitment to Christ. The church should, therefore, accommodate itself as much as possible to the world to reduce tensions with outsiders (Horrell 2007a, 113). Elliott, on the other hand, argued that 1 Peter fostered the internal cohesion of the community of believers in order to create a distinctive community identity that would help them resist the external pressures to conform (Horrell 2007a, 113). Where Balch saw assimilation and conformity, Elliott saw distinctiveness and resistance. This disagreement became one of the principal debates in the study of 1 Peter over the next twenty-five years (Dubis 2006, 212).

Horrell suggests that the approaches Balch and Elliott chose were not the most appropriate for the task because resistance to imperial or colonizing powers may take diverse and nuanced forms, and either/or answers do not do justice to its complexity. Horrell used as a point of departure the work of the political scientist James Scott, who has studied how subordinate groups and classes practice resistance. He notes that one of the forms of resistance is through "hidden transcripts," that is, "modes of discourse generally kept hidden from the public stage, where the official, sanctioned transcript dominates" (Horrell 2007a, 118). He also notes that Homi Bhabha, an influential postcolonial writer, has shown that the relationship between the colonizer and the colonized is characterized by the ambivalence and complexity of resistance and conformity at the same time (Horrell 2007a, 121–23). Horrell's analysis of 1 Peter suggests that the author urges the addressees to engage in an act of "polite resistance." This resistance takes subtle, malleable, and fluid forms that interweave a "hidden transcript" of resistance into a discourse apparently about conformity and obedience. The author's stance toward the empire can be compared, then, to one who "snarls sweetly" or practices "sly civility," but at times this resistance comes clearly and publicly into view.

Feminist Readings: 1 Peter and Objectivity

Political and/or ideological readings address the objectivity claims of modernism. They try to develop methods and strategies that lay bare the interest of any text or interpretation to promote certain ideologies in benefit of the interests of a class or a group. Suspicion, then, works as a heuristic tool: "interpreters who press you to accept their objectivity are probably concealing an ideological aim [or self-interest], whether consciously or unconsciously" (Adam 1995, 27). In other words, any composition or interpretation involves ideology that reinforces structures that oppress lower classes. Of course, this claim is itself open to the same critique since their interpretations also contain agendas that conceal the ideological aim of putting them in a privileged position of the knowledge of truth.

Feminist criticism is one of these political readings. It explores the interactions of power and gender in a text or its interpretation that function to build ideologies that support power structures. Its purpose is to demonstrate how readers can resist those constructions of power through critical engagement. Feminist criticism does not provide a unified approach or set of tools. It is more a set of political stances and strategies from which texts are read. Its particular contributions are shaped by the historical circumstances, political and theological alliances, social identities, institutional locations, and intellectual interests of the critic (Bible and Culture Collective 1995, 226–34).

The positioning of "man" at the center of objectivity, claiming for him the normative and universal position whose perspective is privileged and subsumes all others, is central to feminist critique. Womanist critique adds to the feminist critique the perspective of women of color, especially black women. It points out that "man" here does not refer to all males but to males of a certain race and class. Feminist approaches follow different strategies. Some attempt to retrieve from the Bible stories about specific women who can serve as strong role models and with whom contemporary women can identify. A second strategy extends its critique to social and political institutions (with their forces and processes of domination) and finds insights for survival in biblical texts. A third strategy challenges the philosophical grounds of biblical claims and takes as a starting point the assumption that biblical texts are androcentric and serve patriarchal functions. This strategy addresses more clearly postmodern concerns about the objectivity of modern discourse. Thus postmodern feminism attempts to undermine the philosophical hegemony of modernism by calling into question the androcentric terms of the argument. Postmodern feminism is less interested than other feminisms, however, in redemptive or recuperative actions. Its focus is on the ideological effects of biblical texts.

First Peter, in particular the household code (2:13–3:9), is especially fertile ground for postmodern feminist critique. *The Feminist Companion to the Catholic Epistles and Hebrews*, edited by Amy-Jill Levine with Maria Mayo Robbins (2004), provides a sample of various methods and reading styles that come under the broad umbrella of feminist critique. The volume contains ten essays, six of which are on 1 Peter. The essays by Warren Carter and James W. Aageson explore the expectations of slaves and women in the context of cultural and ethical pressures to conform. Magda Misset-van de Weg examines Sarah imagery in 1 Peter in light of presentations of Sarah in the Hebrew Bible and subsequent Jewish exegesis. Betsy J. Bauman-Martin surveys the appeal to 1 Peter in feminist theologies of suffering and their relation to current interpretations of instructions to women in the household code.

Conclusion

A cursory reading of literature on 1 Peter shows that scholars have focused mostly on genetic issues of the text (see Dubis 2006, 199–209). Who was the "real" author of 1 Peter? Was the letter written by the apostle or by another person who borrowed his name? From where did the author write? When was the letter written? Who were the addressees? Where did the addressees live? Is the letter a homogeneous or composite document? Did the author urge the readers to adopt or resist the cultural forces of the society in which they were immersed? These questions are certainly important.

Postmodern approaches, however, have driven the research on 1 Peter in a different direction. While modern approaches have mainly focused on the historical meaning of the text and its genesis, postmodern approaches have tried to pry open the political forces that have shaped interpretations of 1 Peter in order to focus attention on the current meaning of 1 Peter. Is the household code relevant to readers today, and if so, in what way? What are the political, cultural, and other forces that have shaped interpretation of 1 Peter in the past and present? What impact has 1 Peter had on contemporary culture and why? These questions are also important and deserve our consideration.

1 Peter in Patristic Literature

Andreas Merkt

For the church fathers, there was no doubt that the letter known to us as 1 Peter was written by the apostle himself. This authorship by Peter is why the letter was regarded from the second century onward as a text of special inspiration and authority.

Together with 1 John, it formed the germinating core of a group of letters that have been called the Catholic Epistles (Schlosser 2004). This designation has been in use since the third century and primarily refers to the status of those letters as accepted by the catholic church in contrast to those writings for which heretical groups claimed apostolic authority. The term *catholic* in this sense was almost equivalent to "canonical." In the sixth century, Leontius of Byzantium in his work *On Sects* came up with another explanation: "catholic" referred to the fact that these letters were not addressed to individual persons but to entire or even several communities (*De sectis* 2.4). "Catholic" (from Greek *kata*, "concerning," and *holon*, "the whole") could indeed mean something like "general" or "encyclical." Although it does not apply to 3 John and Jude, this explanation is supported by the symbolism of seven. The *Fragmentum Muratori* (or Muratorian Canon), a canon list probably from about 200 C.E. (although there are some scholars who date it later, to the third or fourth century), explains that Paul wrote letters to seven communities in order to emulate John, who in Revelation 2–3 also had addressed seven churches; seven thereby signified the church in its entirety (lines 56–59, in Hahnemann 1992). Analogously, the number seven might convey the universal, representative, "catholic" character of the Catholic Epistles since this number represented completeness in ancient thought and there are seven books in this corpus.

We learn from Eusebius of Caesarea, the author of the first *History of the Church*, that about the year 300 C.E. the status of these seven letters was still disputed. He testified that "the seven so-called catholic epistles ... have been read publicly in very many churches" (*Hist. eccl.* 2.23.25, *NPNF*[2] 1:128). However, he counted only 1 John and 1 Peter with certainty among the writings of the New Testament. The other five belong to the "disputed writings, which are nevertheless recognized" (*Hist. eccl.* 3.25.1–3, *NPNF*[2] 1:156).

These five letters were disputed because there were serious doubts that they were authored by the apostles whose names they bear. Despite these doubts, not only 1 Peter and 1 John but also the whole corpus of the seven letters carried the day. Athanasius, who in his Easter letter of 367 included them in his canon list, was probably influential in this respect. Another factor might have been the symbolic value of the number seven. In any case, we find them accepted in almost all churches all over the Mediterranean world at the turn to the fifth century.

There was, however, one notable exception. In Syria, the Catholic Epistles were missing from the canon until the middle of the fourth century. The Peshitta, which was formed in the first half of the fifth century and remains the standard Bible in all Syrian churches today, included only the three major Catholic Epistles (James, 1 Peter, and 1 John). While the East Syrian Nestorian Church has retained this canon, the other Syrian churches came to accept the shorter epistles as well in the sixth and seventh centuries.

The significance attributed to 1 Peter is reflected by its position within the corpus. In most Western lists, manuscripts, and commentaries, it is the first of the Catholic Epistles. This position might also be due to the outstanding role the apostle played in the Latin tradition. In the early Middle Ages, however, the West took over the mostly Eastern order that, in its turn, probably arose from Gal 2:9, where Paul (according to most Greek manuscripts) lists the "pillars" of the Jerusalem community with James heading and Peter and John following.

As a "catholic" epistle, 1 Peter also participates in the theological function of this corpus. According to Augustine, these letters were written to prevent a misunderstanding of Paul.

> As we said above, this opinion [that faith needs no works] originated in the time of the apostles, and that is why we find some of them, for example, Peter, John, James, and Jude, writing against it in their epistles and asserting very strongly that faith is no good without works. And as regards Paul himself, he does not say that any faith in God is good, but he

says clearly that that faith is good and in conformity with the teaching of the gospel which results in works of love: *and faith*, he says, *that worketh by charity*. As for that faith which some think is sufficient for salvation, he says that it profits nothing. (*Fid. op.* 21; Lombardo 1988, 29)

THE RECEPTION OF 1 PETER IN PATRISTIC LITERATURE: A SURVEY

Although 1 Peter was quoted as early as ca. 120/130 C.E. in Polycarp's *Letter to the Philippians* (e.g., Pol. *Phil.* 1.3, quoting 1 Pet 1:8; and 8.1, quoting 1 Pet 2:22, 24), Irenaeus was the first to refer explicitly to Peter as its author. In his work *Against the Gnostics* (*Adversus haereses*, ca. 180), he opposes the gnostic claims to secret revelations by resorting to the apostolic teaching as manifested in the writings read publicly in the churches, including 1 Peter. Some twenty years later, Clement of Alexandria wrote, as part of his *Hypotyposeis* (*Outlines*), the first brief commentary on 1 Peter. This commentary neither covers every verse nor provides comprehensive explanations. Instead, it offers brief "sketches," which is what *hypotyposeis* actually means. The first comprehensive commentary was written by Didymus of Alexandria in the fourth century.

The first Latin commentaries are late and almost as short and scarce as Clement's. Their authors are Cassiodor, an anonymous Irish interpreter, and an otherwise unknown Hilary in the sixth and seventh centuries. It took the Venerable Bede to produce the first full-fledged Latin commentary, around the year 700.

First Peter obviously did not suggest itself as a preferential object of exegesis, as it was used only occasionally. Some images, like the roaring lion for the devil, became popular idioms in patristic language. With its admonitions and encouragements, the letter lent itself especially to pastoral purposes in sermons and letters. In the liturgies, it was mostly read in the context of Easter and the teaching of catechumens and neophytes (Amphoux and Bouhot 1996: 53–74 [C. Renoux on Jerusalem and the Armenian tradition], 75–85 [B. Outtier on the Georgian liturgy]; 239–81 [J.-P. Bouhot on the Latin traditions]).

This liturgical placement demonstrates how the letter was generally understood: it was a letter about redemption, conversion, and its consequences (Merkt forthcoming). This understanding may be illustrated by the reception of two passages with controversial interpretations: Christ's preaching to the spirits in prison in 3:19 and the term *exemplum* applied to him in 2:21.

Christ's Preaching to the Spirits in Prison (1 Peter 3:19): Postmortem Rescue for the Pagan World?

In his letter to Paulinus, Jerome briefly characterizes the Catholic Epistles by writing, "The apostles James, Peter, John, and Jude, have published seven epistles at once spiritual and to the point, short and long, short that is in words but lengthy in substance so that there are few indeed who do not find themselves in the dark when they read them" (*Epist.* 53.9, *NPNF*² 6:102). One of those verses "short in words but lengthy in substance" and thus quite obscure is certainly 1 Pet 3:19, "he went and preached to the spirits in prison." The patristic authors puzzled about its meaning and arrived at quite diverse conclusions.

This verse was associated very early with the idea of Christ's descent into the netherworld, a common belief that found resonance in liturgical texts and creeds. In popular literature such as apocryphal Gospels, sermons, hymns, and mystery plays as well as in iconographical representations, the descent was imagined in picturesque scenes, with Christ talking to the god of the netherworld, breaking its portals, and liberating the dead (Gounelle 2000).

Most theologians, however, were more concerned with the biblical basis and the theological implications of the idea. Clement of Alexandria (ca. 200) was the first author to take 1 Pet 3:19 as a proof text for Christ's descent into the netherworld (*Strom.* 6.6). Most of the Eastern tradition and in particular the other Alexandrians (Origen, Athanasius, and Cyril) followed him. Nevertheless, there was disagreement concerning the identity of the spirits in prison, and this disagreement also pertained to the question of universal salvation.

Clement was quite optimistic. He was sure that Christ—by preaching to the souls in the netherworld—had extended his saving power to those Hebrews who had lived before his incarnation. But what about the just among the heathens? Clement's standpoint is clear.

> And, as I think, the Savior also exerts His might because it is His work to save; which accordingly He also did by drawing to salvation those who became willing, by the preaching [of the gospel], to believe on Him, wherever they were. If, then, the Lord descended to Hades for no other end but to preach the Gospel, as He did descend; it was either to preach the Gospel to all or to the Hebrews only. If, accordingly, to all, then all who believe shall be saved, although they may be of the Gentiles, on

making their profession there; since God's punishments are saving and disciplinary, leading to conversion, and choosing rather the repentance than the death of a sinner; and especially since souls, although darkened by passions, when released from their bodies, are able to perceive more clearly, because of their being no longer obstructed by the paltry flesh. (*Strom.* 6.6.46, *ANF* 2:490–91)

With this interpretation Clement set off a long and robust line of tradition in the East. Many authors understood 1 Pet 3:19 as speaking of Christ's descent into Hades, where he freed the souls of the just of the Old Testament and perhaps even the just of the pagan world. While most authors only thought of the just who had died before Christ's advent, authors such as Origen (*Princ.* 2.5.3; *Cels.* 2.43; *Comm. Jo.* 6.35; *Comm. Matt.* 132) and Maximus the Confessor (*Quaestiones ad Thalassium* [*Questions and Answers Given to Thalassios*] 7) drew an even more far-reaching conclusion, namely, that conversion after death was possible. Otherwise, they argued, there would have been no point in preaching to the dead.

Origen (in the texts given above) also linked 1 Pet 3:19 with the idea of *apokatastasis panton*, the teaching that all created intelligence will be restored to God at the end of time. Although he seems to have pronounced this view as a matter of speculation, not of dogma, it came to be one of the tenets associated with the "Origenist heresy." Nevertheless, the descent interpretation of 1 Pet 3:19 lives on in the East until the present day since it was not necessarily intertwined with the idea of universal salvation.

In the West, the descent interpretation came to an end when Filastrius of Brescia included it in his list of heresies in the late fourth century (*Liber de haeresibus* [*Book on Heresies*] 125 [97].1), and some years later Augustine provided the theological and exegetical argument for this categorization. The bishop of Hippo had to deal with the verse in the early fifth century when his friend Euodius, bishop of Uzalis, asked him for his opinion concerning the exegesis of 1 Pet 3:19. For Augustine, one fact was beyond question: Christ descended into hell. Indeed, Peter taught this, not in his letter, but in his sermon at Pentecost (Acts 2:24–27). According to Augustine, however, it cannot be proven from the Bible that Christ freed anyone other than the just of the Old Testament.

Although Augustine thus was sure that Christ had descended into the netherworld, it left him "perplexed" how someone could find this doctrine in 1 Pet 3:19. In his opinion, the very next verse clearly contradicts such an interpretation. There, Peter speaks about the unbelievers in the time of Noah. "If he [Jesus] preached to all," Augustine asked, "why has Peter mentioned only these, and passed over the innumerable multitude of others?" (*Ep.* 164.1 [2], *NPNF*¹ 1:515).

Hence, verse 20 made clear that the spirits were none other than the people in the time of Noah. "Spirits" here designates "souls which were at that time still in the bodies of men, and which, being shut up in the darkness of ignorance, were, so to speak, 'in prison,'—a prison such as that from which the Psalmist sought deliverance in the prayer, 'Bring my soul out of prison, that I may praise Thy name' [Ps 142:7]" (*Ep.* 164.5 [16], *NPNF*¹ 1:519). Christ before his incarnation had visited humankind several times, not in his body but spiritually. The cryptic verse thus has a simple "historical" meaning: Christ came to the people in the age of Noah.

According to Augustine, however, there is more to it: what happened then with the flood and the ark also has a typological meaning that is expressed in the ensuing verse 21: "This prefigured baptism, which saves you now." The flood thus served as a *typos*, an image prefiguring baptism. In patristic literature, 1 Pet 3:21 was indeed often employed to legitimize a typological understanding of the flood as symbolizing the baptism in which all sins were washed away. Augustine, however, drew from this verse and from several others a far-reaching conclusion that was to exert a tremendous impact on the history of Western Christianity: baptism is necessary for salvation. Whoever dies without having been baptized and without having joined the church stands no chance of entering heaven, just as all humankind except the eight persons in the ark (an image of the church) were destroyed in the flood.

Is Christ an Example Only?
The Problem of Grace and Freedom (1 Peter 2:21)

While Augustine used 1 Peter to underline the necessity of baptism, another passage in the same letter helped him demonstrate the insufficiency of this sacramental act. First Peter 2:21 reads: "For you Christ suffered, leaving you an example, so that you may follow his footsteps." Augustine quoted this verse in a sermon from the year 397. This was said, he explained, against those who believe that in order to be Christian, it suffices to be baptized and go to church. Following in the *forma sacramenti* ("the form of the sacrament"), that is, by receiving the sacraments, is not enough, argued Augustine. One must follow Christ in *opere exempli* ("in the work of his example"), that is, by acting as he did, as well (*Serm.* 37).

Augustine was not alone in resorting to 1 Pet 2:21. Indeed, this verse became quite popular in sermons of that time. The general historical background explains why. For decades the church had been supported by the emperors, and some years earlier Christianity had gained the status of a state religion. Hence, many people entered the church for opportunistic reasons. Some might also have been attracted by the promise of an easy way of salvation through baptism. Jerome stated: "After the emperors had begun to support the church the Christians grew in number but lost their moral power" (*Vit. Malch.* 1, in Mierow 1946).

Preachers tried to oppose this tendency by highlighting the moral obligations implied in conversion to Christianity. This tendency was also what motivated the Pelagians, a group of thinkers named after Pelagius, an ascetic from Britain who in the early fifth century had become influential in the Roman upper class. Between 411 and 420, several early Pelagian authors quoted the verse to emphasize that one must imitate Christ by living according to high moral standards (e.g., *De divitiis* [*On Wealth*] 9.5; *De castitate* [*On Chastity*] 6.91; *Epistula ad quondam matronam* [*Letter to a Matron*] 1). It was so popular among the Pelagians because it fit their theology, and thus it was not only used in exhortations but also in theological tractates.

In particular, Julian, bishop of Eclanum in southern Italy, exploited the verse dogmatically, as we know from Augustine's work *Against Julian*, where he amply quotes from his Pelagian counterpart. Julian had uttered a basic conviction that all Pelagians shared: *Homo libero arbitrio emancipatus a deo* (*C. Jul.* 1.78), meaning that humans are emancipated from God, set free from God's tutelage, because God has endowed them with a free will to decide for doing good or evil works. This idea diametrically opposed the widespread doctrine of original sin, according to which sin has become so much a part of human nature that no one is capable of making free decisions and acts without the help of God's grace.

To refute this doctrine of original sin, which was strongly advocated by Augustine, Julian quoted 1 Pet 2:21 together with the ensuing sentence, the citation from Isaiah: "He did not commit sin, nor was deceit found on his lips" (1 Pet 2:22). Like others before him, Julian found this statement confirmed by the Lord's saying, "The prince of this world comes, and he finds nothing in me" (John 14:30).

What was new with Julian was that he turned 1 Pet 2:22, which speaks of Christ's sinlessness, into an argument against natural sin in general. He asserted that Peter

> did not say: He assumed no sin, but: *He committed no sin*. ... If he had any thought of natural evil, he would have more carefully and precisely mentioned this point and would have written: Christ left us an example; he neither committed sin, nor did he inherit the sin which we contract by being born. ... But if the apostle had this in mind, he would never have made mention of his example. After all, whom would he have presented to human beings for their imitation, if the nature of a strange flesh set him apart and if the difference of his substance undermined the severity of his teaching? (*C. Jul.* 4.85–86)[1]

We see how Julian employed the call to follow in Christ's footsteps as an argument against natural sin (*in natura crimen, peccatum per naturale virus, naturale malum, peccatum naturale*): Christ can only be seriously set as an example before us if he shared our starting conditions. That means one of two things. If there is a *peccatum naturale* in us, then there is natural sin in Christ as well. This conclusion was, according to Julian, unthinkable. But this is how far, in his eyes, Augustine's impiety had gone. If Christ was born with a sinless nature, Julian reasoned, then we too must have been born without sin. Hence, there cannot be natural sin. "And so it is established," Julian concluded, "that there is no innate sin, since Christ had none, who without loss to the honor of his deity became incarnate in order that he might be imitable by us" (*C. Jul.* 4.87).

Augustine's reply was twofold. On the one hand, he dismissed Julian's *argumentum e silentio* ("argument from silence"): "When he [Peter] was, of course, proposing to human beings an example in Christ for their imitation, what need was there for the apostle Peter to say anything about original sin" (*C. Jul.* 4.86). On the other hand, Augustine tried to lead Julian's argument *ad absurdum* ("to an absurdity"). Of course, imitation cannot be related to anything beyond our will. Our nature, however, is beyond our will. We cannot cause it to be that we are born without sin as Christ was, in the same way that we cannot cause it to be that we were "born as he was born of the Holy Spirit and the Virgin Mary." But the question remains: if we are born in sin, how can we imitate Christ at all? "In order to imitate Christ," Augustine said, "our will is reformed, but in order to be free from original evil, our nature is reborn" (*C. Jul.* 4.86). Hence, natural sin does not necessarily preclude, as Julian insinuated, that we follow Christ's example.

---

1. All translations of *Against Julian* (*C. Jul.*) are from the edition of Teske 1999.

While Augustine was directly replying to a Pelagian in his *Against Julian*, we find traces of the Pelagian controversy in other nonspecific writings as well, including his preaching. Whereas in his sermon of 397 he had felt no need to emphasize that imitating Christ presupposes grace, the case was quite different when, some twenty years later in *Serm*. 284, he again quoted the same verse. Here too he emphasized that Christ taught not only by words but also by giving an example. But now, however, Augustine added that Christ's teaching, namely his hanging on the cross, was at the same time the work of a physician, a *medicus*: "He was hanging there [on the cross], and healing them." He healed by begging his father to forgive those who "do not know what they are doing [Lk 23:34]. ... With his blood he was making a medicine [*medicamentum*]" (*Serm*. 284.6, Hill 1994).

Augustine then proceeded to present Peter as the prototype of those following in Christ's footsteps. At first Peter was presumptuous. He felt self-confident and thought himself capable of following Christ, but he betrayed him. "Peter had in fact presumed on his strength, had trusted in his own strength, not on the grace of God, but in his capacity to choose [*de libero arbitrio*]." Then the Lord looked at him, and he sent his Spirit. Peter became a witness. From the example of Peter, Augustine draws the general conclusion: "So, my brothers and sisters, let us imitate, as far as we can, the example of the Lord in his passion. We shall be able to carry this out if we ask him for his assistance, not by going ahead of him, like Peter in his self assurance; but by following him and praying to him, like Peter, when he was making progress" (*Serm*. 284.6, Hill 1994).

With Augustine and even more after him, *exemplum et sacramentum* ("example and sacrament") became an anti-Pelagian slogan (Studer 1975, 124–39). Christ through his passion and dying is not only an example but also a saving mystery. Leo the Great explicitly linked this slogan with the passage from 1 Peter. In *Serm*. 63, held on Wednesday of Holy Week 452, he said: "Our Savior, the son of God, gave both a mystery [*sacramentum*] and an example to all who believe in him, so that they might attain the one by being reborn, and arrive at the other by imitation. Blessed Peter the apostle teaches this." Then followed the quote of 1 Pet 2:21–24. Although Leo did not comment on this passage, we may assume that he found the sacramental aspect of Christ's passion in verse 24: "He himself bore our sins in his own body on the cross, so that, dead to sin, we might live for holiness" (*Serm*. 63.4, Leo the Great 1996).

These findings may be quite predictable: Pelagianism influenced the reception of 1 Pet 2:21 with its key term *exemplum* (Greek *hypogrammon*).

However, the debate about the term *example* cannot be reduced to the Pelagian controversy. The christological and soteriological interpretation of Christ's depiction as example or paradigm in 1 Peter is considerably older than the Pelagian controversy.

The history of a christological reading of 1 Pet 2:21 begins as early as the third century, when Origen gave a homily on Joshua 8 and explicated the twofold wood mentioned there. The "king of Ai" was said "to be hanged on the twofold wood" (Josh 8:29). "In this place," Origen commented, "a mystery is hidden very deeply. But with your prayers we shall attempt to uncover these things, not from our opinions but from the testimonies of divine Scripture" (*Hom. Jes. Nav.* 8.3, Origen 2002).

The twofold wood prefigured the "double reason for the cross of the Lord." One reason is stated by Peter in his letter: Christ was crucified to leave behind an example for us. The other reason is mentioned in Col 2:14–15: "What was contrary to us, he bore away from the midst, fixing it to his own cross; stripping principalities and authorities, he exposed them openly to public ridicule, triumphing over them on the wood of the cross." The cross thus is a "token of victory over the Devil." Both aspects of the cross were mentioned by Paul in Gal 6:14, where he says: "Let me not glory except in the cross of my Lord Jesus Christ, through whom the world has been crucified to me and I to the world." "You see," Origen commented, "that even here the Apostle brought forth a twofold understanding of the cross. For he says, that for him, two opposing things have been crucified: himself as a saint and the world as a sinner" (*Hom. Jes. Nav.* 8.3, Origen 2002).

Thus, long before Augustine and other anti-Pelagian authors, Origen demonstrated that in 1 Pet 2:21 one finds expressed only one aspect of the passion of Christ: the visible example he gave for imitation. This aspect has to be supplemented by resorting to other verses, with the invisible aspect: the victory over the devil and over sin.

Conclusion

In a generalizing (and thus inevitably simplifying) way, we may say that patristic reception of 1 Peter centers on redemption, conversion, and the consequences for the Christian. This description applies not only to the two passages whose reception I have tried to sketch but also to several other themes, among them most notably the priesthood of the faithful. This theme designates the outstanding dignity of the Christians as part of the body of Christ, the one and only priest mediating between God and humanity (Sandevoir 1980, 219–29).

The two case studies also suggest some remarks on patristic interpretation of biblical texts in general:

(1) It is misleading to talk in absolutes about patristic interpretation of the Bible as if the "church fathers" formed a homogenous group always agreeing with one another. A supposed consensus of the fathers often proves to be a construct of later times. *In most cases, we encounter a diversity of patristic readings.* The interpretation of Christ's preaching to the spirits in prison, for example, demonstrates that one and the same verse could inspire even contradicting readings (supporting universal salvation, or supporting salvation for the baptized only).

(2) *Interpretation is obviously dependent on rather accidental factors.* Not only the theological presuppositions of a specific church father but also his temperament and character may determine a specific exegesis. The literary genre also shapes the way a biblical text is received. A commentary or a theological tractate is usually more complex; it weighs the pros and cons of several interpretations, whereas sermons or letters with their particular purposes tend to favor eclectic and one-sided receptions. The wider historical and cultural background also plays a role with its changing pastoral demands and varying theological challenges. Augustine preached differently on Christ as *exemplum* after the Pelagians had come to the fore. Clement embraced the idea of universal salvation as an erudite member of a religious minority in the multicultural city of Alexandria, whereas two centuries later Augustine tried to strengthen the ties of the new state religion by stressing the need for baptism and church affiliation when he felt that Christian identity was seriously jeopardized from both inside and outside the church. Indeed, the patristic era provided countless soundboards that gave a variety of different sounds and resonances—sometimes amplifying, sometimes distorting—to the voices of the New Testament.

(3) *Nevertheless, occasionally there is to be found a timeless consensus.* Authors as different with regard to character, theological principles, and historical conditions as Origen and Augustine arrived at the same interpretation of the term *exemplum* ascribed to Christ in 1 Pet 2:21. Such cases of consensus may indicate a meaning of the text itself in a certain sense independent of its recipient. The biblical text itself seems to imply and supply a range of explanations that are made explicit on special occasions. (By the way: if there is no good survey at hand for the reception of a certain biblical passage, it is feasible to read at least Origen and Augustine.

In most cases one finds with them the most original and comprehensive discussion. And whenever they agree—although often they do not—it is almost certain that most other patristic authors do as well.)

(4) *Such consensus readings might be due to the fact that the patristic authors basically used the same exegetical method.* Patristic authors are sometimes blamed for their "atomistic" reading of the Bible because they single out certain verses to prove their preconceived opinions without considering the immediate context. Indeed, in some cases this criticism is justified. The examples I presented above, however, prove that most authors knew how to take the context into consideration. What really marks their approach is that they considered the literary context of the Bible to be more important than the historical situation that had caused the production of a special text that later became part of the canon. They took the immediate context into consideration. Augustine's interpretation of Christ's preaching was based on the ensuing verses, and Leo suggested that 1 Pet 2:21 has to be read in combination with 2:24, alluding to Christ's sacramental function. But they cast their net more widely: not only the immediate context but also the whole Bible provides the frame of reference for understanding a single verse or word. First Peter 2:21 may be counterbalanced, as we learn from Origen, by the verses from Colossians and Galatians. The ancient Christian authors applied a kind of mental system of "hyperlinks": whenever they clicked on a biblical verse or term, a window opened offering helpful links to other biblical passages. Some links only serve to corroborate an obvious understanding of a passage. That is the function, for example, of 1 John 3:16 to 1 Pet 2:21 and vice versa. Other links offer checks and balances, such as what Gal 6:14 and Col 2:14–15 do for 1 Pet 2:21. This method constrains the impact of a single suggestive verse by directly linking it hypertextually with other verses that only in the linear structure of the material Bible seem to be remote. The mechanism of mutual elucidations of various verses reduces opportunities for exegetical tyranny or monopoly. It is aimed at maintaining balance of interpretation within the canon. One verse (or better, the meaning it seems to have at first glance) is checked by other verses.

(5) *This method* that takes the entire Bible as the decisive frame of reference for interpreting single passages *reflects a certain hermeneutics that we may call a canonical approach.* For the church fathers, the whole Bible formed one "body of the truth," and every verse and expression had to be understood from "its proper position" within this body (Irenaeus, *Adversus haereses* 1.9.4). All parts of it are interlinked because behind the vari-

ous human writers, there is one and the same author at work: the divine Spirit (e.g., Origen, *Princ.* 4.1; *Comm. Jo.* 5.5–6; Augustine, *Enarrat. Ps.* 103.4.1). This conviction of divine inspiration yields another consequence for interpreting the Bible: one must rely on the help of the same divine Spirit to grasp it (e.g., Origen, *Comm. Matt.* 16.11). Hence, the fathers recommend that the canonical reading be accompanied by praying when searching for the meaning of an obscure biblical text.

Biblical and Nonbiblical Traditions in Jude and 2 Peter: Sources, Usage, and the Question of Canon

Eric F. Mason

The authors of Jude and 2 Peter make ample use of texts and traditions from books that have long been classified as either "biblical" or "nonbiblical." In addition, the author of 2 Peter demonstrates knowledge of Jesus traditions similar to those in the Gospels and also an awareness of Paul's letters. This chapter focuses on three major questions. First, what biblical and nonbiblical sources have the authors of Jude and 2 Peter used? Second, how are these sources utilized? Third, how might these authors have understood the concept of "canon"?

Admittedly this third question must be approached cautiously so as not to make the anachronistic mistake of reading later assumptions and notions of canon back onto these New Testament texts. Indeed, some scholars would argue that this question reveals more about the concerns of later readers than the concerns of the ancient authors themselves. Alternately, other scholars would question whether the term *canon* is appropriate for such an investigation and instead would ask if an ancient interpreter considered a particular text "authoritative." The rationale for such a position is that certain texts could be very highly esteemed and function as authoritative literature if they circulated before canon became a widespread concept, or even if they were not deemed canonical but nevertheless persisted alongside canonical literature.[1] Still other scholars assert that

---

[1]. Examples include the importance of *Jubilees* and the *Protevangelium of James*. The former is essentially an interpretative rewriting of Genesis-Exodus that was read alongside the books of the Pentateuch by the community responsible for the Dead Sea Scrolls (and others). The latter is a noncanonical Gospel that describes the miraculous birth and perpetual virginity of Mary, doctrines that are very important in some Christian traditions despite the silence about such things in the New Testament.

Judaism had already settled on the contents of its canonical Scriptures and that the early church simply inherited this canon and already had a clearly delineated understanding of which books were canonical and which were not in the New Testament era.

The question here concerns what we may infer about how the authors of Jude and 2 Peter understood the sources they used. It is important to remember, however, that use of what ultimately were deemed nonbiblical traditions (especially the prophecy attributed to Enoch in Jude 14–15) was a major point of contention for several centuries as early church leaders debated whether these epistles were worthy of inclusion in the New Testament canon. (See the chapter in this volume on patristic reception of Jude and 2 Peter by Wolfgang Grünstäudl and Tobias Nicklas.) Thus these questions of canon have raised the interest of both ancient and modern interpreters. Also important is the observation that even today there is no one "Old Testament" canon for Christianity, as Orthodox, Catholic, and Protestant Christians use differing collections, so diversity of thought about such matters among ancient churches should not be surprising.

The discussion of the sources used by the authors of Jude and 2 Peter includes the question of the literary relationship between the two books themselves. Various positions have been articulated in the history of New Testament scholarship to explain this relationship, and Jeremy F. Hultin addresses the issue in depth elsewhere in this volume. It will suffice here to affirm the modern consensus that the author of 2 Peter used Jude as a source. One must remember, however, that this relationship does not mean that the authors of the two epistles ultimately have the same outlook or address the same sorts of problems. Indeed, one notices several differences in how these authors use their source traditions, both in passages where the author of 2 Peter is indebted to Jude and elsewhere.

Jude

This investigation begins with Jude, an extremely short but fiery missive that "verse for verse … includes more denunciations and condemnations than any passage of equivalent length in the NT" (Brosend 2008, 3:442).[2] The epistle is attributed to "Jude [literally *Ioudas*, or Judas], a slave [*doulos*]

---

2. See Wasserman 2006 for a thorough study of the manuscript evidence for Jude. Nicholas J. Moore (2013, 510) proposes that the short length of the book and the obscure nature of both the content and figure of Jude adversely affected the recep-

of Jesus Christ and brother of James [literally *Iakōbos*, or Jacob]." Almost all scholars understand this fraternal reference as intended to denote James the Just, that is, James the brother of Jesus (Mark 6:3//Matt 13:55; Acts 12:17; 15:13; 21:18; 1 Cor 15:7; Gal 1:19–2:12). Thus Jude would also be the Lord's brother (*Iouda* in Mark 6:3//*Ioudas* in Matt 13:55). The present discussion does not hinge on one's decision about whether this text was written by Jude or else is pseudepigraphic (see the chapter by Lewis R. Donelson in this volume). Scholarly opinion is roughly divided, and often those who opt for pseudepigraphy do so cautiously. Instead, what matters is the identity that is *asserted*.

The letter's attribution implies the authority of the brother of Jesus, yet the epistle includes no explicit appeal to the words or life of Jesus. Admittedly the Epistle of James also lacks direct appeals to Jesus traditions, although it has materials similar to some sayings in the Gospels. As will be discussed later, however, this lack of explicit appeal to Jesus traditions in Jude stands in sharp contrast to how the author of 2 Peter grounds that epistle's authority in the apostle's eyewitness testimony and experiences with Jesus.

Indeed, the closest analogy in Jude to such an appeal is found in verses 17–18: "But you, beloved, must remember the predictions of the apostles of our Lord Jesus Christ; for they said to you, 'In the last time there will be scoffers, indulging their own ungodly lusts.'"[3] The author distinguishes Jude from the "apostles" ("*they* said to you"), but in doing so he also validates the authenticity of apostolic prophecy by pitching it in continuity with the certain words of God's earlier prophet Enoch (albeit from a book that now is usually considered nonbiblical; see below). The expectation of rebellious behavior in the last days is a very common apocalyptic motif in the New Testament (as discussed by Kelley Coblentz Bautch in her chapter in this volume), and commentators debate whether use in verse 18 of the imperfect *elegon* (literally "they were saying," but normally translated "they said" as in the NRSV and NIV) means that the author was emphasizing the repeated nature of such predictions. In light of how the author presents this statement in parallel with earlier prophetic words, one might

---

tion of the book in the early church (before the citation of Enoch became viewed as problematic).

3. All Scripture quotations are from the NRSV unless otherwise noted.

also suggest that he intends the apostolic statement to be heard as a Spirit-inspired utterance of early Christian prophecy.[4]

As with other New Testament writers, the author of Jude is steeped in language reminiscent of the Scriptures.[5] Even with consideration of its short length, however, the epistle surprisingly lacks any certain, explicit biblical quotations. Instead, its several uses of biblical examples (characters and events) reflect theological developments common in Second Temple–period Jewish interpretation and are interwoven with materials from nonbiblical texts.[6] Indeed, the epistle's *only* explicit literary quotation (setting aside the apostolic prediction noted above) is from the Book of the Watchers, the first section of a group of Enochic materials collected as *1 Enoch*, a book today normally classified among the Pseudepigrapha.[7] This quotation of *1 En.* 1:9 appears in Jude 14–15, and one finds elsewhere in Jude other allusions to the Book of the Watchers (*1 En.* 1–36) and perhaps other Enochic materials.[8]

---

4. Bauckham (1983, 8) finds a similar situation elsewhere and suggests that v. 11 may be "a quotation from an oracle of a Christian prophet."

5. Several scholars argue that the author of Jude read the Hebrew rather than the Septuagint and made independent translations into Greek for use in the letter (see especially Bauckham 1983, 7, but also the response of Davids 2006, 26). See Carson 2007a for detailed discussion of biblical allusions in Jude and Carson 2007b for the same in 2 Peter.

6. Davids asserts that "every reference to narrative material in 2 Peter and Jude that can be checked reveals that the narrative is being read through the lens of what is known to modern readers as Second Temple literature" (2009, 407). See also Davids 2004.

7. The Ethiopian Orthodox Church is an exception, as it considers both *1 Enoch* and *Jubilees* to be canonical. For a recent discussion of the use and status of these books in contemporary EOC liturgy and thought, see Baynes 2012.

8. The several "booklets" collected in what today is called *1 Enoch* originally circulated independently: the Book of the Watchers (chs. 1–36), the Book of Parables (or Similitudes, chs. 37–71), the Astronomical Book (or Book of the Luminaries, chs. 72–82), the Book of Dreams (chs. 83–90), and the Epistle of Enoch (chs. 91–108). They were composed in Aramaic—the Watchers and Astronomical Books as early as the third century B.C.E., the Parables possibly as late as the first century C.E.—and all but the Parables are found among the Dead Sea Scrolls. Some sections also survive in Greek translation, but the five booklets are collected as a unified text only in Ethiopic manuscripts dating since the fifteenth century C.E. The related Book of the Giants is also extant in the scrolls; J. T. Milik famously argued that at Qumran this booklet stood in place of the Parables, but he found few followers. See J. J. Collins 2010, 585 (but note the typographical error for the chapters of the Astronomical Book) and

Jude opens with standard epistolary features (identification of the author, a vague description of the recipients, and a greeting in vv. 1–2) followed by brief comments about the purpose of the letter and the antinomian opponents whose threat prompted the author to write. Verse 4 is particularly significant. The author lists the errors of the opponents "who pervert the grace of our God into licentiousness and deny our only Master and Lord, Jesus Christ," and he also asserts that they "long ago were designated [*progegrammenoi*] for this condemnation as ungodly." The term *prographō* (used in v. 4 as a perfect participle) literally means "write beforehand" (BDAG 867), and some interpreters find here an allusion to specific documents, whether earlier Christian texts, heavenly books (a reasonable suggestion given Jude's apocalyptic influences), or the Jewish Scriptures (along with the prophecy of Enoch; see Carson 2007a, 1069–70, for discussion). If such specificity is intended, a reference to Scripture (in a collective sense) seems most likely in light of the argumentation that follows in the epistle, even if the author of Jude works with examples from Scripture and Jewish tradition rather than explicit biblical quotations.

In Jude 5–7, the author begins to explain this certain judgment on his opponents by noting three examples of God's actions in the past, followed by his comments about the applicability of these examples for his opponents. But, however, the nature of the traditions he cites has prompted much discussion. The first example (v. 5) concerns God's judgment on the wilderness generation of the exodus; he destroyed those who did not enter Canaan at the first opportunity because they "did not believe." Similarly, the third example (in v. 7) recalls God's destruction of Sodom and Gomorrah, which "serve as an example by undergoing a punishment of eternal fire." Such examples of destruction presumably point to the fate of those whom the author of Jude opposes.

Both of these examples have clear referents in the Pentateuch, but they surround a second example whose origins (in the form cited) lie elsewhere, in Second Temple–period traditions about God's judgment on the Watchers (i.e., the fallen angels).[9] The author of Jude writes: "And the angels who did not keep their own position, but left their proper dwelling, he has kept

---

Nickelsburg 2000, 1:249–53. Bauckham (1983, 7) asserts that the author of Jude demonstrates knowledge of all five booklets of *1 Enoch* except perhaps the Parables and Epistle.

9. See Harkins, Coblentz Bautch, and Endres 2014 for a broad survey of Watchers traditions in Jewish and Christian literature. My chapter in that volume (Mason 2014)

in eternal chains in deepest darkness for the judgment of the great day" (v. 6). This tradition ultimately derives from Gen 6:1–4, but with considerable development. The imprisonment of the Watchers is not mentioned there but became a standard assumption for Second Temple–period interpreters of this passage, most notably in the Enochic Book of the Watchers.

While the author of Jude undoubtedly chose these particular examples because he thought they best conveyed his point, it is also interesting to note that appeals to these three stories are common in Second Temple-period literature. In fact, they are among a small group of "stock" examples that cluster in the following groups: Watchers or giants (the offspring of the Watchers and human women); the flood generation; Sodom and Gomorrah; and the wilderness generation (including themes like the spies, Kadesh, and Korah's rebellion).[10] Of these, the Watchers (or giants) and Sodom examples very frequently appear together, and in Jude their association is particularly close.

Bauckham (1983, 46–47, 54) notes that these examples are linked grammatically by *hōs ... homoion* ("just as ... likewise" in RSV; NRSV has changed the sentence structure), with the sin both of the Watchers and Sodom and Gomorrah doubly defined in verse 7 as sexual immorality (from the broad [*ek*]*porneuō* root) and going after *sarkos heteras*. The latter phrase is best translated as "strange flesh" (so KJV and NASB). This rendering is much preferable to "unnatural lust" (RSV/NRSV; NAB "unnatural vice") and especially "perversion" (NIV) because these latter translations obscure the boundary-crossing aspect of the sexual contact involving angels and humans that characterizes both examples.

The author of Jude turns to address the nature of his opponents in verse 8 and charges "these dreamers" with defiling the flesh, rejecting authority, and slandering (or reviling) the "glories" (presumably spiritual or celestial beings).[11] These three charges reflect the offenses in the three examples in

---

addresses these traditions in 1–2 Peter and Jude; some discussion of Jude and 2 Peter there and here appears in similar form.

10. See the chart in Bauckham 1983, 46, which details the examples (including a few falling outside the traditional clusters) listed in Sir 16:7–10; CD 2:17–3:12; *3 Macc.* 2:4–7; *T. Naph.* 3:4–5; *m. Sanh.* 10:3; 2 Pet 2:4–8; and the present passage. Use of these examples in Jude and 2 Peter admittedly is distinctive because they function as types for contemporary antitypes encountered by the recipients of the letters, not warnings about the personal conduct of the letters' recipients themselves.

11. Jude does not explain the nature of this slander by his antinomian opponents, but see the appealing suggestion of Davids (2006, 62): "The false teachers slander

verses 5–7, but not with clear one-to-one correlations. The strongest link is the statement in Jude 8 that the false teachers "defile [*miainousin*] the flesh." Here the author of Jude likely alludes to the frequent comments in the Book of the Watchers that the fallen angels "defile themselves" (*miainesthai*) with women.[12]

The arrogance of Jude's villains is contrasted in verse 9–10 with the respect the archangel Michael showed even to the devil. The reference here almost certainly is to a pseudepigraphical tradition about the disposal of Moses' corpse from the lost ending of *Assumption* (or the *Testament*) *of Moses* (see detailed discussion in Bauckham 1983, 65–76; G. L. Green 2008, 80–84). Yet the statement attributed to Michael (*epitimēsaisoi kyrios*, "the Lord rebuke you!") also corresponds well to God's rebuke of the devil in Zech 3:2 LXX (*epitimēsai kyrios en soi*), when Satan opposes the high priest Joshua in Zechariah's vision (G. L. Green 2008, 81). The closest thing to a direct quotation in the epistle of what today would be considered canonical Scripture thus appears within an example from a nonbiblical text!

In verse 11 the author of Jude adds three more traditional examples of rebellious figures—Cain, Balaam, and Korah—and ascribes their errors directly to his opponents. Cain (Gen 4:1–16) and Korah (Num 16) clearly are negative figures in their original biblical contexts, and their infamy is reinforced in subsequent interpretative traditions (including references elsewhere in the New Testament; see relevant discussions in Kugel 1998). In contrast, the initial description of Balaam in Num 22–24 is mostly positive, but subsequent references to the figure in the Hebrew Bible (Num 31:16; Deut 23:3–6; Josh 13:22; 24:9–10; Neh 13:2) and Second Temple–period literature are less favorable (see additional references and discussion in G. L. Green 2008, 91).

---

angels, probably accusing them of foisting the law with its moral requirements upon Moses." A tradition developed in Second Temple–period Judaism that angels mediated or delivered the law to Moses (see, e.g., *Jub.* 1:27; Acts 7:38, 53; Gal 3:19; cf. Deut 33:2 LXX; Josephus, *Ant.* 15.136), but this was not normally viewed negatively.

12. The likelihood that this is an intentional allusion rests in large part on the assumption that the author of Jude knows the extant Greek translation of the Book of the Watchers. Elsewhere, however, the author of Jude may know Enochic traditions in Aramaic, not just in Greek translation. Bauckham (1983, 56) cites *1 En.* 7:1; 9:8; 10:11; 12:4; 15:3–4.

Second Temple–period interpreters tended to remove any ambiguity from the moral evaluation of biblical characters, with the flaws of righteous figures like Abraham and Moses normally vindicated through exegetical "polishing" while failings of other figures were emphasized so as to render them as purely negative types. Balaam suffered significantly in this process; he chiefly devolved in exegetical tradition into a caricature of a prophet for hire who taught the Moabites how to seduce the Israelites with sexuality and idolatry. This negative portrait is exegetically justified in part because Israel's sin at Shittim was narrated in Num 25, the very next chapter after the discussion of Balaam in Num 22–24 when Balak, king of Moab, hired him to curse Israel. (Balaam could only bless Israel instead; see Num 24:17 and discussion below of 2 Pet 1:19.) Later one reads in Num 31:16 that those who tempted Israel sexually followed Balaam's advice (see Kugel 1998, 799–810, 818–23). The author of Jude has indeed used biblical examples, but he demonstrates familiarity with common interpretative traditions as shown by his use of Balaam as an example of avarice.

The author continues his denunciation of his opponents in verses 12–13 with a series of metaphors drawn from nature. The language may reflect allusions to biblical or other texts (Bauckham 1983, 78–79), although most of the imagery seems common or general enough that no precise referent may be identified. A possible exception is the reference to "wandering stars." This term could be used in the classical tradition for planets as opposed to "fixed" stars (G. L. Green 2008, 98). Alternately, this term may be indebted to *1 En.* 18:15–16; 21:5–6, where stars that did not rise at the appointed time were subsequently punished (Bauckham 1983, 89–91).

Next, the author of Jude continues his critique with the quotation in Jude 14–15 from *1 En.* 1:9. This quotation concerns the judgment of the ungodly and reflects the theophoric introductory comments in *1 Enoch* that in turn draw heavily from Jer 25:30–31; Isa 66:15–16; and especially Deut 33:1–3 (Nickelsburg 2001, 143–44, 148–49). Numerous correspondences between the wording of the quotation in Jude and the Greek of this Enochic passage preserved in Codex Panopolitanus confirm that this is a quotation, but several divergences may also imply knowledge of the Enoch text both in Greek translation and in the original Aramaic (Bauckham 1983, 94–96; G. L. Green 2008, 104–5).

The author's presentation of this Enochic material is striking. Enoch "prophesied" (*proephēteusen*), a term that implies profound—even divinely inspired—authority for the statement. This language is even stronger than that used for the "predictions" of the apostles in verse 17, where the Greek is *tōn rhēmatōn tōn proeirēmenōn*, literally "the foretold words," with the connotation of warning (*proeipon*, BDAG 868). The identity of the figure bringing judgment and the timing of this event are less clear. God is the active figure in *1 En.* 1:9 since he comes (*erchetai*) with "his myriads and his holy ones" (following Codex Panopolitanus) at some future time, whereas in Jude 14 "the Lord came" (*ēlthen kyrios*) to bring judgment. Most interpreters assert that the author of Jude has recast this quotation as a prophecy of Jesus' Parousia. For example, Bauckham (1983, 93, 96–97) understands *kyrios* in Jude 14 as Jesus and the aorist verb as a prophetic perfect (see similar interpretations in Kelly 1969, 276; Perkins 1995, 153; Watson 1998, 12:494; G. L. Green 2008, 105–6). Such a contextual adaptation in Jude is very possible, and Nickelsburg (2001, 149) likewise notes that in *1 En.* 52:5–9 the coming of the Anointed and Chosen One is described with language reflecting *1 En.* 1:3–7.

While this certainly is the mainstream interpretation, one might also consider the possibility that Jude 14–15 denotes God's judgment in the *past*. The language admittedly may be read as that of final judgment (although the Deut 33:1–3 language to which this passage is strongly indebted describes a theophany at Sinai, not an eschatological event). However, the author next turns in Jude 17–23 to remind the audience that the apostles *also* foretold of events of the last days, both of the presence of the ungodly and the return of Jesus. The pattern in Jude has been to relate the wicked of the past (and their fates) with "these" opponents of the author's generation.[13] Since the biblical chronology in Genesis placed Enoch prior to any of the negative examples in Jude 5–7, Enoch's prophecy of judgment by the *kyrios* God in Jude 14–16 might be read as the precedent guaranteeing the validity of the apostolic foresight in Jude 17–23,

---

13. Numerous scholars note the author's pattern of citing past examples in vv. 5–7, 9, 11, and 14–15, followed by application of these comments to the contemporary opponents ("these" [*houtoi*, from the demonstrative pronoun *houtos*]) in vv. 8, 10, 12–13, and 16, respectively. "These" also appears in v. 19 after discussion of the apostolic prediction. In contrast, the recipients of Jude are "beloved" (*agapētoi*; vv. 3, 17, 20; cf. *ēgapēmenois* in v. 1 according to the best manuscripts). See the very helpful discussion of these terms and their implications for understanding the genre of Jude (chiefly whether "midrash" is the proper designation) in G. L. Green 2008, 39–41. One should note that the opponents are already in view when the errors of Cain, Balaam, and Korah are cited in v. 11, and the prophecy of Enoch in v. 14 is also about "these" (*toutois*, also a form of *houtos*).

thus affirming that the *kyrios* Jesus Christ will also bring judgment on a later generation of scoffers.

Ultimately such interpretation hinges on the identity of "these" in verse 14—are they the contemporary opponents of the author of Jude (as most interpreters assume), or are they the ancient prototypes of evil who have already faced God's wrath? Regardless, the letter continues in verses 17–23 with discussion of the apostolic prediction and a charge for the "beloved" to remain faithful. Its language is infused especially in verse 23 with allusions to the vision in Zechariah (the imagery of snatching something from fire and filthy clothes, Zech 3:2–4) and in Amos (again the image of snatching from fire, now connected with Sodom and Gomorrah traditions in Amos 4:11). Consistent with those images, Jude hopes for repentance by his opponents, calling his audience to extend mercy to them in a way that reflects the mercy the faithful also receive (vv. 21–23; Bauckham 1983, 114–17; Chester and Martin 1994, 78–79). The letter concludes in verses 24–25 with a doxology.

To summarize, one finds in Jude much use of biblical traditions, but these are intertwined with related materials from nonbiblical sources and Second Temple–period exegetical traditions. The only explicit quotation comes from the Enochic Book of the Watchers, and it seems to be paired with an apostolic teaching. The author implies the authority of Jude, the Lord's brother, but does not exploit this authoritative identification with use of Jesus traditions.

2 Peter

Whereas scholarship is divided on the authorship of Jude, the dominant scholarly consensus is that 2 Peter is pseudepigraphical (as discussed by Lewis R. Donelson elsewhere in this volume). This position is increasingly common even among interpreters who otherwise reject pseudonymity in the New Testament. As with Jude, however, the important matter for interpretation of 2 Peter is not actual authorial *identity* but rather the authorial *authority* claimed for the epistle. Unlike Jude, where appeals to the authority of the author are not exploited, the apostolic authority of "Peter" is at the forefront in this epistle.

The letter opens with an attribution to "Simeon Peter, a servant and apostle of Jesus Christ" (1:1). Later, a significant portion of the first chapter (1:12–18) builds on the assumption that the author is repeating a message previously communicated to the recipients (1:12) that he desires for them to continue pondering (1:13–15). "Peter" is presented as the person who evangelized the recipients (1:16), and the author appeals to the apostle's experience of the divine voice affirming Jesus at the transfiguration (1:17–18). "Peter" knows via revelation from the Lord Jesus Christ that his death is imminent (1:14).[14] This setting heightens the urgency of his message, and it has contributed to the common—but debated—classification of this epistle as a testament.

Much of chapter 2 is an adaptation and expansion of materials from Jude (see further below), but appeals to "Peter's" relationship to the recipients resume in chapter 3. In 3:1 the author describes the present text as his "second letter" to the audience, and in 3:15–16 he discusses letters of "our beloved brother Paul."[15] The latter are deemed difficult to interpret and liable to misinterpretation by those who also twist "the other scriptures" (*tas loipas graphas*).

That last statement is intriguing, as it places the Pauline letter collection on par with the Jewish Scriptures and affirms that this author indeed is working with some consciousness of what is *authoritative* literature. Bauckham (1983, 333; compare also Senior and Harrington 2003, 296), however, rightly cautions against taking this a step further toward a *canonical* consciousness. Bauckham also suggests the possibility that the Gospels might be among "the other scriptures," and his proposal is reasonable pending the identification of the source of the transfiguration tradition cited earlier in 1:16–18. He determines, however, that 2 Peter reflects an independent transfiguration tradition (210), not materials from a New Testament Gospel (see the different assessment by Wolfgang Grünstäudl and Tobias Nicklas in their chapter in this volume), but that the author likely draws on John 21:18 (rather than several other possible early Christian sources) for the comment in 2 Pet 1:14 that Jesus has revealed the apostle's impending death. Generally, however, scholars are reluctant to

---

14. Compare the recent argument of Markley (2013) that the author of the Gospel of Matthew presents Peter as an apocalyptic seer.

15. Most interpreters assume this is a reference to 1 Peter in 2 Pet 3:1, even though most recent scholars agree that similarities between the two books are very limited. See the discussion in Bauckham 1983, 143–47, and the chapter by Jeremy F. Hultin in this volume. A century earlier, Bigg (1902, 232) had argued that "no document in the New Testament is so like 1 Peter as 2 Peter," and Boobyer (1959) argued similarly (G. L. Green 2008, 310–11). Despite the reference to a Pauline corpus, "there is little sign of Pauline influence in 2 Peter" (Bauckham 1983, 147).

affirm a particular source for the transfiguration account. As for the statement in 1:14, Kelly (1969, 314; followed by Kraftchick 2002, 105) notes that it likely was common for early Christians to assume that their leaders had premonitions of death and thus no specific source text need be sought.

In addition to the emphasis placed on apostolic identity, *discussion* of the importance of Scripture in 2 Peter also is striking in comparison to the relative silence in Jude. This is the case even though, as Elliott asserts, "not once is the OT cited explicitly [in 2 Peter] though the letter abounds with OT allusions" (1992, 5:284).[16] As with the book's materials appealing to the figure of "Peter," the comments about Scripture appear in the first and third chapters of 2 Peter (i.e., not the section adapted from Jude). The first (in 1:19–21) follows immediately upon the transfiguration account, in which the apostle heard "this voice borne from heaven" (1:18 RSV).[17] The author links that divine testimony with the "prophetic word" of 1:19. The latter almost certainly is a reference to Scripture, as the phrase "prophetic word" is used uniformly in this sense elsewhere in Second Temple Jewish and early Christian literature (see Bauckham 1983, 224, for examples). While scholars debate the precise relationship implied here (chiefly how to construe the word *bebaioteron*), the point is that the testimony of God about Jesus at the transfiguration and that of Scripture stand as dual foundations and affirmations of the apostolic message (Davids 2006, 208; in distinction to the clever myths of 1:16a for Bauckham 1983, 223).[18]

---

16. Some disagree with Elliott's assessment. The first of the two proverbial statements cited in 2 Pet 2:22 ("the dog turns back to its own vomit") reflects Prov 26:11 ("Like a dog that returns to its vomit is a fool who reverts to his folly"). Köstenberger (2006, 247) considers this a "formal citation" and a "quotation." Other scholars, however, note that the Greek wording in 2 Pet 2:22 only loosely reflects that of the LXX, and the dog proverb is paired in the epistle with another about a sow that does not derive from Scripture. They are introduced in 2 Pet 2:22 as "the true proverb" (note the singular language), but nothing implies that the author consciously quotes Scripture. Bauckham observes that while "the two sayings ... originally derive from distinct sources ... they are so closely parallel as given here ... that the author probably found them together in the form he quotes, no doubt in some Hellenistic Jewish collection of proverbs" (1983, 278–79).

17. Tasker (1954, 131) finds an earlier reference to Scripture in 2 Pet 1:4 ("his precious and very great promises"), but this is vague.

18. *Bebaioteron* (from *bebaios*) in 1:19 may be read to imply that God's statement at the transfiguration confirms the teaching of the "prophetic word" (thus the NRSV: "So we have the prophetic message more fully confirmed"). Some scholars have understood this confirmation in reverse, appealing to a rabbinic tradition that Scrip-

The recipients are thus called to regard the message of Scripture (perhaps in conjunction with the voice of God; see the note on *bebaioteron*) as "a lamp shining in a dark place, until the day dawns and the morning star rises in your hearts."[19] The comparison of Scripture to a lamp is traditional (Ps 119:105; Wis 18:4; see Bauckham 1983, 225, for other examples; see also Davids 2006, 208, for discussion of a lamp in a "dark place" in *4 Ezra* 12:42), but the imagery here takes on an eschatological tint that points to the return of Christ. Note also the possible allusion to "the day of the Lord" tradition in prophetic literature and perhaps also to the "star" language of Num 24:17 (from Balaam's fourth oracle, and often read as messianic in Second Temple Judaism; compare Bauckham 1983, 225–26; Neyrey 1993, 183–84; and Carson 2007b, 1048).

Interpretation of 1:20–21 is also complicated. One may find in 1:20 a dismissal of the idea that prophecy originates with the prophet himself (see NIV: "no prophecy of Scripture came about by the prophet's own interpretation of things"), or else one may read the verse as a condemnation of novel, independent interpretations, perhaps with those of the author's opponents in view (see NRSV: "no prophecy of scripture is a matter of one's own interpretation"; see Davids 206, 210–13, for discussion of both approaches). Regardless, the overall thrust is clear in 1:21 that prophecy has its source in God (through the Holy Spirit).

This discussion of prophecy provides an excellent transition to chapter 2, which is chiefly composed of materials adapted from Jude.[20] One also finds here (2:1–3) the first explicit discussion of the opponents in 2 Peter (but see the "cleverly devised myths" of 1:16). Whereas in Jude the opponents were immoral antinomians, now the threat comes from

---

ture is more reliable than a "voice from heaven," but that does not fit the argument in 2 Peter, where the author mentions the apostle's testimony about hearing the voice of God in order to remind the recipients of what they already know (1:12–15). Alternately, *bebaioteron* may be read to affirm the absolute trustworthiness of Scripture apart from any sense that either it or the transfiguration statement affirms the other (as in the NAB: "Moreover, we possess the prophetic message that is altogether reliable"; the 2011 revision of the NIV has "something completely reliable," but earlier editions read "made more certain"). See Bauckham 1983, 223; Davids 2006, 207; and Neyrey 1993, 178–80, for varying perspectives.

19. "Rises in your hearts" is a standard translation (NRSV, NAB, NIV), but commentators are eager to note that the subject is the Parousia and not a personal psychological or existential experience. See, e.g., G. L. Green 2008, 229.

20. See Callan 2004 for detailed examination of 2 Peter's use of Jude.

false teachers and scoffers who also deny the Parousia (among many other offenses). In contrast to the certainty of the God-inspired message, the words of these false teachers are destructive and deceptive.

As in Jude, divine judgment on such people is certain, and so begins the litany of examples of God's wrath in the past. Jude's examples of the wilderness generation, Watchers, and Sodom and Gomorrah are revamped in multiple ways. The examples in 2 Pet 2:4–10 are the Watchers (with adaptations addressed below), the flood generation, and Sodom and Gomorrah, now arranged according to the biblical chronology and supplemented with reflections on how God simultaneously delivered the righteous Noah and Lot in the midst of the latter two judgments. Lot clearly has been rehabilitated significantly via Jewish tradition, much as Balaam declined in the same process. Now both Lot and Noah exemplify those who are righteous in the midst of wickedness, as the recipients of 2 Peter also find themselves.[21]

Although the flood reference has replaced the wilderness account and the positive remarks about Noah and Lot have been added, still all of these derive from the collection of "stock" Second Temple–period judgment examples mentioned above. Yet as in Jude, the author of 2 Peter has chosen particular examples because they best make his point. The inclusion of Noah is particularly appropriate because he comes to be hailed in traditional interpretation for his patience, and God's own patience is emphasized later in 2 Peter.[22] Together, these examples in 2 Peter testify to God's ability to deal appropriately with both the righteous and the unrighteous until the appointed time (2:9).

The castigation of the author's opponents continues through the end of the chapter (2:10–22). It broadly follows Jude's pattern of criticizing their arrogance and slander of the "glories" (in distinction to respectful angelic behavior) and their avarice (like that of Balaam, who now receives expanded discussion, whereas Jude's references to Cain and Korah have been dropped). The author of 2 Peter then illustrates the folly of the opponents with a series of nature metaphors, all with significant supplementary material. Much scholarly attention has been devoted to how the author of

---

21. The view of Lot as a righteous figure is common among interpreters of the Second Temple period, but this positive rehabilitation is not unanimous. See Kugel 1998, 328–32, 345.

22. I am indebted to Jenny DeVivo for this observation.

2 Peter adapts the Watchers and Michael language from Jude, but it is helpful to consider use of nonbiblical traditions in the epistle more broadly.

As noted above, four passages in Jude appear to have significant Enochic influence. Although most of the contents of Jude are taken over in some form in 2 Peter, two Enochic passages were not: the comment about "wandering stars" in Jude 13, and the quotation of *1 En.* 1:9 in Jude 14–15.[23] Also, the defilement language of Jude 8 may have been deleted if one assumes the condemnation of 2 Pet 2:13–14 is instead an expansion of Jude 12. Elsewhere, other materials from Jude are "domesticated" in 2 Peter, as is the case with the Michael tradition from Jude 9. Jude's explicit discussion of the verbal restraint of the archangel Michael in his dispute with the devil for the body of Moses becomes considerably more vague in 2 Pet 2:11.

The fourth major Enochic passage discussed above is the example of God's judgment of the Watchers from Jude 6. The "strange flesh" link with the Sodom story has been deleted, and only a minimal number of common terms remain (chiefly various forms of the verb *tēreō*, "keep"). Compared to Jude 6, the 2 Peter adaptations seem paraphrastic.

> Jude 6—And the angels who did not keep their own position, but left their proper dwelling, he has kept in eternal chains in deepest darkness for the judgment of the great Day.

> 2 Peter 2:4—For if God did not spare the angels when they sinned, but cast them into hell and committed them to chains of deepest darkness to be kept until the judgment …[24]

One might ask whether the author of 2 Peter independently utilized Watchers traditions. It is important to note that the *softening* of Enochic traditions present in Jude does not indicate that the author of 2 Peter *rejected*

---

23. Perhaps one might assume that the author of 2 Peter has severely summarized Jude's use of the Enoch citation and the subsequent predictions of the apostles in 2 Pet 3:2: "you should remember the words spoken in the past by the holy prophets, and the commandment of the Lord and Savior spoken through your apostles."

24. Some manuscripts read *seirois* or *sirois* ("pits"; see RSV) rather than *seirais* ("chains"; the term for "chains" in Jude 6 is *desmois*). Bauckham (1983, 249) argues that if "pits" were original, it could imply independent knowledge of the description of the dungeon of the Watchers in *1 Enoch*. See also Carson 2007b, 1050; G. L. Green 2008, 268. For additional discussion of changes made by 2 Peter, see Callan 2004, 49–50.

such materials, as he retains discussion of the imprisoned Watchers from Jude 6 and likely appeals to nonbiblical traditions in 2 Pet 3:4–13.[25] Also, the author of 2 Peter changes the description of the imprisonment of the sinful angels, something that goes beyond what he finds in Jude. The term *tartaroō* in 2 Pet 2:4 ("hold captive in Tartarus," BDAG 991; NRSV "cast into hell") is reminiscent of the story of the confinement of the Titans to Tartarus by Zeus, the Olympian gods, and the "Hundred-handers" in Hesiod, *Theog.* 617–819.[26] Although one might argue that the author of 2 Peter has connected the Watchers story with the Greek mythological tradition in the course of his own paraphrase of Jude, it is also important to note that Tartarus language appears in the Greek translation of the Book of the Watchers (and elsewhere in Second Temple–period texts, including the Septuagint).[27] It may be the case that the author of 2 Peter has personal knowledge of this Greek translation of the Enochic text and is not solely dependent on Jude for this tradition.

Much has been said already about the contents of chapter 3, including the presumed reference to 1 Peter in the comment that presents 2 Peter as a "second letter" (3:1) and the discussion of the Pauline corpus and "other scriptures" (3:15–16). The heart of this chapter concerns further repudiation of the scoffers in favor of reliance on the words of the prophets and Jesus (the latter conveyed by the apostles, 3:2). Evocative language from

---

25. See the discussion of literary relationships between 2 Peter and texts of the Jewish Pseudepigrapha in Bauckham 1983, 139–40. His explanation for 2 Peter's omission of most of the nonbiblical materials in Jude is that they (other than the ubiquitous story of the imprisoned Watchers) were unfamiliar to the author, who presumed the same would be true for his audience (see also Callan 2004, 49–50). Bauckham notes that *1 Enoch* was very popular in Greek translation among Christian writers of the second century C.E., but the author of 2 Peter presumably could not read these texts in Aramaic as did the author of Jude. Bauckham asserts, however, that both the author of 2 Peter and *1 Clement* utilized traditions from the *Book of Eldad and Modad*. Nickelsburg (2001, 14) argues that at least the Book of the Watchers must have been in Greek translation by the late first century because of the quotation of *1 En.* 1:9 in Jude 14–15 (but see comments above) and use of the book by the author of Revelation.

26. See especially B. A. Pearson 1969. Bauckham (1983, 249) is sympathetic and notes precedents in Hellenistic Jewish texts. See also the survey of possible influences of the Titans' story elsewhere in Second Temple Jewish literature in B. W. R. Pearson 1999, 41–47.

27. See G. L. Green (2008, 250–51), who lists Job 41:24 LXX; *1 En.* 20:2; Philo, *Embassy* 49, 103; Philo, *Rewards* 152; Josephus, *Ag. Ap.* 2.240; *Sib. Or.* 1.98–103; 2.303; 4.186.

the flood narrative, apocalyptic traditions, and even Stoic cosmological thought marks much of the chapter (3:3–7), as the author emphasizes the certainty of God's future judgment and explains the delay of the "day of the Lord" as an act of divine mercy (3:8–10; cf. 3:15; the correlation of day and a thousand years in 3:8 reflects Ps 90 [LXX 89]:4). In the meantime, believers should be both diligent and vigilant (3:11–18).

This survey of 2 Peter has focused on two things, the author's discussion of Scripture and his adaptation of materials from Jude. His discussion of Scripture is much more explicit than anything one finds in Jude. Rhetoric about Scripture is prominent and is linked with appeals to the authority and experiences of the ascribed author, but still one notices a significant intermingling of biblical and nonbiblical traditions. In some cases, use of nonbiblical texts has been softened compared to Jude, but such usage has not been eliminated—and still other texts appear to have been utilized.

Reflections

This discussion began with three questions, asking what biblical and nonbiblical sources have been used by the authors of Jude and 2 Peter; how these sources are utilized; and how these authors might have understood the concept of "canon." The various sources used in Jude and 2 Peter have been addressed above, and some attention has been given to how they were used. More remains to be said on that second question and the third, and the ideas that follow are only suggestive.

On close examination, the lack of explicit biblical quotations in these two epistles is surprising. As noted earlier, the only explicit textual quotation in *either* epistle is the citation of Enoch in Jude 14–15. Beyond that quotation, the closest thing to a biblical citation is the wording of the angel Michael's rebuke to Satan in Jude 9. Likewise, the closest thing to a citation formula in the two epistles is also found in Jude, when one reads that Enoch "prophesied."[28]

---

28. Many scholars argue that use of certain citation formulas signals that an author considers a source to be authoritative or even canonical, something recognized uncomfortably in the awkward assessment by Beckwith (1985, 402): "if 1 Enoch were a canonical book, one would be inclined to regard this as an endorsement of its canonicity, since it is not, the statement may just be a repetition of what 1 Enoch says happened." See McDonald 1995 for criticism of Beckwith's assumptions and argumentation.

Equally surprising—though more understandable in light of the absence of quotations—is the way biblical examples and allusions are used. The examples tend to be from an apparently "stock" collection used in numerous texts of the period, with stories derived both from biblical and nonbiblical materials. Second Peter can take over several of these examples from Jude but also may exchange some examples from others in the traditional "kit" as desired. In Jude and 2 Peter, these examples are simply presented as reminders and warnings, with the assumption that their audiences understand the intended references, agree with their evaluations of various characters, and accept them as authoritative. While one certainly should assume these examples were used with definite intention and purpose by the authors of Jude and 2 Peter, there is no explicit *exegesis* of these materials presented in the epistles themselves. Instead, whatever interpretation involved in their use appears to be *received* interpretation, inherited from Second Temple–period Jewish tradition.

Similarly, observation of the use of these materials in Jude and 2 Peter is an excellent reminder for contemporary interpreters of the great difficulty often encountered in attempts to distinguish between what texts ancient writers considered biblical and nonbiblical. Both Jude and 2 Peter use texts that fall in both categories from the perspective of later canonical opinions. While the author of 2 Peter does omit the explicit Enochic quotation when reusing those materials, this omission is not a repudiation of such traditions, as is evident by the materials that author introduces elsewhere. Likewise, examples from both (subsequent) canonical categories appear mixed together in the traditional example materials.

Even if one might argue that the "stock" nature of these examples means that their use in Jude and 2 Peter implies little about the authors' conscious decisions to use them, still materials from nonbiblical books appear elsewhere in both epistles. (Though beyond the scope of this chapter, the inclusion of such materials in the stock collection also raises questions about the status of such traditions when these examples were assembled.) Similarly, it is impossible to argue that the authors used only Gen 6:1–4 when discussing the Watchers and not materials from nonbiblical sources because both authors include specific details that go far beyond information in the Genesis text.

In short, nothing in either Jude or 2 Peter allows one to distinguish between texts that later will be deemed biblical and nonbiblical. While both authors clearly cite texts and traditions they consider authoritative and 2 Peter demonstrates an awareness of the concept of "Scripture," neither epistle comes anywhere close to demonstrating the canonical distinctions that later will be of much importance to the early church.[29] This lack of awareness is problematic only if one is certain that the New Testament authors were already working with clearly defined canonical parameters for the "Old Testament." This assumption was long held by scholars and found strenuous defense in Beckwith (1985). In recent decades, however, many have questioned traditional assumptions about matters such as how quickly the Jewish canon of Hebrew and Aramaic texts came to be "closed" in its three-part arrangement (Law, Prophets, Writings) and how to understand the church's preference for a larger collection of books in its Greek "Old Testament" (the Septuagint, also of Jewish origin). Both of these issues are very complicated and cannot be addressed appropriately in this chapter, but it will suffice to say that the neat, tidy explanations of previous generations of scholarship have been found wanting.

Beyond that, it is important to note two other factors. First, one should not underestimate how strongly traditions recorded in certain nonbiblical texts became *the* standard interpretations of biblical passages, such as reading the cryptic Gen 6:1–4 through the lens of the Watchers tradition. (Later, however, this approach would be opposed in rabbinic Jewish interpretation and by some early Christian writers; see Wenham 1987, 139–40.)

---

29. Compare the very different evaluation of Beckwith (1985, 395–405), which seems driven by two faulty assumptions. His insistence that New Testament authors already observed later canonical distinctions leads him to consider whether Jude intentionally sought to popularize Pseudepigraphical literature (401). Also, his conviction that anything said in New Testament books must be factual in the modern sense demands his rationalization that Jude uses Watchers and Michael traditions because they are "pieces of narrative haggadah—edifying, but not necessarily historical" (403). Beckwith argues that such distinctions clearly were understood in early Jewish Christianity but later were misunderstood by Gentile converts. Jewish Christians "would have seen edifying stories not as history but as edifying stories, and if Jude had selected two such edifying stories from books which he may even have regarded as otherwise unedifying, this would neither have impugned his own authority nor have conferred authority upon the pseudonymous apocalypses from which he drew" (405). Gene L. Green's approach, while still very cautious, is more reasonable: "Jude's esteem of 1 Enoch was not out of harmony with the honor ascribed to the book by some circles within Judaism, even though 1 Enoch was not accepted widely" (2008, 28), yet his assessment of 2 Peter's use of similar sources does not fully reflect the evidence surveyed here ("wherever Jude made explicit use of apocryphal literature, [2] Peter left that material to one side"; 2008, 30).

In such cases, one finds what were widely deemed to be correct *interpretations* (at least in particular eras) in books that ultimately later would not be accepted as biblical. Second, it is also important to recognize that use of nonbiblical texts by Christians continued alongside and even after consensus was reached as to what texts (including the New Testament texts) are canonical. Numerous church fathers could affirm interpretations and ideas from nonbiblical texts as proper and even necessary supplements for understanding Scripture *even if* ultimately they considered the texts so used to be nonbiblical or even corrupted otherwise (Adler 2002). The most important consideration in such cases was whether materials from such texts helped illuminate Scripture or advance an orthodox argument.

Perhaps this last observation is instructive for considering Jude and 2 Peter. While we cannot know exactly what the authors of these epistles thought of the status of the Enochic and similar books, it is clear that neither would have used such texts in their epistles if they did not find them beneficial for their purposes.

Are the Others Too Other?
The Issue of "Others" in Jude and 2 Peter

Peter H. Davids

Jude and 2 Peter are sometimes treated as literature too short, obscure, and controversial for serious study. Sitting as they do toward the end of the New Testament, they often warrant only cursory treatment at the end of a course on New Testament letters or the end of a volume on multiple letters. Furthermore, it is clear to most scholars that 2 Peter has used Jude much as Matthew and Luke have used Mark. Because of this, the two works are often treated together in such a manner that they almost merge, with Jude considered the junior partner and 2 Peter assumed to be condemning the same individuals or group of individuals as Jude does. The result has been a failure to hear the distinctive voices of each of these two works and, in particular, to understand what each of the two was addressing and how their situations related to the development of the post-Easter Jesus movement out of which both of these letters arose.

Diversity and Conflict in the Jesus Movement

Initial Diversification

The Jesus movement started out as a relatively cohesive movement both culturally and theologically. This beginning does, of course, contradict Walter Bauer's hypothesis that the earliest Christian communities were very diverse and only later grew to be more uniform (Bauer 1971). Bauer's thesis has been critiqued by a number of later writers, and in claiming relative original homogeneity we are not asserting that this cohesion would have been accepted as "orthodox" in the second and third centuries. It is just that movements usually start out relatively homogenous and then diverge as various influences and challenges encounter them (Desjardins

1991, 65–82). The evidence that we have in both the Synoptic Gospels and elsewhere points to the observations that the Jesus movement originally was composed of Jews, its leaders were mostly Galilean Jews, and it was centered in Jerusalem. Acts presents it as a localized movement for which temple piety was important (e.g., Acts 3).

However, even on the witness of Acts, a work that views the developing Jesus movement in as irenic a manner as possible, tensions soon developed as the movement grew.[1] Some of these tensions were inevitable. Whatever one makes of the Ananias and Saphira incident in Acts 5, it is clear that the author of Acts states that there were dissenters (even if private ones) from the prevailing ethos. In Acts 6:1, he refers to conflict between two culturally distinct groups, the "Hellenists" and the "Hebrews," with the former group ostensibly claiming that their widows were being treated unfairly. This account is presented as a linguistically based conflict, Greek-speakers versus Aramaic-speakers, but one immediately asks why this became an issue. Given the nature of first-century Palestine, many, if not most, with Aramaic as their mother tongue also spoke Greek, although the reverse was not necessarily true (see Sevenster 1968). Could it be that Acts is reflecting cultural differences? Jews from the coastal plain or from outside Palestine, who did not speak Aramaic and had lived as a Jewish minority within predominately Greco-Roman cultures, would surely have different perspectives from Jews coming from a Jewish majority culture. This would be true even if the Jews from a Jewish majority culture often interacted in Greek with Gentiles (including those Gentiles living in predominately Gentile towns and cities within Palestine). Acts claims that the issue was bridged by appointing a second set of leaders who were from the aggrieved group and therefore shared its values.

However, again according to Acts, the Jesus movement soon spread to Samaria (Acts 8). While we read of leaders from Jerusalem who traveled to Samaria and gave their seal of approval to the newly baptized followers of Jesus, we do not hear of Samaritan followers of Jesus who traveled to Jerusalem and took part in the temple piety that Acts attributes to the mother group. Did the Samaritan followers continue to be involved in Samaritan

---

1. Our working hypothesis is that the tendency in Acts is to show that all in the developing Jesus movement were "of one heart and soul" (Acts 3:32) and thus the reporting of conflict is counter to this tendency. One may not be certain that all were as happy with the solutions to the conflicts as Acts implies, but one may be relatively certain that the author would not invent conflicts within the community.

religious piety? Whether they did or not, they were from a distinct culture and probably had different ideas of what Jesus would do when he returned, for example, what he would do to the Jerusalem temple. Furthermore, did all of the Jewish followers of Jesus in Jerusalem and Judea fully accept the Samaritan followers of Jesus as brothers and sisters? Did none of the suspicion and resentment from the past centuries of mutual hostility remain? Acts is silent on this issue, although it is perhaps significant that Samaria is not mentioned again in any of the New Testament documents. We should note that both 2 Peter and Jude are attributed to men who were identified with the "Jerusalem" side of the Jerusalem-Samaria divide.

Diversification beyond the Palestinian Area

Yet from our contemporary perspective, the Samaritans were part of the Jewish "family," even if both the main Jewish groups and the Samaritans treated the other group as (sometimes hostile) outsiders. The big challenge would come with the integration of Gentiles into the Jesus movement. Both Acts and the far-earlier Paul claim that this is exactly what happened. Acts presents Peter as the first one to evangelize Gentiles (Acts 10; Philip's encounter with the Ethiopian eunuch in 8:26–40 is not appealed to as such elsewhere in Acts). Even if they were Gentiles with some forms of Jewish piety, it is clear in both Acts (chapters 10, 11, and 15) and in Paul's writings (particularly Galatians) that for some there was a real issue as to whether the "others" (in terms of their being taboo and in terms of their religious practice) remained too "other" after they committed themselves to following Jesus, unless they also became proselytes to Judaism, that is, became "like us."[2] In contrast to this position, Paul argues that such initiates into the Jesus movement were fully "in" and acceptable and that it would be inappropriate, indeed disloyal, to Jesus for them to become Jewish proselytes. That Paul has to argue this point so vigorously in Galatians shows that there were others in the Jesus movement who disputed this theology, including the "some from James" that trigger the famous conflict in Antioch in Gal

---

2. "Taboo" is a better term than "unclean," since the anthropological term *taboo* indicates that one group should not come in contact with an object or group because of its nature or usage, while "unclean" suggests in contemporary English that there is some dirt or lack of hygiene associated with the object, person, or group. Pigs, for example, were taboo to Jews, not because they were dirty, but because they were pigs.

2:11–14.³ Note that one with whom Paul disputes is that very Peter to whom 2 Peter is attributed (Gal 2:11).

It is also clear that twenty-five or so years after the Jesus movement began, Paul can write about differing factions in the community in Corinth (1 Cor 1) that we might surmise are organized around cultural (and perhaps theological) differences. We do not know how hostile they were to one another, but we do know that they were distinct enough for Paul to describe them as recognizable groups, and that this distinction in itself was unacceptable to him. One can only wonder how many other communities in the Jesus movement were undergoing similar differentiation.

It is also apparent that while Paul insists in Galatians that Gentiles ought not to become Jews after committing to Jesus as Lord, he had his own limits when it came to how un-Jewish they could remain. For instance, while Paul argues in 1 Cor 5:1 that a certain man has transgressed the ethical boundaries of not just Jewish mores but also Greco-Roman culture, Paul's perception appears to differ from that of the Corinthians. The deed was apparently not as problematic to the Corinthian community as it was to Paul (1 Cor 5:2). Had it been otherwise, Paul would clearly not have had to intervene. Then in 1 Cor 6:12–19, Paul appears to confront behavior that would have been acceptable in Greco-Roman culture but that he found unacceptable within the Jesus movement.⁴ However, 1 Cor 6:12 may well contain slogans in support of this behavior that stem from Paul himself, in other words, slogans that Paul found useful in his context but that he did not accept in the context in which the Corinthians were using them. What is clear is that Paul qualifies these slogans rather than refutes them. We also notice that it is behavior more than doctrine that is at issue, which is also the case in Jude and 2 Peter.

---

3. Naturally, we recognize that in Galatians we are getting Paul's presentation of both his own position and that of those he opposes, so we know how he perceives them as other than himself but not how they would present themselves nor how they perceived Paul's position.

4. He would also have found this behavior unacceptable within his Pharisaic value system, for even had the prostitutes been Jewish, they were considered taboo—that is, sinners—because they could not observe Pharisaic purity regulations and keep on working. However, since they were almost certainly pagan and Gentiles, they would also have been taboo due to their idolatry and their ethnicity. It is these latter issues that seem to lie behind Paul's concern in 1 Corinthians. Within Greco-Roman culture, of course, visiting a prostitute was not a problem; it was only the wives who were supposed to remain chaste so that the parentage of the children would be clear.

What we have argued, then, is that the Jesus movement grew across linguistic and cultural boundaries, including the subcultural boundaries within first-century Judaism. For example, what was acceptable to the writers of the Dead Sea Scrolls differed from what was acceptable to a Pharisee, and presumably at least some of this difference carried over if they became part of the Jesus movement. Indeed, it is quite possible that the concept of "heretic" as meaning an "unacceptably doctrinally deviant group" first arose in Judaism and was taken over into the Jesus movement (Desjardins 1991; Segal 1986, 133–61).

Thus, as the Jesus movement developed and crossed cultural and subcultural boundaries, various fissures appeared. Some were matters of individual behavior about which a given group of Jesus devotees might or might not have taken a stand, while others were surely group phenomena, positions championed and actively propagated by an identifiable group (such as those Paul opposes in Galatians). Some of these positions were inevitably viewed as acceptable differences within the movement, even if their proponents were viewed as wrong-headed, while others were viewed as serious enough to exclude their proponents from the movement. Generally the surviving literature, especially what became the canonical literature, preserves one side of the discussion with the proponents of the other side never being heard, for the surviving literature from "the other side" is either fragmentary (e.g., the *Gospel of the Hebrews*) or later than the literature included in the New Testament, (e.g., the anti-Pauline Pseudo-Clementines).

Furthermore, later some apparently felt the need to bridge the divides among major leaders of the movement. For example, there are later icons of Peter and Paul together (often kissing), the earliest extant ones being in the fourth-century-C.E. collection in the tomb of a Roman noblewoman in the Santa Tecla catacomb in Rome. One wonders how much these icons reflect actual traditions of Peter and/or Paul and how much they reflect the need of the church to view the gulf as bridged?[5]

A Theoretical Framework

As one may have noted above, there were (and are) various ways of dealing with difference. Differences that one considers minor, of course, would not

---

5. Acts 15 does indeed present Paul and Peter as being in harmony, but Paul's writings do not present the two as having met again after their conflict in Antioch (Gal 2).

be an issue, but as differences become more significant in one's perception, a situation of cognitive dissonance is set up (Festinger 1957; Festinger and Carlsmith 1959, 203–10; and the original 1954 study, published as Festinger, Rieken, and Schachter 1956). This dissonance occurs especially when the differences involve behavior.[6]

How can one deal with such cognitive dissonance? First, one can change one's belief, as Paul certainly did when confronted with an experience of the risen Jesus. However one values the Acts narrative (Acts 9; 21; 26), Paul obviously had a major paradigm shift between his upbringing as a Jew (2 Cor 11:22, expanded in Phil 3:5–6 and consistent with Gal 1:13–14) and his championing Gentile inclusion in the community of the followers of Jesus, a community that he once persecuted. He attributes this change to "a revelation of Jesus" (Gal 1:12, 15–16), which is what Acts has in narrative form.

Second, one can also change actions to conform with one's belief, which on the group level would mean how one treats those who are setting up the dissonant situation. This conformity could take the shape of hostility toward the group viewed as producing the dissonance and culminate in their expulsion (as Paul instructs in 1 Cor 5:4–5) or of withdrawal from that group. Thus 1 John 2:19 speaks of a group that "went out from us."

Third, one can have a change in perception. For instance, 1 John 2:19 states, "they did not belong to us." Surely before the dissonance that led to the rupture, the author would not have made this statement, but once the rupture happened, it was clear to him that "they" never were part of "us" (whom the unnamed author addresses as "children"). Not only are they not "children," but they are also "antichrists," a radical change in perception indeed. Once "they" are expelled or "they" withdraw and the perception of "them" as ever having been part of "us" is adjusted, then the group can continue to see itself as a unified group, as "one" in Johannine terminology.

We do not mean that the psychological explanation implies that the process is therefore illegitimate. A community without boundaries ceases to exist, so at some point those who are dissonant in behavior or belief must withdraw or be expelled. One may debate where that point is and what the separation should look like, but one can hardly debate that a point where dissonant behavior becomes intolerable exists if the

---

6. Strictly speaking, cognitive dissonance is between one's beliefs and actions, but the theory was developed by observing how people in groups dealt with dissonant perceptions. As such it is certainly applicable.

community is to continue as an identifiable community or movement. Likewise, a community that cannot adapt to changing circumstances ceases to exist (often slowly, as members age and die), but such necessary change also causes dissonance and often leads to the rupture of the community. So both the process of maintaining boundaries (and reducing dissonance) and the process of necessary adaptation that can lead to dissonance are necessary to community survival. One sees them played out in the first century in the tensions between the ethnic Jewish groups and the followers of Jesus, and these tensions ultimately led to a rupture.

In the case of Jude and 2 Peter, we have two communities of the Jesus movement that are similar in that each is experiencing internal conflict, and we have two related letters. Although this essay is not the place to lay out the data once again (Davids 2006, 136–43; see also the chapter by Jeremy F. Hultin in this volume), we are assuming that the author of 2 Peter is using Jude. Furthermore, we are assuming that his technique in using Jude is the ancient rhetorical practice of *aemulatio*, that is, reshaping the material to fit one's own rhetorical needs and context while retaining enough of the original so that the (ideal) auditors should recognize the authority that one is adapting (Kloppenborg 2004). However, while there is documentary commonality and a similar situation, the two letters address different perceived threats and arrive at somewhat different solutions.

The Others in Jude

Jude is referring to those he presents as outsiders who have "slipped stealthily into" the community (Jude 4).[7] This reference would appear to indicate that they originally came from outside the community, although it may only mean that Jude does not view them as really part of the community but rather as a foreign influence. While vilification language is stereotyped in all literature of this period and thus one must be careful about how

---

7. The name "Jude" is almost certainly intended to attribute authorship to a younger brother of Jesus. While Bauckham (1990) makes a decent case for its having been written in the last quarter of the first century by that Jude, this present author is only making the assumption that it is a late first-century work written in a place where the relatives of Jesus were valued, which appears to have been the eastern end of the Mediterranean. Wherever it was written, it was apparently valued in the community to which the author of 2 Peter belonged. See further Davids 2006, 8–17.

much information one draws from it, it is too extreme to say that it carries no information about those critiqued (Du Toit 1994, 403–12).

In this case, the fact that Jude says that *they* snuck in while 2 Peter says that they snuck in *ideas* gives evidence that in the one case the people are viewed as coming from outside while in the other case it is only the ideas.[8] These "Others" (Reese 2007) in Jude are never said to have authority in the community, so they are never called (true or false) teachers, prophets, elders, or any of the other terms used for recognized leaders in the early Jesus movement.

The presence of the "Others" means that the "Beloved" (Jude's repeated term for what is rhetorically the majority in the community, who in his view are faithful) must "contend for the faith" (v. 3, not that surprising in an agonistic society). The "Others" are never accused of theological deviation (that will be the major issue in a later era) but of "transforming God's grace into self-abandonment." The latter phrase translates *aselgeia*, a "lack of self-constraint that involves one in conduct that violates all bounds of what is socially acceptable" (BDAG 141). This word is often used together with sexual terms, and it is likely that this connection is what Jude intends, for they "defile the flesh" (v. 8) and they "follow their own desires" (v. 16). They are also accused of rebelliousness (v. 11) and slandering angels (v. 8).

While, as noted above, we do need to realize that at least some of this vilification was part of the standard rhetorical treatment of those with whom one had a sharp disagreement (i.e., pointing out that they are morally corrupt as well as having dangerous ideas), it is noteworthy that these "Others" are not said to "deny our only Master and Lord" (v. 4) in any other way. Therefore, it is likely that this critique at least points to the category of behavior at issue. In other words, it looks like these "Others" are a group that views the teaching about God's grace as allowing behavior that Jude (and the "Beloved") viewed as "beyond the bounds of what is socially acceptable."

The "Others" may have justified this by rejecting the authority of the Torah as something foisted on humanity by angels, although this justification is admittedly a hypothesis explaining a very obscure passage (vv. 8–9).[9] Could it be that what one has here is a clash between a more

---

8. The "sneaking" is the stuff of vilification, for it attributes a negative motive to the behavior. We shall try to exercise similar caution elsewhere in drawing conclusions from this vilificatory language.

9. The passage refers to the slandering of angels. The issue is why they would

Jewish-influenced group (whom Jude represents) and a more Hellenistic group? In that case, the Hellenistic group is being viewed as "outsiders" who have penetrated the community without giving up their Hellenistic mores. They may well have justified their lifestyle by appealing to the community's teaching about God's grace. Their critique of "angels" may indicate that they viewed the attempt to impose Jewish mores on them as an attempt to bring them under the law, a law that angels had foisted on the Jews in the first place.

Again, this scenario is obviously somewhat hypothetical, for we have no writings or other communication from these "Others." However, this hypothesis makes sense of the data. Vilifying a group with which one is in conflict as immoral is one aspect of Greco-Roman rhetoric, and what Jude considers "immorality" (whether expressed in the extreme or not) is the only thing that he appears to have against this group.

This scenario also makes sense of how Jude advises the "Beloved" to treat the "Others." Although he has used very strong language about the "Others" ("those causing divisions," "not having the Spirit," v. 19), he instructs the "Beloved" not only to strengthen their own commitment but also to "have mercy on" "those who are at variance" or "disputing" with them (*diakrinō*, BDAG 231, meaning 5). They show mercy by rescuing them, "snatching them from the fire." (The repeated *de* gives further information about this "being merciful" and indicates that it is a rescue operation and that it is a risky operation.) They do need to be aware that there is some risk in this action, so they are to "show mercy in fear" and, metaphorically speaking, to "hate even the *chiton* stained by the flesh." The *chiton* was the garment worn next to the body, so it was the one most likely to be stained by any spilled bodily fluids. It thus forms a metaphor for the immoral activities of the "Others"; so Jude is advising the "Beloved" to be careful to avoid such activities totally.

In summary, Jude speaks strongly about the "Others" and roundly condemns them. One would expect them to be simply consigned to their fate. Jude surprises us in indicating that the "Others" are redeemable, although the operation of rescuing them needs to be done with care. This

---

have done that. Several New Testament books (including Acts 7:38; Gal 3:19; and Heb 2:2) refer to the Second Temple tradition clearly found in *Jubilees* that the Torah was mediated by angels, since Moses could not have actually had contact with God and have lived. This makes it reasonable to believe that a group might slander angels as the givers of the Torah. See Davids 2006, 54–64.

"having mercy" sets Jude apart from 2 Peter, who will not pick up this rescue operation from Jude, even though he picks up so much else from the letter.

The Others in 2 Peter

Turning to 2 Peter, we discover that while the author does freely borrow from Jude's polemic, he views his situation somewhat differently.[10] In 2:1 he describes those he opposes as "false teachers" who arise from within ("in you"). These false teachers are parallel to the "false prophets" in Israel, and this parallel allows the author to segue from a discussion of true prophecy to a condemnation of the "false teachers." There is something that is "snuck in" or "brought in," but what is "brought in" is not the people themselves but "destructive opinions." Thus it is the ideas being taught that are foreign to the faith, not the people foreign to the community.

This perspective fits with the first part of the work, where knowledge of "our Lord Jesus the Anointed One" needs to be confirmed by the development of virtue (1:5–8). The one who fails to develop virtue "has forgotten the cleansing of his or her past sins" and by implication is stumbling and so not entering the "eternal kingdom of our Lord and Savior Jesus the Anointed One" (1:9–11). This description would fit people who started as "normal" members of the community (in the eyes of the author) but whom the author of 2 Peter views as swerving from the right path.

The "false teachers" are roundly condemned in terminology adapted from Jude. For instance, while the imprisonment of "the angels who sinned" is cited (2 Pet 2:4//Jude 6), 2 Peter adds the Deluge (which will come up again in the next chapter) and that Noah was delivered. When the author of 2 Peter refers to Sodom and Gomorrah (2 Pet 2:6//Jude 7), his interest is in the "righteous man" Lot, who was also delivered. His point is therefore that "the Lord knows how to deliver the godly" as well as put the ungodly in a place of punishment until the Day of Judgment.

---

10. The "Peter" of 2 Peter is not the same "Peter" as that of 1 Peter, as is clear from Greek style, subject matter, and theology. It is not so much that they are contradictory as that they come from different worlds. Thus we have argued that the letter coheres with late first-century works but lacks the second century's concern with church structure and Christology. It is extremely Hellenistic in outlook, but it seems to share something of the outlook of Revelation. See further Davids 2006, 123–32.

While the influence of Jude is clear, we also see that there is a second agenda operating. It is not only that the "false teachers" are immoral (2 Pet 2:13–14), that is, greedy (including for food and drink) and sexually loose, but also that they promise "freedom" (2 Pet 2:19), a claim not found in Jude. One suspects that this promise was connected to a Pauline phrase, such as freedom from the law or "all things are lawful to me" (1 Cor 6:12), for 2 Peter appears to believe that these "false teachers" were distorting Paul (2 Pet 3:15–16).

It is not only that they are "scoffers" (2 Pet 3:3//Jude 17), but they also mock the idea of providence and in particular "the promise of his coming" (2 Pet 3:4); with the latter they reject resurrection and final judgment (which 2 Pet 3:7 makes clear is certain). Furthermore, the author of 2 Peter is at pains to say that while there may be a dissolution of the heavens and the heavenly bodies (the *stoicheia*, often translated "elements," but in this context the elements of the heavens), the earth is not included in that dissolution, but instead will be "disclosed," and there is a renewed heavens and earth coming (3:10, 13; see note 12 and the related discussion below).[11]

This complex of ideas that 2 Peter opposes is found elsewhere in the ancient world, namely in popular adaptations of Epicureanism, including those adaptations in Judaism (Neyrey 1993, 122–28). Those who hold these ideas argued that freedom (from both pain and fear) is found in realizing that there is no divine providence, no afterlife, and no final judgment but rather just the pleasure of the present life.[12] The end is the end, the world itself having an end in its dissolution into atoms. If there is no

---

11. This interpretation is based on text-critical evidence in that "the earth ... will be disclosed" or "will be discovered" is the reading of Sinaiticus and Vaticanus, among other ancient witnesses; alternative readings that have the earth in some sense destroyed appear to be trying to harmonize this clause with the previous clauses and use a number of differing ways of doing so. This interpretation also agrees with some of the expectations in Second Temple Judaism and related literature. However, because it is unexpected, not all scholars have agreed with Nestle-Aland[27]. Nestle-Aland[28] reads "will not be disclosed" or "will not be found," a reading that is, in our mind, unwarranted. See Davids 2006, 283–93, and the literature cited there.

12. Unlike popular misconceptions of Epicureanism, the maximizing of pleasure was under the control of rationality. Namely, there was a golden mean, a point at which pleasure peaked without causing events that were not pleasurable. That is, one can enjoy food to a point, but after that point, one will end up with gastric distress. Thus rationality dictates that one seeks that mean, the maximum point, and that one does not transgress it. Many members of the Jesus movement, however, may have seen

providence and no judgment, there naturally can also be no prophecy, and any prophecy about the end is a "myth."

This reasoning would explain why 2 Peter takes pains to argue that the inauguration of the rule of Jesus is no "myth" (i.e., prophecy that is unable to be substantiated) but something Peter personally observed, and that therefore the previous prophecies about it are confirmed (1:16–19). The Parousia may have been delayed ("delay" being a telling argument that Epicureans and others used against providence), but it was a purposeful delay so that more people could be rescued (3:9). The idea of future judgment, 2 Peter argues, is no more imaginary than the past judgment of the Deluge (3:5–6), and this event proves that history is not a continuous following of the same laws until the eventual dissolution of the world.

The final judgment, however, will not be identical to the Deluge, for it will be associated with fire. The heaven (firmament) will be affected, but the elements that will melt will be the heavenly bodies (as noted above, a well-documented meaning of *stoicheia* and the most likely, since the context is the heaven), but the earth will *not* dissolve into atoms. Rather the earth will be revealed for judgment, not unlike removing the top of a nest of ants so that their activities are observable.[13] There will, then, be no escape from that judgment.

Second Peter's response to the "false teachers" has been refutation and condemnation, but he also has a response for the "Beloved." They are to avoid the ethical errors of the "false teachers" (i.e., they are to "strive to be found by [our Lord and Savior Jesus Christ] at peace, without spot or blemish," 3:14, amplified in 3:17). They are to deal with the delay of the Parousia as "salvation," perhaps meaning a delay that allowed "the

---

the mean as already transgressing the teaching of Jesus, the Hebrew Scriptures, or the law of love.

13. As previously discussed in note 11, despite the reading in Codex Alexandrinus and the Byzantine tradition (reflected in some English translations such as the KJV), which does have "will be burned up," the oldest manuscripts (Sinaiticus, Vaticanus, and perhaps originally P[72]) clearly read "will be discovered," which fits precisely the point that 2 Peter wishes to make. The reading "will not be discovered" or "will not be found" in Nestle-Aland[28] is strange, because it only appears in some Syriac translations, not in any early Greek manuscript, so it is apparently an attempt to harmonize the existing variants in Greek manuscripts, but does so by conjecturing a missing "not" on the basis of the Syriac. It is more likely that the Syriac tradition misunderstood 2 Peter, for "not" covers up the point that 2 Peter seems to me making, namely, that all will be exposed to God's eye for judgment. See Davids, 2006, 286 n. 51.

Beloved" to come to faith, that is, that they were some of those for whom God had been waiting.

Unlike Jude, however, there is not a word in 2 Peter about rescuing the "false teachers." Instead, these teachers twist Paul and the other writings "to their own destruction" (3:16). The dire predictions of chapter 2 and the warnings of chapter 1 find no modifying hope of rescue in chapter 3. Is it because the author of 2 Peter views them as "false teachers"? Is it because he fears any rescue attempt will destabilize the "Beloved"?

Conclusion

It is clear that in both of these letters, the "Others" have become too "other" and are beyond the boundaries of what Jude or 2 Peter deem acceptable. The originally Jewish Jesus movement was able to integrate people from various cultures into it and indeed be transformed by them, but it would not have a place for some Greco-Roman practices. It could and would integrate Stoic and Neoplatonic ideas, but it does not seem to have accepted Epicurean thought. The "Others" are too "other" for Jude, so he condemns them but advises careful rescue. A different group of "Others," this one arising from within and so once part of the "Beloved," is too "other" for the author of 2 Peter, but in his case, he can only advise the "Beloved" to stay in their safe stance, for the "Others" are too "other" even for rescue.

Searching for Evidence: The History of Reception of the Epistles of Jude and 2 Peter

Wolfgang Grünstäudl and Tobias Nicklas

In the introduction to his still-important 1977 monograph, Tord Fornberg states,

> A hasty glance at bibliographical works such as the *Elenchus* and *New Testament Abstracts* indicates that the interest in Early Christian epistolary literature is focused chiefly on the Corpus Paulinum (including Hebrews) and to some extent on the three major Catholic Epistles, i.e. James, 1 Pet[er], and 1 John. The four minor epistles, 2 Pet[er], 2 John, 3 John and Jude on the other hand, seldom come under consideration. (Fornberg 1977, 1)

The situation described by Fornberg has not really changed during the last decades. Even if the minor Catholic Epistles are considered as part of most New Testament canons (the exception being the Syriac Peshitta), they play only a very minor role in New Testament scholarship and even less in the life and liturgy of modern churches. In the following study, we will focus on the Epistles of Jude and 2 Peter—both perhaps even more neglected than 2 and 3 John. What were the reasons that these two books have been included in the canon? What role did they play in the life of ancient churches? Only a few traces of the reception of these texts in earliest times are left. While these traces do not allow us to draw a complete picture, at least a few lines of their reception can be made visible.[1]

---

1. Of course, the space limitations of this chapter do not allow for a complete discussion of the early reception of both texts. We therefore concentrate on some of the

Before we discuss receptions of Jude and 2 Peter by ancient Christian authors outside the New Testament, it should not be forgotten that the texts are related on the literary level. It is not possible to discuss all of the evidence here, but it is highly probable that 2 Peter used Jude as one of its sources (see Kraus 2001, 368–76; Wasserman 2006, 73–98; and the chapter by Jeremy F. Hultin in this volume). Even if, however, both texts belong together in a certain sense, their paths to canonical status were remarkably different.

Jude—Troubles with Moses and Enoch

Evidence for Commentary and Use of Jude

Interestingly, the earliest evidence we have about the reception of Jude shows that this text had already been used as an authority at a very early point. The so-called Muratorian Fragment (Rome, late second/early third century C.E.) mentions the Epistle of Jude after some "forged" texts like the pseudo-Pauline *Epistle to the Laodiceans* and *Epistle to the Alexandrians* and in a group of texts (including two Johannine letters, Wisdom of Solomon, Revelation, and *Apocalypse of Peter*) that were more or less accepted in the Roman church but remained a matter of discussion.[2]

Much more interesting, however, is the use of the text by two other authors who were writing at the turn of the second to the third century C.E. In his *Adumbrationes in Epistolas Catholicas* (*Comments on the Catholic Epistles*), perhaps the seventh volume of his otherwise lost *Hypotyposes* (*Outlines*; see also Eusebius, *Hist. eccl.* 6.14.1), Clement of Alexandria (140/150–215/216 C.E.) gives a short commentary on Jude (along with 1 Peter and 1–2 John). While the original Greek text has been lost, a later Latin translation by Cassiodorus (ca. 485–580 C.E.) survived. In any case, Clement seems to have read Jude as part of his "New Testament."

Perhaps even more interesting is a short note in Tertullian's (ca. 160–ca. 220 C.E.) writing *De cultu feminarium* (*The Apparel of Women*), dated

---

most important traces. For more information on the reception of 2 Peter, see Grünstäudl 2013.

2. Although often designated as the Muratorian Canon, the Muratorian Fragment should not be taken for a "canon list." It should instead be compared to "prologues" of early manuscripts of the Gospels or the *Corpus Paulinum*. For a thorough discussion of the text's historical background, see Verheyden 2003.

between 197 and 201 C.E. In a passage about fallen angels, Tertullian has to acknowledge that the relevant information about these angels comes from the book of Enoch (*1 Enoch*), which "is not received by some" (1.3, *ANF* 4:14). According to Tertullian, the problems some people have with *1 Enoch* have to do with the question of how this book could have survived the great flood. In his counterargument, Tertullian not only constructs a possible line of transmission of the text via Noah and speaks about questions of inspiration but also finishes the chapter with an additional argument: "To these considerations is added the fact that Enoch possesses a testimony in the Apostle Jude" (*ANF* 4:16). This is a clear reference to Jude 14, where *1 En.*1:9 is quoted (see Hultin 2010). The interesting point here is that Tertullian bases a part of his argument for the disputed authority of *1 Enoch* on the authority of Jude. This argument, however, was only possible if Tertullian expected that the authority of the latter was undisputed by his presumed readers.

Other authors followed the line of Tertullian's argument. The most interesting example is Priscillian of Avila (ca. 345–executed 385 C.E.). In his *Liber de fide et de apocryphis* (*Book on Faith and the Apocrypha*), Priscillian defends his own interest in apocryphal literature with the fact that even apostles like Jude, the brother of the Lord, quote *1 Enoch*. If Jude— and other canonical writings—used apocryphal texts and traditions, the reading of these apocryphal texts cannot be condemned. That is why, according to Priscillian, an absolute ban on reading apocrypha implies a condemnation of the apostles who, at least in some cases, used these texts (see Burrus 1990).

Accepted by Most

While most of the earliest evidence on Jude is clearly positive, interestingly some later authors are a bit more cautious regarding the letter. While Origen (ca. 185–253 C.E.) personally held Jude in high esteem, in his *Commentary on the Gospel of Matthew* 17.30 he also bears testimony to doubts raised against the text. Eusebius of Caesarea (264/265–339/340 C.E.), who mentions Jude several times in his *Ecclesiastical History*, goes even further. Eusebius discusses the letters of James and Jude when concluding a lengthy passage on James the brother of the Lord. Although, according to Eusebius, both texts were publicly read in most communities, he raises some doubts regarding their status because "not many of the ancients [*ou polloi ... tōn palaiōn*] have mentioned it" (*Hist. eccl.* 2.23.25, *NPNF*[2] 1:128).

This judgment is repeated more systematically a bit later when Eusebius gives an overview of the writings of his New Testament (*Hist. eccl.* 3.25). He starts with the four Gospels and the book of Acts, then mentions the *Corpus Paulinum*, continues with 1 John and "the," that is *one*, Letter of Peter, and adds—with some hesitation—the book of Revelation. He counts all these writings among the acknowledged Scriptures. He continues with a category of so-called *antilegomena* ("disputed ones") that, however, were accepted by most: James, Jude, 2 Peter, and 2–3 John. After these two categories, he moves to a third category of texts: among these "spurious" writings (*en tois nothois*) he counts the *Acts of Paul*, Shepherd of Hermas, *Apocalypse of Peter*, *Barnabas*, and others. While Jude seems to be well on the way toward "universal" acceptance in this late stage of the formation of the New Testament canon, it is highly interesting that its authority, which an earlier author like Tertullian had already taken for granted, was, at least in some circles, still (or again) a matter of dispute.

This evidence is affirmed by other fourth-century witnesses. Codex Claromontanus, a sixth-century bilingual manuscript of the Pauline Corpus, offers a catalog of writings (with the numbers of their *stichoi*) that seems to go back to the fourth century.[3] Jude is mentioned here after 1–3 John, but—interestingly—before Barnabas, Revelation, Acts, Shepherd of Hermas, *Acts of Paul*, and *Apocalypse of Peter*. At least in the Codex Claromontanus itself, some of the writings in the list—*Barnabas*, Shepherd of Hermas, *Acts of Paul*, and *Apocalypse of Peter*—are marked by a short horizontal stroke that perhaps serves to distinguish between universally acknowledged and disputed (or apocryphal?) writings. It is, however, not clear whether this distinction goes back to the original fourth-century catalog or was only added in the later Claromontanus. In any case, it seems to attest another—more open—approach to authoritative Christian writings than Eusebius shows, and it clearly includes the Epistle of Jude among the acknowledged writings.

Additionally, the oldest manuscript witness to Jude goes back to about the same era (third/fourth century c.e.; see Nicklas and Wasserman 2006; Nicklas 2005; Wasserman 2006). Actually, the text, identified as P^{72} in Gregory-Aland's standard list of New Testament manuscripts, is part of a larger codex with miscellaneous contents: the *Birth of Mary* (= *Protevangelium of James*), *3 Corinthians*, *Odes of Solomon* 11, Melito of Sardis's *Peri Pascha* (*On the Pascha*), an otherwise unknown hymn, the *Apology*

---

3. For the text, see Preuschen 1910, 40–42.

of Phileas, Pss 33 and 34 LXX, Jude, and 1–2 Peter. Interestingly, however, although Jude is written by the same scribe as 1 and 2 Peter, within the manuscript it is separated from both of those epistles. In addition, Jude, contrary to 1–2 Peter, does not contain marginal notes. Its text is written rather carelessly and differs from our modern critical editions in many ways. If we take the fact into account that the codex contains several writings that today would be considered apocryphal, plus the very free treatment of its text, it should at least be considered that the scribe of this text did not regard Jude as part of a "New Testament canon."

Finally, another Western author who made extensive use of Jude is Lucifer of Cagliari (died 370 c.e.). In his *De non conveniendo cum haereticis* (*Of Not Holding Communion with the Heretics*), written around 355/356 c.e., he argues for the need to separate from the Arians. Interestingly, in his conclusion he quotes more than half of Jude (vv. 1–4, 5–8, 11–13, 17–19). Jude's own (very open) polemic against heretics is thus reused in the new situation created by the Arian schism. This polemical use of Jude, however, is only possible if Lucifer (and his intended audience) considered Jude an authentic apostolic writing.

Rejected by Most?

Our three earliest witnesses, the Egyptian Clement, the North African Tertullian, and the Roman Muratorian Fragment, had little problem understanding Jude as an authoritative writing. Eusebius of Caesarea provides evidence that Jude was accepted as apostolic in most communities. Athanasius of Alexandria lists it among the writings of a New Testament canon in his famous thirty-ninth *Paschal Letter* (367 c.e.). At least some other authors, however, attest different opinions about the authority of the text. The most extreme example is Jerome (347–419 c.e.).

As was discussed earlier, Tertullian and Priscillian defended their use of *1 Enoch* by appealing to the authority of Jude. In Jerome's *De viris illustribus* (*On Illustrious Men*) 4, however, the whole matter is turned on its head. According to Jerome, Jude was rejected by most (*a pleris*) *because* of its use of the apocryphal *1 Enoch*. In light of the other evidence, it seems that Jerome overemphasized the extent of the letter's rejection, but he is not the only one who expresses a problem with Jude on account of its use of apocryphal traditions.

While Jerome focuses on verse 14, others seemingly had trouble with verse 9 and its idea that the archangel Michael fought with the devil for

Moses' corpse. According to Clement of Alexandria (*Adumbrationes in Epistolas Catholicas* [*Comments on the Catholic Epistles*]) and Origen (*Princ.* 3.1), this tradition finds its roots in the pseudepigraphical *Assumption of Moses*.[4] While for Clement, as we saw above, Jude's use of this pseudepigraphical text did not cause a major problem, (pseudo-?)Didymus of Alexandria (*Epistolam beati Judae apostoli enarratio* [*Interpretation of the Epistle of the Saint Apostle Jude*]; PG 39:1811–18) felt the need to attack people who remained skeptical of Jude because of its use of the *Assumption of Moses*.

2 Peter—No Part of the Canon?

Forged and No Part of the Canon

Compared to Jude, the evidence regarding 2 Peter is even more ambiguous. The author of *In Epistulas Catholicas brevis enarratio* (*Short Interpretation of the Catholic Epistles*) explicitly disagrees with 2 Peter's eschatology.[5] He clearly states, "It is not to be ignored that the present epistle is spurious [*praesentem epistolam esse falsatam*], which, although it is published (in the churches), nevertheless is not in the canon [*non tamen in canone est*]."[6] It seems possible that the original (and maybe quite old; see Zahn 1888, 312; and Leipoldt 1907, 239 n. 4) Greek version was much less harsh here than the Latin translation by Cassiodorus (see Leipoldt 1905, 57).[7] A puzzling fact remains, however. In spite of the positive decisions of several fourth-century synods (Laodicea, 360 C.E.; Carthage, 397 C.E.;

---

4. In fact, we do not have any evidence of this motif in the manuscripts of the *Assumption of Moses* currently known to us.

5. This is an ancient commentary on all seven Catholic Epistles that is written in Greek, attributed to Didymus of Alexandria, and translated into Latin in the sixth century C.E. See Cassiodorus, *Instutiones Divinarum et Saecularium Litterarum* (*Institutes of Divine and Human Letters*) 1.8.6. The *status quaestionis* regarding the authorship of the commentary is laid out by Bennett 1997, 27–33.

6. The English translation is taken from Ehrman 1983, 9. Ehrman's judgment "that the commentary must have been an original Latin composition" (10) misinterprets certain explanatory phrases of the translator and does not consider Friedrich Zoepfl's thorough study of the text (1914).

7. If the word *nothos* ("ingenuine," "spurious," "illegitimate") was present in the original Greek, then Eusebius's statement regarding James (*Hist. eccl.* 2.23.25) would provide a striking parallel. It is, in any case, unlikely that this negative comment on

maybe Rome, 382 C.E.; see also Athanasius, *Paschal Letter* 39, 367 C.E.) regarding 2 Peter's canonicity and the presence of 2 Peter in the important majuscules (Codex Alexandrinus, Codex Sinaiticus, and Codex Vaticanus), as late as the sixth century Cassiodorus provided the inhabitants of the monastery Vivariense/Castellum with this translation (intended to aid them in reading Scripture) that plainly does not accept 2 Peter.

The author of *In Epistulas Catholicas brevis enarratio* assessed the eschatological teaching of 2 Peter as nonapostolic.[8] Taking a different approach, Jerome (Hieronymus) informs us in *De viris illustribus* 1 that 2 Peter's apostolic authorship was doubted *by most* because of the stylistic differences between 2 Peter and 1 Peter (*a plerisque propter stili cum priore dissonantiam*, "by most because of its different style compared to the First [Epistle of Peter]"). As in the case of Jerome's note on Jude that was mentioned earlier, this formulation may be somewhat exaggerated. In *Letter* 120.11, he attempts to explain these differences by Peter's alleged use of a secretary in writing his epistle(s).

In the early fourth century, Eusebius, discussing the written legacy of Peter, states that he did not receive 2 Peter as canonical (*ouk endiathēkon … einai pareilēphamen*) but that "many" (*polloi*) judged the text as "useful" (*chrēsimos*) and worthy "to be studied together with the other scriptures" (*meta tōn allōn espoudasthē*; *Hist. eccl.* 3.3.1–4). In his famous categorization of Christian literature, Eusebius lists 2 Peter, like Jude, among the disputed writings (*antilegomena*) but not as forged (*Hist. eccl.* 3.25.3). It seems that his judgment is influenced by two different assessments of 2 Peter. On the one hand, he knows a strong tradition (maybe connected to Origen) that accepted only 1 Peter as an authentic Petrine writing (*Hist. eccl.* 3.3.1, 4). On the other hand, he noticed the emerging authority of the collection of the seven so-called Catholic Epistles (*Hist. eccl.* 2.25.23; see Nienhuis 2007, 63–70).

---

2 Peter stems from Didymus (see n. 5 above), who quotes 2 Peter several times as an apostolic and authoritative writing (see Ehrman 1983, 9–10).

8. In particular, the destruction of the world through fire (see 2 Pet 3:10–13) is said to contradict Jesus' teaching about the end of the world as preserved in Luke 17:26–30. As a consequence, this text does not speak of "Peter" or the "apostle" as the author of 2 Peter, but simply calls him *conscriptor epistulae* ("the writer of the letter"; see PG 39:1773). In a similar way, the Egyptian merchant and later monk Cosmas Indicopleustes struggled with 2 Peter's eschatology in his *Christian Topography* (see, e.g., 7:64–70) at the beginning of the sixth century.

Second Peter's "usefulness," to quote Eusebius, can be seen in two other witnesses. The anti-Marcionite *Dialogues with Adamantius* (late fourth century; see Tsutsui 2004) contain theological discussions between Marcus, a representative of Marcionism, and Adamantius, who follows mainstream orthodoxy. Adamantius challenges the typical Marcionite focus on the apostolic authority of Paul by asking for a witness for this authority besides Paul himself (see 2 Cor 10:18). Limited to the Marcionite canon of "Gospel and Apostle," Marcus is not able to find a satisfying answer. Thus Adamantius triumphs by pointing to Peter's statement in 2 Pet 3:15 (see *Dialogues* 2.12). In this way, the *Dialogues* intend to demonstrate that even a core idea of Marcionism such as the authority of Paul can only be argued by accepting the fuller canon of the orthodox.

A fragment probably falsely attributed to Methodius of Olympus (died ca. 311 C.E.) quotes 2 Pet 3:8 with the introductory phrase "the Apostle Peter wrote."[9] This verse is a modified citation of Ps 90 (LXX 89):4, a text quite often used in early Jewish and early Christian writings (see Bauckham 1983, 306–10). While theologians like the author of Barnabas, Justin, Irenaeus, and Hippolytus (all probably not dependent on 2 Peter; see Otto 1877) employed the psalm in a sort of "divine calculus" (see Schrage 1985, 267–75), 2 Peter's reception attests, by way of contrast, a focus on the incalculability of the coming "day of the Lord" (2 Pet 3:10; cf. 3:12). The fragment follows this latter line of thought in countering a millenarian interpretation of Rev 20:5 by pointing to 2 Pet 3:8, yet it goes even further when it equates the "thousand years" of Revelation with eternity (*ho aperantos aiōn*; cf. 2 Pet 3:18).[10]

Thus the Christian communities that produced and preserved the earliest extant textual witness of 2 Peter—the aforementioned P[72] (third/fourth centuries)—obviously judged 2 Peter to be "useful." Regrettably, it seems impossible to sort out the specific reasons for that judgment (see Haines-Eitzen 2000, 96–104; Nicklas and Wasserman 2006). The same holds true for the fascinating Papyrus Michigan 3520 (see Schenke and Kasser 2003), a Coptic manuscript from the first half of the fourth century. The papyrus contains a rather unusual combination of biblical texts: Eccle-

---

9. See Bonwetsch 1891, 238 (see XXIV) for information on the fragment. Buchheit (1958, 143–53) points to Andreas of Caesarea (sixth/seventh century C.E.) as the possible author.

10. We would like to thank Prof. Dr. Katharina Bracht (University of Jena) for helpful information on this fragment.

siastes, 1 John, and 2 Peter. Interestingly, the oldest Coptic manuscript of 1 Peter, the Crosby-Schøyen Codex (third century?), seems to be unaware of 2 Peter, as it calls 1 Peter (in both the *inscriptio* and *subscriptio*) "*the* Epistle of Peter" (see Bethge 1993, 260).

2 Peter and the "Canon" of Origen

Origen's opinion about 2 Peter is extremely difficult to assess. Without doubt, Origen (ca. 185–255 c.e.) knew *a* second letter of Peter, a fact that is proven when he refers to 1 Peter as the "first epistle of Peter" (*Commentary on the Gospel of Matthew* 15.27). Furthermore, a fragment of his *Commentaries on the Gospel of John* is regarded as the "first absolutely incontrovertible reference in Christian literature" (Chase 1902b, 3:803) to 2 Peter: "And Peter, on whom the Church of Christ is built, 'against which the gates of hell shall not prevail,' has left one acknowledged epistle; perhaps [or: let it be granted] also a second, but this is doubtful" (Origen, *Commentaries on the Gospel of John* 5.3 = Eusebius, *Hist. eccl.* 6.25.8, *NPNF*² 1:273).[11]

It is unclear, however, if the phrase "let it be granted" implies Origen's doubts concerning the apostolic authorship of 2 Peter (this implication would be supported by Origen's use of the phrase in his apology *Against Celsus*, see, e.g., 1.62; 5.7), or if, especially in this context, the phrase betrays Origen's rhetorical interest in minimizing the written legacy of the apostles (see the fragments of the *Commentaries on the Gospel of John*, which are preserved in the *Philocalia* [*Love of the Beautiful*; see Kalin 1990, 279]). In any case, the difference in Origen's attitude toward 1 Peter and 2 Peter is striking and corresponds with the testimony of his other works that are preserved in the original Greek.

The Latin translations made by Rufinus of Aquileia (but not those made by Jerome!) explicitly quote 2 Peter six times (*Homilies on Exodus* 12.4; *Homilies on Leviticus* 4.4; *Homilies in Numbers* 13.8.1; 18.4.6; *Commentaries on Romans* 4.9; 8.7) and list 2 Peter among the books of the New Testament canon (*Homilies on Joshua* 7.1). Given the peculiarities of Rufinus's translation technique (see, e.g. Wagner 1945; Grappone 2007), his strong interest in reconciling Origen with the orthodoxy of the fourth century (see Kalin 1990, 280–81), the absence of a closed canon in Origen's

---

11. Strictly speaking, the fragment does not identify the second letter as 2 Peter, but it is extremely improbable that Origen referred to a different second letter of Peter that perished in later times without a trace.

time, and the differences between the Latin version and Origen's text in Greek (see Chase 1902b, 3:803), it seems doubtful that these references to 2 Peter stem from Origen himself.[12] It follows, therefore, that one should avoid speaking of "quotations" of 2 Peter in Origen, or stating that Origen regarded 2 Peter as "canonical" (see Stenzel 1942, 51–57; Nienhuis 2007, 61–62).

There is, however, at least one solid hint that Origen *did use* 2 Peter. In *Princ.* 1.8.4, while discussing whether preexisting rational souls could be incarnated into animals (and not only into human beings), Origen clearly alludes to 2 Pet 2:16. The comparison of Rufinus's translation with the reports of Jerome and Pamphilus on this topic (see the excellent edition of Görgemanns and Karpp 1992, 263–65) shows that Rufinus tried to conceal possible contradictions between Origen's reflections and later orthodoxy. Given this fact, it seems quite implausible that—just at this place—Rufinus should have interpolated into Origen's text a biblical proof text in support of a problematic doctrine.

Hence, Origen attests the existence of 2 Peter even though he harbors doubts about its apostolic origin (see *Commentaries on John* 5.3; *Commentary on Matthew* 15.27). Thus there appears to be evidence for a use of the epistle in a relatively early Alexandrian work of Origen (*Princ.* 1.8.4), but the explicit quotations of 2 Peter in his other texts are highly dubious (especially *Commentaries on Romans* 8.7; *Homilies on Joshua* 7.1).

Reception of 2 Peter before Origen?

In spite of the numerous testimonies listed by Charles Bigg and Joseph Mayor (see Bigg 1902, 199–215; Mayor 1907, cxv–cxxxiv; further Bauckham 1983, 162–63), there is no clear evidence of the existence of 2 Peter in the time before Origen.[13] Sometimes it is assumed that Clement of

---

12. Chadwick (1959, 21) demonstrates Rufinus's "redrafting" of Origen's texts also to include the change and rearrangement of biblical quotations. As far as 2 Peter is concerned, Origen's *Commentaries on Romans* 8.7 (cf. 5.3; 9.2) shows especially significant traces of alteration by Rufinus (see Chase 1902b, 3:803). Clearly, this "redrafting" cannot be discussed here in any detail (but see Grünstäudl 2013, 59–73).

13. Unlike Jude, 2 Peter is even missing in the Muratorian Fragment. The *Acts of Peter* (see esp. 12.20) contains several similarities to 2 Peter, but a literary relationship cannot be proven. In addition, there is an ongoing debate about the exact date of the *Acts of Peter*.

Alexandria wrote a commentary on 2 Peter, but the information on this subject found in Eusebius (*Hist. eccl.* 6.14.1) and Photius (*Bibliotheca*, cod. 109) is rather vague. Clement's extant commentaries on the Catholic Epistles (*Adumbrationes in Epistolas Catholicas*) and his other works show no knowledge of 2 Peter. Given the extensive use Clement makes of Jude (see above) and his interest in Petrine pseudepigrapha like the *Preaching of Peter* (see Cambe 2003) and the *Apocalypse of Peter* (which is closely related to 2 Peter, see below), Clement's complete silence regarding 2 Peter is remarkable.[14]

Writing some decades before Clement, Justin Martyr provides a striking parallel to 2 Pet 2:1 in his *Dialogue with Trypho* (ca. 160 C.E.; see Bobichon 2003) that deserves quotation.

> And just as there were false prophets [*pseudoprophētai*] contemporaneous with your holy prophets, so are there now many false teachers [*pseudodidaskaloi*] amongst us, of whom our Lord forewarned us to beware. (Justin, *Dial.* 82.1, ANF 1:240)

> But there were also false prophets [*pseudoprophētai*] among the people, just as there will be false teachers [*pseudodidaskaloi*] among you. (2 Pet 2:1 NIV)

The extreme rareness of the term "false teachers" (*pseudodidaskaloi*) in early Christianity (before Origen only these two texts use this term, but see *pseudodidaskalia* in Polycarp, *To the Philippians* 7.2), the comparison of these figures with the "false prophets" in Israel, and the similar syntactical structure make a literary relationship between 2 Peter and Justin highly probable (see Ruf 2011, 361; Kraus 2001, 340 n. 100).

This relationship, however, does not automatically mean that it is Justin who is in the dependent position. It has to be noted that Justin relates the warning about the false teachers not by referring to Peter but by referring to "our Lord" (*ho hēmeteros kyrios*). He thereby presents the logion in terms of an actual instance of Jesus' warnings in Matt 24:11, 24// Mark 13:22. Moreover, the theme of "teaching" is prominent in Justin. If one follows the argument throughout the whole of the *Dialogue* (see espe-

---

14. The Greek fragments of the *Apocalypse of Peter* are edited in Nicklas and Kraus 2004 (79–130), the Ethiopic text in Marrassini 1994. For an English translation and commentary, see Buchholz 1988.

cially *Dial.* 35.80–82), it seems that Justin is developing the concise parallelism of *Dial.* 82.1 step by step.

Finally, the context of *Dial.* 82.1 provides several points of contact with 2 Peter—none of them derived from 2 Peter, but from other sources. In *Dial.* 81.1 the phrase "new heaven and the new earth" (cf. 2 Pet 3:13) is explicitly taken from Isa 65:17. In *Dial.* 81.2 the "holy mountain" (cf. 2 Pet 1:18) recalls Isa 65:25, and in *Dial.* 81.3 the allusion to Ps 90:4 (cf. 2 Pet 3:8) is introduced as "the expression" (*to eirēmenon*). Justin's use of these other sources leads to the quite surprising conclusion that an (early) *patristic* text (Justin, *Dialogue*) might be the source for a *New Testament* text (2 Peter). If this hypothesis holds, any reception of 2 Peter before Justin would be per se impossible.[15]

Nevertheless, one other very early text, the *Apocalypse of Peter*, must be considered here because of its great relevance for recent scholarship on 2 Peter. (See *ANF* 9:141–47 for a translation.) This text, which should not be confused with the Coptic *Apocalypse of Peter* from Nag Hammadi (NHC 7.3; second/third century?), was written in the first half of the second century and shows some striking similarities with 2 Peter.[16] Several different explanations for these similarities have been provided, but the most thorough discussion of the topic is found in the work of Richard Bauckham (see Bauckham 1998; Kraus 2001, 390–96; 2003, 75–84).

Bauckham rightly argues that the relationship between 2 Peter and the *Apocalypse of Peter* should not be investigated primarily by evaluating the Greek fragment of the apocalypse found in Akhmîm (P.Cair. 10759), but by focusing on the Ethiopic text, which probably comes closer to the lost original form of the apocalypse and is, furthermore, supported by two old Greek fragments (Bodl.MS.Gr.th.f. 4 [P] and P.Vindob.G 39756). Building on this important methodological insight, Bauckham is able to demonstrate that the similarities between 2 Peter and the *Apocalypse of Peter*, *taken as a whole*, are best explained by a literary relationship between the two Petrine pseudepigrapha. As in the case of Justin, the direction of dependence is not automatically clear. Arguing that the account of the transfiguration in the *Apocalypse of Peter* makes use of Synoptic tradition

---

15. Picirilli (1988) argues for a reception of 2 Peter in the so-called Apostolic Fathers, but his arguments are not convincing. For a balanced study of the reception of the New Testament writings in the Apostolic Fathers, see Gregory and Tuckett 2005.

16. While B. A. Pearson (1990) thinks that the *Apocalypse of Peter* from Nag Hammadi used 2 Peter, Havelaar (1999, 167) remains skeptical about this dependence.

while in 2 Peter it does not, Bauckham sees the *Apocalypse of Peter* in the dependent position. Robert J. Miller, however, has convincingly questioned 2 Peter's independence of the Synoptic tradition and thereby weakens the decisive force of Bauckham's argument (see Miller 1996).

Moreover, an examination of the presentation of the figure of Peter and the theological implications of this picture in *Apocalypse of Peter* and 2 Peter make it more probable that 2 Peter used the apocalypse than vice versa. If 2 Peter were used by *Apocalypse of Peter*, one would expect that at least some traces of Jude, which was incorporated by 2 Peter, would be found in the apocalypse, but this is not the case. Therefore, the *Apocalypse of Peter* does not appear to be the first text that used 2 Peter, but is rather—like Jude—a *source* text for the epistle (see Grünstäudl 2013, 97–144).

Conclusion

If Jude and 2 Peter are among the most neglected writings of the New Testament today, this neglect is surely more or less in line with their difficult journey into the canon. At least at first sight, our surviving witnesses to Jude's early use seem to show a linear progression from more or less universal acceptance of the text to growing doubts due to the text's use of apocryphal traditions like *1 Enoch* and the *Assumption of Moses*. However, we should be careful not to draw overly simplistic conclusions from our few early testimonies about the text. They do not tell us what "normal" people thought about the text, nor does evidence from Africa (i.e., Tertullian) tell us much about the text's reception in Syria or Asia Minor. Therefore, we think that we are on quite safe ground if we conclude that from early times Jude was interpreted as an authoritative, apostolic Christian writing by some (or perhaps even many), but that the text remained disputed for a long time (even after Athanasius). The most negative voice surely comes from Jerome, but even though he regards the letter as rejected by most, many other witnesses—even among his contemporaries—point in a different direction.

Interestingly, 2 Peter's inclusion was much more difficult than Jude's. On the one hand, 2 Peter seems not to be used in the whole of the second century and was, owing to its style and eschatology, doubted until the end of antiquity. On the other hand, 2 Peter was assessed as "useful" in the third and fourth centuries, and therefore it eventually made its way into the canon of the New Testament. The study of this complex process of rejection and reception opens a fascinating window through which to view the Bible "in the making." In addition, however, the insights gleaned along the way encourage us to ask questions about 2 Peter's and Jude's ongoing "usefulness" today.

Bibliography

Aageson, James W. 2004. "1 Peter 2:11–3:7: Slaves, Wives, and the Complexities of Interpretation." Pages 34–49 in *The Feminist Companion to the Catholic Epistles and Hebrews*. Edited by A.-J. Levine with M. Mayo Robbins. London: T&T Clark.

Achtemeier, Paul J. 1988. "New-born Babes and Living Stones: Literal and Figurative in 1 Peter." Pages 207–36 in *To Touch the Text: Biblical and Related Stories in Honor of Joseph H. Fitzmyer*. Edited by M. P. Horgan and P. J. Kobeleski. New York: Crossroad.

———. 1993. "Suffering Servant and Suffering Christ in 1 Peter." Pages 176–88 in *The Future of Christology: Essays in Honor of Leander E. Keck*. Edited by A. Malherbe and W. Meeks. New York: Crossroad.

———. 1996. *1 Peter: A Commentary on First Peter*. Hermeneia. Minneapolis: Fortress.

Adam, A. K. M. 1995. *What Is Postmodern Biblical Criticism?* GBS. Minneapolis: Fortress.

———, ed. 2001. *Postmodern Interpretations of the Bible: A Reader*. St. Louis: Chalice.

———. 2006. *Faithful Interpretation: Reading the Bible in a Postmodern World*. Minneapolis: Fortress.

Adams, Edward. 2007. *The Stars Will Fall From Heaven: Cosmic Catastrophe in the New Testament and Its World*. LNTS 347. London: T&T Clark.

Adams, Sean A. 2010. "Paul's Letter Opening and Greek Epistolography: A Matter of Relationship." Pages 33–55 in *Paul and the Ancient Letter Form*. Edited by S. E. Porter and S. A. Adams. Pauline Studies 6. Leiden: Brill.

Adler, William. 2002. "The Pseudepigrapha in the Early Church." Pages 211–28 in *The Canon Debate*. Edited by L. M. McDonald and J. A. Sanders. Peabody, Mass.: Hendrickson.

Aichele, George, Peter Miscall, and Richard Walsh. 2009. "An Elephant in the Room: Historical Critical and Postmodern Interpretations of the Bible." *JBL* 128:383–404.

Aland, Kurt. 1961. "The Problem of Anonymity and Pseudonymity in Christian Literature of the First Two Centuries." *JTS* n.s. 12:39–49.

Albl, Martin C. 1999. *"And Scripture Cannot Be Broken": The Form and Function of the Early Christian Testimonia Collections.* NovTSup 96. Leiden: Brill.

Amphoux, Christian-Bernard, and Jean-Paul Bouhot, eds. 1996. *La lecture liturgique des Épîtres Catholiques dans l'Église ancienne.* HTB 1. Lausanne: Zèbre.

Anderson, R. Dean. 1999. *Ancient Rhetorical Theory and Paul.* Rev. ed. CBET 18. Leuven: Peeters.

Aristotle. 1885. *The Politics of Aristotle.* Translated by B. Jowett. 2 vols. Oxford: Clarendon.

Aristotle. 1926–2011. Translated by H. Rackham et al. 23 vols. LCL. Cambridge, Mass.: Harvard University Press.

Arnold, Bill T. 2010. "Old Testament Eschatology and the Rise of Apocalypticism." Pages 23–39 in *The Oxford Handbook of Eschatology.* Edited by J. Walls. Oxford: Oxford University Press.

Arzt-Grabner, Peter. 2010. "Paul's Letter Thanksgiving." Pages 129–58 in *Paul and the Ancient Letter Form.* Edited by S. E. Porter and S. A. Adams. Pauline Studies 6. Leiden: Brill.

Ashcroft, Bill, Gareth Griffiths, and Helen Tiffin. 2000. *Post-Colonial Studies: The Key Concepts.* London: Routledge.

———. 2002. *The Empire Writes Back: Theory and Practice in Post-Colonial Literatures.* 2nd ed. New Accents. London: Routledge.

———, eds. 2006. *The Post-Colonial Studies Reader.* 2nd ed. London: Routledge.

Augustine. 1900. *De fide et operibus.* Pages 35–97 in *De fide et symbolo, De fide et operibus, De agone christiano, De continentia, De bono coniugali, De virginitate, De bono viduitatis, De adulterinis coniugiis, De mendacio, Contra mendacium, De opere monachorum, De divinatione daemonum, De cura pro mortuis gerenda, De patientia.* Edited by J. Zycha. CSEL 41. Vienna: Tempsky.

———. 1961. *Sermo 284.* Pages 446–73 in *Sermones de vetere testamento (1–50).* Edited by C. Lambot. CCSL 41. Turnhout, Belgium: Brepols.

———. 2004a. *Contra Julianum opus imperfectum.* Edited by M. Zelzer. CSEL 85/2. Vienna: Austrian Academy of Sciences.

———. 2004b. *Sermo 37.* Pages 131–39 in *Sermones ad populum.* Edited by H. Drobner. Patrologia 13. Frankfurt am Main: Peter Lang.

Aune, David E. 1987. *The New Testament in Its Literary Environment.* LEC 8. Philadelphia: Westminster.

———. 2003. *The Westminster Dictionary of New Testament and Early Christian Literature and Rhetoric.* Louisville: Westminster John Knox.

———. 2008. "Lists, Ethical." *NIDB* 3:670–72.

Avruch, Kevin. 2003. "Culture and Ethnic Conflict in the New World Disorder." Pages 72–82 in *Race and Ethnicity: Comparative and Theoretical Approaches.* Edited by J. Stone and R. Dennis. Blackwell Readers in Sociology. Oxford: Blackwell.

Balch, David L. 1981. *Let Wives Be Submissive: The Domestic Code in 1 Peter.* SBLMS 26. Atlanta: Scholars Press.

———. 1986. "Hellenization/Acculturation in 1 Peter." Pages 79–101 in *Perspectives on First Peter.* Edited by C. H. Talbert. North American Baptist Professors of Religion Special Studies Series 9. Macon, Ga.: Mercer University Press.

———. 1988. "Household Codes." Pages 25–50 in *Greco-Roman Literature and the New Testament.* SBLSBS 21. Edited by D. E. Aune. Atlanta: Scholars Press.

Barr, David L., ed. 2003. *Reading the Book of Revelation: A Resource for Students.* SBLRBS 44. Atlanta: Society of Biblical Literature.

Bartlet, James Vernon. 1899. *The Apostolic Age: Its Life, Doctrine, Worship and Polity.* New York: Charles Scribner's Sons.

Barton, John. 1998. "Historical-Critical Approaches." Pages 9–20 in *The Cambridge Companion to Biblical Interpretation.* Edited by J. Barton. Cambridge Companions to Religion. Cambridge: Cambridge University Press.

Bauckham, Richard J. 1980. "The Delay of the Parousia." *TynBul* 31:3–36.

———. 1983. *Jude, 2 Peter.* WBC 50. Waco, Tex.: Word.

———. 1990. *Jude and the Relatives of Jesus in the Early Church.* Edinburgh: T&T Clark.

———. 1998. *The Fate of the Dead: Studies on the Jewish and Christian Apocalypses.* NovTSup 93. Leiden: Brill.

Bauer, Walter. 1971. *Orthodoxy and Heresy in Earliest Christianity.* 2nd ed. Philadelphia: Fortress.

Bauman, Zygmunt. 1991. *Modernity and Ambivalence.* Ithaca, N.Y.: Cornell University Press.

Bauman-Martin, Betsy J. 2004. "Feminist Theologies of Suffering and Current Interpretations of 1 Peter 2.18–3.9." Pages 63–81 in *The Feminist Companion to the Catholic Epistles and Hebrews*. Edited by A.-J. Levine with M. Mayo Robbins. London: T&T Clark.

———. 2007. "Speaking Jewish: Postcolonial Aliens and Strangers in First Peter." Pages 144–77 in *Reading First Peter with New Eyes: Methodological Reassessments of the Letter of First Peter*. Edited by R. L. Webb and B. Bauman-Martin. LNTS 364. London: T&T Clark.

Baynes, Leslie. 2012. "*Enoch* and *Jubilees* in the Canon of the Ethiopian Orthodox Church." Pages 799–818 in vol. 2 of *A Teacher for All Generations: Essays in Honor of James C. VanderKam*. Edited by E. F. Mason et al. 2 vols. Leiden: Brill.

Bechtler, Steven R. 1998. *Following in His Steps: Suffering, Community, and Christology in 1 Peter*. SBLDS 162. Atlanta: Scholars Press.

Beckwith, Roger. 1985. *The Old Testament Canon of the New Testament Church and Its Background in Early Judaism*. Grand Rapids: Eerdmans.

Bede the Venerable. 1983. *In Epistulas Septem Catholicas*. Pages 179–342 in *Opera exegetica*. Edited by M. L. W. Laistner and D. Hurst. CCSL 121. Turnhout, Belgium: Brepols.

Bennett, Byard John. 1997. "The Origin of Evil: Didymus the Blind's *Contra Manichaeos* and Its Debt to Origen's Theology and Exegesis." Ph.D. diss., University of St. Michael's College, Toronto School of Theology.

Berger, Klaus. 1974. "Apostelbrief und apostolische Rede/Zum Formular frühchristlicher Briefe." *ZNW* 65:190–231.

Bethge, Hans-Gerhard. 1993. "Der Text des ersten Petrusbriefes im Crosby-Schøyen Codex (Ms. 193 Schøyen Collection)." *ZNW* 84:255–67.

Bhabha, Homi K. 1994. *The Location of Culture*. London: Routledge.

Bible and Culture Collective, The. 1995. *The Postmodern Bible*. New Haven: Yale University Press.

Bigg, Charles. 1902. *A Critical and Exegetical Commentary on the Epistles of St. Peter and St. Jude*. 2nd ed. ICC. Edinburgh: T&T Clark.

Bird, Jennifer G. 2011. *Abuse, Power and Fearful Obedience: Reconsidering 1 Peter's Commands to Wives*. LNTS 442. London: T&T Clark.

Bobichon, Philippe. 2003. *Justin Martyr: Dialogue avec Tryphon*. Paradosis 47. 2 vols. Fribourg: Département de Patristique et d'Histoire de l'Eglise de l'Université de Fribourg/Fribourg Academic Press.

Boismard, Marie-Emile. 1956. "Une liturgie baptismale dans la *Prima Petri*." *RB* 63:182–208.

Bömer, Franz. 1958–63. *Untersuchungen über die Religion der Sklaven in Griechenland und Rom*. 4 vols. Akademie der Wissenschaften und der Literatur. Abhandlungen der geistes- und sozialwissenschaftlichen Klasse. Mainz: Franz Steiner.

Bonwetsch, Gottlieb Nathanael. 1891. *Methodius von Olympus I: Schriften*. Erlangen/Leipzig: Deichert.

Boobyer, G. H. 1959. "The Indebtedness of 2 Peter to 1 Peter." Pages 34–53 in *New Testament Essays: Studies in Memory of Thomas Walter Manson, 1893–1958*. Edited by A. J. B. Higgins. Manchester: Manchester University Press.

Boring, M. Eugene. 1999. *1 Peter*. ANTC. Nashville: Abingdon.

———. 2007. "Narrative Dynamics in First Peter: The Function of Narrative World." Pages 8–40 in *Reading First Peter with New Eyes: Methodological Reassessments of the Letter of First Peter*. Edited by R. L. Webb and B. Bauman-Martin. LNTS 364. London: T&T Clark.

Brosend, William. 2008. "Jude, Letter of." *NIDB* 3:440–43.

Brox, Norbert. 1975. *Falsche Verfasserangaben: Zur Erklärung der Frühchristlichen Pseudepigraphie*. SBS 79. Stuttgart: Bibelwerk.

Buchheit, Vinzenz. 1958. *Studien zu Methodios von Olympos*. TUGAL 69. Berlin: Akademie.

Buchholz, Dennis D. 1988. *Your Eyes Will Be Opened: A Study of the Greek (Ethiopic) Apocalypse of Peter*. SBLDS 97. Atlanta: Scholars Press.

Buell, Denise Kimber. 2001. "Rethinking the Relevance of Race for Early Christian Self-Definition." *HTR* 94:449–76.

———. 2002. "Race and Universalism in Early Christianity." *JECS* 10:429–68.

———. 2005. *Why This New Race: Ethnic Reasoning in Early Christianity*. New York: Columbia University Press.

Burrus, Virginia. 1990. "Canonical References to Extra-Canonical 'Texts': Priscillian's Defense of the Apocrypha." Pages 60–67 in *Society of Biblical Literature Seminar Papers, 1990*. SBLSP 29. Atlanta: Scholars Press.

Callan, Terrence. 2004. "Use of the Letter of Jude by the Second Letter of Peter." *Bib* 85:42–64.

———. 2010. "Rhetography and Rhetology of Apocalyptic Discourse in Second Peter." Pages 59–90 in *Reading Second Peter with New Eyes: Methodological Reassessments of the Letter of Second Peter*. Edited by D. F. Watson and R. L. Webb. LNTS 382. London: T&T Clark.

Cambe, Michel. 2003. *Kerygma Petri: Textus et commentarius*. Corpus Christianorum: Series Apocryphorum 15. Turnhout, Belgium: Brepols.

Campbell, Barth L. 1998. *Honor, Shame, and the Rhetoric of 1 Peter*. SBLDS 160. Atlanta: Scholars Press.

Candlish, J. S. 1891. "On the Moral Character of Pseudonymous Works." *The Expositor* 4:91–107, 262–79.

Carey, Greg. 1999. "Introduction: Apocalyptic Discourse, Apocalyptic Rhetoric." Pages 1–17 in *Vision and Persuasion: Rhetorical Dimensions of Apocalyptic Discourse*. Edited by G. Carey and L. G. Bloomquist. St. Louis: Chalice.

Carroll, Robert P. 1998. "Poststructuralist Approaches, New Historicism and Postmodernism." Pages 50–66 in *The Cambridge Companion to Biblical Interpretation*. Edited by J. Barton. Cambridge Companions to Religion. Cambridge: Cambridge University Press.

Carson, D. A. 2007a. "Jude." Pages 1069–79 in *Commentary on the New Testament Use of the Old Testament*. Edited by G. K. Beale and D. A. Carson. Grand Rapids: Baker Academic.

———. 2007b. "2 Peter." Pages 1047–61 in *Commentary on the New Testament Use of the Old Testament*. Edited by G. K. Beale and D. A. Carson. Grand Rapids: Baker Academic.

Carson, D. A., Douglas J. Moo, and Leon Morris. 1992. *An Introduction to the New Testament*. Grand Rapids: Zondervan.

Carter, Warren. 2004. "Going All the Way? Honoring the Emperor and Sacrificing Wives and Slaves in 1 Peter 2:13–3:6." Pages 14–33 in *The Feminist Companion to the Catholic Epistles and Hebrews*. Edited by A.-J. Levine with M. Mayo Robbins. London: T&T Clark.

Chadwick, Henry. 1959. "Rufinus and the Tura Papyrus of Origen's Commentary on Romans." *JTS* n.s. 10:10-42.

Charles, J. Daryl. 1993. *Literary Strategy in the Epistle of Jude*. Scranton, Pa.: University of Scranton Press.

Chase, Frederic Henry. 1902a. "Jude, Epistle of." Pages 799–806 in vol. 2 of *A Dictionary of the Bible*. Edited by J. Hastings et al. 5 vols. Edinburgh: T&T Clark.

———. 1902b. "Peter, Second Epistle of." Pages 796–818 in vol. 3 of *A Dictionary of the Bible*. Edited by J. Hastings et al. 5 vols. Edinburgh: T&T Clark.

Chester, Andrew, and Ralph P. Martin. 1994. *The Theology of the Letters of James, Peter, and Jude*. New Testament Theology. Cambridge: Cambridge University Press.

Chilton, Bruce, and Jacob Neusner, eds. 2001. *The Brother of Jesus: James the Just and His Mission*. Louisville: Westminster John Knox.

Clement of Alexandria. 1981. *Stromata V*. Edited by A. LeBoulluec and P. Voulet. SC 278–79. Paris: Cerf.

———. 1997. *Stromata VII*. Edited by A. LeBoulluec. SC 428. Paris: Cerf.

Clifford, Richard. 1998. "The Origin and Early Development of Themes of Apocalyptic." Pages 1–38 in vol. 1 of *The Encyclopedia of Apocalypticism*. Edited by J. J. Collins. 3 vols. New York: Continuum.

Clines, David J. A. 2010. "Psalm 23 and Method: Reading a David Psalm." Pages 175–84 in *The Fate of King David: The Past and Present of a Biblical Icon*. Edited by T. Linafelt, C. V. Camp, and T. Beal. OTS 500. New York: T&T Clark.

Coblentz Bautch, Kelley. 2003. *A Study of the Geography of 1 Enoch 17–19*. JSJSup 81. Leiden: Brill.

Collins, Adela Yarbro. 1986. "Introduction: Early Christian Apocalypses." *Semeia* 36:1–11.

Collins, John J. 1979. "Introduction: Towards the Morphology of a Genre." *Semeia* 14:1–20.

———. 1998. *The Apocalyptic Imagination: An Introduction to the Jewish Matrix of Christianity*. 2nd ed. Grand Rapids: Eerdmans.

———. 2010. "Enoch, Ethiopic Apocalypse of (1 Enoch)." Page 585 in *The Eerdmans Dictionary of Early Judaism*. Edited by J. J. Collins and D. C. Harlow. Grand Rapids: Eerdmans.

Collins, Raymond F. 2010. "A Significant Decade: The Trajectory of the Hellenistic Epistolary Thanksgiving." Pages 159–84 in *Paul and the Ancient Letter Form*. Edited by S. E. Porter and S. A. Adams. Pauline Studies 6. Leiden: Brill.

Cook, John Granger. 2010. *Roman Attitudes Toward the Christians: From Claudius to Hadrian*. WUNT 261. Tübingen: Mohr Siebeck.

Cook, Stephen L. 2003. *The Apocalyptic Literature*. Interpreting Biblical Texts. Nashville: Abingdon.

Crouch, James E. 1972. *The Origin and Intention of the Colossian Haustafel*. FRLANT 109. Göttingen: Vandenhoeck & Ruprecht.

Dalton, William Joseph. 1989. *Christ's Proclamation to the Spirits: A Study of 1 Peter 3:18–4:6*. 2nd ed. AnBib 23. Rome: Pontifical Biblical Institute.

Davids, Peter H. 1990. *The First Epistle of Peter*. NICNT. Grand Rapids: Eerdmans.

———. 2004. "The Use of Second Temple Traditions in 1 and 2 Peter and Jude." Pages 409–31 in *The Catholic Epistles and the Tradition*. Edited by J. Schlosser. BETL 176. Leuven: Peeters.

———. 2006. *The Letters of 2 Peter and Jude*. Pillar New Testament Commentary. Grand Rapids: Eerdmans.

———. 2009. "The Catholic Epistles as a Canonical Janus: A New Testament Glimpse into Old and New Testament Canon Formation." *BBR* 19:403–16.

Debrunner, Albert, et al. 1967. "λέγω, κτλ." *TDNT* 4:69–192.

Deissmann, Adolf. 1901. *Bible Studies*. Translated by A. Grieve. Edinburgh: T&T Clark.

———. 1927. *Light From the Ancient East*. Translated by L. R. M. Strachan. New York: Doran.

Dennis, John. 2008. "Cosmology in the Petrine Literature and Jude." Pages 157–77 in *Cosmology and New Testament Theology*. Edited by J. T. Pennington and S. M. McDonough. London: T&T Clark.

Desjardins, Michael. 1991. "Bauer and Beyond: On Recent Scholarly Discussions of Αἵρεσις in the Early Christian Era." *SecCent* 8:65–82.

Dibelius, Martin. 1936. *A Fresh Approach to the New Testament and Early Christian Literature*. London: Ivor Nicholson and Watson.

———. 1976. *James*. Revised by H. Greeven. Translated by M. A. Williams. Hermeneia. Philadelphia: Fortress.

Dio Chrysostom. 1932–51. Translated by J. W. Cohoon and H. L. Crosby. 5 vols. LCL. Cambridge, Mass.: Harvard University Press.

DiTommaso, Lorenzo. 2011. "The Apocalyptic Other." Pages 221–46 in *The "Other" in Second Temple Judaism: Essays in Honor of John J. Collins*. Edited by D. C. Harlow et al. Grand Rapids: Eerdmans.

Donelson, Lewis R. 1986. *Pseudepigraphy and Ethical Argument in the Pastoral Epistles*. HUT 22. Tübingen: Mohr Siebeck.

———. 2010. *I and II Peter and Jude*. NTL. Louisville: Westminster John Knox.

Doty, William G. 1973. *Letters in Primitive Christianity*. GBS. Philadelphia: Fortress.

Dryden, J. de Waal. 2006. *Theology and Ethics in 1 Peter: Paraenetic Strategies for Christian Character Formation*. WUNT 2/209. Tübingen: Mohr Siebeck.

Dubis, Mark. 2002. *Messianic Woes in First Peter: Suffering and Eschatology in 1 Peter 4:12–19*. Studies in Biblical Literature 33. New York: Peter Lang.

———. 2006. "Research on 1 Peter: A Survey of Scholarly Literature Since 1985." *Currents in Biblical Research* 4:199–239.

Dunn, James D. G. 2006. *Unity and Diversity in the New Testament: An Inquiry into the Character of Earliest Christianity*. 3rd ed. London: SCM.

———. 2009. *Beginning from Jerusalem*. Vol. 2 of *Christianity in the Making*. Grand Rapids: Eerdmans.

Du Toit, Andreas. 1994. "Vilification as a Pragmatic Device in Early Christian Epistolography." *Bib* 75:403–12.

Ehrman, Bart D. 1983. "The New Testament Canon of Didymus the Blind." *VC* 37:1–21.

———. 2013. *Forgery and Counterforgery: The Use of Literary Deceit in Early Christian Polemics*. Oxford: Oxford University Press.

Elliott, John H. 1976. "The Rehabilitation of an Exegetical Step-Child: 1 Peter in Recent Research." *JBL* 95:243–54.

———. 1981. *A Home for the Homeless: A Sociological Exegesis of 1 Peter, Its Situation and Strategy*. Philadelphia, Fortress. [see Elliott 1990 below]

———. 1982. *I–II Peter, Jude*. ACNT. Minneapolis: Augsburg.

———. 1986. "1 Peter, Its Situation and Strategy: A Discussion with David Balch." Pages 61–78 in *Perspectives on First Peter*. Edited by C. H. Talbert. North American Baptist Professors of Religion Special Studies Series 9. Macon, Ga: Mercer University Press.

———. 1990. *A Home for the Homeless: A Social-Scientific Criticism of 1 Peter, Its Situation and Strategy, With a New Introduction*. 2nd ed. Minneapolis: Fortress. [see Elliott 1981 above]

———. 1992. "Peter, Second Epistle of." Pages 282–87 in vol. 5 of *Anchor Bible Dictionary*. Edited by D. N. Freedman. 6 vols. New York: Doubleday.

———. 1993. *What Is Social-Scientific Criticism?* GBS. Minneapolis: Fortress.

———. 1995. "Disgraced yet Graced: The Gospel according to 1 Peter in the Key of Honor and Shame." *BTB* 25:166–78.

———. 2000. *1 Peter: A New Translation with Introduction and Commentary*. AB. New York: Doubleday.

———. 2007a. *Conflict, Community, and Honor: 1 Peter in Social-Scientific Perspective*. Cascade Companions. Eugene, Ore.: Cascade.

———. 2007b. Review of Bonnie Howe, *Because You Bear This Name: Conceptual Metaphor and the Moral Meaning of 1 Peter*. *Review of Biblical Literature*. Online: http://www.bookreviews.org/pdf/5321_5610.pdf.

Engberg-Peterson, Troels. "The Concept of Paraenesis." Pages 47–72 in *Early Christian Paraenesis in Context*. Edited by J. Starr and T. Engberg-Pedersen. BZNW 125. Berlin: De Gruyter.

Eriksson, Anders, Thomas H. Olbricht, and Walter Übelacker, ed. 2002. *Rhetorical Argumentation in Biblical Texts: Essays from the Lund 2000 Conference*. Emory Studies in Early Christianity 8. Harrisburg, Pa.: Trinity Press International.

Esler, Philip F. 1987. *Community and Gospel in Luke-Acts: The Social and Political Motivations of Lucan Theology*. SNTSMS 57. Cambridge: Cambridge University Press.

———. 1998. *Galatians*. New Testament Readings. London: Routledge.

———. 2003. *Conflict and Identity in Romans*. Minneapolis: Fortress.

Eusebius of Caesarea. 1903–1909. *Historia Ecclesiastica*. Edited by E. Schwartz and T. Mommsen. Eusebius Werke 2/1–3. Griechischen Christlichen Schriftstellern der ersten drei Jahrhunderte 9/1–3. Leipzig: Hinrichs.

Feldmeier, Reinhard. 1992. *Die Christen als Fremde: Die Metapher der Fremde in der antiken Welt, im Urchristentum und im 1. Petrusbrief*. WUNT 64. Tübingen: Mohr Siebeck.

———. 2008. *The First Letter of Peter: A Commentary on the Greek Text*. Translated by P. H. Davids. Waco, Tex.: Baylor University Press.

———. 2009. "Salvation and Anthropology in First Peter." Pages 203–13 in *The Catholic Epistles and Apostolic Traditions*. Edited by K.-W. Niebuhr and R. W. Wall. Waco, Tex.: Baylor University Press.

Festinger, Leon. 1957. *A Theory of Cognitive Dissonance*. Evanston, Ill.: Row & Peterson.

Festinger, Leon, and J. M. Carlsmith. 1959. "Cognitive Consequences of Forced Compliance." *Journal of Abnormal and Social Psychology* 58:203–10.

Festinger, Leon, Harry W. Rieken, and Stanley Schachter. 1956. *When Prophecy Fails: A Social and Psychological Study of a Modern Group that Predicted the Destruction of the World*. New York: Harper & Row.

Fiore, Benjamin. 2009. "Parenesis." *NIDB* 4:382–83.

Foerster, Werner, and Johannes Herrmann. 1965. "κλῆρος, κτλ." *TDNT* 3:758–85.

Forbes, Christopher. 1986. "Comparison, Self-Praise and Irony: Paul's Boasting and the Conventions of Hellenistic Rhetoric." *NTS* 32:1–30.

Fornberg, Tord. 1977. *An Early Church in a Pluralistic Society: A Study of 2 Peter*. ConBNT 9. Lund: Gleerup.

Frey, Jörg. 2009. "The Epistle of Jude between Judaism and Hellenism." Pages 309–30 in *The Catholic Epistles and Apostolic Traditions*. Edited by K.-W. Niebuhr and R. W. Wall. Waco, Tex.: Baylor University Press.

Freyne, Sean. 2011. "Apocalypticism as the Rejected Other: Wisdom and Apocalypticism in Early Judaism and Early Christianity." Pages 247–61 in *The "Other" in Second Temple Judaism: Essays in Honor of John J. Collins*. Edited by D. C. Harlow et al. Grand Rapids: Eerdmans.

Friesen, Steven J. 2004. "Poverty in Pauline Studies: Beyond the So-called New Consensus." *JSNT* 26:323–61.

Gager, John G. 1975. *Kingdom and Community: The Social World of Early Christianity*. Englewood Cliffs, N.J.: Prentice-Hall.

Gammie, John G. 1990. "Paraenetic Literature: Toward the Morphology of a Secondary Genre." *Semeia* 50:41–77.

Gandhi, Leela. 1998. *Postcolonial Theory: A Critical Introduction*. Edinburgh: Edinburgh University Press.

Gentner, Dedre. 1989. "The Mechanisms of Analogical Learning." Pages 199–241 in *Similarity and Analogical Reasoning*. Edited by S. Vosniadou and A. Ortony. London: Cambridge University Press.

Gerdmar, Anders. 2001. *Rethinking the Judaism-Hellenism Dichotomy: A Historiographical Case Study of Second Peter and Jude*. ConBNT 36. Stockholm: Almqvist & Wiksell.

Gilmour, Michael J. 2001. "Reflections on the Authorship of 2 Peter." *EvQ* 73:291–309.

Gloag, Paton J. 1887. *Introduction to the Catholic Epistles*. Edinburgh: T&T Clark.

Görgemanns, Herwig, and Heinrich Karpp, eds. 1992. *Origenes: Vier Bücher von den Prinzipien*. 3rd ed. Darmstadt: Wissenschaftliche Buchgesellschaft.

Gounelle, Rémi. 2000. *La descente du Christ aux enfers. Institutionnalisation d'une croyance*. Collection des Études Augustiniennes, Série Antiquité 162. Paris: Institut d'Études Augustiniennes.

Grappone, Antonio. 2007. *Omelie Origeniane nella traduzione di Rufino: Un confronto con i testi greci*. SEAug 103. Rome: Institutum Patristicum Augustinianum.

Green, Gene L. 2008. *Jude and 2 Peter*. BECNT. Grand Rapids: Baker Academic.

Green, Joel B. 2006. "Body." *NIDB* 1:283–85.

———. 2007. *1 Peter*. Two Horizons New Testament Commentary. Grand Rapids: Eerdmans.

Green, Michael B. 1987. *The Second Epistle General of Peter and the General Epistle of Jude: An Introduction and Commentary.* 2nd ed. TNTC. Grand Rapids: Eerdmans.

Gregory, Andrew W., and Christopher M. Tuckett, eds. 2005. *The Reception of the New Testament in the Apostolic Fathers.* Vol. 1 of *The New Testament and the Apostolic Fathers.* Edited by A. W. Gregory and C. M. Tuckett. Oxford: Oxford University Press.

Grünstäudl, Wolfgang. 2013. *Petrus Alexandrinus: Studien zum theologischen und historischen Ort des Zweiten Petrusbriefes.* WUNT 2/353. Tübingen: Mohr Siebeck.

Gudemann, Alfred. 1894. "Literary Frauds among the Greeks." Pages 52–74 in *Classical Studies in Honour of Henry Drisler.* New York: Macmillan.

Gunkel, Hermann. 1895. *Schöpfung und Chaos in Urzeit und Endzeit: eine religionsgeschichtliche Untersuchung über Gen 1 und Ap Joh 12.* Göttingen: Vandenhoeck & Ruprecht.

———. 2006. *Creation and Chaos in the Primeval Era and the Eschaton: A Religio-Historical Study of Genesis 1 and Revelation 12.* Translated by K. W. Whitney. Grand Rapids: Eerdmans.

Guthrie, Donald. 1962. "The Development of the Idea of Canonical Pseudonymity in New Testament Criticism." *Vox Evangelica* 1:43–59.

———. 1990. *New Testament Introduction.* 4th ed. Downers Grove, Ill.: InterVarsity.

Hahnemann, Geoffrey Mark. 1992. *The Muratorian Fragment and the Development of the Canon.* Oxford Theological Monographs. Oxford: Clarendon.

Haines-Eitzen, Kim. 2000. *Guardians of Letters: Literacy, Power, and the Transmitters of Early Christian Literature.* Oxford: Oxford University Press.

Hanson, Paul D. 1975. *The Dawn of Apocalyptic: The Historical and Sociological Roots of Jewish Apocalyptic Eschatology.* Philadelphia: Fortress.

Harkins, Angela Kim, Kelley Coblentz Bautch, and John C. Endres, eds. 2014. *The Watchers in Jewish and Christian Traditions.* Minneapolis: Fortress.

Harnack, Adolf von. 1904. *The Expansion of Christianity in the First Three Centuries.* Vol 1. London: Williams & Norgate.

Havelaar, Henriette W., ed. 1999. *The Coptic Apocalypse of Peter (Nag Hammadi-Codex VII,3).* TUGAL 144. Berlin: Akademie.

Hill, Edmund. 1994. *Sermons 273–305A*. Works of Saint Augustine: A Translation for the 21st Century 3/8. New York: New City Press.
Hillyer, Norman. 1992. *1 and 2 Peter, Jude*. NIBCNT. Peabody, Mass.: Hendrickson.
Hodgson, Robert, Jr. 1979. "The Testimony Hypothesis." *JBL* 98:361–78.
Hoffman, Robert R., ed. 1985. *Metaphor: A Bibliography of Post-1970 Publications*. Amsterdam: Benjamins.
Holloway, Paul A. 2009. *Coping with Prejudice: 1 Peter in Social-Psychological Perspective*. WUNT 244. Tübingen: Mohr Siebeck.
Horrell, David G. 2002. "Social Sciences Studying Formative Christian Phenomena: A Creative Movement." Pages 3–28 in *Handbook of Early Christianity: Social Science Approaches*. Edited by A. J. Blasi, J. Duhaime, and P.-A. Turcotte. Walnut Creek, Calif.: Alta Mira.
———. 2007a. "Between Conformity and Resistance: Beyond the Balch-Elliott Debate Towards a Postcolonial Reading of First Peter." Pages 111–43 in *Reading First Peter with New Eyes: Methodological Reassessments of the Letter of First Peter*. Edited by R. L. Webb and B. Bauman-Martin. LNTS 364. London: T&T Clark.
———. 2007b. "The Label Χριστιανός: 1 Peter 4:16 and the Formation of Christian Identity." *JBL* 126:361–81.
———. 2008. *1 Peter*. NTG. London: T&T Clark.
———. 2009a. "The Themes of 1 Peter: Insights from the Earliest Manuscripts (the CrosbySchøyen Codex ms 193 and the Bodmer Miscellaneous Codex Containing P72)." *NTS* 55:502–22.
———. 2009b. "Whither Social-Scientific Approaches to New Testament Interpretation? Reflections on Contested Methodologies and the Future." Pages 6–20 in *After the First Urban Christians: The Social-Scientific Study of Pauline Christianity Twenty-Five Years Later*. Edited by T. D. Still and D. G. Horrell. London: T&T Clark.
———. 2012. "'Race,' 'Nation,' 'People': Ethnic Identity-Construction in 1 Peter 2.9." *NTS* 58:123–43.
———. 2013. *Becoming Christian: Essays on 1 Peter and the Making of Christian Identity*. LNTS/Early Christianity in Context 394. London: Bloomsbury T&T Clark.
———. Forthcoming. "'Honor Everyone…' (1 Pet. 2.17): The Social Strategy of 1 Peter and Its Significance for the Development of Christianity." In *To Set at Liberty: Essays on Early Christianity and Its Social World in Honor of John H. Elliott*. Edited by S. K. Black. Sheffield: Sheffield Phoenix.

Horsley, Richard A., ed. 1997. *Paul and Empire: Religion and Power in Roman Imperial Society.* Harrisburg, Pa.: Trinity Press International.
———, ed. 2000. *Paul and Politics: Ekklesia, Israel, Imperium, Interpretation.* Harrisburg, Pa.: Trinity Press International.
———, ed. 2004a. *Paul and the Roman Imperial Order.* Harrisburg, Pa.: Trinity Press International.
———, ed. 2004b. *Hidden Transcripts and the Arts of Resistance: Applying the Work of James C. Scott to Jesus and Paul.* SemeiaSt 48. Atlanta: Society of Biblical Literature.
Howe, Bonnie. 2008. *Because You Bear This Name: Conceptual Metaphor and the Moral Meaning of 1 Peter.* Society of Biblical Literature Biblical Interpretation Series 81. Atlanta: Society of Biblical Literature.
———. 2009. Review of Robert L. Webb and Betsy Bauman-Martin, *Reading First Peter with New Eyes: Methodological Reassessments of the Letter of First Peter.* Review of Biblical Literature. Online: http://www.bookreviews.org/pdf/6447_6965.pdf.
Hultin, Jeremy F. 2010. "Jude's Citation of 1 Enoch: From Tertullian to Jacob of Edessa." Pages 113–28 in *Jewish and Christian Scriptures: The Function of "Canonical" and "Non-Canonical" Religious Texts.* Edited by J. H. Charlesworth and L. M. McDonald. Jewish and Christian Texts in Contexts and Related Studies 7. Edinburgh: T&T Clark.
Hunzinger, Claus-Hunno. 1965. "Babylon als Deckname für Rom und die Datierung des 1. Petrusbriefes." Pages 67–77 in *Gottes Wort und Gottesland. Hans-Wilhelm Hertzberg zum 70.* Edited by H. G. Reventlow. Göttingen: Vandenhoeck & Ruprecht.
———. 1968. "ῥαντίζω, ῥαντισμός." *TDNT* 6:976–84.
Hurst, David. 1985. *Bede the Venerable: Commentary on the Seven Catholic Epistles.* Cistercian Studies 82. Kalamazoo, Mich.: Cistercian.
Isocrates. 1928–45. Translated by G. Norlin and L. Van Hook. 3 vols. LCL. Cambridge, Mass.: Harvard University Press.
Jerome. 1910. *Epistulae 1–70.* Edited by I. Hilberg. CSEL 54. Vienna: F. Tempsky.
———. *Vita Malchi.* [see C. C. Mierow]
Jobes, Karen H. 2005. *1 Peter.* BECNT. Grand Rapids: Baker Academic.
Johnson Hodge, Caroline. 2007. *If Sons, then Heirs: A Study of Kinship and Ethnicity in the Letters of Paul.* Oxford: Oxford University Press.
Jülicher, Adolf. 1904. *An Introduction to the New Testament.* Translated by J. P. Ward. London: Smith, Elder & Co.

Kalin, Everett R. 1990. "Re-examining New Testament Canon History 1: The Canon of Origen." *CurTM* 17:274-82.
Käsemann, Ernst. 1964. *Essays on New Testament Themes*. Translated by W. J. Montague. SBT 41. Naperville, Ill.: Allenson.
———. 1969. *New Testament Questions of Today*. Translated by W. J. Montague. Philadelphia: Fortress.
Kelly, J. N. D. 1969. *The Epistles of Peter and of Jude*. BNTC. London: Black.
Kennedy, George. 1984. *New Testament Interpretation through Rhetorical Criticism*. Chapel Hill: University of North Carolina Press.
Kimmel, Michael. 2002. "Metaphor, Imagery and Culture: Spatialized Ontologies, Mental Tools and Multimedia in the Making." Ph.D. diss., University of Vienna.
Klauck, Hans-Josef. 2006. *Ancient Letters and the New Testament: A Guide to Context and Exegesis*. Translated by D. P. Bailey. Waco, Tex.: Baylor University Press.
Kloppenborg, John. 2004. "The Reception of the Jesus Tradition in James." Pages 93-141 in *The Catholic Epistles and the Tradition*. Edited by J. Schlosser. BETL 176. Leuven: Peeters.
Köstenberger, Andreas J. 2006. "The Use of Scripture in the Pastoral and General Epistles and the Book of Revelation." Pages 230-54 in *Hearing the Old Testament in the New Testament*. Edited by S. E. Porter. Grand Rapids: Eerdmans.
Kraftchick, Steven J. 2002. *Jude, 2 Peter*. ANTC. Nashville: Abingdon.
Kraus, Thomas J. 2001. *Sprache, Stil und historischer Ort des zweiten Petrusbriefes*. WUNT 2/136. Tübingen: Mohr Siebeck.
———. 2003. "Die griechische Petrus-Apokalypse und ihre Relation zu ausgewählten Überlieferungsträgern apokalyptischer Stoffe." *Apocrypha* 14:73-98.
Kugel, James L. 1998. *Traditions of the Bible: A Guide to the Bible as It Was at the Start of the Common Era*. Cambridge, Mass.: Harvard University Press.
———. 2007. *How to Read the Bible: A Guide to Scripture Then and Now*. New York: Free Press.
Kuhn, Karl Georg. 1964. "Βαβυλών." *TDNT* 1:514-17.
Kvanvig, Helge S. 2011. *Primeval History: Babylonian, Biblical, and Enochic. An Intertextual Reading*. JSJSup 148. Leiden: Brill.
Lakoff, George. 1993. "The Contemporary Theory of Metaphor." Pages 202-51 in *Metaphor and Thought*. Edited by A. Ortony. Cambridge: Cambridge University Press.

Lakoff, George, and Mark Johnson. 1980. *Metaphors We Live By*. Chicago: University of Chicago Press.

Lampe, Peter. 2010. "Rhetorical Analysis of Pauline Texts—Quo Vadit?" Pages 3–21 in *Paul and Rhetoric*. Edited by J. P. Sampley and P. Lampe. London: T&T Clark.

LaVerdiere, Eugene A. 1974. "A Grammatical Ambiguity in 1 Pet. 1:23." *CBQ* 36:89–94.

Lawrence, Louise J. 2005. *Reading with Anthropology: Exhibiting Aspects of New Testament Religion*. Carlisle, U.K.: Paternoster.

Legaspi, Michael C. 2010. *The Death of Scripture and the Rise of Biblical Studies*. Oxford Studies in Historical Theology. Oxford: Oxford University Press.

Leipoldt, Johannes. 1905. *Didymus der Blinde von Alexandria*. Leipzig: Pries.

———. 1907. *Geschichte des neutestamentlichen Kanons: Erster Teil/Die Entstehung*. Leipzig: Hinrich.

Leo the Great. 1973. *Tractatus [Sermones 39–96]*. CCSL 138a. Edited by A. Chavasse. Turnhout, Belgium: Brepols.

———. 1996. *Sermons*. Translated by J. P. Freeland and A. J. Conway. FC 93. Washington, D.C.: Catholic University of America Press.

Levine, Amy-Jill, with Maria Mayo Robbins, eds. 2004. *The Feminist Companion to the Catholic Epistles and Hebrews*. London: T&T Clark.

Lewis, Scott, S.J. 2004. *What Are They Saying about New Testament Apocalyptic?* Mahwah, N.J.: Paulist.

Lieu, Judith M. 2002. *Neither Jew Nor Greek? Constructing Early Christianity*. Studies of the New Testament and Its World. Edinburgh: T&T Clark.

———. 2004. *Christian Identity in the Jewish and Graeco-Roman World*. Oxford: Oxford University Press.

Lincicum, David. 2008. "Paul and the *Testimonia*: Quo Vademus?" *JETS* 51:297–308.

Lohse, Eduard. 1986. "Parenesis and Kerygma in 1 Peter." Pages 37–59 in *Perspectives on First Peter*. Edited by C. Talbert. North American Baptist Professors of Religion Special Studies Series 9. Macon, Ga.: Mercer University Press.

Lombardo, Gregory J. 1988. *St. Augustine on Faith and Works*. Ancient Christian Writers 48. Mahwah, N.J.: Newman.

Longenecker, Bruce W. 2009. "Exposing the Economic Middle: A Revised Economy Scale for the Study of Early Urban Christianity." *JSNT* 31:243–78.

———. 2010. *Remember the Poor: Paul, Poverty, and the Greco-Roman World*. Grand Rapids: Eerdmans.

Lyotard, Jean-Francois. 1984. *The Postmodern Condition: A Report on Knowledge*. Translated by G. Bennington and B. Massumi. Theory and History of Literature 10. Minneapolis: University of Minnesota Press.

———. 1993. *The Postmodern Explained*. Translated by D. Barry, B. Maher, J. Pefanis, V. Spate, and M. Thomas. Minneapolis: University of Minnesota Press.

Malherbe, Abraham J. 1986. *Moral Exhortation, A Greco-Roman Sourcebook*. LEC. Philadelphia: Westminster Press.

———. 1988. *Ancient Epistolary Theorists*. SBLSBS 19. Atlanta: Scholars Press.

Malina, Bruce J. 2001. *The New Testament World: Insights from Cultural Anthropology*. 3rd ed. Louisville: Westminster John Knox.

Markley, John R. 2013. *Peter—Apocalyptic Seer: The Influence of the Apocalypse Genre on Matthew's Portrayal of Peter*. WUNT 2/348. Tübingen: Mohr Siebeck.

Marohl, Matthew J. 2008. *Faithfulness and the Purpose of Hebrews: A Social Identity Approach*. Princeton Theological Monographs. Eugene, Ore.: Pickwick.

Marrassini, Paolo. 1994. "L'Apocalisse di Pietro." Pages 171–232 in *Etiopia e oltre: Studi in onore di Lanfranco Ricci*. Edited by Y. Beyene et al. Studi Africanistici: Serie Etiopica 1. Naples: Istituto Universitario Orientale.

Martin, Troy W. 1992. *Metaphor and Composition in 1 Peter*. SBLDS 131. Atlanta: Scholars Press.

———. 2007. "The Rehabilitation of a Rhetorical Step-Child: First Peter and Classical Rhetorical Criticism." Pages 41–71 in *Reading First Peter with New Eyes: Methodological Reassessments of the Letter of First Peter*. Edited by R. L. Webb and B. Bauman-Martin. LNTS 364. London: T&T Clark.

———. 2010a. "Invention and Arrangement in Recent Pauline Rhetorical Studies: A Survey of the Practices and the Problems." Pages 48–118 in *Paul and Rhetoric*. Edited by J. P. Sampley and P. Lampe. London: T&T Clark.

———. 2010b. "Investigating the Pauline Letter Body: Issues, Methods, and Approaches." Pages 185–212 in *Paul and the Ancient Letter Form*. Edited by S. E. Porter and S. A. Adams. Pauline Studies 6. Leiden: Brill.

———. 2011. "Clarifying a Curiosity: The Plural *Bloods* (αἱμάτων) in John 1:13." Pages 175–85 in *Christian Body, Christian Self: Concepts of Early Christian Personhood*. Edited by C. K. Rothschild and T. W. Thompson with R. S. Kinney. WUNT 284. Tübingen: Mohr Siebeck.

Mason, Eric F. 2014. "Watchers Traditions in the Catholic Epistles." Pages 69–79 in *The Watchers in Jewish and Christian Traditions*. Edited by A. K. Harkins, K. Coblentz Bautch, and J. Endres. Minneapolis: Fortress.

Mason, Eric F., and Kevin B. McCruden, eds. 2011. *Reading the Epistle to the Hebrews: A Resource for Students*. SBLRBS 66. Atlanta: Society of Biblical Literature.

May, Margaret Tallmadge. 1968. *Galen On the Usefulness of the Parts of the Body*. Ithaca, N.Y.: Cornell University Press.

Mayor, Joseph B. 1907. *The Epistle of St. Jude and the Second Epistle of St. Peter: Greek Text with Introduction, Notes, and Comments*. London: Macmillan.

Mbuvi, Andrew M. 2007. *Temple, Exile and Identity in 1 Peter*. LNTS 345. London: T&T Clark.

McDonald, Lee M. 1995. *The Formation of the Christian Biblical Canon*. Rev. ed. Peabody, Mass.: Hendrickson.

McKenna, Mary Margaret. 1981. "The 'Two Ways' in Jewish and Christian Writings of the Greco-Roman Period: A Study of the Form of Repentance Parenesis." Ph.D. diss., University of Pennsylvania.

McMillen, R. Melvin. 2011. "Metaphor and First Peter: The Essential Role of the Minds of Father-God's Children in Spiritual Conflict with a Special Focus on 1:13." Ph.D. diss., University of South Africa.

Meade, David G. 1986. *Pseudonymity and Canon: An Investigation into the Relationship of Authorship and Authority in Jewish and Earliest Christian Tradition*. Grand Rapids: Eerdmans.

Meeks, Wayne A. 1972. "The Man from Heaven in Johannine Sectarianism." *JBL* 91:44–71.

———. 1983. *The First Urban Christians: The Social World of the Apostle Paul*. New Haven: Yale University Press.

Merkt, Andreas. Forthcoming. *1 Petrus*. Novum Testamentum Patristicum 21. Göttingen: Vandenhoeck & Ruprecht.

Metzger, Bruce. 1972. "Literary Forgeries and Canonical Pseudepigrapha." *JBL* 91:3–24.

Michaels, J. Ramsey. 1987. "Jewish and Christian Apocalyptic Letters: 1 Peter, Revelation, and 2 Baruch 78–87." Pages 268–75 in *Society of*

Biblical Literature Seminar Papers, 1987. SBLSP 25. Atlanta: Scholars Press.

———. 1988. *1 Peter*. WBC 49. Waco, Tex.: Word.

———. 1993. Review of Troy W. Martin, *Metaphor and Composition in First Peter*. *JBL* 112:358–60.

Mierow, C. C. 1946. "Sancti Eusebi Hieronymi Vita Monachi Captivi" [edition and translation of Jerome, *Vita Malchi*]. Pages 33–60 in *Classical Essays Presented to J. A. Kleist*. Edited by R. E. Arnold. St. Louis: Classical Bulletin.

Miller, Robert J. 1996. "Is There Independent Attestation for the Transfiguration in 2 Peter?" *NTS* 42:620–25.

Misset-van de Weg, Magda. 2004. "Sarah Imagery in 1 Peter." Pages 50–62 in *The Feminist Companion to the Catholic Epistles and Hebrews*. Edited by A.-J. Levine with M. Mayo Robbins. London: T&T Clark.

Moore, Nicholas J. 2013. "Is Enoch also Among the Prophets? The Impact of Jude's Citation of *1 Enoch* on the Reception of Both Texts in the Early Church." *JTS* n.s. 64:498–515.

Moore, Stephen D. 1989. *Literary Criticism and the Gospels: The Theoretical Challenge*. New Haven: Yale University Press.

———. 1992. *Mark and Luke in Poststructuralist Perspectives: Jesus Begins to Write*. New Haven: Yale University Press.

———. 1994. *Poststructuralism and the New Testament: Derrida and Foucault at the Foot of the Cross*. Minneapolis: Fortress.

———. 2010. *The Bible in Theory: Critical and Postcritical Essays*. SBLRBS 57. Atlanta: Society of Biblical Literature.

Moule, C. F. D. 1959. *An Idiom Book of New Testament Greek*. 2nd ed. Cambridge: Cambridge University Press.

Murphy, Frederick J. 2012. *Apocalypticism in the Bible and Its World: A Comprehensive Introduction*. Grand Rapids: Baker Academic.

Neyrey, Jerome H. 1980. "The Form and Background of the Polemic in 2 Peter." *JBL* 99:417–31.

———. 1993. *2 Peter, Jude*. AB. New York: Doubleday.

Nickelsburg, George W. E. 2000. "Enoch, Books of." Pages 249–53 in vol. 1 of *Encyclopedia of the Dead Sea Scrolls*. Edited by L. H. Schiffman and J. C. VanderKam. 2 vols. Oxford: Oxford University Press.

———. 2001. *1 Enoch 1: A Commentary on the Book of 1 Enoch, Chapters 1–36; 81–108*. Hermeneia. Minneapolis: Fortress.

Nicklas, Tobias. 2005. "Der lebendige Text des Neuen Testaments: Der Judasbrief in P^{72} (P. Bodmer VII)." *Annali di storia dell'esegesi* 22:203–22.

Nicklas, Tobias, and Thomas J. Kraus. 2004. *Das Petrusevangelium und die Petrusapokalypse: Die griechischen Fragmente mit deutscher und englischer Übersetzung*. Die griechischen christlichen Schriftsteller der ersten Jahrhunderte, Neue Folge 11 (= Neutestamentliche Apokryphen I). Berlin: de Gruyter.

Nicklas, Tobias, and Tommy Wasserman. 2006. "Theologische Linien im Codex Bodmer Miscellani." Pages 161–88 in *New Testament Manuscripts: Their Texts and Their World*. Edited by T. J. Kraus and T. Nicklas. Texts and Editions for New Testament Study 2. Leiden: Brill.

Niebuhr, Karl-Wilhelm, and Robert W. Wall, eds. 2009. *The Catholic Epistles and Apostolic Traditions: A New Perspective on James to Jude*. Waco, Tex.: Baylor University Press.

Nienhuis, David. 2007. *Not by Paul Alone: The Formation of the Catholic Epistle Collection and the Christian Canon*. Waco, Tex.: Baylor University Press.

Noppen, Jean-Pierre van, and Edith Hols, eds. 1990. *Metaphor II: A Classified Bibliography from 1985–1990*. Amsterdam: Benjamins.

Ogden, Schubert. 1982. *The Point of Christology*. San Francisco: Harper & Row.

Olbricht, Thomas H., and Anders Eriksson, eds. 2005. *Rhetoric, Ethic, and Moral Persuasion in Biblical Discourse: Essays from the 2002 Heidelberg Conference*. Emory Studies in Early Christianity 11. London: T&T Clark.

Olbricht, Thomas H., and Jerry Sumney, eds. 2001. *Paul and Pathos*. SBLSymS 16. Atlanta: Society of Biblical Literature.

Origen. 1960. *Homiliae in Josuam*. Edited by A. Jaubert. SC 71. Paris: Cerf.

———. 2002. *Homilies on Joshua*. Translated by B. J. Bruce. FC 105. Washington, D.C.: Catholic University of America Press.

Otto, Johann Karl Theodor von. 1877. "Haben Barnabas, Justinus und Irenäus den zweiten Petrusbrief (3,8) benutzt?" *ZWT* 20:525–29.

Pearson, Birger A. 1969. "A Reminiscence of Classical Myth at 2 Peter 2:4." *GRBS* 10:71–80.

———. 1990. "The Apocalypse of Peter and Canonical 2 Peter." Pages 67–75 in *Gnosticism and the Early Christian World: In Honor of James M. Robinson*. Edited by J. E. Goehring et al. ForFasc 2. Sonoma, Calif.: Polebridge.

Pearson, Brook W. R. 1999. "Resurrection and the Judgment of the Titans: ἡ γῆ τῶν ἀσεβῶν in LXX Isaiah 26.19." Pages 33–51 in *Resurrection*.

Edited by S. E. Porter, M. A. Hayes, and D. Tombs. JSNTSup 186. Roehampton Institute London Papers 5. Sheffield: Sheffield Academic.

Perkins, Pheme. 1995. *First and Second Peter, James, and Jude.* IBC. Louisville: John Knox.

———. 1999. "Hebrews and the Catholic Epistles." Pages 121–33 in *The New Testament Today.* Edited by M. A. Powell. Louisville: Westminster John Knox.

Petersen, Norman R. 1985. *Rediscovering Paul: Philemon and the Sociology of Paul's Narrative World.* Philadelphia: Fortress.

Phillips, Gary. 1989. "The Authority of Exegesis and the Responsibility of the Critic: The Ethics and Ethos of Criticism." Paper presented at the AAR/SBL Annual Meeting, Chicago.

Philo. 1929–53. Translated by F. H. Colson et al. 12 vols. LCL. Cambridge, Mass.: Harvard University Press.

Picirilli, Robert E. 1988. "Allusions to 2 Peter in the Apostolic Fathers." *JSNT* 33:57–83.

Popkes, Wiard. 2005. "Paraenesis in the New Testament: An Exercise in Conceptuality." Pages 13–46 in *Early Christian Paraenesis in Context.* Edited by J. Starr and T. Engberg-Pedersen. BZNW 125. Berlin: de Gruyter.

Preuschen, Erwin. 1910. *Analecta. Kürzere Texte zur Geschichte der Alten Kirche und des Kanons II. Zur Kanongeschichte.* 2nd ed. Sammlung ausgewählter kirchen- und dogmengeschichtlicher Quellenschriften 1. Reihe. Tübingen: Mohr.

Procksch, Otto, and Karl Georg Kuhn. 1964. "ἅγιος, κτλ." *TDNT* 1:88–115.

Rad, Gerhard von. 1993. *Wisdom in Israel.* Translated by J. Martin. London: SCM.

Reese, Ruth Anne. 2007. *2 Peter and Jude.* Two Horizons New Testament Commentary. Grand Rapids: Eerdmans.

Reicke, Bo. 1964. *The Epistles of James, Peter, and Jude.* AB. Garden City, N.Y.: Doubleday.

Richard, Earl. 1986. "The Functional Christology of First Peter." Pages 121–39 in *Perspectives on First Peter.* Edited by C. H. Talbert. North American Baptist Professors of Religion Special Studies Series 9. Macon, Ga.: Mercer University Press.

Rist, Martin. 1972. "Pseudepigraphy and the Early Christians." Pages 75–91 in *Studies in New Testament and Early Christian Literature: Essays in Honor of Allen P. Wikgren.* Edited by D. E. Aune. Leiden: Brill.

Robinson, John A. T. 1976. *Redating the New Testament*. Philadelphia: Westminster.
Robson, E. Iliff. 1915. *Studies in the Second Epistle of St Peter*. Cambridge: Cambridge University Press.
Rothschild, Clare K. 2009. *Hebrews as Pseudepigraphon: The History and Significance of the Pauline Attribution of Hebrews*. WUNT 235. Tübingen: Mohr Siebeck.
Rowland, Christopher. 1982. *The Open Heaven: A Study of Apocalyptic in Judaism and Early Christianity*. London: SPCK.
Rowston, Douglas J. 1975. "The Most Neglected Book in the New Testament." *NTS* 21:554–63.
Ruf, Martin G. 2011. *Die heiligen Propheten, eure Apostel und ich: Metatextuelle Studien zum zweiten Petrusbrief*. WUNT 2/300. Tübingen: Mohr Siebeck.
Sandevoir, Pierre. 1980. "Un royaume de prêtres?" Pages 219–29 in *Études sur la première lettre de Pierre*. Edited by C. Perrot. LD 102. Paris: Cerf.
Sandnes, Karl Olav. 2005. "Revised Conventions in Early Christian Paraenesis: 'Working Good' in 1 Peter as an Example." Pages 373–403 in *Early Christian Paraenesis in Context*. Edited by J. Starr and T. Engberg-Pedersen. BZNW 125. Berlin: de Gruyter.
Schenke, Hans-Martin, and Rodolphe Kasser, eds. 2003. *Papyrus Michigan 3520 und 6868(a): Ecclesiastes, Erster Johannesbrief und Zweiter Petrusbrief im fayumischen Dialekt*. TUGAL 151. Berlin: de Gruyter.
Schlosser, Jacques. 2004. "Le corpus des épîtres Catholiques." Pages 3–41 in *The Catholic Epistles and the Tradition*. Edited by J. Schlosser. BETL 176. Leuven: Peeters.
Schmidt, Karl Ludwig. 1964. "διασπορά." *TDNT* 2:98–104.
Schmidt, Karl Ludwig, Martin Anton Schmidt, and Rudolf Meyer. 1967. "πάροικος, παροικία, παροικέω." *TDNT* 5:841–53.
Schmitz, Otto, and Gustav Stählin. 1967. "παρακαλέω, παράκλησις." *TDNT* 5:773–99.
Schnider, Franz, and Werner Stenger. 1987. *Studien zum Neutestamentlichen Briefformular*. NTTS 11. Leiden: Brill.
Schrage, Wolfgang. 1985. "'Ein Tag ist beim Herrn wie tausend Jahre, und tausend Jahre sind wie ein Tag' (2 Petr 3,8)." Pages 267–75 in *Glaube und Eschatologie: Festschrift für Werner Georg Kümmel zum 80. Geburtstag*. Edited by E. Gräßer and O. Merk. Tübingen: Mohr Siebeck.
Schüssler Fiorenza, Elisabeth. 1983. *In Memory of Her: A Feminist Theological Reconstruction of Christian Origins*. New York: Crossroad.

Scroggs, Robin. 1975. "The Earliest Christian Communities as Sectarian Movement." Pages 1–23 in *Christianity, Judaism and Other Greco-Roman Cults: Studies for Morton Smith at Sixty. Part Two: Early Christianity*. Edited by J. Neusner. Leiden: Brill.

Sechrest, Love L. 2009. *A Former Jew: Paul and the Dialectics of Race*. LNTS 410. London: T&T Clark.

Seeman, Christopher. 2014. "The Watchers Traditions and Gen 6:1–4 (MT and LXX)." Pages 25–38 in *The Watchers in Jewish and Christian Traditions*. Edited by A. K. Harkins, K. Coblentz Bautch, and J. Endres. Minneapolis: Fortress.

Segal, Alan F. 1986. "Judaism, Christianity, and Gnosticism." Pages 133–61 in *Separation and Polemic*. Edited by S. G. Wilson. Vol. 2 of *Anti-Judaism in Early Christianity*. Studies in Christianity and Judaism 2. Waterloo, Ont.: Wilfrid Laurier University Press.

Selwyn, Edward Gordon. 1947. *The First Epistle of St. Peter: The Greek Text with Introduction, Notes, and Essays*. 2nd ed. New York: St. Martin's.

———. 1954. "Eschatology in 1 Peter." Pages 394–401 in *The Background of the New Testament and Its Eschatology: Studies in Honour of C. H. Dodd*. Edited by W. D. Davies and D. Daube. Cambridge: Cambridge University Press.

Senior, Donald P., and Daniel J. Harrington. 2003. *1 Peter, Jude and 2 Peter*. SP. Collegeville, Minn.: Liturgical.

Sevenster, J. N. 1968. *Do You Know Greek? How Much Greek Could the First Jewish Christians Have Known*? NovTSup 19. Leiden: Brill.

Sherlock, Thomas. 1725. *The Use and Intent of Prophecy in the Several Ages of the World: Discourses Preached at the Temple Church*. London: Pemberton.

Soards, M. L. 1988. "1 Peter, 2 Peter, and Jude as Evidence for a Petrine School." *ANRW* 25.2:3828–49.

Sollors, Werner. 1996. "Foreword: Theories of American Ethnicity." Pages x–xliv in *Theories of Ethnicity: A Classical Reader*. Edited by W. Sollors. New York: New York University Press.

Speyer, Wolfgang. 1971. *Die literarische Fälschung im heidnischen und christlichen Altertum: Ein Versuch ihrer Deutung*. Handbuch der klassischen Altertumswissenschaft, vol. 1, part 2. Munich: Beck.

Spicq, Ceslas. 1966. *Les Épîtres de Saint Pierre*. Paris: Gabalda.

Starr, James. 2005. "Was Paraenesis for Beginners?" Pages 73–111 in *Early Christian Paraenesis in Context*. Edited by J. Starr and T. Engberg-Pedersen. BZNW 125. Berlin: de Gruyter.

Starr, James, and Troels Engberg-Pedersen. 2005. "Introduction." Pages 1–10 in *Early Christian Paraenesis in Context*. Edited by J. Starr and T. Engberg-Pedersen. BZNW 125. Berlin: de Gruyter.

Stenzel, Meinrad. 1942. "Der Bibelkanon des Rufin von Aquileia." *Bib* 23:43–61.

Stone, John. 2003. "Max Weber on Race, Ethnicity, and Nationalism." Pages 28–42 in *Race and Ethnicity: Comparative and Theoretical Approaches*. Edited by J. Stone and R. Dennis. Oxford: Blackwell.

Stowers, Stanley K. 1986. *Letter Writing in Greco-Roman Antiquity*. LEC. Philadelphia: Westminster.

Studer, Basil. 1975. "'Sacramentum et exemplum' chez saint Augustin." *Recherches augustiniennes* 10:87–141.

Sumney, Jerry L., ed. 2012. *Reading Paul's Letter to the Romans*. SBLRBS 73. Atlanta: Society of Biblical Literature.

Tajfel, Henri, and John Turner. 2001. "An Integrative Theory of Intergroup Conflict." Pages 94–109 in *Intergroup Relations: Essential Readings*. Edited by M. A. Hogg and D. Abrams. Philadelphia: Psychology Press. Originally published in *The Social Psychology of Intergroup Relations*. Edited by W. G. Austin and S. Worchel. Monterey, Calif.: Brooks/Cole, 1979.

Talbert, Charles H. 1986. "Once Again: The Plan of 1 Peter." Pages 141–51 in *Perspectives on 1 Peter*. Edited by C. H. Talbert. National Association of Baptist Professors of Religion Special Studies Series 9. Macon, Ga.: Mercer University Press.

Tasker, R. G. V. 1954. *The Old Testament in the New Testament*. 2nd ed. Grand Rapids: Eerdmans.

Temkin, Owsei, et al. 1956. *Soranus' Gynecology*. Baltimore: Johns Hopkins University Press.

Teske, Ronald J., trans. 1999. Augustine, *Answer to the Pelagians, III: Unfinished Work in Answer to Julian*. Works of Saint Augustine: A Translation for the 21st Century 1/25. New York: New City Press.

Theissen, Gerd. 1979. *Studien zur Soziologie des Urchristentums*. WUNT 19. Tübingen: Mohr Siebeck.

———. 1982. *The Social Setting of Pauline Christianity: Essays on Corinth*. Minneapolis: Fortress.

———. 1992. *Social Reality and the Early Christians: Theology, Ethics, and the World of the New Testament*. Minneapolis: Fortress.

Thurén, Lauri. 1990. *The Rhetorical Strategy of 1 Peter: With Special Regard to Ambiguous Expressions*. Åbo, Finland: Åbo Academy Press.

———. 2004. "The Relationship between 2 Peter and Jude—A Classical Problem Resolved?" Pages 451–60 in *The Catholic Epistles and the Tradition*. Edited by J. Schlosser. BETL 176. Leuven: Peeters.
Tite, Philip L. 1997. *Compositional Transitions in 1 Peter: An Analysis of the Letter-Opening*. San Francisco: International Scholars Publications.
———. 2009. "Nurslings, Milk and Moral Development in the Greco-Roman Context: A Reappraisal of the Paraenetic Utilizations of Metaphor in 1 Peter 2:1–3." *JSNT* 31:371–400.
———. 2010. "How to Begin, and Why? Diverse Functions of the Pauline Prescript within a Greco-Roman Context." Pages 57–99 in *Paul and the Ancient Letter Form*. Edited by S. E. Porter and S. A. Adams. Pauline Studies 6. Leiden: Brill.
Tsutsui, Kenji. 2004. *Die Auseinandersetzung mit den Markioniten im Adamantios-Dialog: Ein Kommentar zu den Büchern I–II*. PTS 55. Berlin: de Gruyter.
Turner, Nigel. 1963. *Syntax*. Vol. 3 of J. H. Moulton, W. F. Howard, and N. Turner, *A Grammar of New Testament Greek*. Edinburgh: T&T Clark.
VanderKam, James C. 1984. *Enoch and the Growth of an Apocalyptic Tradition*. CBQMS 16. Washington, D.C.: Catholic Biblical Association of America.
———. 1995. *Enoch: A Man for All Generations*. Studies on Personalities of the Old Testament. Columbia: University of South Carolina Press.
Van Unnik, W. C. 1980. "The Teaching of Good Works in 1 Peter." Pages 83–105 in vol. 2 of *Sparsa Collecta: The Collected Essays of W. C. Van Unnik*. 3 vols. NovTSup 30. Leiden: Brill.
Verheyden, Joseph. 2003. "The Canon Muratori: A Matter of Dispute." Pages 487–556 in *The Biblical Canons*. Edited by J.-M. Auwers and H. J. de Jonge. BETL 163. Leuven: Peeters.
Vermes, Géza. 1975. "The Targumic Versions of Genesis 4:3-16." Pages 92–126 in *Post-Biblical Jewish Studies*. SJLA 8. Leiden: Brill.
Wagner, Maria Monica. 1945. *Rufinus, the Translator: A Study of His Theory and His Practice as Illustrated in His Version of the Apologetica of St. Gregory Nazianzen*. Patristic Studies 73. Washington, D.C.: Catholic University of America Press.
Wasserman, Tommy. 2005. "Papyrus 72 and the Bodmer Miscellaneous Codex." *NTS*. 51:137–54.
———. 2006. *The Epistle of Jude: Its Text and Transmission*. ConBNT 43. Stockholm: Almqvist & Wiksell.

Watson, Duane F. 1988. *Invention, Arrangement, and Style: Rhetorical Criticism of Jude and 2 Peter*. SBLDS 104. Atlanta: Scholars Press.

———. 1997. "Letter, Letter Form." Pages 649–55 in *Dictionary of the Later New Testament and Its Developments*. Edited by R. P. Martin and P. H. Davids. Downers Grove, Ill.: InterVarsity.

———. 1998. "The Letter of Jude." Pages 471–500 in vol. 12 of *The New Interpreter's Bible*. Edited by L. E. Keck. 12 vols. Nashville: Abingdon.

———. 2002. "The Oral-Scribal and Cultural Intertexture of Apocalyptic Discourse in Jude and 2 Peter." Pages 187–214 in *The Intertexture of Apocalyptic Discourse in the New Testament*. Edited by D. F. Watson. Leiden: Brill.

———. 2010a. "The Role of Style in the Pauline Epistles." Pages 119–39 in *Paul and Rhetoric*. Edited by J. P. Sampley and P. Lampe. London: T&T Clark.

———. 2010b. "The Three Species of Rhetoric and the Study of the Pauline Epistles." Pages 25–47 in *Paul and Rhetoric*. Edited by J. P. Sampley and P. Lampe. London: T&T Clark.

Watson, Duane F., and Terrance Callan. 2012. *First and Second Peter*. Paideia. Grand Rapids: Baker Academic.

Watson, Duane F., and Robert L. Webb. 2010. *Reading Second Peter with New Eyes: Methodological Reassessments of the Letter of Second Peter*. LNTS 382. London: T&T Clark.

Webb, Robert L. 1990. "'Apocalyptic': Observations on a Slippery Term." *JNES* 49:115–26.

———. 1996. "The Eschatology of the Epistle of Jude and Its Rhetorical and Social Functions." *BBR* 6:139–51.

———. 2004. "The Petrine Epistles: Recent Developments and Trends." Pages 373–90 in *The Face of New Testament Studies: A Survey of Recent Research*. Edited by S. McKnight and G. R. Osborne. Grand Rapids: Baker Academic.

———. 2007. "Intertexture and Rhetorical Strategy in First Peter's Apocalyptic Discourse: A Study in Socio-Rhetorical Interpretation." Pages 72–110 in *Reading First Peter with New Eyes: Methodological Reassessments of the Letter of First Peter*. Edited by R. L. Webb and B. Bauman-Martin. LNTS 364. London: T&T Clark.

Webb, Robert L., and Betsy Bauman-Martin, eds. 2007. *Reading First Peter with New Eyes: Methodological Reassessment of the Letter of First Peter*. LNTS 364. London: T&T Clark.

Webb, Robert L., and Peter Hugh Davids, eds. 2009. *Reading Jude with New Eyes: Methodological Reassessments of the Letter of Jude.* LNTS 383. London: T&T Clark.

Webster, Jane, and Nicholas J. Cooper, eds. 1996. *Roman Imperialism: Post-Colonial Perspectives.* Leicester Archaeology Monographs 3. Leicester: School of Archaeological Studies, University of Leicester.

Weima, Jeffrey A. D. 2010. "Sincerely, Paul: The Significance of the Pauline Letter Closings." Pages 307–345 in *Paul and the Ancient Letter Form.* Edited by S. E. Porter and S. A. Adams. Pauline Studies 6. Leiden: Brill.

Weinrich, Harald. 1976. *Sprache in Texten.* Stuttgart: Klett.

Wenham, Gordon J. 1987. *Genesis 1–15.* WBC 1. Dallas: Word.

White, John L. 1972. *The Body of the Greek Letter.* SBLDS 2. Missoula, Mont.: Scholars Press.

———. 1984. "New Testament Epistolary Literature in the Framework of Ancient Epistolography." *ANRW* 25.2:1730–56.

———. 1986. *Light from Ancient Letters.* Philadelphia: Fortress.

———. 1988. "Ancient Greek Letters." Pages 85–105 in *Greco-Roman Literature and the New Testament.* Edited by D. E. Aune. SBLSBS 21. Atlanta: Scholars Press.

Williams, Travis B. 2012a. *Persecution in 1 Peter: Differentiating and Contextualizing Early Christian Suffering.* NovTSup 145. Leiden: Brill.

———. 2012b. "Suffering from a Critical Oversight: The Persecutions of 1 Peter within Modern Scholarship." *Currents in Biblical Research* 10:275–92.

Witherington, Ben, III. 2007. *A Socio-Rhetorical Commentary on 1–2 Peter.* Vol. 2 of *Letters and Homilies for Hellenized Christians.* Downers Grove, Ill.: IVP Academic.

Wright, N. T. 1992. *The New Testament and the People of God.* Minneapolis: Fortress.

Zahn, Theodor. 1888. *Geschichte des neutestamentlichen Kanons: Erster Band/Erste Hälfte.* Erlangen: Deichert.

Zerbe, Gordon M. 1993. *Non-retaliation in Early Jewish and New Testament Texts: Ethical Themes in Social Contexts.* JSPSup 13. Sheffield: JSOT Press.

Zoepfl, Friedrich. 1914. *Didymi Alexandrini in epistolas canonicas brevis enarratio.* NTAbh 4/1. Münster: Aschendorff.

Contributors

Kelley Coblentz Bautch (Ph.D., University of Notre Dame) is associate professor of religious studies at St. Edward's University, Austin, Texas.

Félix H. Cortez (Ph.D., Andrews University) is assistant professor of New Testament literature at the Seventh-Day Adventist Theological Seminary, Andrews University, Berrien Springs, Michigan.

Peter H. Davids (Ph.D., University of Manchester) is visiting professor in Christianity at Houston Baptist University, Houston, Texas.

Lewis R. Donelson (Ph.D., University of Chicago) is the Ruth A. Campbell Professor of New Testament Studies at Austin Presbyterian Theological Seminary, Austin, Texas.

Wolfgang Grünstäudl (Dr. theol., University of Regensburg) is assistant professor at the University of Wuppertal, Germany.

David G. Horrell (Ph.D., University of Cambridge) is professor of New Testament studies and director of the Centre for Biblical Studies at the University of Exeter, United Kingdom.

Jeremy F. Hultin (Ph.D., Yale University) is lecturer in New Testament at Murdoch University, Perth, Australia.

Steven J. Kraftchick (Ph.D., Emory University) is professor in the practice of New Testament interpretation at Candler School of Theology, Emory University, Atlanta, Georgia.

Troy W. Martin (Ph.D., University of Chicago) is professor of religious studies at Saint Xavier University, Chicago, Illinois.

Eric F. Mason (Ph.D., University of Notre Dame) is professor of biblical studies at Judson University, Elgin, Illinois.

Andreas Merkt (Dr. theol., University of Mainz) is professor of early church history and patristics at the University of Regensburg, Germany.

Tobias Nicklas (Dr. theol., University of Regensburg) is professor of New Testament exegesis and hermeneutics at the University of Regensburg, Germany.

Nancy Pardee (Ph.D., University of Chicago) is administrator, Chicago Center for Jewish Studies, University of Chicago, and teaches at Saint Xavier University and Catholic Theological Union in Chicago, Illinois.

Duane F. Watson (Ph.D., Duke University) is professor of New Testament studies at Malone University, Canton, Ohio.

Index of Ancient Sources

Hebrew Bible

Genesis
2–3	66
2:10–14	121
3:6	74
4:1–16	187
4:8	36–37
5:21–24	65, 71
6–9	79
6:1–4	61, 73, 186, 198–99
9:4	93

Exodus
5:23	140
6:6	93
19:5–6	53, 140
24	118
24:24	140

Leviticus
11:44–45	119
17:11	93
18:24	140
19:2	119
20:7	119
20:26	119
26:12	140

Numbers
16	187
16:1–35	61
22–24	187–88
24:14	61
24:17	188, 193
24:25	61
25	188
26:9–10	61
31:16	187–88

Deuteronomy
7:6	140
7:6–7	140
23:3–6	187
30:15–20	122
33:1–3	188–89
33:2 LXX	187

Joshua
8	176
8:29	176
13:22	187
24:9–10	187

Isaiah
8:14	53
13:6–16	63
26:21	78
28:14	79
28:16	53
34:4	79
38:12	77
43:20	140
43:20–21	53
51:11	93
52:3	93
52:3–4	93
53	95, 127
53:4–5	95
53:7	93, 95

Isaiah (cont.)

53:9	95
53:11–12	95
55:6	95
55:10	95
65:16–17	63
65:17	81, 226
65:25	226
66:15–16	188
66:22	81

Jeremiah

21:8	122
25:30–31	188
29:1–23	122

Hosea

1:6–7	53
1:9	53
1:10 LXX	53
2:1	53
2:23 LXX	53
2:25	53

Amos

4:11	190

Zechariah

3:2	71, 187
3:2–4	190

Malachi

4:1	79

Psalms

23	158
33	111
33 LXX	219
33:5	111
33:6	111
33:9 LXX	111
33:13–17	54, 111
34 LXX	219
34:12–16	54
34:13–17	129
89:4 LXX	59, 80, 197, 222
90:4	59, 80, 197, 222, 226
117	53
118 LXX	53
119:105	193
142:7	172

Proverbs

26:11	42, 192

Job

41:24 LXX	196

Daniel

12:1–2	79

Nehemiah

13:2	187

DEUTEROCANONICAL BOOKS

Tobit

4:5–9	117
12:6–10	117

Wisdom of Solomon

9:15	77
14:25–27	122

Sirach

16:7–10	73, 186

2 Maccabees

1:1–10	51, 76
1:10–2:18	51, 76

3 Maccabees

2:4–7	73, 186

DEAD SEA SCROLLS

CD

1:14	79
2:17–3:12	73, 186

INDEX OF ANCIENT SOURCES

1QS		
4:2–11	122	

1QH		
3:29–35	79	
10:8	70	

4QpIsaiah[b]		
2:6–10	79	

Pseudepigrapha

2 Baruch		
78–87	51, 76	

1 Enoch		
1–36	184	
1:3–7	189	
1:9	23, 78, 184, 188–89, 195–96, 217	
7:1	187	
9:8	187	
10:11	187	
12:4	187	
15:3–4	187	
17–36	72	
18:15–16	188	
20:2	196	
21:5–6	188	
34–35	61	
37–71	69, 184	
40:9	119	
52:5–9	189	
61:10	69	
72–82	184	
72:1	81	
83–90	184	
91–108	184	
91:16	81	

2 Enoch		
22:7	70	
22:10	70	

4 Ezra		
7:9	119	

| 7:17 | 119 |
| 12:42 | 193 |

Jubilees	
1:27	187
1:29	81
4:26	81
32:19	119

Odes of Solomon	
11	218

Psalms of Solomon	
14:10	119

Sibylline Oracles	
1.98–103	196
2.303	196
4.186	196

Testament of Levi	
3:1–8	69

Testament of Moses	
8	79
10	79

Testament of Naphtali	
3:4–5	73, 86

Ancient Jewish Writers

Josephus, *Ag. Ap.*	
1.1–2	140
2.240	196

Josephus, *Ant.*	
1.52–66	61
4.126–130	61
15.136	187

Josephus, *J.W.*	
1.667	133

Philo, *Alleg. Interp.*		3:31–34	23
1.63	121	4:13	63
		6:3	22, 183
Philo, *Contempl. Life*		10:45	93
12	133	13	67
		13:22	225
Philo, *Decalogue*			
31.165–166	126	Luke	
		6:16	22
Philo, *Embassy*		8:19–21	23
3–4	140	12:35	119
49.10	196	17:26–30	221
		23:34	175
Philo, *Moses*		24:21	93
1.295–300	61		
		John	
Philo, *Posterity*		14:30	173
38–39	61	21:18	191
Philo, *Rewards*		Acts	
152	196	2:24–27	171
		3	202
Philo, *Sacrifices*		3:32	202
32	121	5	202
		6:1	202
Philo, *Spec. Laws*		7:38	187, 209
1.45	70	7:53	187
		8	202
New Testament		8:26–40	203
		9	206
Matthew		10	203
3:10	79	11	203
10:2–4	22	11:26	146
10:24–25	19	12:17	183
12:46–50	23	15	203, 205
13:55	22, 183	15:13	183
21:43	141	15:14	19
24:3	71	15:22	22
24:7	79	15:27	22
24:11	225	15:32	22
24:24	225	20:28	93
24:43	80	21	206
		21:18	183
Mark		23–29	52
3:16–19	22	26	206

INDEX OF ANCIENT SOURCES

26:28	146	2:11–14	203–4
		3:19	187, 209
Romans		5:22–23	115
1:1	19	6:14	176, 178
1:28–31	122		
3:24	93	Ephesians	
3:24–25	93	4:32	123
6:19	118	5:21–6:9	126
6:22	118	5:22–23	130
8:30	119		
8:38	69	Philippians	
12:1–15:3	115	1:1	19
13:1–7	127	3:5–6	206
15:4	134		
		Colossians	
1 Corinthians		2:14–15	178
1	204	2:18	70–71
1:30	118	3:1–4:6	115
3:1–3	112	3:18–19	130
5:1	204	3:18–4:1	126
5:2	204		
5:4–5	206	1 Thessalonians	
5:9	42	5:1–11	63
6:3	71, 81	5:2	80
6:12	204, 211		
6:12–19	204	2 Thessalonians	
7	115	2:13	118
9:5	15	2:16–17	134
15:7	83		
15:24	69	1 Timothy	
		1:4	70
2 Corinthians		2:1–2	127
5:1–4	77	2:9–10	128
10:18	222	2:11–14	126
11:22	206	2:15	118
		5:1–2	126
Galatians			
1:12	206	Titus	
1:13–14	206	2:14	93
1:15–16	206		
1:19–2:12	183	Hebrews	
2	205	2:2	209
2:1–14	15	2:7	71
2:9	8, 168	5:12	112
2:11	204	6:2	112

Hebrews (cont.)

6:4–8	148
9:12	93
11:9	118
11:13	118
12:5	134
12:14	118
13	116

James

1:1	23, 52, 76

1 Peter

1:1	11, 55, 75–76, 85, 91, 95, 99–100, 110–11, 118, 136, 143, 162
1:1–2	52, 55, 74, 117
1:1–12	52
1:2	14, 44, 52, 55, 84, 91, 94, 96, 110, 118–20, 162
1:3	53, 80, 84–85, 87–89, 92, 110, 169
1:3–9	120, 131
1:3–12	52, 119
1:4	75, 80, 86, 92, 119
1:4–7	91
1:4–9	118
1:5	43, 88–90, 94, 111
1:5–7	80
1:6	51, 86, 146
1:6–7	43–44, 51, 55, 79
1:6–9	119
1:7	43, 84, 86, 90, 94
1:7–9	84
1:8	92
1:9	80, 88, 91
1:9–10	89
1:10–11	84, 89
1:10–12	42, 111, 119
1:11	87, 90, 96
1:12	70, 81, 90, 160
1:13	79, 84, 88, 90, 92, 93, 113, 119–20, 131
1:13–16	53, 120
1:13–17	104
1:13–21	93
1:13–22	120
1:13–2:10	52–53
1:13–5:11	52–53
1:14	53, 85, 93, 99–100, 114–20
1:14–15	94
1:14–16	51
1:14–2:10	105
1:15	93
1:15–16	87, 119–20
1:16	43, 119
1:16–18	19
1:17	53, 75, 87–88, 92–93, 114, 117–18, 127, 136
1:17–18	93
1:17–21	53, 85, 92
1:18	76, 85, 88, 93–94, 99, 114
1:18–19	84, 91, 94, 96, 110
1:18–21	92–93
1:19	94
1:20	74, 88, 90, 92, 94, 96
1:20–21	94
1:21	84, 88–94, 120, 131
1:22	119–20, 122–23
1:22–25	53
1:23	75, 85, 88, 89, 110, 120, 131
1:23–25	110
1:24–25	43
1:25	92
2:1	111, 122–123
2:1–3	53, 102–4, 106, 110
2:2	85, 88–89, 100, 104, 109, 111–12, 120, 131
2:2–3	107
2:3	111
2:4	53, 84, 92, 94–95, 111
2:4–7	91
2:4–8	53
2:4–10	53, 94, 140, 144, 162
2:5	53, 89, 119–20, 162
2:6	43, 92, 95
2:7	94–95
2:8	74
2:9	75, 95, 99, 112, 119–20, 139–40
2:9–10	53, 90
2:10	87–88, 90, 99–100, 114, 119, 160

INDEX OF ANCIENT SOURCES

2:11	53, 75, 86, 91, 93, 96, 111, 117–18, 133, 136, 162	3:2	88
		3:3	87
2:11–12	53, 94, 120, 144	3:4	120, 131
2:11–17	129	3:5	90, 120, 160
2:11–25	43	3:5–6	128
2:11–3:12	105, 120, 142	3:6	87–88, 120
2:11–4:11	52–53	3:7	128–29
2:12	51, 54, 85, 87–88, 113–14, 124, 131	3:8	122–23
		3:8–9	129
2:12–15	144	3:8–12	54
2:12–17	51	3:8–17	98
2:12–3:17	144	3:9	9, 51, 87, 91, 113, 120, 131
2:13	126	3:9–12	129
2:13–17	53, 126–27	3:9–17	43
2:13–3:7	53	3:9–18	55
2:13–3:9	163, 165	3:10	100
2:13–3:12	123	3:10–12	43, 111
2:14	124	3:12	120, 131
2:14–15	176	3:13	54, 86, 114, 131
2:15	51, 86–88, 96, 114, 131	3:13–17	51, 54, 113, 144
2:16	130	3:13–18	87
2:17	88, 127, 144	3:13–22	54
2:18	54, 114, 130	3:13–5:11	105
2:18–19	54, 95	3:14	86, 88–89
2:18–25	54–55, 87	3:14–16	54
2:18–3:7	123, 127	3:14–17	146
2:19	54, 86–87, 127	3:14–18	89, 114, 131
2:19–20	120, 131, 146	3:15	84, 89, 92, 120, 130
2:19–21	86, 114, 131	3:15–16	86
2:19–23	51, 89	3:15–18	96
2:20	54, 86–88	3:16	51, 86, 91, 93, 114, 131
2:21	9, 86–88, 91, 95–96, 169, 172–73, 175–78	3:16–18	95
		3:17	54, 86–87, 96, 124, 131
2:21–23	51, 84, 132	3:17–18	88
2:21–24	85, 91, 175	3:18	51, 54, 75, 84, 87–88, 90–91, 132
2:21–25	54, 87, 92–95, 162	3:18–19	84
2:22	95, 169, 173	3:18–22	54
2:22–24	127	3:19	72, 81, 92, 169–71
2:22–25	90	3:19–20	44, 75
2:23	51, 95–96	3:20	44, 90, 160
2:24	88, 91, 96, 169, 178	3:21	54, 88–90, 160, 172
2:25	90, 95, 160	3:22	69, 81, 92
3:1	93, 96, 114	4:1	53, 84, 86–87, 91, 132, 146
3:1–2	128, 131, 144	4:1–2	88–89, 120
3:1–7	54, 129	4:1–3	54

1 Peter (cont.)
4:1–4	54–55, 94
4:1–5	113
4:1–6	54, 86–87
4:2	124
4:3	85, 114, 122, 124
4:3–4	76, 99, 114
4:4	51, 86, 113
4:5	92, 132
4:5–6	54
4:6	80
4:7	43, 53–54, 86
4:7–10	54
4:7–11	54–55
4:8	89
4:11	53–54, 88, 90
4:12	51–52, 86, 146
4:12–19	43, 55, 113–14, 131, 146
4:12–14	86
4:12–16	87
4:12–5:11	52
4:12–5:14	55
4:13	84, 87, 90–91, 94, 96, 120, 131–32
4:13–14	86, 90
4:13–15	91
4:13–16	94
4:14	51, 87–89, 113, 120, 131, 146
4:14–16	89
4:14–17	96
4:15	122, 124
4:15–16	86, 146
4:16	51, 84, 86–88, 96, 100, 146–47
4:17	86, 88, 97, 100, 132, 162
4:17–18	87
4:18–19	43
4:19	51, 86–88, 91
5:1	16, 43, 52–53, 84, 86–87, 90, 94, 133
5:1–4	132
5:1–5	126, 129
5:1–11	52, 55
5:4	84, 90, 94, 120, 131
5:5	43, 114, 120, 131
5:6	53, 88, 120, 131
5:6–10	85, 91
5:8	70
5:8–9	120
5:9	87, 92, 99, 131
5:9–10	51, 98, 113–14, 131, 146
5:10	43, 80, 86, 88–91, 120, 131
5:12	41, 52, 55, 85, 120, 133, 148
5:12–14	15, 52, 55
5:13	55, 99, 118, 162
5:13–14	52
5:14	52, 55

2 Peter
1:1	11, 44, 56, 190
1:1–2	56
1:2	27, 44, 56
1:2–3	57
1:3	56
1:3–4	56
1:3–11	56
1:4	56, 77, 192
1:5	28
1:5–6	57
1:5–8	210
1:5–10	56
1:5–11	43
1:6–7	56
1:8	57
1:9–11	210
1:11	56
1:12	28, 40, 57, 190
1:12–15	20, 56, 193
1:12–18	190
1:13–14	77
1:13–15	191
1:14	191
1:16	57, 77, 191–93
1:16–18	57, 191
1:16–19	57, 212
1:16–21	55, 58
1:16–2:10	55, 57
1:16–3:13	56–57
1:17–18	191
1:18	192, 226
1:18–19	77

INDEX OF ANCIENT SOURCES 267

1:19	57, 188, 192	3:1–2	4, 41, 58
1:19–21	35–36, 42, 192	3:1–3	30
1:20	57, 193	3:1–4	55
1:20–21	57, 193	3:1–5	63
1:21	193	3:1–7	55
2	193	3:1–13	55, 78
2:1	28, 55, 77, 210, 225	3:2	36, 41–43, 195–96
2:1–3	32, 36, 38, 57, 193	3:3	32–33, 36, 38–39, 79, 211
2:1–22	77	3:3–4	41, 59
2:1–3:3	4, 30	3:3–7	81, 197
2:2	43, 77	3:3–13	57–58
2:3	58, 77	3:4	56, 77–78, 211
2:3–10	55, 58	3:4–13	33, 196
2:4	28, 30, 34, 72, 81, 195–96, 210	3:5	36
2:4–8	73, 186	3:5–6	59, 212
2:4–10	58, 194	3:5–7	35, 59, 79
2:5	33–35, 39, 44, 81	3:5–10	59
2:5–6	56	3:7	39, 59, 211
2:5–9	35	3:7–13	77
2:6	28, 39, 78–79, 210	3:8	43, 57, 59, 80, 197, 222
2:6–8	35	3:8–9	33
2:7–8	81	3:8–10	197
2:9	56, 77–78, 81, 194	3:8–13	55
2:10	28, 30, 38, 71, 77	3:9	36, 43–44, 56, 59, 212
2:10–11	81	3:10	43, 59, 80, 211, 222
2:10–22	36, 57, 55, 58, 194	3:10–11	79
2:11	29, 71, 195	3:10–12	74
2:12	29, 39, 56, 71	3:10–13	221
2:13	29, 31, 56	3:11	56, 79
2:13–14	195, 211	3:11–13	59
2:14	38, 57	3:11–18	197
2:15–16	29–30	3:12	79, 211, 222
2:15–17	35	3:13	56, 63, 74, 81, 211, 226
2:16	224	3:14	43, 56, 212
2:17	29, 72	3:14–18	56, 59
2:18	29, 38	3:15	43, 197, 222
2:18–19	43	3:15–16	35, 45, 191, 196, 211
2:19	211	3:16	36, 213
2:20	77	3:16–17	57
2:20–21	57	3:17	36, 212
2:20–22	56	3:18	56–57, 222
2:21	28, 36		
2:22	42, 192	1 John	
3	213	2:19	206
3:1	27, 41–42, 191, 196	3:16	178

Jude	
1	11, 60, 189
1–2	60, 185
1–3	30, 37
1–4	219
2	27, 60
3	28, 60, 189, 208
3–4	60
3–23	60
4	23, 28, 32, 59–61, 185, 207–8
4–18	4, 30, 34
5	28, 34, 40, 80, 185
5–7	61, 185, 187, 189
5–8	219
5–10	61
5–16	60–61
6	23, 28, 30, 34, 78, 186, 195–96, 21
6–7	73
6–8	59
7	28, 35, 39, 185–86, 210
8	28, 30, 33, 59, 70, 186–87, 189, 195, 208
8–9	208
8–10	59, 61
9	29, 35, 38, 71, 189, 195, 197, 219
10	29, 39, 59, 81, 189
11	29, 30, 33, 35–36, 61, 76, 184, 189, 208
11–13	59, 61, 219
12	29, 31, 195
12–13	23, 34, 61, 188–89
13	74, 195
14	189–190, 217, 219
14–15	23, 35, 59, 61, 64, 182–84, 188–89, 195–97
14–16	59, 61, 189
15	39
15–16	34
16	23, 29, 38, 59, 61, 76, 189, 208
17	36, 40, 189, 211
17–18	30, 32–33, 36, 62, 183
17–19	59, 62, 219
17–23	60, 62, 189–90
18	38–39, 59, 64
19	33, 59, 62, 76, 189, 209
19–25	30
20	189
20–23	37, 62
21	59–60, 81
21–23	190
22–23	59
23	59, 76, 190
24	60
24–25	37, 60, 62, 190
25	23

Revelation
1:1	65
2–3	167
3:3	80
19:10	70
20:5	222
21:1	63, 81
22:8	70

APOSTOLIC FATHERS

Barnabas
18–21	122

Didache
1–6	122
5:1	123
16:2	119

Diognetus
1	100, 141
6:8	77

Martyrdom of Polycarp
10:1	147
10:1–2	145
12:1	147

Polycarp, *To the Philippians*
1:3	169
7:2	225
8:1	169

INDEX OF ANCIENT SOURCES

OTHER EARLY CHRISTIAN WRITINGS

Acts of Peter
12.20   224

Acts of the Scillitan Martyrs
8–9   145

Acts of Thomas
31   22
39   22

Adamantius, *Rect. fid.*
2.12   222

Apostolic Constitutions and Canons
7.46   22
8.13   111

Athanasius, *Paschal Letter*
39   221

Augustine, *C. Jul.*
1.78   173
4.85–86   174
4.86   174
4.87   174

Augustine, *Enarrat. Ps.*
103.4.1   179

Augustine, *Ep.*
164.1   172
164.5   172

Augustine, *Fid. op.*
21   168–69

Augustine, *Serm.*
37   172
284   175

Cassiodorus of Alexandria, *Institutiones divinarum et saecularium litterarum*
1.8.6   220

Clement of Alexandria, *Hyp.*
7   216

Clement of Alexandria, *Strom.*
5.14.98.4   141
6.5.41.6–7   141
6.6   170–71

Cosmas Indicopleustes, *Topography*
7.64–70   221

Cyprian or [Pseudo-Cyprian], [*De Pascha computus*]
17   141

Cyril of Jerusalem, *Catechetical Lecture*
23.20   111

Cyril of Jerusalem, *Mystagogic Catechesis*
3.20   111

Eusebius, *Epistula*
120.11   18

Eusebius, *Hist. eccl.*
2.23.25   217, 220
2.25.3   221
2.25.23   221
3.3.1   221
3.3.1–4   12, 221
3.3.4   221
3.25   218
3.25.1–3   167–68
3.25.3   12
4.5.3   22
5.1.20   147
6.14.1   216, 225
6.25.8   223

Filastrius of Brescia, *Liber de haeresibus*
125 [97].1   171

Irenaeus, *Haer.*
1.9.4   178

Jerome, *Epist.*		16.11	179
53.9	170	17.30	217
71.6	111		
120.11	41, 223	Origen, *Hom. Jes. Nav.*	
		8.3	176
Jerome, *Vir. ill.*			
1	40, 221	Origen, *Princ.*	
4	219	1.8.4	224
		2.5.3	171
Jerome, *Vit. Malch.*		3.1	121
1	173	4.1	179
Justin Martyr, *Dial.*		Photius, *Bibliotheca*	
35.80–82	226	109	225
81.1	226		
81.2	226	Rufinus, *Orig. Comm. Rom.*	
81.3	226	4.9	223
82.1	225–26	5.3	224
		8.7	223–24
Leo the Great, *Serm.*		9.2	224
63	175		
		Rufinus, *Orig. Hom. Exod.*	
Leontius of Byzantium, *De sectis*		12.4	223
2.4	167		
		Rufinus, *Orig. Hom. Jos.*	
Martyrdom of Apollonius		7.1	223–24
3.6.37	145		
		Rufinus, *Orig. Hom. Lev.*	
Maximus the Confessor, *Quaestiones ad Thalassium*		4.4	223
7	171	Rufinus, *Orig. Hom. Num.*	
		13.8.1	223
Origen, *Cels.*			
1.62	223	Theophilus, *Ad Autolycum*	
2.43	171	1.11	145
5.7	223		

Greek and Latin Sources

Origen, *Comm. Jo.*			
5.3	223–24	Aristotle, *Gen. an.*	
5.5–6	179	1.19	108
6.35	171	1.20	107
		2.4	108
Origen, *Comm. Matt.*		4.8	107–8, 110
13.2	171		
15.27	223–24		

Aristotle, *Historia animalium*		3	116
3.20	110	5	116
		7	116
Aristotle, *Poet.*		8	116
21.7	100	9–12	116
		15	116
Aristotle, *Pol.*		45–46	116
1.3	125	48	116
Aristotle, *Rhet.*		Pliny, *Epistula*	
3.2.12	99	10.96	145–47
3.3.4	100		
3.10.7	100	Seneca, *Epistula*	
		94.1	125
[Pseudo-Aristotle], [*Virt. vit.*]			
1.3–4	121	Soranus, *Gynecology*	
		1.15	109
Dio Chrysostum, *Or.*		2.11–15	107, 110
2.75–76	121		
		Suetonius, *Nero*	
Epictetus, *Diatr.*		16.2	146
3.2	125		
		Tacitus, *Ann.*	
Galen, *UP*		15.44	146
2.292	109		
14.8	109	Tertullian, *De cultu feminarium*	
14.10–11	108	1.3	216–17
Galen, *De Sem.*		Tertullian, *Nat.*	
1.12	108	7–8	141
Hesiod, *Theog.*		RABBINIC LITERATURE	
617–819	196		
		Targum Pseudo-Jonathan	
Hippocrates, *Aphor.*		Num 16:1–35	61
5.39	109	Num 24:14	61
5.50	109	Num 24:25	61
5.52	109	Num 26:9–10	61
5.60	108		
		Mishnah Sanhedrin	
Hippocrates, *Epid.*		10:3	73, 186
2.3.17	107		
Isocrates, *Demon.*			
2	116		

Index of Modern Authors

Aageson, James W. 165
Achtemeier, Paul J. 2, 6, 41, 54, 69, 73, 76, 80, 83, 85, 90, 93, 95, 107, 110, 112–14, 117, 119, 122–32, 138
Adam, A. K. M. 151–53, 155, 158, 161, 164,
Adams, Edward 66, 77, 79, 81
Adams, Sean A. 48
Adler, William 200
Aichele, George 156–57
Aland, Kurt 13
Albl, Martin C. 39
Amphoux, Christian-Bernard 169
Anderson, R. Dean 48
Arnold, Bill T. 66
Arzt-Grabner, Peter 48
Ashcroft, Bill 143
Aune, David E. 48, 101, 114–15, 121–22, 126
Avruch, Kevin 139
Balch, David L. 7, 92, 125–28, 130–32, 142, 144, 163–64
Barr, David L. 2
Bartlet, James Vernon 31
Barton, John 153–56
Bauckham, Richard J. 1–2, 18–20, 23–24, 35, 39, 44, 55, 64, 70–74, 77–78, 80–81, 184–93, 195–96, 207, 222, 224, 226–27
Bauer, Walter 201
Bauman, Zygmunt 156
Bauman-Martin, Betsy J. 6, 140, 143, 158, 161–62, 166
Baynes, Leslie 184
Bechtler, Steven R. 138–44

Beckwith, Roger 197, 199
Bennett, Byard John 220
Berger, Klaus 48
Bethge, Hans-Gerhard 223
Bhabha, Homi K. 143, 164
Bigg, Charles 32–33, 41, 44, 191, 224
Bird, Jennifer G. 145
Bobichon, Philippe 225
Boismard, Marie-Emile 107
Bömer, Franz 127
Bonwetsch, Gottlieb Nathanael 222
Boobyer, G. H. 41, 191
Boring, M. Eugene 84–85, 87, 89–90, 95–97, 126, 159–60
Bouhot, Jean-Paul 169
Brosend, William 182
Buchheit, Vinzenz 222
Buchholz, Dennis D. 225
Buell, Denise Kimber 141
Burrus, Virginia 217
Callan, Terrance 30, 52, 68, 79, 81, 193, 195–96
Cambe, Michel 225
Campbell, Barth L. 52
Candlish, J. S. 13
Carey, Greg 67
Carlsmith, J. M. 206
Carroll, Robert P. 156–57
Carson, D. A. 37, 184–85, 193, 195
Carter, Warren 145, 165
Chadwick, Henry 224
Charles, J. Daryl 60
Chase, Frederic Henry 37, 223–24
Chester, Andrew 1, 190
Chilton, Bruce 22

Clifford, Richard 68
Clines, David J. A. 158
Coblentz Bautch, Kelley 5, 63, 72, 74, 183, 185
Collins, Adela Yarbro 65
Collins, John J. 64–66, 184
Collins, Raymond F. 48
Cook, John Granger 147
Cook, Stephen L. 64
Cooper, Nicholas J. 143
Cortez, Félix H. 8, 151
Crouch, James E. 126
Dalton, William Joseph 73, 75
Davids, Peter H. 6, 9–10, 19, 24, 37, 69, 78–79, 81, 184, 186, 192–93, 201, 207, 209, 212
Debrunner, Albert 118
Deissmann, Adolf 47
Dennis, R. 69, 72–73
Desjardins, Michael 201, 205
Dibelius, Martin 36, 115–16
DiTommaso, Lorenzo 63
Donelson, Lewis R. 4, 11, 13, 41, 69–71, 74, 76, 81, 84, 95–96, 122, 124, 127–28, 131, 183, 190
Doty, William G. 48
Dryden, J. de Waal 113, 115, 132
Dubis, Mark 68, 74–75, 79, 146, 164, 166
Dunn, James D. G. 1, 99, 114
Du Toit, Andreas 208
Ehrman, Bart D. 12–13, 220–21
Elliott, John H. 1–2, 7–8, 13, 15, 17, 70, 73, 75–76, 80, 85, 88, 92–93, 103, 113–15, 117, 122–32, 136–38, 142–44, 146, 158, 163–64, 192
Endres, John C. 72, 185
Engberg-Peterson, Troels 114, 133
Eriksson, Anders 50
Esler, Philip F. 136, 147
Feldmeier, Reinhard 80, 90, 110, 112, 138
Festinger, Leon 206
Fiore, Benjamin 115, 133
Foerster, Werner 119
Forbes, Christopher 76
Fornberg, Tord 215
Frey, Jörg 70, 76, 81
Freyne, Sean 63
Friesen, Steven J. 136
Gager, John G. 135
Gammie, John G. 115
Gandhi, Leela 143
Gentner, Dedre 104
Gerdmar, Anders 32
Gilmour, Michael J. 18
Gloag, Paton J. 37
Görgemanns, Herwig 224
Gounelle, Rémi 170
Grappone, Antonio 223
Green, Gene L. 2, 24, 187–89, 191, 193, 195–96, 199
Green, Joel B. 75, 107, 114
Green, Michael E. 19, 37, 39, 42
Gregory, Andrew W. 226
Grünstäudl, Wolfgang 10, 182, 191, 215–16, 224, 227
Gunkel, Hermann 65–66
Guthrie, Donald 45
Hahnemann, Geoffrey Mark 167
Haines-Eitzen, Kim 222
Hanson, Paul D. 68
Harkins, Angela Kim 72, 185
Harnack, Adolf von 141
Harrington, Daniel J. 16, 18, 191
Havelaar, Henriette W. 226
Herrmann, Johannes 119
Hill, Edmund 175
Hillyer, Norman 17
Hodgson, Robert, Jr. 39
Hoffman, Robert R. 101
Holloway, Paul A. 113, 147
Hols, Edith 101
Horrell, David G. 7–8, 45, 86, 92, 100, 135–36, 140–41, 143–45, 147, 163–64
Horsley, Richard A. 136
Howe, Bonnie 100–102, 104–7, 160
Hultin, Jeremy F. 4, 21, 27, 35, 182, 191, 207, 216–17
Hunzinger, Claus-Hunno 119, 143
Jobes, Karen H. 15, 17

Johnson, Mark	101	May, Margaret Tallmadge	109
Johnson Hodge, Caroline	141	Mayor, Joseph B.	39, 44, 224
Jülicher, Adolf	36	Mbuvi, Andrew M.	138
Kalin, Everett R.	223	McCruden, Kevin B.	2
Karpp, Heinrich	224	McDonald, Lee M.	197
Käsemann, Ernst	1, 64	McKenna, Mary Margaret	122
Kasser, Rodolphe	222	McMillen, R. Melvin	99, 101–5, 107
Kelly, J. N. D.	24, 85, 96, 107, 111, 189, 192	Meade, David G.	13, 17
		Meeks, Wayne A.	135
Kennedy, George	50	Merkt, Andreas	8–9, 167, 169
Kimmel, Michael	101	Michaels, J. Ramsey	69–70, 73, 76, 79–80, 85, 107, 127, 129, 144
Klauck, Hans-Josef	47		
Kloppenborg, John	207	Mierow, C. C.	173
Köstenberger, Andreas J.	192	Miller, Robert J.	227
Kraftchick, Steven J.	6, 18, 37, 83, 192	Miscall, Peter	156–57
Kraus, Thomas J.	216, 225–26	Moo, Douglas J.	37
Kugel, James L.	152–53, 187–88, 194	Moore, Nicholas J.	182
Kuhn, Karl Georg	118, 144	Moore, Stephen D.	157
Kvanvig, Helge S.	68,	Morris, Leon	37
Lakoff, George	101	Moule, C. F. D.	38
Lampe, Peter	48	Murphy, Frederick J.	64, 67
LaVerdiere, Eugene A.	110	Neusner, Jacob	22
Lawrence, Louise J.	136	Neyrey, Jerome H.	36–37, 70–73, 76–80, 193, 211
Legaspi, Michael C.	152		
Leipoldt, Johannes	220	Nickelsburg, George W. E.	72, 185, 188–189
Levine, Amy-Jill	165		
Lewis, Scott, SJ.	64	Nicklas, Tobias	10, 182, 191, 215, 218, 222, 225
Lieu, Judith M.	141, 147		
Lincicum, David.	39	Nienhuis, David	221, 224
Lohse, Eduard	96, 130	Noppen, Jean-Pierre van	101
Lombardo, Gregory J.	169	Ogden, Schubert	83, 97
Longenecker, Bruce W.	136	Olbricht, Thomas H.	50
Lyotard, Jean-Francois	152, 155–57	Otto, Johann Karl Theodor von	222
Malherbe, Abraham J.	47, 115, 120–21, 125, 132	Pardee, Nancy	7, 113
		Pearson, Birger A.	196, 226
Malina, Bruce J.	135	Pearson, Brook W. R.	196
Markley, John R.	191	Perkins, Pheme	2, 73–74, 79–81
Marohl, Matthew J.	147	Petersen, Norman R.	136
Marrassini, Paolo	225	Phillips, Gary	157
Martin, Ralph P.	1, 190	Picirilli, Robert E.	226
Martin, Troy W.	1, 6–7, 48, 50–52, 76, 99, 102, 106, 108, 111–15, 117–18, 132, 138	Popkes, Wiard	115
		Preuschen, Erwin	218
		Prochsch, Otto	118
Mason, Eric F.	1–2, 9, 35, 72–73, 78, 181, 185	Rad, Gerhard von	68
		Reese, Ruth Anne	208

Reicke, Bo	37, 39, 71, 73	Theissen, Gerd	135
Richard, Earl	88	Thurén, Lauri	34, 37, 52
Rieken, Harry W.	206	Tite, Philip L.	48, 107
Robbins, M. Mayo	165	Tsutsui, Kenji	222
Robinson, John A. T.	31	Tuckett, Christopher M.	226
Robson, E. Iliff	37	Turner, John	38, 147–48
Rowland, Christopher	65	Übelacker, Walter	50
Rowston, Douglas J.	1	VanderKam, James C.	68, 72
Ruf, Martin G.	225	Van Unnik, W. C.	87
Sandevoir, Pierre	177	Verheyden, Joseph	216
Sandnes, Karl Olav	51, 115, 128	Vermes, Géza	36
Schachter, Stanley	206	Wagner, Maria Monica	223
Schenke, Hans-Martin	222	Walsh, Richard	156–57
Schlosser, Jacques	167	Wasserman, Tommy	45, 182, 216, 218, 222
Schmidt, Karl Ludwig	118		
Schmidt, Martin Anton	118	Watson, Duane F.	5, 6, 24, 34, 47–48, 50–52, 55, 60, 64, 68, 73–74, 76–78, 81, 189
Schmitz, Otto	133–34		
Schnider, Franz	48		
Schrage, Wolfgang	222	Webb, Robert L.	6, 64, 68–69, 76, 78–79, 81, 146, 158
Schüssler Fiorenza, Elisabeth	130		
Scott, James C.	164	Webster, Jane	143
Scroggs, Robin	135	Weima, Jeffrey A. D.	49
Sechrest, Love L.	141	Weinrich, Harald	102
Seeman, Christopher	73	Wenham, Gordon J.	199
Segal, Alan F.	205	White, John L.	48
Selwyn, Edward Gordon	63, 85	Williams, Travis B.	145, 147
Senior, Donald P.	16, 18, 191	Witherington, Ben, III	114, 120, 127
Sevenster, J. N.	202	Wright, N. T.	66
Sherlock, Thomas	37	Zahn, Theodor	220
Soards, M. L.	13	Zerbe, Gordon M.	87
Sollors, Werner	139–40	Zoepfl, Friedrich	220
Spicq, Ceslas	39		
Stählin, Gustav	133–34		
Starr, James	114		
Stenger, Werner	48		
Stenzel, Meinrad	224		
Stone, John	139		
Stowers, Stanley K.	47, 51, 115		
Studer, Basil	175		
Sumney, Jerry L.	2, 50		
Tajfel, Henri	147–48		
Talbert, Charles H.	132		
Tasker, R. G. V.	192		
Temkin, Owsei	109		
Teske, Ronald J.	174		

www.ingramcontent.com/pod-product-compliance
Lightning Source LLC
Chambersburg PA
CBHW032002220426
43664CB00005B/113